On Not Being Able to Play

On Not Being Able to Play

Scholars, Musicians and The Crisis of Psyche

Marla Morris
Georgia Southern University

SENSE PUBLISHERS
ROTTERDAM / TAIPEI

A C.I.P. record for this book is available from the Library of Congress.

ISBN: 978-90-8790-775-4 (Paperback)
ISBN: 978-90-8790-776-1 (Hardback)
ISBN: 978-90-8790-777-8 (ebook)

Published by: Sense Publishers,
P.O. Box 21858, 3001 AW Rotterdam,
The Netherlands

Printed on acid-free paper

This Book is Dedicated to Mary Aswell Doll

TABLE OF CONTENTS

ACKNOWLEDGMENTS

I would like to thank Mary Aswell Doll for all of her support throughout my musical and scholarly struggles. I would like to thank Naomi Rucker who encouraged me to go back to my music after twenty years of silence. I would like to thank Mary Virre who gave me a psychic foundation that allowed me to live again and who I carry with me in my psychoanalytic mind. I would like to thank my musical peers, Hari Simran Khalsa for being there over the hard years of not playing. Twenty some years of talking about the problems of the music world has always given me great comfort. A kindred spirit. I would like to thank Vivus Dorwin for introducing me to the cello and always being there for me. Vivus and I were always together at CMU. Vivus is my musical brother. I would like to thank Annie Allman for teaching me about the beauty of the acoustic guitar. Annie gave me the space to explore the unfamiliar territory of the acoustic guitar world. I would like to thank my piano teachers for giving me the knowledge needed to play and to know when to stop playing because of my physical limitations. Here I would like to thank the late Harry Franklin, the late Jack Roberts, the late Aube Tzerko. I would like to thank Margaret Rose, Ralph Zitterbart and Nancy Weems. I would like to thank Gary Graffman and Leon Fleisher for giving me the courage to play when I can and accept the hard times when I cannot play. Graffman and Fleisher are models of perseverance and strength especially for those of us who suffer from injury. In the scholarly world I would like to thank William F. Pinar for giving me a home in Curriculum Studies. Bill has been there for me through it all and is the most inspiring, big hearted scholar I know. I would again like to thank Mary Doll for teaching me the art of writing. I've learned everything I know about writing from you. Our ongoing discussions of the scholarly life have always been a source of great inspiration to me. I want to thank Joe Kincheloe and Shirley Steinberg who have supported me throughout my academic career and have opened up spaces for me to do my work. Joe and Shirley's ongoing friendship and support of my work has meant the world to me. I would like to tank Michel Lokhorst for taking my work seriously and allowing me the opportunity to publish this book.

IN MEMORY

While working on the page proofs for this book Joe Kincheloe died. His sudden, untimely death shocked the curriculum community. He meant a lot to me. He was a dear person and a dear friend. I am deeply saddened by this loss. He was always there for me as a young scholar. He was one of the most generous people I have ever known.

PART ONE

ON NOT BEING ABLE TO PLAY

Introduction

The idea for my book, *On Not Being Able to Play: Scholars, Musicians and the Crisis of Psyche*, came about after reading two groundbreaking texts: Joanna Field's (a pseudonym for Marion Milner) (1957) *On Not Being Able to Paint* and William F. Pinar's (1994) *Death in a Tenured Position*. Both of these texts deal with psychic wounds. Milner, a psychoanalyst, is primarily interested in what psychoanalysis can teach about the art of painting as it relates to the unconscious. Milner shows that the art of painting is hindered when psyche is blocked. Her book is basically about unblocking psyche so the artist can paint more freely. Painting is a metaphor for living, as I read Milner. Living is limited when psyche gets blocked and we must work to unblock psyche. This is her larger point. The way we work through psychic blocks is through developing the ability to freely associate. Milner raises some general questions like, What is artistic creation about? How can one become a better artist of one's life? What happens when the painter cannot paint as she would like to? It is this last question about which I am particularly curious. I will address this more in a moment, but briefly I want to talk about the second book that influenced my thinking and that is William F. Pinar's (1994) ground breaking essay, *Death in a Tenured Position* which raises similar questions. Pinar, a curriculum theorist, asks what happens when scholarly life gets blocked psychically? What happens to the scholar who symbolically "dies in a tenured position?" Pinar suggests that tenure is a signifying moment that gives pause. The academy, generally speaking, for Pinar becomes problematic if it blocks the scholar's work. Pinar wonders how the scholar can keep the burning flame of his work alive in a deadening atmosphere.

Marion Milner (1957) talks of the painter and her psychic blocks. Here, drawing on her work, I want to talk of musicians—since I am one—who suffer psychic blocks. The question I am interested in here is what happens when the musician is no longer able to play? Extending Pinar's (1994) discussion of the scholar who gets blocked, I want to raise the question about the scholar who can no longer work. What happens then?

Although drawing on Milner's and Pinar's work, my work differs from theirs in many ways. My book is about connections between musicians and scholars. More to the point, my book concerns the problems that both musicians and scholars face in their professions. Psychic blocks trouble musicians and scholars. I want to explore this trouble. My home discipline is curriculum studies and it is from here that I ground my study. My theoretical frame combines psychoanalysis and phenomenology because I am interested in psyche, emotions and the working through of emotions. I am interested in exploring what I call the crisis of psyche which is this: What do you do when you cannot do what you were called to do? This is the main question in my book. This book is distantly autobiographical. I

3

became a scholar in my late thirties, thanks to the guidance and generosity of William Pinar's mentorship. But before entering the academy, I studied as a classical pianist at Carnegie-Mellon University. I studied with Aube Tzerko at the Aspen Music Festival in the early '80s. He was the biggest influence on me, even though my time with him was relatively brief. His teacher was Artur Schnabel and one of his most famous students is Misha Dichter. I studied with a host of other people, but Tzerko is the one with whom I identify the most. So I am a musician and a scholar. But more to the point here, my music career ended when I injured my right hand. *On Not Being Able to Play* is distantly about that experience.

This book is a theoretical study of play and work, the play of the musician and the work of the scholar. John Dewey (1991) in a book titled *How We Think*, talks of the intellectual life as a life of play. He states:

> Mental play is open-mindedness, faith in the power of thought to preserve its own integrity without external supports and arbitrary restrictions. Hence free mental play involves seriousness, the earnest following of subject-matter. It is incompatible with carelessness or flippancy. . . . (p. 219)

Dewey suggests here that there is nothing frivolous about play. Play is serious business. This is the case for both musicians and scholars. Musicians play with musical ideas and scholars play with intellectual ideas. Lay people do not really think much about how serious musicians have to be to be committed to their art. In a book on Juilliard, Judith Kogan (1989) tells us that some students at the school practice ten hours a day. When I was in music school I practiced some five hours a day and that is probably why I got injured. But the point here is that playing an instrument is serious business. Playing an instrument is also about playing with musical ideas. In the classical music world, there is no room for "carelessness" as Dewey puts it. Mistakes are not allowed, period. And this is part of the problem that I address later on in this book.

At any rate, this book is also about my struggles as a scholar who worries about psychic blocks and tries to work through them. I am interested in what happens when the scholar gets psychically blocked and cannot do her work. This is something that not many people in academe talk about, although in the artistic community writer's block is a common topic of discussion. But here I am not talking of writer's block per se; I am talking about a much larger and more serious problem of psychic inertia that is a result of working in the academy. Working in the academy can serve to undermine the scholar's task. The academy is a hard place to work especially for women and minorities and I will look at these problems as the book progresses.

In the first part of the book I will discus in some depth the world of the musician and her art. I use psychoanalytic theory to flesh out the implications of suffering from a damaged musical psyche. In the second part of the book I turn to the life of the scholar. Here, I use psychoanalytic theory to tease out the implications of suffering from a damaged scholarly psyche. Psychic blocks come about both because of one's psychic predisposition and because of the potentially toxic environment into which that psyche is thrown. Both music conservatories and universities can become potentially hazardous places for musicians and scholars.

I am not alone in my plight. Two well known pianists suffer from problems similar to mine. One is Gary Graffman, the other is Leon Fleisher. Graffman performs only with his left hand. Graffman injured his right hand years ago and has made his career amazingly by playing repertoire that is written exclusively for the left hand. Fleishman's use of his right hand is on again off again; sometimes he can use his right hand and sometimes he cannot. Of course the difference between these successful artists and me is that they both went on with their careers despite their handicaps, whereas I did not go on with mine. I could not find a way to make a music career out of a very unreliable hand. I had neither the support nor the resources to make my career work even if I had decided to play exclusively with one hand. I dropped out of music school and basically disappeared into the humdrum of a working class life for nearly ten years before I figured out what I wanted to do with the rest of my life. That is when I met Bill Pinar. I knew then that I wanted to become a scholar because that was, for me, the closest thing to being a classical musician. I feel extraordinarily lucky to have met Bill because he gave me a new lease on life. I started my life over again in my late thirties and began the second phase of my life as a scholar.

I began writing about music in 1999 in my piece *Curriculum as Musical Text* (1999) in an edited book titled *How We Work* which I co-edited with Mary Aswell Doll and William F. Pinar. In that piece I talked about not being able to play but I hadn't really fleshed out my ideas in any detail probably because psychologically I was not ready to. But it was here that I began thinking about this problem. There are many musicians who suffer from injury, like athletes. Many have to give up music careers because of injuries, as I did. My problem is not isolated by any means. One of the most famous pianists who suffered from injury was Paul Wittgenstein, Ludwig Wittgenstein's brother. Paul got his arm blown off from gunfire during WW1. The Wittgenstein's were a family of musicians, with the exception of Ludwig who became a philosopher. How could Paul *not* go on as a pianist? He did go on playing repertoire written exclusively for the left hand.

In the field of curriculum studies, I know of no other book that deals with the inter-related problems that both musicians and scholars face. As a matter of fact, there are very few books in the field of curriculum studies on music. However, there are three full length books on music of note. One is by jan jagodzinski (2005). In his book titled *Music in Youth Culture: A Lacanian Approach,* jagodzinski explores a wide range of musical genres from Rap to Hip Hop, from Punk to Heavy Metal, from Techno to Goth. His Lacanian approach explores such topics as desire, jouissance, the death drive, the Lacanian Real with a mix of Deleuze and Guattari. Greg Dimitriadis (2005)–in a full length book– explores Hip Hop and African American youth from a cultural studies perspective. He argues that identities of youth are negotiated more out of school than in. In a fascinating study of skaterpunks—punk rockers who also skate board—Curry Malott and Milagros Pena (2004) suggest that punk rock can serve as a revolutionary art form. The authors of this book – *Punk Rockers' Revolution: A Pedagogy of Race, Class, and Gender* – are careful not to homogenize and sanitize the brutal history that is Punk Rock, as some of it is racist, sexist and homophobic. But the authors argue that there are strands of skaterpunk that involve "extreme environmentalism" (p. 32); there are strands of skaterpunk that are Marxist! In fact, Peter and Jonathan McLaren—who wrote the afterward to the book—claim that skaterpunk can serve revolutionary purposes. For me, the book is more about the politics of Punk than the music itself.

There are some shorter pieces on music—in the field of curriculum studies–mostly in edited books of note that I list here. Greg Dimitriadis and co-author Cameron McCarthy (2001) write about postcolonial art, literature and music. Here they argue that educators can learn much from postcolonial studies and the arts. However, this book devotes only one chapter to postcolonial music. Rosalie Romano (2002) contributes a short chapter on music in an edited volume titled *Passion and Pedagogy: Relation, Creation and Transformation in Teaching (Eds., Mirochnik & Sherman)*. Here, Romano talks about being a classically trained violinist and how that training influences her pedagogy. She suggests that the musician needs to be focused and at one with her work and her fellow musicians, especially when playing chamber music. So too should the pedagogue be passionate and at one with her work and with her students in the classroom. *Sound Identities* (1999) edited by Cameron McCarthy et al., deals with popular music and politics; Ted Aoki (2005) talks about jazz as a metaphor for scholarly work. Likewise, Adrienne Dixson (2006) talks—in a short chapter– in an edited book on critical race theory and education (Eds., Dixson & Rousseau). She talks about jazz as a metaphor for epistemology and methodology in qualitative research as it relates to critical race theory. Peter Appelbaum (2008) also talks about jazz as a metaphor for curriculum studies; Brent Davis (1996) talks about listening and the importance of the ear as a metaphor for making sense of mathematics and curriculum studies; Maxine Greene (1995) talks of Wallace Steven's *Blue Guitar* as a metaphor for difference within the context of education. Greene's (1995) *Releasing the Imagination* turns on the literary arts, not the musical arts. Most books in the field of curriculum studies on aesthetics or arts-based education deal with the visual arts. These scholars are interested—generally speaking– in why we need to keep art in the curriculum. One such book is by Margaret Macintyre Latta (2001). I want to ruminate on the title of her book for a moment. Her book is called *The possibilities of play in the classroom: On the Power of Aesthetic experience in Teaching, Learning, and Researching*. I am struck by the first part of this title because it is exactly opposite of the title of my book which is *On Not Being Able to Play*. Latte's concern turns on the "possibilities" of play. My concerns are obviously very different from those of Latta's. I am interested not in 'possibilities' but in impossibilities.

My book deals with the unique problems facing musicians and scholars when they find that they are psychically blocked and are not able to do their work. In *How We Work* (1999), some of the writers in the book talked about writer's block, but none of the writers—except me—talked about not being able to play and the implications for curriculum studies and scholarship. My book is an extension of a discussion I began in 1999. Thus, I argue that *On Not Being Able to Play: Scholars, Musicians and the Crisis of Psyche* contributes to the field of curriculum studies in a unique way.

This book is broadly divided into two sections. The first section deals with issues around musicians who are unable to play. The second section deals with issues concerning scholars who are unable to do their work because of some sort of psychic block. Again, this book is written from the perspective of curriculum theory as it intersects with both phenomenology and psychoanalysis. Thus, all of the chapters will be grounded in curriculum theory, phenomenology and psychoanalysis. Here I outline in brief each of the chapters that are to follow.

Part One is comprised of chapters one through six. Part Two is comprised of chapters seven through chapter nine. Chapter One is titled *The Mystery of Music: A Psychoanalytic Exploration.* Here I examine the psychic components of music. I ask the question about where music comes from. That is, why do people turn to music to express their feelings? I ultimately argue that this question remains a mystery but there are some clues along the way that we can unpack. Drawing on Donnel Stern's (1997) notion of "unformulated experience" (p. 81) and Christopher Bollas' (1987) notion of "the unthought known" (p. 282), I suggest that pre-verbal experience plays some role in the development of a musical psyche.

Chapter two is titled *A Phenomenology of a Musical Psyche.* Here I ask questions that tease out what a musical imagination might look like from a phenomenological perspective drawing on the work of two phenomenologists, Gaston Bachelard (1988a; 1988b; 1990; 1994; 1999; 2000a; 2002b) and Maurice Merleau-Ponty (1968). I argue that neither Bachelard nor Merleau-Ponty take their work far enough when talking about the ways in which psyche relates to the world. I turn the conversation to a more negative note and ask the question that they do not: What happens when psyche *cannot* relate to the world? Not being able to play a musical instrument is such a problem. I begin making implications early on about what this also means for the scholarly life when it too gets interrupted. I also develop what I call a phenomenology of pain in this chapter and talk about why pain is so difficult to articulate. I talk toward the end of the chapter about the tragic life of cellist Jacqueline du Pres who had to stop playing the cello at 27 because she was struck down by Multiple Sclerosis.

Chapter three is titled *Listening: The Regressive Movement of Currere.* In this chapter I talk about the intersections between curriculum studies and music focusing on William Pinar's (1995) notion of Currere. Currere, for me, in the context of this book, points toward the ways in which memory, music and childhood interconnect. This chapter focuses on the importance of popular music for children and the ways in which popular music—especially the music we listen to as children—shapes our adult lives. More specifically, I focus on the popular music of *Pink Floyd.* This band has been a large influence for my generation. I think that of my generation *The Floyd* is one of the most important rock groups around. Later in the chapter I focus specifically on the founding member of *The Floyd,* namely, Syd Barrett who was unable to play the guitar because of his mental collapse which some attribute to drug use and the onset of Asperger's syndrome. Syd Barrett's story is a tragedy much like the story of Jacqueline du Pres in that both left a hole in the music world when they stopped playing. The rock world was as devastated by Barrett's psychic decline just as the classical world was devastated by the loss of du Pres.

Chapter four is titled *Educating Moods: Regression, Repetition Compulsion and Minimalism.* From a psychoanalytic perspective, I examine the notion of a mood and the ways in which moods shape what we do, what we repeat and what we act out. More specifically, in this chapter I make a comparison between the groundbreaking work that has been done in curriculum studies– since the Reconceptualization of the field (see Pinar et al., 1995) – to the experimental music called minimalism. I take a closer look here at the minimalist music of Philip Glass and Steve Reich. In this chapter, I compare, broadly, musicianship and scholarship as they relate to regression, repetition compulsion and moods.

Chapter five is titled *On Waiting: States of Interiority and Intentionality.* Psychoanalyst Masud R. Khan (1989), in his book called *The Long Wait,* argues that waiting is a "core experience" (p.188). Waiting is certainly a core experience for the injured musician who thinks that she will eventually get better. And this waiting is at root a psychological experience, it is an experience of deep interiority. The problem I want to address here is what happens when a musician waits for a future that never comes. What happens when the injury never heals? What to do then? At root, this is a problem of the notion of hope. To hope for a future that does not come only serves to devastate a psyche already torn apart. Samuel Beckett's (1958) *Waiting for Godot,* also deals with the absurdity of waiting for a future that does not come. But the characters in his play are waiting for a god who never comes. In this chapter I talk some about Paul Wittgenstein who had his right arm blown off in WW1 and the ways in which he made his career as a pianist playing with only his left hand.

Chapter six is titled *On Not Being Able to Heal: Dread and Nachtraglichkeit.* This chapter is a continuation of the discussion in chapter five in that I ask the question about what it feels like to give up the idea that one will be able to play again. As the realization sinks in—that one will no longer be able to play– dread is at hand. I explore dread from a psychoanalytic perspective and tie it to issues around time and memory. In this chapter I talk about the ways in which archaic emotional problems stemming from early childhood can compound problems in adult life—like not being able to play—. Specifically, I talk about child abuse and the ways in which lingering after- effects (*nachtraglichkeit*) compound problems later in life.

Part two is comprised of chapters seven, eight and nine. Here I examine the scholarly life and the connections between the lives of musicians and the lives of scholars. Thus, in chapter seven, titled, *On Not Being Able to Work: A Scholar's Dilemma,* I tease out implications– for my own work– of William Pinar's (1994) *Death in a Tenured Position.* From a psychoanalytic perspective I explore the problems of life inside of the university. Pinar suggests that scholars need to find a way out of their difficulties so as to not die in a tenured position, as it were. I suggest—as a link to previous chapters in the book—that one way out of the scholar's dilemma might be in the form of a Parabola. The scholar who gets psychically blocked might turn to music to get unstuck; the musician who can no longer play might turn to scholarship as a way to heal a damaged psyche. Doing scholarly work can heal.

Chapter eight is titled *Institution as Intrusive Mother: A School for Scandal.* Here I deepen my discussion of the university as a problematic place for scholars by using the analogy of Winnicott's (1990; 1992) not good enough mother. In the second part of the chapter I turn to the work of the WPA (Works Progress Administration) and show how artists of the WPA– who lived during the Depression in the United States– were able to continue doing their art despite living in bad times. I argue that scholars can learn lessons from these admirable artists who painted murals. Many of these murals reflected the struggles of minorities during the Depression and many of them were displayed, interestingly enough, in public schools. What we learn from these artists is that they found their way out of bad times by working on their art.

Finally in chapter nine titled *The Scholar and the Musician: On Not Being Able to Work or Play,* I tie together sections one and two of the book by showing relations between music and scholarship. More specifically, I unpack relations between language, music and thought. I argue that on a fundamental level, music and scholarship have much in common, even though they are different disciplines. I discuss in this chapter subjugated knowledges of Native American scholars, women and Jewish scholars and talk about the ways in which the academy oppresses these differing minority groups making it hard for minorities to get tenure. More specifically, I look at scholars who have had trouble doing their work. I discuss William James, Ludwig Wittgenstein, Ruth Benedict and Nadia Boulanger as they all had difficulties working at some point during their careers. My point in drawing from the various disciplines of philosophy, anthropology and musical composition is to show that the problem of not being able to work is a cross– disciplinary problem.

I am hoping that scholars and musicians from many different backgrounds will read this book as it might help them find a way out of their dilemmas. From classical musicians, to rock stars, from curriculum theorists to music teachers, from anthropologists to philosophers, this book takes the reader on a journey that opens up a discussion that has long been ignored in academe.

CHAPTER ONE

THE MYSTERY OF MUSIC

A Psychoanalytic Exploration

I am interested in unpacking, from a psychoanalytic perspective, what music is. Instrumental music is not easily explained because it is not verbal. How to represent that which is beyond representation? Music comes from the gut. Or maybe from the heart. Some people argue that Bach is too intellectual. I think not. Bach, for me, is gutsy, full of heart, deep, profound and warm. Some people argue that Bach is cold and mathematical. I don't feel this way. But what is it about Bach that moves me so deeply? Every day for the last several months I have been playing Pablo Casals' recordings of the *Six Unaccompanied Cello Suites*. Casals is my favorite cellist. He is a master. His interpretation of Bach is idiosyncratic. There is nothing slick about Casals. What I don't like about younger more technically oriented cellists is their slickness, their smooth shifting and even expression. Casals takes time in unusual places. This is called rubato. Casals is able to make the cello sing like the human voice. I even hear the cello weeping. But what is it about this music? Music–as an object of my affection–is something to which I am deeply drawn. In this depth is mystery.

I want to use psychoanalytic concepts to explore where music might come from in the human psyche. First, I would like to talk about Donnel B. Stern's (1997) idea of what he calls "unformulated experience" (p. 81). Stern suggests that there is a part of the human psyche which is un-touchable. There are aspects of the human psyche which are simply beyond reach. Whatever is 'unformulated' is before language and therefore hard to put into language. When put into language, that which is 'unformulated' gets expressed as "creative disorder" (p. 79). Stern explains.

> When a patient is finally able to think about a previously unacceptable part of life, seldom are fully formulated thoughts simply waiting to be discovered, ready for exposition. Instead, what is usually experienced is a kind of confusion–a confusion with newly appreciable possibilities. . . . (p. 79)

I argue that music gets expressed through unformulated experience. There is some mysterious part of us that demands expression. Why something unformulated needs to be expressed is not clear. The creation of musical expression is never clear. It just is. It is before language. It is psychically older than language. If psyche is not in touch with its unformulated experience, one cannot express music. Now, being in touch with unformulated experience does not mean understanding it or being able to articulate what it is. When one reads Marion Milner's (1957) book

On Not Being Able to Paint, she addresses a similar issue throughout much of her book. She talks about painting by just letting the brush lead her. By letting go of ego, the painting comes alive almost by itself. Milner says that she is surprised by what emerges on the canvas. Is freely associated painting unformulated experience? Does unformulated experience get expressed as a surprise? Unconscious surprises startle. Unformulated experience gets expressed in the analytic situation when the patient freely associates. What the patient says sometimes is surprising even to herself; the patient's narrative takes on its own life. This narrative comes out of some deep unconscious place. That which is unformulated always surprises.

When improvising music, the musician might start out with a form, a pattern, perhaps some clearly patterned chord progressions, but if the musician lets herself go and lets go of ego the music seems to take on its own life and direction. Too much direction from the observing ego can spoil the surprises. But getting lost in tonal transitions can also be maddening. Stern (1997) explains.

> As artists tell it, the unformulated often does coalesce without conscious intervention, but it must brew, and it takes its own time to do it. Mozart is one famous example: He could compose in a room full of noise and traffic, and could be interrupted at any point without being disturbed, because by the time he sat down to write, he was merely copying onto the page a piece of music which already existed in its entirety in his mind. (p. 95)

Mozart was, of course, a genius. Letting the unformulated experience "brew" can take months or even years. I am thinking here of the process of writing a book. For me, it takes years to formulate what is unformulated. Sleeping on it, getting distance and taking great care and time to do revisions lead to the forming of ideas. And ideas must take "form" otherwise they are merely disconnected and nonsensical. But this process is most mysterious. Perhaps it is the unconscious which "brews" the material. Like Mozart, scholars might be able "brew" up books completely in their minds before writing them down. How is it that some people can compose a symphony in a summer, while others can barely write an email that makes sense? The 'how', or the 'why' behind musical or scholarly creativity—especially when genius is involved—remains a mystery.

Prolific composers like Mozart and Beethoven were not poster children for mental health. Many schizophrenics plaster their walls with words. Dr. Paul Schreber (2000)—a schizophrenic who penned a diary—which Freud analyzed—about his madness wrote and wrote and wrote and wrote to get out the madness. When he wasn't writing, he was playing the piano, when he wasn't playing the piano or writing he was psychotic. Now, I'm not saying that all artists are mad, but there certainly is a mad component to excessive expression—there is a mad urge to formulate what is unformulated, to make conscious that which is unconscious.

Like Stern's notion of unformulated experience, Christopher Bollas (1987) talks about what he calls the "unthought known" (p. 282). My take on Bollas' notion of the unthought known is that at some level what is unthought is, indeed, known. However, what is unthought cannot in some sense be thought. But it is known on a deeper level, perhaps on an unconscious level. Bollas says that the unthought known is made up of "inarticulate elements of psychic life" (p. 210). I would argue that most of what goes on with people is, in fact, inarticulate. There is much going on in the psyche that is impossible to understand. On a certain level, psyche might know that there is some feeling, some mood, some frame of mind, some trouble at hand. But what these inarticulate experiences are, remain, for the most part, unthinkable. Every now and then, though, part of the unthought known does get known. And I think that this is the moment of artistic expression. Bollas even talks about music in his work. He claims that "it may well be that musical representation is somewhere between the unthought known and thought proper" (p. 282). Musical expression is made of thought, sound and sometimes image. Patients in psychoanalysis express thoughts, ideas and feelings. Sometimes they even breakthrough to the known of what is unthought, making the unconscious conscious. But in musical expression the experience is not the same. Musical expression bursts in on the scene. Sounds are not words, but they are like words. Sounds are elusive. Sounds breaking in on the scene puzzle. Sometimes these sounds disturb. The unthought known(s) that make up what Bollas (1987) calls our 'personal idioms' are shaped by history and culture. We are highly historical creatures. So too are our unthought knowns.

Winnicott (2005) argues that playing a musical instrument, like playing with the teddy bear, serves to transition the musician away from her primal object relations. The instrument, in other words, is a substitute mother. It is the primary object with which the child relates. When children begin to learn instruments very young one must wonder what this early transition away from the mother and toward the instrument does to the child. How does the child's relation with the mother change? Playing an instrument is akin to playing the mother, or in some cases escaping from the mother. Instruments–like teddy bears–serve to 'hold'–in the Winnicottian sense. If the mother does not serve as a holding environment, instruments become even more important for children. Instruments 'hold' and can serve to heal the child who is not loved enough or loved at all. Playing an instrument can serve as a holding environment. Christopher Bollas (1987) talks about "being held by the object" (p. 30). Sound 'holds' the child in nurturing ways. Sound is the way the child expresses deep felt needs that perhaps the mother did not 'hear.' The more the mother does not hear the child–symbolically– the more the child wants to be heard. Why would a child want to play the trumpet or the drums? These are very loud instruments. How loudly does the child have to play to be heard? The instrument 'holds' the child in the sound produced. Sounds have sustaining qualities. In sustain-ment, if you will, the child's message resonates. The child's cry will be heard through the playing. Playing creates a safe space for the child. The instrument, like the human voice, becomes a cry for attention. Listen to me!! Perhaps, in some cases–especially if the child is abused by the mother– playing an instrument allows a space for the expression of psychic damage.

Perhaps all expression of music is generated from the unconscious. Michael Eigen (2004), drawing on Wilfred Bion, states that musicians work from unconscious states. For Bion, 'alpha' represents that which is unconscious. 'Beta' reflects that which is conscious. Utilizing these concepts, Eigen (2004) interestingly points out that,

> An amazing tap dancer has alpha feet, a pianist has alpha hands, an analyst has alpha intuition at times. Of course, things are in movement, subject to change. A baseball player makes an alpha catch one day, and on another he is leaden and unable to move. Life is uneven. A pianist with alpha hands and a heart for music may be unable to love a person—music reaches alpha function but people remain beta objects. (p. 77)

Eigen points out here that the alpha musician may not be able to relate to people. Child prodigies sometimes suffer from this problem. Practicing ten hours a day does not lend itself to building inter-relations with others.

If the musician cannot let go of ego the playing becomes overly mechanical. Here all musicality is lost. Unfortunately, the world of competitions force musicians to become mechanically oriented while losing what Eigen terms 'alpha hands.' This is the world of loud and fast, as my teacher Aube Tzerko used to say. Once–while I was studying with him– a student brought to him a showy piece by Franz Liszt. I was wowed by the performance thinking I could never do that!! Shockingly at the end of the student's performance, Tzerko closed the score and chastised the student for bringing him such 'junk.' Tzerko's lesson was over!! He told the student to leave!! Shades of Lacan's two minute session?? Tzerko was not interested in the wow of technical ability. He was interested in interpreting music and making meaning out of musical ideas. Liszt does not lend itself to these things—some musicians feel– because his music is all dazzle and show. One of the reasons I believe that Tzerko accepted me into his studio was certainly not because of my technique, for at the time I was having serious troubles with technique. Tzerko accepted me into his studio because of my ability to interpret music. Of all my music teachers, Tzerko stands out the most, even though I only studied with him for a very short period of time. Tzerko was a master at phrasing. He would spend entire lessons on the first page of a piece encouraging the student to listen more carefully to her phrasing and dynamics. Now, the piano–being a very percussive instrument– is not really a singing instrument, like a violin for instance. You have to work at getting the piano to sing. For one thing, you really have to listen. So many pianists do not listen!! They just play loud and fast. Of course, playing loud and fast is important when the music calls for it–but what is more difficult is playing slower pieces that demand attention to the musical line. As a student of Schnabel's, Tzerko worked at music like Schnabel. Konrad Wolff (1972) says of Schnabel that his "analysis was inside out. It was concrete inasmuch as he treated each piece as though it were the only composition in existence" (p. 120). Working a piece from the inside out is getting into every detail of every phrase and that means getting into the mystical side of the music. When the pianist pays careful attention to interpretation she becomes at one with the piece. You cannot be at one with a piece unless you have really given a lot of thought to the "inside-outness" of what the piece can potentially express. And you have to make that piece your own through your own idiosyncratic interpretation. Wolff says that

Schnabel taught that good playing involved "a penetration of the spirit" (p. 102). Tzerko, too, worked music in a way that did get at the spiritual side of interpretation. Every phrase was treated with awe and care. The lessons I learned from Tzerko—especially about the care with which one should take interpreting a musical score—have served me well as a scholar. I work very hard to pay close attention to the work of other scholars and try to unpack as carefully and thoughtfully as I can the spirit of the piece at hand. For me, interpreting music and scholarship are similar activities.

MUSIC AS TRANSITIONAL OBJECT

If music serves as a transitional object because of its holding qualities, then where in the psychoanalytic literature is this discussed? Surprisingly, the connection between hearing, music and the function of the transitional object is rarely talked about. Marjorie McDonald (1990) comments,

> Psychoanalytic interest in "transitional phenomena" has focused almost exclusively upon tangible objects which infants use as their first "not me" possession–objects which make their appeal through sight, smell, feel and taste. A musician would have to ask why the sense of hearing is not included in this list of significant sensations. (p. 85)

It is interesting to me that in curriculum studies, music tends to be an overlooked art form, even though some scholars have mentioned the importance of the ear as a metaphor for connectedness (Aoki, 2005; Davis, 2006). McDonald argues that a good enough mother who sings, speaks, or even whispers to her child will enable the child to develop better listening capacities than children who are not sung to and so forth. The musician is born out of a loving, singing holding environment, says McDonald. Well, this may be the case for some. But certainly there are melancholic musicians and poets who became artists in order to unconsciously express unstable relations with "not good enough mothers"—as Winnicott put it—or tyrannical fathers. The destructive capacity of the mother or father can actually spur creativity. Or, a chemical and biological imbalance that causes, say, bipolar disorder can serve to heighten creativity. Why would a well-balanced person be an artist anyway? Aren't artists known to be temperamental, crazy, eccentric? Adam Kirsch (2005) examines biographies, memoirs, personal letters and other primary source documents of Robert Lowell, Elizabeth Bishop, John Berryman, Randall Jarrell, Delmore Schwartz and Sylvia Plath to show that all of these poets had psychological problems. Would they have been poets or writers had they not suffered from some sort of problem of the psyche? These poets were either alcoholics or committed suicide, or wrote out of a state of madness or melancholy. Kirsch (2005) claims that Robert Lowell "suffered all his life from severe manic depression and was hospitalized almost annually for decades" (p. 28). Elizabeth Bishop, says Kirsch (2005), suffered from alcoholism and "bouts of severe depression" (p. 86). Moreover, her life "was shadowed by mental illness: when she was four years old, her mother was committed to an insane asylum . . . her father died when she was an infant" (p. 64). And to top it off, her lover, Lota de Macedo, committed suicide. Alice Miller (1991) argues that Picasso's memory from childhood of an earthquake shaped the way he saw the world. *Guernica*, according to Miller, was an expression of this experience. Nietzsche, claims Miller, wrote what he did because of being abused as a child. Miller (1991) argues,

> And yet today it seems to me a simple matter to recognize that what Nietzsche wrote was his hopeless attempt, which he didn't abandon until his breakdown, to free himself from his prison by expressing his unconscious but present hatred for those who raised and mistreated him. His hatred, and his fear of it, became all the more vehement the less he succeeded in becoming independent of its objects, his mother and his sister. (p. 90)

In Miller's (2005) book titled *The Body Never Lies: The Lingering Effects of Cruel Parenting*, she makes her argument even clearer than she did in her 1991 book. She argues in her book on the body (2005) that people who suffer from child abuse and repress their feelings about that abuse often create art as a way to express this unthinkable past. For the most part, artists do not know what drives their work. But for some, repression drives the work. A result of this splitting off—which is what repression does– is often the manifestation of illness, says Miller. Miller's main thesis in the book is that the body has a memory and will present bodily symptoms of psychological problems as long as the problems are not dealt with. It is no accident, Miller claims, that many artists who were abused as children get seriously ill when they are adults and die young. Miller talks about Dostoevsky's abusive childhood. His father was tyrannical. Clearly his work *The Brothers Karamozov*, Miller argues, reflects the relationship that Dostoyevsky had with his tyrannical father. It is well known that Dostoyevsky suffered from epileptic fits but he also suffered from "chronic insomnia and complained of dreadful nightmares" (p. 44). Rimbaud, suffered at the hands of an abusive mother, says Miller. Drawing on one Yves Bonnefoy, Miller (2005) says that "Mme. Rimbaud did everything in her power to curb and thwart her son's development as a poet, albeit to no avail" (p. 60). Often victims of child abuse will internalize the abuse and begin to blame themselves and turn hate inward. Self hatred is a common problem for victims of child abuse. Miller claims that Rimbaud's poetry is filled with self hatred. She tells us that his poetry "reflects not only his self-hatred but also his quest for the love so completely denied him in the early stages of his life" (p. 61). It is interesting that repressed memories demand expression and often that expression comes in the form of art.

Here the Kleinians are helpful. Hannah Segal (2000), in an interesting book titled *Dream, Phantasy and Art*, argues that artistic expression springs from the depressive position. Segal (2000) explains,

> The act of creation at depth has to do with an unconscious memory of a harmonious internal world and the experience of its destruction; that is, the depressive position. The impulse is to recover and recreate that lost world. (p. 94)

I don't know if the impulse of many artists is to recover the lost world so much as it is to express destruction. The shattering of internal objects is what gets projected– I think— into artistic creations. Perhaps the gift of the creative object is a form of reparation. Recall, for Kleinians the depressive position is connected to reparation. To make repair (*Tikkun*) is to work through psychic damage. However, if one does not work through psychic disaster it becomes impossible to heal "damaged bonds," as Michael Eigen (2001a) might say. Art can and does at times express shattered or damaged internal objects. If one thinks of the music of Arnold Schoenberg what is one to make of the ugly sounds? His music is deadly, ugly, awful. What is Schoenberg attempting to express? It could be that he is simply applying the strict rules of composing serial music and what you hear is what you get. The serial composers did not really care what their music sounded like as long as the music followed the rules of the twelve tone method. Perhaps it is a bit of a stretch to say that his music mirrored some kind of inner psychic catastrophe. But it sure sounds that way!! Serial music—at least for me—is a catastrophe. It seems so wrong headed to put logical rules of composition in front of the sound produced. It is curious to me why Adorno (2004) – in his book on aesthetics and music –devotes so much time to Schoenberg. I cannot understand how anyone can make sense of Schoenberg's music. Beauty is in the ear of the beholder, I suppose.

At any rate, Michael Parsons (2000) points out that there is a strong link between aggression and creativity. What is the aggression in Schoenberg about? Perhaps Freud (1908) had it right. Artistic expression is a projection of unconscious conflict. Maybe some composers become more drawn to the death drive as they age. Perhaps some composers are drawn to the death drive because of early childhood traumas they can't fully articulate or understand or even remember. Michael Eigen (2005) points out in his book *Emotional Storm* that "[t]here are "creative as well as destructive storms" (11). For some, creativity and destruction are of a piece. Eigen (2005) talks much of "psychic annihilation" (p. 23) throughout his work. Music can be made in the service of psychic annihilation. This can be deconstructed in many different ways. One might write or play music to obliterate the self, or to obliterate others symbolically. One plays an instrument, in some cases, to make the self disappear. Playing music might be an expression of breakdown. Eigen (2005) says, "[o]fen we are pushed to a limit, a point of last resort, and sometimes we go under. A collapse lasts an hour, a week, months or years" (p. 50). Is playing music a form of mental collapse? Collapsing into music may be a way for the psyche to take refuge from a brutal world, or a brutal childhood.

Composing music, too, might be a way to express repressed memory. On the other hand, maybe it is not so complex. Maybe some composers are just bad tempered, hot headed. Maybe certain composers are just plain gloomy. One gets that impression from reading Beethoven's (1972) letters. In a letter to Dr. Von Schaden written early in his life (1787) Beethoven complains. "I have been troubled with asthma and I much fear that it will lead to consumption. I also suffer from melancholy which is as great an evil as my illness itself" (p. 2). In 1800, Beethoven writes to Carl Amenda,

> How often do I wish you were with me, for your Beethoven is most unhappy, and at strife with nature and Creator. The latter I have often cursed for exposing His creatures to the smallest chance, so that frequently the richest buds are thereby crushed and destroyed. Only think that the noblest part of me, my sense of hearing, has become very weak. Already when you were with me I noted traces of it, and I said nothing. Now it has become worse, and it remains to be seen whether or not it can ever be healed. (p. 17)

Over and over again in his letters he "curses his existence" (p. 20). What a cruelty for a composer to lose his hearing!! No wonder he was depressed. But he probably was a depressive sort long before he lost his hearing. Interestingly enough, Martin Nass (1990b) points out that it is not unusual for musicians to suffer from some sort of hearing disturbance. He explains,

> Instances of hearing disturbance or ear disease are common in the history of musicians and might be one of several factors in hypercathecting the ear. Experiences of pain in the ear and ringing or buzzing in the head during childhood appear frequently in biographical and clinical material. While this is a dimension independent of talent, it may serve to heighten auditory cathexis. (p. 189)

Perhaps talented musicians with hearing disturbances are more sensitive to sound. Buzzing in the head invites the constant playing of music to cover up the buzzing. I know this from personal experience. I suffered many ear problems as a child all the way up into my early twenties. One of my ear doctors even told me that eventually I would go deaf. But I'm still not deaf and I'm well into my forties. The buzzing, though, is always there. I cannot tolerate silence, it is almost painful. Music covers it up. I probably do not hear as well as other people because of all those years of practicing in small rooms with large pianos. Perhaps the loudness of those pianos in those tiny practice rooms damaged my hearing. Imagine being a drummer or a rock musician. I wonder if they can hear after twenty years of playing. At any rate, Beethoven was a moody sort, a melancholic to be sure. He was a conflicted man and I think you can hear this in his music, much more so than, say, in Mozart.

Playing music, at least for me, is directly connected with going into a mood. Beethoven was a moody sort of fellow. I think his music reflects this. But what does it mean to be in a mood? Christopher Bollas (1987) explains that

> A person if often described as being 'in' a mood, giving those of us who are not in such a condition the sense that the one in a mood is 'inside' some special state. How far inside the mood is someone? How long will it last? Spatial and temporal metaphors register something of a special nature of this phenomenon. 'Don't worry,' a friend may say of another, 'he will come out of it sooner or later.' (p. 99)

Suffering from depression my entire life, I know exactly what it means to not be able to get out of a mood. Once in a funk, it's almost impossible for me to get out of it. Funks are not brought on necessarily by events, but by chemical imbalance.

How can you shift a chemical imbalance? Anti-depressants only do so much and then you are stuck with your mood. When someone says 'snap out of it grump-bucket' it's like saying change the chemical imbalance in your brain. How can you do that?

For some musicians, playing well means being in a mood. Depression can be used in the service of music. Playing sad music means getting inside of a depression. I have often wondered how musicians who have never suffered from depression can play sad music. I suppose happy musicians can play sad music, but experiencing depression first hand helps to express a piece that is sad. This sad state needs to be honoured, not pushed away. Moods can be used, then, in the service of creativity. The problem, however, is that these moods disturb others. Being in a mood is an annoying trait. Why are you in such a mood? One might get stuck in a mood. That is not a good feeling. So one must learn to work with one's moods so that they do not disturb others, but are used in the service of creative expression. For me, I have to be in a mood to play. That is not hard for me, because I am always in a mood. Like Beethoven, I am a very moody sort. Being in a mood allows one to explore surprises and play in new keys. Being in a mood allows one to experiment. As Bollas (1987) might say, being in a mood allows one to hear "[r]eception of news from within" (p. 239). Bollas explains,

> For here lies a paradox: the aspect of mental life activates when tranquillity is achieved. Reception of news from within (in the form of dream, phantasy, or inspired observation for instance) arrives through evocation, a mental action characterized by a relaxed, not a vigilant state of mind. (p. 239).

Being in mood is like being inside of a dream state, being inside of a sort of fog. A curtain comes down over the ego. When id seeps through psyche one can play music. Without being in touch with foggy states, or dreamy states, or id states, the musician cannot express deep unconscious feeling. Bollas is right to suggest that this takes a sort of tranquillity, a relaxed state of mind. Playing music, improvising for example, cannot happen if one is overly rational, overly logical. There is a certain letting go that happens when the improvised music clicks. I think one could say the same thing for writing. When the writer lets go of the observing ego, the words just seem to appear on the page by themselves. Like music, the notes just come out, as if they are doing things by themselves. Playing music can be mystical. Playing music allows one to be in a mystical state. The difficulty of performing in front of others is that that mystical state is interrupted, almost ruined by nervousness and the gaze of the other(s) in the audience.

Playing music, for me, is an intensely private act, like writing. The thing I like about writing is that it is done in private, nobody watches. The privacy of writing, for me, is a blessing, a sanctuary, a refuge. I cherish this privacy. In music, I guard my playing. Although I have performed in many different kinds of venues over the years, I have finally come to the conclusion that I don't like performing. Performing gets me outside of myself too much, gets me out of my mood. The nerves ruin the mood. The fight against self-consciousness gets in the way of genuine expression for me. I take great comfort in the words of the late Glenn

Gould (1991) who tells us that "there was something a little bit degrading about giving concerts. The process was essentially distasteful" (p. 90). Yes. Degrading. Playing in hotel lobbies, or at weddings or even in coffee houses is degrading. Gould retired from playing concerts at the young age of 32. I don't blame him. There is something creepy about people watching you express your deepest emotions. And there is something exhibitionist about playing in front of people. For me, performing was always a horrible experience perhaps because I am an introverted person. Interestingly enough, Chopin also hated performing! In a biography of Chopin by Benita Eisler (2003), we learn that some time during his life "[h]is [Chopin's] horror of performing before strangers–akin to feelings of violation–had worsened" (p. 83). Chopin remarks, "I am not fit to give concerts; the crowd intimidates me and suffocates me and I feel suffocated by its eager breath, paralyzed by its alien faces" (qtd. in Eisler, 2003, p. 83).

I was a performance major in college. What was I thinking? I hated performing. I was interested to learn that jazz pianist Keith Jarrett–who attended the Berklee School of Music–tells us that the faculty "kicked him out" (cited in Carr, 1991, p. 19). Jarrett is just too 'out there' for music school. Ian Carr (1991) tells us that while in counterpoint classes, Jarrett would "read paperbacks" (p. 19). When Jarrett would explore chord progressions with the teacher, one Rogert Share, Share "would say 'No, no, no! You can't go from here to there! Then the class would laugh" (cited in Carr, 1991, p. 19). Shockingly Jarrett had the chance to study with the famous Nadia Boulanger but said NO!! Can you imagine that?

Jazz is a more acceptable genre in the academy than rock. There are many schools in the US that have departments of Jazz, such as The University of North Texas where Lyle Mays went to school. Mays is the keyboardist for jazz guitarist Pat Methany. Tori Amos (2005), who was a child prodigy and attended the Peabody Institute *at the age of 5*, remarks on her disappointment with the classical music world. What she really wanted to do was to get involved in popular music. But most music schools don't teach popular music– the word popular, as Amos points out, is "blasphemy" (p. 50) in music conservatories. Amos followed her dream and became a famous and well respected popular musician and left her classical life behind. Amos (2005) comments,

> I started to let people know that I loved this other kind of music. I think I was ten when I said to one of my teachers, "What about the idea of John Lennon? Lennon and McCartney the modern day Mozarts" That was just blasphemous. There wasn't a place for the idea of being a contemporary composer, working in the pop idiom. Jazz was acceptable; in fact it's a big peace of the Peabody program. (p. 50)

Tori Amos is an accomplished pianist. I am impressed with her playing and I am impressed with her compositions. She has the career that I always wanted! I could have been Tori Amos—except that I was not a child prodigy and certainly did not go to a music conservatory at the age of five! When I watch Tori Amos perform on stage I say to myself, that should have been me.

When I was in music school I began to take an interest in composing because I really wanted to write down my improvisations. So I asked a professor if I could take a composition class. He was taken aback and said emphatically NO. You can't do that! You are a performance major!! I was shocked. Later that summer, I tried to write my improvisations down on staff paper and one of my teachers who saw me doing this said, 'why are you doing that, there is already enough music in the world!' I was so discouraged that I just quit trying. My lack of mathematical skills has really hurt me as a musician. I simply cannot count!! When I was in college I actually failed a course in Dalcroze Eurhythmics because I did not understand the value of an 8th note. As a child I think I was playing mostly by ear by imitating my teacher but not understanding the music on the page. I played things by ear more than by reading the score and this got me into great trouble when I entered music school. I can read music, of course, and I can even sight read pretty well. But reading music is still a struggle for me. I prefer improvising to reading music. This is another no no in the classical music world. Improvising doesn't count.

Improvisation, I think, is a lost art. Eisler (2003) tells us that Chopin was a master of improvisation. Eisler (2003) comments that "[as] always, it was his improvisations that left audiences–kings or commoners–ecstatic" (p. 96). Keith Jarrett, the contemporary jazz pianist, also leaves his audiences ecstatic. He is the only person I know of who has the guts to do entire performances played off the top of his head. Jarrett's imagination and command of the instrument astounds. I've learned a lot from Jarrett, although I have little interest in playing jazz.

When I was in music school in the early 1980s I just couldn't deal with the idea that in order to graduate I would have to play a recital. It was bad enough to have to play juries every semester. When I was in my teens, playing a recital did not seem so bad, but as I got a little older my nerves became frayed and I suffered from serious stage fright. Once, while in a Master Class at Carnegie-Mellon with a well known pianist named James Tocco from the Mannes School of Music, I nearly fainted before I started to play. I remember seeing spots and things going black on me. I had to stop and start over again. Anathema in the music world. You just can't do things like that!! Feeling ashamed and humiliated I went through with the Master Class but heard nothing Tocco said to me, I was too embarrassed. I went through terrible phases of blanking out. Sometimes I could not even start a piece, even though I knew the music by memory. I never developed the steely nerves one needs for performing live. Now, some people do not get nervous but I'm certainly not one of them. At any rate, performing is a nightmare for some musicians. Pianist Claudio Arrau (1992) speaks to these issues psychoanalytically. Arrau says,

> Eros may be within us, but so is the Death wish. . . and we do the most inexplicable things. We frustrate ourselves constantly. Out of fear–fear of failure and, strange, as it may seem, fear of success as well–we artists suddenly fall sick before major appearances. We create frightful emotional upsets, we risk losing what we hold dearest. We fall and break an arm [or in my case develop tendonitis]. We have car accidents. Singers suddenly

become hoarse. . . . Instrumentalists suddenly lose the use of some fingers or suddenly can't play the simplest (or most difficult) passages. (p. 242)

Arrau speaks to many experiences that are very familiar to me. Even at the young age of 17 or so, I had a complete memory loss and sudden inability to play pieces that I knew well from memory when I auditioned at the Juilliard School of Music. I was so freaked out at this audition that I felt like I had a mental collapse right there in front of three of the most well known piano teachers in the country. I started to play and then conveniently forgot everything. There is no second chance at Juilliard. The judges were polite and nice to me, they asked me who I studied with and basically said goodbye. Needless to say the experience of this dreadful audition stayed with me all these years. It was one of the biggest embarrassments of my musical life. It was one of the worst performances of my life. I am not the only one who has ever suffered from blanking out and memory loss while performing. This seems to be a rather common problem, even the great ones suffer from this. Misha Dichter (1991) a fabulously successful concert pianist—who studied with the same teacher I did, Aube Tzerko— talks about memory problems. Dichter tells us that,

Then again my mind used to play games on me, during a performance. I would think, "Where will you forget this time?" and, of course I *would* forget Naturally! I was waiting for it, and it arrived. If it was a small lapse, my mind was pleased, if a big one, it was even more pleased! I had to learn to turn this off by having the positive impulses to keep going and not even allowing the devil to work. (p.70)

This is a remarkable passage! I never thought that concert pianists suffered from the same problems that I had. They always look so composed and look like they know what they are doing. I've never seen a concert pianist blank out or have a memory loss, but whenever I do go to a concert, I sit on the edge of my seat nervous for them, hoping to God that it doesn't happen. It's almost as if I can't wait for it to be over because I don't want to see them blank out.

Interestingly enough, another very famous and well respected and I might add here too fabulously successful concert pianist talks about his struggles with blanking out and memory loss. Here I am thinking of concert pianist Andre Watts. Watts (1991) tells us that,

. . . I had a season of almost nothing but memory lapses which sort of became a cycle. I knew I had a memory failure in a previous concert, so I waited for one in the present performance. It went on and on. Eventually it passed and, even though now occasionally I have a memory lapse, nothing ever equalled that particular year. (p. 188)

This is another remarkable passage coming from someone who is so successful and someone who has such great command over the instrument. I wish that when I was a music student someone would have told me these stories. I think it would have helped me to understand that even the famous musicians have problems. I used to think that it was a great failing of mine and that I was doomed because I blanked out occasionally, especially when the situation was very nerve wracking. Of course, performing in public is very nerve wracking. I don't know how these concert artists deal with this all the time. I cannot imagine going out onto a concert stage in front of three thousand people and not being nervous!!

The next audition I played to get into college was at Carnegie-Mellon University. It was flawless. Go figure? The problem with my playing had always been a lack of consistency due to technique. Sometimes I was on, sometimes I was off. When studying with Aube Tzerko at The Aspen Music Festival, I just couldn't play. I went through a terrible phase where my technique was so awful that I couldn't play anything. When I was much younger, say, around 12, I thought I played better!! It was so embarrassing and I just couldn't figure out what the problem was. He taught in the master class format where all of his students would sit around the piano and watch him teach one of us. How utterly humiliating for me. I was up against child prodigies, Curtis students. Once again, I just couldn't make my hands work. Tzerko—who had little patience for the whiz kids—was so sensitive to my situation that he asked me to come over to his house to take a private lesson. Unheard of!! I could never understand why he was so kind to me. I was the worst pianist there and knew then that I would never make it in the music world. But unlike the teachers at Juilliard, I felt like Tzerko gave me that second chance. At Tzerko's house, I played well. He asked me if I played tennis. I said yes, I've played the game. He said when you hit the ball do you think about it or just hit it? I said, of course, just hit it. Well, he said, then just play, don't think about it. But I had more problems than just not thinking about it. I had all sorts of technical problems as well as nerve problems. I just couldn't figure out how to play anymore. I got to the point where I couldn't figure out how to depress one key. Part of the problem was that I got too much conflicting advice from too many teachers. I think I suffered from too many obsessive thoughts about how to play that got in the way of my playing. Interestingly, looking back, I suffered from a similar problem in my Masters Program in Religious Studies. I got to a point in writing my Masters Thesis where I couldn't figure out how to write a sentence. Tzerko was right! Thinking got in the way of my writing as it got in the way of my playing. I got beyond that problem and wrote my thesis but I did it with much struggle.

I studied piano seriously since I was 8 years old, I won two competitions for young people, performed in front of large audiences. But as Arrau says, there are psychological reasons why musicians self-destruct. Something deep in me said, don't do this. Don't go there. Don't continue on this track. Several years later, I felt as if I had recovered from these ridiculous upsets and played perhaps the best audition of my life for Nancy Weems (who placed in the Van Cliburn Competition and was also nominated for a Grammy Award) at the University of Houston. I finally felt like I mastered my technique. But then this audition came too late as I was playing on top of an injured hand and it all came crashing down on me when the pain got so bad that I had to stop. I kept playing on the injury only to damage my hand more, until Nancy said "you must go to a doctor." I loved Nancy as a teacher and pianist. She was clearly one of the best pianists I ever studied with. But it was too late for me. I engaged in much magical thinking while in her studio pretending that nothing was really the matter. The injury over time forced me to stop playing. The pain became too much. The trips to the hand surgeon seemed interminable. And that was the end of my music career. I was 22 years old. I am now 46 years old and in my heart of hearts, I am still a musician.

The music world, at least the classical music world, is so sadistic. Performances must be flawless, perfect. Solo performances are usually done from memory. Will my memory fail me? Will my fingers forget? Will I blank out? What is the point of practicing 5 -7 hours a day? What is the point? But this is what classical musicians do. The instrument becomes a torture machine. The piano becomes the enemy. Cellist Pablo Casals (1959) surprisingly remarks,

> But it was the first trip, in 1901, that stands out sharply in my memory, because in California I almost ended my career as a cellist. While I was climbing a mountain, a rock fell on my hand and crushed it. Although the hand healed in a few months and I was soon scratching away again as nimbly as ever, I remember thinking that my reaction at the time of the accident was: "Well, thank God, I won't have to play the cello any more. I can now devote myself composing and conducting." This may sound strange, but I knew then that I had become a slave to the cello. I love the cello, but there are times when I feel it is a wilful instrument dominating my life and from which there is no escape. (pp. 33–34)

I must say when first came across this passage in Casals' autobiography I laughed aloud and finally felt vindicated in my negative feelings about the piano that I always felt too ashamed of to admit. Of course, Casals became one of the greatest cellists of the 20th century, while I became nothing—at least in the music world. I am a failure in the music world. I never made it. And that is something very difficult to admit.

And yet I read autobiographies of musicians because I am still drawn to that world. Tori Amos' (2005) book is perhaps one of the most intelligent and sensitive books written by a pop musician. She interests me especially because she was trained in the classical world and dropped out of it to become a pop star. Casals (1956; 1959; 1991) Arrau (1991; 1992) and Dimitri Shostakovich (2000) write greatly introspective autobiographies. Casals was almost mythic because not only did he play beautifully; he also had strong ethical convictions. He was not just a cellist. He was a fighter for social justice. Jim Hargrove (1991) calls Casals a "cellist of conscience" as the title of his book reflects this. Casals (1959) remarks,

> My life has been a search for perfection in art and for justice. In my music I have tried to give of myself, to do everything to the utmost of my ability. In the search for artistic perfection, perhaps I have contributed something. In the search for justice, I have tried to stand fast by the things I believe in: liberty, honesty and plain human dignity. This is no merit. It is natural and normal, an egotistical desire to live at peace with one's self. I have sought all my life to live at peace with myself. (p. 1)

Casals would never play in any country that was fascist, including his own, Spain. Casals became a musician of exile. It would have been easy for him to accept large sums of money to play in fascist countries but he never did. There are musicians who would sell their soul to the devil just to play. Thomas Mann's (1999) novel *Doctor Faustus* speaks exactly to this issue. And Klauss Mann (1995), Thomas Mann's son, speaks also to this issue in his novel *Mephisto*, which was also made into a striking film. Interestingly enough, in a letter by Thomas Mann (1954/1956), we read a statement about Pablo Casals, and his admiration for Casals' political steadfastness. Mann comments,

> This great creative artist will set foot in no country where liberty and right are not respected. Nor will he go to those countries which call themselves free, but make opportunistic deals with injustice. He withholds his genius from a world which, though steeped in wrong, would still like the aesthetic pleasure of hearing him–notably from Spain, the land of his birth. He no longer accepts invitations or leaves the village near the Franco-Spanish frontier which he has chosen as his refuge–Prades. This name, almost unknown till linked with his, has become universally known as a symbol of art devoid of all compromise–of the unbreakable union of art and morality. (cited in J. Ma. Corrdor, iii, 1954)

Since Casals wouldn't leave Prades, other musicians came to him. Hence the famous Prades Festival was born. I grew up listening to recordings of Casals playing at the Prades festival. At the time I listened to him I was not aware of the political background against which he played. I was only 12 years old when I discovered these recordings of Casals. What did I know of social justice at 12? Or fascism? It was only as I grew older and more interested in issues of social justice that the Prades Festival became an important sociological study for me. As is well known, too, many European musicians made pacts with the devil during the rise of fascism and Nazism. One need only comb the literature, for example, on Hitler's army of Nazi musicians.

SECRETS, PSYCHOANALYSIS AND MUSIC

Adam Phillips (1993) talks about secrets and their connection to psychoanalysis. The purpose of psychoanalysis is to uncover secrets. Not so easy. Secrets are partly conscious and partly unconscious attempts to cover over something painful. Music can be an expression of secrets. But most musicians– whether they have gone through analysis or not– probably do not pay attention to their own secrets. They are too busy memorizing and repeating phrases for hours on end.

How can one play out of a site of a secret? Secrets are coded memories, hovering between the conscious and the unconscious. Where music comes from remains a mystery and is for many a secret. Does music express a deeply repressed secret? Is sadness in music just sadness? One must wonder what performers are really thinking about when playing sad music. What goes through their minds? What are they connecting to? Perhaps the musicians do not even know. I bet that most of them do not know what drives their playing. Is the secret that drives musicians' playing an obstacle? What if the obstacle were removed? Does the removal of the obstacle also remove the musician's drive to play? If musicians do not have secrets, what are they expressing? Does not knowing the secret cripple? Are musicians who are driven by unconscious secrets emotionally crippled? Adam Phillips (1997) suggests that one uses obstacles in the service of concealing. "The obstacle is used to conceal–to pack up, as it were– the unconscious desire" (1997, p. 81). What is the unconscious desire of music making? Is music an obstacle? Does it serve to cover over and deny a past? Is music making a form of forgetting? Is it a form of denial? Is playing music a defense mechanism?

Is music an expression of desire? Is it a form of seduction? Is the purpose of music to seduce? Lacan argued that all of life is about seduction, really. I am thinking here of Paderewski. His playing was highly charismatic and dramatic. He seduced his audience through his playing. James Cooke (1999) claims that he "cast a personal spell" (p. 17) over his audience. Is casting a spell over people what music is really about? Is it a form of witchcraft or voodoo?

Does music just come out of nowhere? Freud, according to Christopher Bollas (1995), talked about ideas seemingly coming out of nowhere. The term he used to express this is *einfall*. Does music just fall into or out of the psyche by accident? I don't think so. Music comes from somewhere, some deep psychic place. For some, music comes out of what Michael Eigen calls "the ongoing disaster" (p. 64, 2004). And the 'ongoing disaster' is a remnant of a wrecked childhood. I am thinking of Dimitri Shostakovich. His symphonies are so depressing to listen to. They are depressing because they are expressions of his experience of living through the catastrophe that was the Soviet Union. In his memoirs, he states, " [l]ooking back, I see nothing but ruins, only mountains of corpses" (p. 3). For Shostakovich, composing music was a way to "unburden" his soul. He states, "[s]o many unsaid things collect in the soul, so much exhaustion and irritation lie as a heavy burden on the psyche. And you must, you *must* unburden your spiritual world or risk a collapse" (p. 29). Music prevents collapse. Or music is collapse. Music serves to keep the psyche together or rips it apart. Music is in the service of holding or destroying. Michael Eigen (2005) argues that "[a] specialty of psychoanalysis is focusing on unbearable emotions" (p. 4). The purpose of music is expressing the unbearable. Certainly for Shostakovich music was the expression of an unbearable situation. As Joan Symington (2000) might put it, music expresses "imprisoned pain" (p. 2).

On **not** being able to play is what this book is about. Michael Parsons (1999) tells us that identity-formation—from a psychoanalytic perspective—is not about who we are but about who we are not; the story of a life is not about what we have become but what we have not become. And that is exactly what my book is about. Parsons (1999) states:

> All ego-developments and any experience of ourselves as subjects has to be achieved against an essential background of loss and absence. We become who we are by how we deal with the fact that we cannot have what we want

nor be who we wish to be. . . . In considering the *fort-da* game. . . [Freud's] emphasis would not be first on the *da*, the child's successful recovery of the cotton-reel. . . but on the *fort,* his throwing away of the cotton-reel. . . . (p.71)

Interestingly enough, Parson's makes much of Freud's game playing with a child. The child who throws away the cotton-reel symbolizes the loss of relation with the mother according to Parsons. The throwing away of the cotton-reel is a symbol, then, of loss. The game of life is partly about dealing with loss. The lost cotton-reel is also a symbol, not of wholeness but of being split off in some way. Early trauma splits the self, especially when the mother—for the child—is not attentive. This plays a big role in how the adult—who deals with loss later in life—deals with life's blows and disappointments.

Listening to music—because it is primarily an emotional activity—can bring up these archaic losses and can remind psyche of a troubled past. This is what is so powerful about music. As Gilbert Rose (2004) puts it, listening to music may "provoke us with disunion rather than welcome us with union" (xxi). This disunion that music evokes might be the unconscious memory of the lost mother, the thrown away cotton-reel. The disunion that might be felt listening to music might also be the reminder of not being able to play music or to play with ideas. At bottom, these losses are a crisis of psyche. And this crisis splits us into pieces psychically. Although some Jungians talk about finding wholeness in the personality, here I am not interested in wholeness. I am interested in the broken shards, the shattered psyche. Who we are is what we have lost. And dealing with that loss tells much about our character. What do you do when you cannot do what you've been called to do? What happens then? What is the way out? Is there a way out? This book is an attempt to find a way out.

CHAPTER TWO

A PHENOMENOLOGY OF A MUSICAL PSYCHE

Thinking phenomenologically about not being able to play a musical instrument is the task at hand. We must ask first what a musical imagination is and what happens when that musical imagination is wounded. In order then to talk about being wounded we must think about a phenomenology of pain as it exiles a person from both her psyche and body. When pained, one tends to psychically over-invest in the painful limb or dissociate from it altogether. Depersonalization can be a consequence of woundedness.

This chapter will be divided into two sections that tease out differing layers of phenomenological thought around being unable to play. First, it is crucial to examine what a phenomenology of a musical imagination might be. Secondly I will tease out a phenomenology of pain. Thought through together, these two sections of this chapter will help us think about what a phenomenology of a pained musical psyche might feel like.

A PHENOMENOLOGY OF A MUSICAL IMAGINATION

What is it to have a musical imagination? To imagine music suggests that one can express musical images–or sound-images– by playing an instrument. The musical imagination is akin to what I call a painting imagination. Marion Milner (1957)– after whose work this one is built–obviously had a painterly imagination. Her book, *On Not Being Able to Paint* (1957) deals with what that painterly imagination can do once let loose from the chains of ego. We don't often think of someone possessing an intellectual imagination, but scholars, if they do not have an imaginative capacity cannot do groundbreaking work. They only imitate. But in order to think through the new– whether expressed through music, art or scholarship— developing an imaginative capacity becomes necessary. To do something new calls for imagination. Intellectual work is a mix of ideas and images. A musical imagination mixes ideas, images and sounds. The scholar and musician work in similar ways both intellectually and emotionally. The question is what happens when the work breaks down? Here, I look at the breakdown of the musical imagination all the while thinking about the implications for what this might mean for the scholar who is unable to work on ideas.

What is a musical imagination? What does it feel like? These questions are inherently phenomenological. Let us turn to some of the work of Maurice Merleau-Ponty and Gaston Bachelard (2002b) to help flesh out our topic. First I turn to Merleau-Ponty's (1968) work *The Visible and the Invisible* to articulate what I mean when I talk of a musical imagination. Merleau-Ponty (1968) talks in this rather difficult book about two realms: the visible and the invisible. Let us start with the invisible because it is harder to grasp than the visible. The invisible realm is that place where thinking and imagining happen. Thinking for Merleau-Ponty is a sort of mysterious something that goes on within us but we really don't understand much about it. It is the invisible something that makes us what we are. I am reminded here of Descartes' *Cogito Ergo Sum*. I think therefore I am. But Descartes doesn't really tell us what thinking is. Neither does Merleau-Ponty. Thinking is an 'ing.' 'Ing' is obscure, the very nature of the 'ing' makes it so. The act of imagine—'ing', I suggest, is connected to thinking but differs from thinking proper. To imagine is a bit different from thinking because imagining is broader. Sometimes imagine-'ing' encompasses images, sounds and ideas. Thinking—for the scholar—might only encompass ideas and images. But the scholar might also think in terms of ideas, images and sounds—especially if she is a scholar of music or musician. So imagining and thinking overlap in some cases. To imagine, however, seems to be a more mystical activity than thinking proper. To imagine suggests that psyche is up in the clouds. The act of Thinking moves psyche downward toward the ground. Later we will see that Gaston Bachelard (2002b) deals with these earthly images to ground his phenomenology. At any rate, images, ideas and sounds are complexly meshed together. To think at all baffles, to imagine at all baffles, to imagine sound baffles. Thinking and imagining or creating sounds are largely invisible processes. Now, the key for Merleau-Ponty (1968) is that the invisible (thinking or imagining) cannot be separated from the visible. The instrument which is played upon is visible, yes? I see the guitar. I act on it through touching it. Touch is a major category for Merleau-Ponty. It is through touch that the invisible and the visible get connected. The visible, broadly speaking, is what is sensible. The body is sensible. Merleau-Ponty is one of the first philosophers in the Western canon to talk of the body. His argument is that thinking (and I would add imagining) cannot happen without being instantiated in the visible, in the body. Thinking is not separated from that which is thought about. Merleau-Ponty (1968) explains that

> the sensible world is visible and relatively continuous, and because the universe of thought, which is invisible and contains gaps, constitutes at first sight a whole and has its truth only on condition that it be supported on the canonical structures of the sensible world. (p. 12)

Essentially, Merleau-Ponty's position diverges from that of Descartes because Descartes drives a wedge between thought and what is thought about. There seems to be a hole between thinking and that which is thought. Descartes did not discount that we have a body but he did place the body in a diminished position–which of course pleased the Church, for Descartes straddled the world of Church and State. The Church still had a stranglehold on Europe. Father of the Enlightenment, Descartes privileged reason over against perception and imagination. But Merleau-Ponty does not privilege one term over against another. He suggests basically that everything is connected to everything else. This more ecologically sensitive position becomes a problem for philosophy as a discipline because Merleau-Ponty introduces the importance of the body into the canon. The body, historically speaking, has always been a scandal for philosophers. It is unpredictable, sexual, soft and can get wounded. Merleau-Ponty, like the feminists, turned to the body to make sense of the world. But of course feminists had been talking about the body long before Merleau-Ponty came along but they got burned at the stake for doing so.

What is the connection between thinking and that which is thought? (Again, here I would also ask for our purposes here, what is the connection between imagining and that which is imagined ?) As against the history of Western philosophy, Merleau-Ponty suggests that there is no chasm between these two realms, there is no wedge, but rather they are sort of "tangle [d]" up by the flesh. In the tangled web one part is "contiguous" with the other. Merleau-Ponty (1968) claims that:

> it is that this distance [between thinking and what is thought about] is not the contrary of this proximity, it is deeply consonant with it, it is synonymous with it. It is the thickness of the flesh between the seer and the thing is constitutive for the thing of its visibility as for the seer of his corporeity, it is not an obstacle between them, it is their means of communication. (p. 135)

Against Descartes, Merleau-Ponty makes the claim that the "thickness of the flesh" is what holds these two parts [the seer and that which is seen, the thinker and that which is thought about]] together. The introduction of the flesh into philosophy is a scandal. The flesh is weak. The flesh is not eternal. Unlike Plato's notions of the Forms or Ideas which are eternal, Merleau-Ponty emphasizes that the glue to lived experience-the flesh—is precisely what Plato denigrated. The flesh bleeds. Plato and Descartes had no use for bloody flesh. Theirs was a world of purity and wholeness. But when we think of Descartes and his deep connections with the Church, we must wonder about what happened to that image of the bloody Christ on the cross? The Church Fathers—or the Patristics—cleaned up that image of Christ. Yet in some regions of the world like Mexico for example, the image of Christ on the cross is rather bloody. It is curious how some Europeans and European-Americans sanitize images.

The difficult phenomenological question is always already this: How does a thinking, feeling and imagining person communicate with another who thinks, feels and imagines? Phenomenology is the study of what is intensely private. How to translate the private? How does one person translate her fleshy experiences and feelings, thoughts and imaginings to another person? Is it even possible? The nagging phenomenological question plagues. Merleau-Ponty suggests that there is a limit to communication because of the complications of our invisible, private worlds. It is the private world that is really interesting because in the privacy of thinking or imagining, we really do not understand how it is that we come to think or imagine to begin with. Relevant to this study, Merleau-Ponty (1968) suggests that it is through music that a person might be able to communicate her feelings to another. Music might serve as a bridge between one person and another. He states:

But at the very moment that I think I share the life of another, I am rejoining it only in its ends, its exterior poles. . . . it is through the music that I enter into his musical emotion, it is the thing itself that opens unto me the access to the private world of another. (p. 11)

Merleau-Ponty is on to something here as he suggests that music helps us communicate with the other. Music is primarily emotional. It is both played and listened to with the ear of the emotions, even if it is highly intellectual. But primarily music moves people through emotions. Music connects people. As I will discuss later in the book, the group *Pink Floyd* has been so successful because they have been able to connect with generations of people because they express emotions that resonate with many. The band expresses a deep anguish to which many can relate. Music is deeply psychological. Private worlds can be made public through the expression of sound. And for the scholar, her private world can be made public through the expression of ideas. Yet, expression of any sort is limited. Parts of the private world remain private. There is always already an impenetrable place in the psyche. The psyche is Other to the other as it is Other to the self. At a certain point, communication between two people stops. One can only understand another person up to a certain point. Understanding is limited. And this is always the problem of phenomenology. Lacan, in a typical postmodern fashion, argues throughout his work that–at the end of the day– we really do not communicate with each other at all. We live in a world of continual misunderstanding and missed meaning. Well, he does have a certain point here. And perhaps this is what pains us.

One problem of a phenomenological approach to pain is that no matter how hard one tries to express what pain feels like, pain defies explanation. And Merleau-Ponty points this out. He asks "how could I conceive, precisely. . . his pain" (p. 11). I cannot 'precisely' understand anybody else's pain but my own, and even then I am not sure I can conceptualize it. Pain is the greatest problem for phenomenology because it is beyond representation, behind language, pre-verbal and primordial. And it is private. I might try to express my pain to you but I will always fail. Pain is deeply enfleshed. But what does enfleshed really mean? It is not clear exactly what the flesh is. Flesh, for Merleau-Ponty is not a substance, matter or an essence, but rather a "texture" (p. 146) and interestingly enough an "element." (p. 139). We will see later on in Bachelard's (2002b) work how important fundamental elements (like earth, air, water and even dreams) are to creativity and imagination. At any rate, Merleau-Ponty (1968) claims that "[t]he flesh . . . is not contingency, chaos, but a texture that returns to itself and conforms to itself' (p. 146). The flesh as texture is dense and kind of strange. What is meant by texture? What is a texture that is flesh? It is not clear. The texture of flesh for Merleau-Ponty (1968) is:

this interiorly worked-over mass, [and] has no name in any philosophy. As the formative medium of the object and the subject, it is not the atom of being, the hard in itself that resides in a unique place and moment: one can indeed say of my body that it is not elsewhere, but one cannot say that it is here or now in the sense that objects are. . . . (p. 147)

I argue, against Merleau-Ponty, that in pain the body does become elsewhere either in psychic overinvestment or dissociation. Now, it might be strange to think that overinvestment is an elsewhere, but it can be if the limb is so focused upon that the rest of the body disappears psychically. The psychic place of elsewhere is the seemingly disappearing body.

Imagining and playing music are fundamentally grounded in the flesh, in the touch. To play guitar, one must have a certain touch that allows the strings to resonate. Some people have it and others don't. The ideas and sounds which create the music are expressed through touch. The point of touch, a fleshy textured touch, is that it is inextricably connected to what gets expressed. Some people are heavy-handed while some have a light touch. The more nuanced and sensitive the touch the better the musician. But what is it about touching that is so special? Touching is what connects us to the world. To touch the sky. This is a metaphor for being light. To soar like a bird. Some musicians have no touch. Perhaps these people should not be called musicians at all. Playing a Rachmaninoff piano concerto, for example, without a sensitive touch, without nuance, playing heavy handed grates on the ear. The pianist might get all the notes right but communicate little to her audience. This is the school of loud and fast. Many can play loud and fast, technique can be taught, but musicianship cannot. Musicianship is a gift. Pianist Alicia de Laroccha (1991) comments on the problem of competitions and the way in which they make technical "*machines*" out of musicians. She states:

> I think the whole system is wrong, completely wrong. It has nothing to do with music or the artist. It's like an Olympic which is artificial and mechanical. It's work work, work to make the competition, but then what? If pianists are any good, they don't need a competition. Besides, if they do, they merely receive a prize and a series of concerts which sometimes turns the pianists into mere machines. (p. 56)

Competitions, as de Laroccha says, are the real tragedy in the classical music world. Music is not a competition and it certainly is not about the machinery of playing. The competition takes the soul out of playing.

Now Mozart had soul. How did he hear an entire symphony in his head before putting it on paper? Where did the music come from? Where do musical ideas come from? From the soul? That is the mystery. Some people have musical ideas and some people do not. Music is either *in you* or it isn't. The techniques of composition can be taught, but getting the musical ideas in the first place cannot. What does it mean to be an expressive musician? Merleau-Ponty (1968) turns this question on its head by remarking that,

> We do not possess the musical or sensible ideas, precisely because they are negativity or absence circumscribed; they possess us. The performer is no longer producing or reproducing the sonata: he feels himself, and the others

feel him to be at the service of the sonata; the sonata sings through him or cries out so suddenly that he must "dash his bow" to follow it. (p. 151)

It is the music that possesses us, not the other way around—Merleau-Ponty points out. Good musicians do indeed feel possessed by the music. It is as if the music speaks through the body. If music is a 'negativity' or an 'absence'–as Merleau-Ponty suggests– some interesting problems arise. In the psyche there are holes or as Merleau-Ponty suggests "open vortexes" (p. 151). Lacan talks similarly about lacks. It is through the lack, the hole, the blank spot that musical expression emerges. Going backwards and downwards to the lack one might think that the lack is nothing at all. Is this a Buddhist question? If there is nothing at bottom in the heart of being how can something (i.e. music) come out of nothing? This Leibnizian question rears its head . Again we are back to square one. From whence does music spring? Who knows. Perhaps the search for origins is misguided. And since we do not know the origins of anything really, musical imagination refuses explanation. The secret of musical expression remains.

Like Merleau-Ponty, Gaston Bachelard (2002b) speaks to issues that turn on the topic at hand. Bachelard is helpful to us as he fleshes out phenomenology in such a way that might be related to musical imagination. Bachelard does not talk about a musical imagination per se, but his phenomenology lends itself nicely to thinking about what a musical imagination might be. Here I would like to explore some of Bachelard's ideas on what he calls material imagination and think about the ways in which a material imagination might offer clues to thinking about musical imagination. Bachelard's phenomenology moves our thinking in a different direction from that of Merleau-Ponty's. It is to this different direction that I would like to turn. The major book upon which I draw is Bachelard's (2002b) *Earth and Reveries of Will: An Essay On the Imagination of Matter.* I will also touch on a (s)mattering of ideas throughout his other works as well to fill out the picture.

Generally speaking, Bachelard's work is rather difficult to penetrate, like Merleau-Ponty's. But the difficulties are a little different from those that we find in Merleau-Ponty's work. A key to reading Bachelard– like reading Derrida–is that much of his work turns on aporias. Like Deleuze, the key word for Bachelard is **And. And** this conjunction signals a paradox. Bachelard's work is filled with paradoxes and puzzles. These paradoxes do not easily resolve. The paradoxes are sometimes synthesized, but still there is always an uneasy read when working on Bachelard. The uneasy read may frustrate, but in the frustration much depth emerges.

Bachelard is interested in creativity and how the creative spirit works with objects. There is something about objects and relations to objects that fascinates. Bachelard's work leads to questions like what is the imagination after all? How does that imaginative spirit connect to objects? How does the imagination connect with the outside world? What is it about the inside and outside that puzzle? Bachelard suggests that the imagination is not some free floating thing or a thing-in-itself, rather it is always already instantiated in matter. Matter is both inside the body and in objects. Objects are primarily made up of the stuff of the earth, air, fire and water. These basic elements are inside us and in the larger cosmos. One must remember that Bachelard was a philosopher of science so it makes perfect sense that basic elements would take on meaning for him. If it is the case that the elements are inside us and outside in the world and in objects then imagination–being housed in the body–is also made up of the elements. For Bachelard the imagination is material. This is a touchstone of his thought. This is not dissimilar to Merleau-Ponty's point that the visible (that which is touched, the body, or an object) and that which is invisible (touching, thinking or imagining) are inextricably tied. Interestingly enough, for Bachelard the imagination (which is material) gets expressed through the hand. The hand that works matter connects the imagination to the body and to objects in the world. Now, Bachelard, unlike Merleau-Ponty, is a Jungian so he is interested in talking about related psychological principles. For example, he makes much of dreaming. He suggests that working on objects, in dreamlike states, or states of reverie, connect the person who is working upon objects better with both her own embodied, or enmattered, imagination as well as to the object upon which she "works." "Working" is a key term for Bachelard. One must "work" the imagination he argues. This has implications for both musicians and scholars because both must work at what they do. Some musicians wait until they are inspired to practice, some scholars wait until they are inspired to write. But the real work is in the everyday practice and everyday writing. Bachelard might suggest that waiting for inspiration is not working the matter (of music or writing I would conjecture) enough. It is through work–with the hands and the imagination–that one becomes healed. Bachelard suggests that working in a dreamlike state is a form of therapy. So we might dream better to work better. Hard work, Bachelard says, is necessary to enliven the imagination.

Let us turn now to the text at hand (Bachelard's (2002b) *Earth and Reveries of Will*) to better flesh out–as it were–Bachelard's key points. Once this is accomplished, I will make use of Bachelard in my own way as I attempt to connect his phenomenological principles to my question about thinking through a musical phenomenology.

Now, it seems an oxymoron that the imagination is material, that is, that the imagination is "enmattered" as Bachelard puts it. This is the first difficult paradox around which we must deal. The imagination is that faculty which dwells on images. When one thinks of images, one thinks of free floating, static forms. One might think of Plato's Forms as images of the True, the Beautiful and the Good. But Plato's Forms are static, eternal. Bachelard moves away from Plato by suggesting that images are not static at all, in fact, he suggests that we might think of them as 'de-formed', rather than formed. To de-form an image is to liquidify it in a way, to melt it, to watch it move and change. Images are, therefore, moving, changing, breathing creatures for Bachelard. However, these moving, living, swelling images which are de-formed are also and paradoxically enmattered. That is, images are instantiated in matter which we usually think of as hard and immovable. But Bachelard argues that matter is not static, rather it is in motion. The earth–the matter that makes up the earth–is alive and moving and changing.

The earth is a living thing. If we are born from the earth we are part of the earth and therefore matter is in our being and therefore the imagination is enmattered. Bachelard suggests that to better understand this difficult paradox is through reverie and dream. Bachelard (2002b) states,

> Indeed, before the spectacle of fire or water or sky, the reverie that seeks substance beneath ephemeral appearance is in no way obstructed by reality. In these circumstances, imagination is exactly what is called for: one must dream up a deeper substance for vibrant, colorful fire; fix the fluid substance of running water; and finally, amid the airy whisperings of breezes and birds in flight, imagine the very stuff of airiness, the very stuff of atmospheric freedom. (p. 1)

Imagining what is ephemeral does not detract from reality. Reality is embedded in the elements, the elements are reality, the ephemeral is reality. The real is the imagined, the imagined is the real. What is imagined –or fantasized–is made of the matter of the real. Imagination is encased in matter, it is matter, and it does matter. Just because someone imagines or dreams or fantasizes doesn't mean that these things are not real; imagination is real and dreams are real. Freud often pointed out throughout his work that fantasies–just because they are made up–are real. In fact, Freud suggested that psychic reality is all we really have. We live in made up worlds.

Bachelard suggests that the more we think on matter or about matter (i.e. the elements), the more likely images will emerge from thinking on matter. Thinking about images emerging from matter complicates. The more I look at and think about a rock, for example, the more I will start to dream the rock into another sphere and imagine qualities about the rock which might be psychological in nature. The rock conjures up thoughts of heaviness or even depression for example. In other words, dwelling on basic elements that seem impenetrable or ethereal (like air for example) gets the psychological imagination to move, to do its work to enliven spirit-bodies. Imagination– because it is made up of matter–is housed in the body-matter. This brings us back to ourselves and psychological musings. Thinking on a rock, is thinking on what rocks psyche.

What is the motivating force that moves us to dwell on matter and the imagination? Bachelard argues that it is the will that makes us work on matter in an imaginative way. In fact, Bachelard suggests that *imagination and will* come together in a "synthesis", even though they seem to stand at polar ends of the psyche. Bachelard (2002b) states

> By approaching the dialectic of Imagination and Will at the outset, I am preparing the ground for a possible synthesis of the imagination of matter and the imagination of energy. (p. 8).

Matter, when one casually thinks about it, seems to be still. But there is also at bottom a mobility of earthy things. Even rocks that are seemingly still, move, change. Just think of the Grand Canyon. Or think of Bryce Canyon and its hoodoos. The hoodoos are living, changing rock formations. Yet, as one stands at the top of Bryce it seems that all is quiet on the hoodoo front. Thus, matter is seemingly hard and still and yet it is also moveable. Bryce is on the move, even though we can't see that with our eyes. When infused with energy a still thing like a rock becomes a moving thing. The will, however, must do something with the rock, or work on the rock. Does the earth have a will? Bachelard seems to think so. The will is the earth's energy. Of course, the will inside of us is a driving force behind doing something. It is the *working on the matter* that gives a seemingly inert thing a push toward mobility. Bachelard (2002b) states:

> The hardness and softness of things engage us in an entirely other kind of dynamic life. The resistant world lifts us out of our static reality, beyond ourselves, initiating us into the mysteries of energy. Henceforth we are awakened beings. Hammer or trowel in hand, we no longer stand alone–we have an adversary, something to accomplish. (p. 14)

The will to "hammer" the earth into new forms brings energy to what is seemingly inert. The earth, for Bachelard, is a symbol of what is most resistant and perhaps most difficult to think about because it seems as if it is a solid form that will not budge, like a diamond that one cannot break open, or a hard rock. *Working* these material things with the hand by hammering, for example, energizes the imagination to create something out of hard substance and enliven that substance. This is what sculptors do. Bachelard says that "it is human beings who awaken matter; it is the contact of the marvelous human hand, a contact imbued with all our tactile dreams, that gives life to the qualities slumbering in things" (p. 18).

What fascinates is that both Bachelard and Merleau-Ponty make much of the hand. Recall that for Merleau-Ponty the key term for him is touch. Likewise, for Bachelard the key term is the hand. There is something about the hand's touch that connects us to the outside world in profound ways. It is the hand that creates life from seemingly lifeless matter. It is the touch which allows us to express feelings and effect objects outside of our bodies simultaneously. Recall, for Merleau-Ponty, the touch and the flesh is that thickness that connects the visible and invisible realms.

One of the differences between these two phenomenologists is that Bachelard is more interested in the psychological qualities of lived experience. Bachelard makes much of feelings. What is it that causes one to have the feeling of being weighed down or buoyant? One might soar to the heights via imagination by working on enmattered images; but one also plummets into the depths in "troubled waters". Merleau-Ponty, on the other hand, is a philosopher who is more interested in the ways in which we *think* through embodied states of lived experience. Bachelard is a psychological phenomenologist whereas Merleau-Ponty is a philosophical phenomenologist. Bachelard emphasizes, in the passage below, that what he is after is exploring ways in which to move the psyche into a mobile state so that the imagination can do its work. A dead psyche, or an inert psyche cannot imagine matter into existence. The inert psyche only sinks into the belly of the earth. Here, Bachelard (2002b) tells us that:

In describing the union of imagination and will with specific examples, one can clarify the psychology of a dream which occurs in a heightened awakeness, a dream which the worker becomes attached to the object worked, penetrates its substance fully with desire, and achieves as great a solitude thus as in the deepest sleep. (p. 38)

Talking about the specific example of rocks–for instance–Bachelard suggests that one can better focus the imagination on that piece of hard matter and work to carve out– while, say hammering that matter– something that comes to life or seems alive rather than inert. Hammering rocks, one might make an object alter its shape and form, become "de-formed" and movable, shifting like a piece of art.

An important part of the above passage relates to the connection between the worker and the object which is worked. Here, I am reminded of W.D. Winnicott's (2005) theory of transitional objects and transitional phenomena. Transitional objects serve as a mother substitute. The teddy bear, Winnicott (2005) points out, is one such object. The teddy bear transitions the child away from the mother and toward the world. The love the child has for the mother is now transferred onto the teddy bear, or toward the world. Likewise, Bachelard suggests that it is crucial that the worker connect to an object in a way that is loving. That is, there must be a certain "attachment" to the object. If someone works with objects without this attachment and love one toils in misery. Objects, in this instance, alienate, rather than warm. Marx made a similar point about the worker and her work. Alienation happens when the worker does not love her work.

To connect to an object or to be attached to an object–as Bachelard puts it–one might think more about the way in which one *touches* the object. What does it mean to hammer life into a rock? Think of Italy for a moment. Italy is beautiful partly because of its sculptures. There is something about the way in which rock is carved into such beautiful things that stun. Standing before the statue of David or Moses one might weep–the beauty astounds. When rock is carved with love and attachment, Bachelard suggests the worker-of-rock has developed a "poetry of touch" (p. 62). Bachelard states,

If poetry is to reanimate the powers of creation in the soul or help us relive our natural dreams in all their intensity and all their meaning, we must come to understand that the hand as well as the eye has its reveries and poetry. We must discover the poetry of touch, the poetry of the kneading hands. (p. 60)

Bachelard makes much of the *hands* throughout his work. The hands are what connect us to the material imagination, the hands set dreaming to work in material form. The poetry of the hand is that which links the physical and the psychological while working on matter and this work from matter moves us into an aesthetic realm–i.e. the statue of David–whereby the elements (earth, air, fire, water) play a role in what is worked over. In fact, Bachelard (1988b) argues in his book *The Right to Dream*, that the elements are "principles of artistic creation" (p. 28). Bachelard (1988b) says,

And so the elements–fire, water, air and earth–which for so long served philosophers for thinking grandly of the universe, still remain principles of artistic creation. Their action upon the imagination may seem remote and it may seem metaphorical. And yet as soon as we find a work of art's proper appurtenance to the elemental cosmic force, we have a feeling of having discovered a ground of unity that strengthens the unity of even the best composed works. (p. 28)

What is striking about Bachelard's work is that he combines philosophy, Jungian psychology, science and the arts in such a seamless way. The combination of these various disciplines is what gives Bachelard's work a kind of poetic flare. He claims (2002b) that "this phenomenology is essentially a dynamology and that a material analysis of work must be accompanied by an analysis of the energies involved" (p. 33). What confounds is the idea that solid substance is inherently in motion and that solid substance is also inert. The earth is the element which most troubles because it is the hardest one, I think, to think on and work on. When I think of the earth, I think of a planet with a solid core, unlike, say, the planets that are made up of only gas, like Saturn. How can a planet made up of a solid core also be worked in such a way to make that solid liquidify? Working on matter (i.e. the earth) makes imagination come alive. It is not enough to gaze at the landscape, one must do something with it, one must work it. Is that not what both artists and scholars do? Scholars, for example, work on words and work on hard matter, (the difficult subject at hand as well as literally on the matter of the computer). A seemingly inert thing (a dead subject for example) comes alive if the scholar makes it come alive through words. Working on words is another way of working on matter. Working words into shape, finding patterns in words is as difficult as chiselling out a statue from rock.

In connection with words and matter, Bachelard suggests that the element of fire is the one upon which the poet draws inspiration. Fire is the element which gets the poet going, sets words in motion. In his book *The Flame of a Candle*, Bachelard (1988a), tells us that:

Of all images, images of the flame–the most artless as well as the most refined, the wisest as well as the most foolish–bear the mark of the poetic. Whoever dreams of a flame is a potential poet. All reverie in the presence of a flame is admiring reverie. Whoever dreams of a flame is in a state of primal reverie. (p. 2)

Reverie is a basic concept for Bachelard; throughout his work he speaks of reverie. Reverie is an interesting yet difficult notion to articulate. Reverie is not exactly memory and it does not happen exactly in the here and now–it sort of hovers between the two. Reverie is like a dream- state I suppose. Bachelard uses dreams and reverie in similar ways. Reverie seems, however, to be a little different from dreams. Dreams, whether conscious or unconscious, might get expressed in story-form with a whole cast of characters. Reverie, I think, is hazier, vague. Reverie is that space where one might just zone out. Psyche is absent and yet present but not depersonalized. Psyche is a step removed from the present and yet is fully in the now, the present. I don't know whether Bachelard would define reverie in this way, but I don't think he would disagree with this interpretation. Interestingly, Wilfred Bion (1991) – the well known psychoanalyst –argues that if the mother does not open herself to spaces of reverie, the child will not be able to connect to things or relate fully to her environment. The child is somehow psychologically arrested because the mother did not open a space through which the child could project feelings, imaginings and so forth. A mother without reverie is as good as a dead mother–as Andre Green (1991) might put it. The dead mother, for Green, is not psychically there for the child. For Green (1993) the more psychically dead the mother is to the child, the more the introject or imago of the dead mother gets fixed in the psyche of the child. And then we have a host of problems because psyche is occupied with and by a corpse.

Back to fire for a moment, though. Symbolically, fire is what moves poets musicians, artists and scholars–if they are worth their salt (salt is an element too). I am on fire in my writing. I am burning to get to my work. Sometimes burning brings up images of anger. I think of Richard Wright's work. Angry. Bachelard makes a connection between anger and creativity. In fact, he suggests that anger may be an important component in creating a work of art. Bachelard (2002b) claims,

> The hostility of hard matter is thus the sign of an old grudge. All the resentments of life resurface with each shoe to be worked. . . . Philippe concludes with a formula that deserves to become a motto for the philosophy of labor. "To be a shoemaker, you have to be angry". (p. 41)

In this passage, Bachelard is not talking about fire but earthen matter which is mostly resistant to altering and "de-forming." The shoemaker is the one who works with hard matter or the material of the shoe. In order to craft the shoe, anger is a necessary emotion to get the shoe into shape. Fire might fuel anger. When one gets angry, the ears often turn red, or the face might turn red. One might start to sweat and get overheated. The expression 'hot under the collar' is an expression of anger; one is inflamed. Something that is inflamed in the body, like a tendon, feels hot because it is hot, it catches the fire of in-flame-ation. An inflamed tendon pushes against nerves and hurts. The sheaths of the tendon fill with *fluid* and the arm feels like it is about to burst.

Speaking of things fluid, let us move to the element of water. Bachelard states that water is akin to the liquidity of speech. When one gives a lecture extemporaneously, and things go well, we might say that the lecture just flowed as if it had its own current. When speaking flows between people a spark (of fire) might be ignited. The elements are enfolded into each other. Bachelard tends to separate out the elements in his work (i.e. one book on fire, another on water, another on dreams, another on the earth) but as a whole Bachelard seems to suggest that the elements are webbed ecologically. It might be more convenient to treat them separately as Bachelard does and as I am doing here–but really everything is in everything else. Elements make up planets, the earth and our bodies. Back to water for a moment. Bachelard (1999), in his book *Water and Dreams,* emphasizes the negativity of water by suggesting that many dwell in "troubled waters" (p. 139). He states:

> There are dreamers who concentrate on troubled water. They gaze in wonder at black ditch water, at water permeated by bubbles, at water that shows the veins within its substance and that raises, as if by itself, a swirl of salt. Then it seems as though water itself dreams and is covered over with a nightmarish vegetation. (p. 139)

In this passage I am reminded of the Simon and Garfunkel song "Like a bridge over troubled water." Why are waters troubling? What troubles water? And if one is troubled in speech then liquidity dries up. Is this what it means to be dried up? If one feels dried up as a teacher, it's time to stop teaching. If one dries up as a musician, it's time to put the instrument down. If one's ideas dry up, it's time to put the pen down. But when the water flows again (in liquidity), and the speech seems to come as if on its own, all is good again.

The interesting thing about Bachelard is that there are places in his work where he does dwell on states of depression, but most of his work seems to be light and airy. He makes a point, though, throughout his work to suggest that all good things have their bad counterparts. In fact he says that the heights and the abysses are always already interconnected. Falling and rising are all part of lived experience. And water takes on another characteristic relevant to our study here–water makes birds and people sing, says Bachelard (1999). He explains that:

> murmuring waters teach birds and men to sing, speak, recount; and that there is, in short, a continuity between the speech of water and the speech of man. Conversely, I shall stress the little noted fact that, organically human language has a liquid quality. (p. 15)

Inextricably connected to water is air. In his book *Air and Dreams*, Bachelard (2002a) states that air (uplift or ascension) and water (the abyss) work in tandem and or paradoxically. He says, "imagination of the fall [into the abyss of water] will be present only insofar as it is an inverted ascent" (p. 15). Emotionally this presents a problem. Everybody has ups and downs. But when those ups and downs are at extreme poles one can get sick from that roller coaster ride. Some call this bipolar dis-ease; others might call it manic-depression. Interestingly enough, Michael Hedges–the well known experimental guitarist–has a piece entitled *Ariel Boundaries*. His guitar is so light, so buoyant so liquidified as to seem magic. How does he play like that? If you have heard Hedges you would know what I mean when I say his music is magic. I don't know how he does it. How does one become so *fluid* with an instrument? Not many people can do.

Another genre that is *liquidy* is painting. Here I look back to Marion Milner (1957) and her book on painting. Painting is all about making colors look liquidy. Bachelard (1988b) writes about Chagall in his book *The Right to Dream*. He says:

And what a delight it is for us to see an artist create quickly, for Chagall creates quickly. Creating quickly is the secret of creating live. Life will not wait; life never stops to think. No rough drafts, just flashes. All Chagall's creatures are first flashes. (p. 8)

When art comes it comes in waves (i.e. water) and painting has a liquidy feel to it. Pulling the brush across a canvass with oils feels liquidy, even gooey. To paint with such fluidity is like playing the guitar fluidly. Quickness is what the artist needs in order to create, Bachelard points out. Quickness helped Chagall paint. Bachelard says of Chagall that everything he sees he turns into colours. A painter's world (unless she is colour-blind) is one of colour. A musician's world is made up of sound. Interestingly enough, sounds–for many musicians–are connected with colours. Some instruments–like the cello–open up a vast array of colour. Tone, phrasing, touch, if they are highly nuanced allow the musician to play in colourful ways.

MUSIC AND PSYCHE

Now that we have unpacked some of Bachelard's work, we can move on to discuss how these ideas might help us develop a phenomenology of a musical imagination. Music opens spaces in which to dream. Playing an instrument, say guitar, allows one to drift off into an airy state, one not dissimilar to Bachelard's notions of air and ascension. The guitar lends itself to air, especially in the higher registers. The way in which the guitar is tuned changes what kind of air one can enter. Sometimes the guitar produces haunting sounds through overtones and harmonics. The *Ariel* guitar–as Bachelard might put it– travels mostly in the higher registers. When the musician moves downward on the frets we enter into the depths of an abyss. The abyss of sound paints dark colours, clouded watery colours. Bachelard talked of troubled waters. The lower register of the guitar is engulfed in troubled waters. Sometimes the notes even sound a little muddy. But the thing that is most striking about the guitar– and what we have learned from Bachelard– is a connection between the earth the guitar. Bachelard suggests that earthy substances are hard, and in turn are hard to work on. The acoustic guitar is made up of earthy elements: wood and steel. These matter(s) are hard and extremely resistant. Steel strings are particularly intimidating. One wonders how a soft, fleshy hand moves steel. Depending on the gauge of the string, steel, once put into action by the hand, vibrates by its motion. The hand learns to work with and against the immobility and mobility of the steel strings. Some gauges are tighter and heavier than others and are harder to bend. The harder the strings are to bend, the richer the sound. Overtones are easier to generate with heavy gauged steel. Steel strings are particularly unfriendly when hands are cold. The earthiness of steel feels rough and even ugly in the wrong environment. The resistance of the strings–like the resistance of earthy matter–requires a sort of angry mobility—as Bachelard might put it– to get things going. But one must never force the matter. Forcing strings with the hands is the quickest way to get injured. Sounds sink into the abyss of muddied waters on cold days, or when the steel just won't move in sync with the hands. Following Bachelard, the musician needs fire to get the hands warm. The psyche must be aflame. The hands on fire sets what is inert (steel strings at rest) in motion. The easy mobility of the hands working the steel is what we are after. A warm fleshy hand does this when the tension of the strings is just right. Paradoxically, the musician should use strings that have the greatest resistance in order to get the greatest depth, drive and punch from the guitar. The harder the guitar is to play, the better it sounds. If the strings have little resistance, the sounds produced will be weak and without depth. But more resistance demands more strength from the hands and also risks injury. And here we arrive at the problem.

The interesting thing about guitars is that there are many kinds of wood that the guitar maker can use to make a guitar and each wood has a different sound and different colour and tone to it. This is why, I think, guitar players usually have more than one guitar. I have eleven guitars partly because each one opens up a new world of sound. The combination of wood and steel (and again there are different kinds of steel strings which resonate in different ways) together, create the vast variety of guitars. Some guitars are warmer than others, some are balanced and some have too much bass, some sound dead because they do not resonate, some sound alive because they do resonate. Bachelard's work on the earth is particularly helpful when thinking about the guitar because it is an earthy instrument. Wood and steel are of the earth and so too are we. There is something about wood and steel that alters psyche–tunes into it. There is also something about tuning in that is telling about the person doing the tuning up. Some days it takes upwards of two hours to tune a guitar. Other days it takes five minutes. If the player cannot tune the guitar, perhaps her psyche is out of tune. The psyche that is out of tune might just be tired. When one is tired one cannot listen in a deep way. So it is best to tune up in the morning. Of course, there are other psychological reasons why one is out of tune. The inability to tune might be a precursor to not being able to play.

The connection or attachment between the musician and her instrument is highly symbolic. What does the bond between the player and that which is played mean psychologically? Why do some attach themselves to the object that is the guitar? There is something almost mystical about such attachments a musician might have with a particular instrument. There is something uncanny about the way in which particular combinations of wood and steel allow the musician to express something deep within her psyche. It is as if the player and the guitar blend into one. The player becomes the guitar. This loss of boundaries harkens back to an archaic state of psyche. This fusion reminds one of another older fusion with the mother. I suppose one could call this transference. Losing oneself while playing feels good because one has always already felt this in the womb. Maybe a bit far fetched– but still there is something to it. When everything seems right, one soars to airy places, to the heights as Bachelard would put it. When everything is wrong, especially when the hands are cold and the strings too resistant, sounds sink in to the muddy waters of the abyss.

Playing music on the guitar is about creating spaces of rest (inertia) and mobility (moving the strings by plucking or pushing or strumming or attacking or sliding).

Recall what Bachelard says of earthen matter, it is both at rest and in motion. Always the dialectic. Rests are created by inertia and can be used effectively for emphasis. The unique combination of rests and sound plus overtones can pull one up to the heights. The guitar can create both hard and soft sounds, depending on who is doing the playing. The hard and the soft sounds are both qualities of earthen matter. The musician uses both hard and soft sounds to get the most from the guitar. Some people like to play very softly and some play with a heavy hand.

A musical imagination is what is needed to play in the first place. If you have got a musical mind to begin with I suppose you could express your musical ideas and feelings on any instrument. But I do think that some temperaments are better suited for different instruments. The acoustic guitar is a particularly hard instrument to master. It takes a rather precise hand to find the notes. One step off the correct site on the fret board and the sounds get a little squeaky. But even more so, the cello demands absolute precision. And here, you are playing in the dark because there are no frets.

Let us for a moment return to Bachelard to help tease out what a musical imagination might be. If we think of the elements, fire, water, air and earth as part of us, part of our make up, and think about the make up of an instrument, fire, air, water and earth, we might think about the connections between sentient and non sentient things. It is the meeting of the two (the elements in the instrument and the elements within us) that matter, that makes matter mobile and produces sound. The imagination has to meet with–if you will– a difficult and resistant object (a guitar made of wood and steel, for example) in order to express musical thoughts and feelings onto and into the instrument. How this connection happens is a bit of a mystery though. Some people are able to make connections with an inert object, and others are not able to do this. You can have all the fancy guitars you want but just because you have high end instruments doesn't mean you can actually transfer you musical imaginings onto the instrument. Most people try to copy or imitate songs that they have heard on the radio. But this is not an authentic connection. A real "meeting", as Martin Buber (2002) would put it, is when the soul of the player meets the soul of the instrument. Now, how this happens is a bit of a mystery, but it can happen. When there is "genuine meeting"– drawing on the words of Martin Buber–between player and instrument a mystical epiphany may be at hand. But experiencing a mystical epiphany is rare. When psyche is in the middle of a mystical epiphany the connection is so real that it is almost surreal. It seems during this epiphany as if the guitar speaks on its own. The musician is simply the channel for what the guitar– or any instrument for that matter–wants to tell you. Recall, Bachelard talks about the relationship between the physical and the psychological. The imagination is *enmattered* in the flesh and in the hand. This imagination therefore is both physical and psychological. I am interested mainly in the psychological aspect of matter. What matter matters psychically? The acoustic guitar is *enmattered* in wood and steel and it allows our musician to dig deep into psyche when played. The depth of the matter of sound depends a lot on both the quality of the instrument and the musician's musicality and skill. Playing tells a lot about psyche. A seeming fluidity across the fret board tells us that the player is at one with the instrument, that the watery sounds are coming from the musician's heart. But when the sound is fragmented and bumpy, squeaky, disconnected and nonsensical, something is amiss in the psyche of the player. It takes a rather precise hand to find the notes. One step off the correct site on the fret board and the sounds get a little squeaky. But even more so, the cello demands absolute precision. And here, as I said earlier, you are playing in the dark because there are no frets.

Some days nothing seems to be going right. There are days when the guitar will not allow the player to express anything. Falling into the depths of despair and frustration, the player puts the instrument down. Putting the instrument down means putting the psyche to rest for a while. Sometimes the psyche needs repose, as Bachelard points out in much of his writing. Without repose, psyche cannot function. Repose is sometimes psychologically the best thing, especially if one feels frustrated. Stepping away allows the musician to regenerate and think about music away from the instrument. Sometimes distance is needed from the instrument. The best thing to do, sometimes, is to stop playing for a week or two or even several months—or maybe even for a few years. The hands need repose, for they do get tired and sore and sometimes get hurt. The psyche needs to rest in the space of nothing for a while to get the musical imagination to be re-generative. The fire(s) of inspiration burn out after awhile. On the other hand, keeping up technique requires an everydayness because the muscles in the hand wither very quickly without practice.

And too, the musical imagination becomes tired and even bored sometimes. When one feels stuck, nothing seems to come from the musical imagination. The psyche seems literally stuck. How to move that stuckness into mobility becomes problematic when one is stuck too long. Get that fire burning again. But the question is how? Sometimes stepping away creates a space of reverie—as Bachelard suggests— that allows one to re-find the fire of inspiration. What if it never comes back? This is the problem at hand.

Now it is worth thinking through psychic movements that make up a musical consciousness. Rest, activity, fluidity, paralysis, moods. Yes, moods are particularly important for building a musical imagination. It is interesting that Bachelard does not address the notion of moods. Moods are hard to articulate but I think different moods can be described by talking about colour. Some moods are red, some blue. A Blue mood as we all know is a sad mood. Red moods might signify anger. Yellow moods might feel like hum drum. Grey moods might signify boredom and so on.

Bachelard talks about the abyss. Musicians who can no longer play fall into an abyss. Falling into a black hole depresses. What is the abyss of feeling? Ironically it may be that there is no feeling left inside of the abyss. When one cannot play, shutting down emotions and moods might serve as a defense mechanism against suicidal tendencies. Depression—as many in the psychoanalytic community suggest— is actually a step on the way toward healing. One must become ill to become well again.

But there is more to the musical imagination than moods. Recall what we learn from Bachelard about the interconnection between the will and the imagination. It is not enough to imagine a sound, but one must *work* that sound via the *will*. Bachelard makes much of the notion of matter being worked on. The musical imagination is a working imagination. Working on wood and steel takes time, commitment and a great deal of patience. Some people are unwilling to *work* at what they do and will never become good players. One must work at playing an instrument. To be able to express oneself–via earthy matters of wood and steel–takes much work. The will that works the earthly matters so as to make musical sounds can become tyrannical–though– and that is when one risks injury. Bachelard does not use the language of the superego or sadism to describe a tyrannical will. I think, however, that this aspect of working must be addressed especially in connection with injury. Playing requires much repetition; the hand is slow to learn new things. And it is the constant repetition that might result in injury. The hand likes to repeat in order to remember where it has been. Amazingly the hand does have a memory, it knows where to go on its own, but only after it has been trained. The working musician knows about working through long stretches of repetition. To repeat takes much patience and determination. Sometimes beginners are put off because of the work involved in being able to play. Developing a will to play is therefore part of the story. At first one might think that it should not take much time to be able to play fluidly, but for most, playing fluidly requires much practice. And practice quickly becomes boring. It is boring to repeat phrases over and over. But because the hand is slow to learn, one must practice phrases slowly over and over. After a while, the phrase will come on its own, but the groundwork must be done in advance. Developing a musical will is difficult when the boredom of repetition sets in. One must somehow make the repetitions interesting and educative. After finally getting a passage down or getting the phrasing just right, the musician might feel elated because the work was so hard. Working matter–as Bachelard says–is no easy matter. Working matter is rather difficult. Matters– like wood and steel–are resistant to the human touch. The hand must learn how to shape the matter psychically and physically. One must never force matter. If the musician forces things, injury is at hand. Some have a strong will to play, and some will be able to work matter through the tediousness of repetition–others cannot get past the tedium. The musical will must be strong enough to get past the technical problems of bending wood and steel through the human hand.

Let us talk on a more ephemeral level now about the musical imagination. On a higher level of consciousness our musician needs to get in touch with basic vibrations both within the psyche and within the instrument. When a string is out of tune it will sound wobbly and will have a grating sound. To get a string in tune means to flatten out the vibrations so two strings merge together in sound. For example, when a guitar is in tune notes blend together. When the guitar is out of tune–and more often than not this is the case–strings will jut out, the vibrations become jarring. Getting a guitar in tune is no easy matter either. There is such a thing as a tired ear. When one is tired one cannot hear– fatigue affects a musical capacity. The musician should never play when tired–ah but this requirement is only possible in a utopic condition. We do not live in utopias, so we play when we can and sometimes this means playing when fatigued.

This merging together–of musician and instrument– is no easy task. It takes years of practice, hard work, patience and a basic musical ability to be able to feel at one with the instrument. It takes a long time –and here we are talking about years–to be able to express feelings and musical ideas. It is not an easy task to get to the point where it seems that the hand becomes the guitar and the guitar becomes the hand.

Stringed instruments are particularly healing. The vibrations of the strings go right *through* the chest. A guitar is something to be held; the vibrations seem to move directly *through* the body. The cello, too, because of the way in which the strings vibrate, can be a healing instrument. But to get to that healing stage requires a lot of practice. Mastering the cello is particularly difficult because the fret board is not marked. Learning where the notes are on a cello takes a lot of time. The guitar is a bit easier because the fret board is marked. Playing the cello takes a particular kind of work that not many are willing to endure. Learning one scale can take a year. Yes, there may be only four strings, but the relations between notes, the patterns of scales are hidden from the novice. It seems as if one must learn a secret code to get beyond the stage of 'where is that note in relation to another note.' The patterns on the guitar are a bit easier to figure out again because the fret board is marked. Markings help the player find the sounds that she wants.

How to enliven this connection between the body (namely the hand) and the object (the instrument) is a key question. Playing is about bringing to life an inert and resistant object. Vibrations that sound right together demand a certain harmony between body and psyche. Being able to play means that our musician is in touch with both physical and psychological aspects of making music. When the musician is not able to play, the physical or psychological has broken down. The psychological is the physical for Bachelard because psyche is enmattered.

The transfer of musical ideas onto an inert and resistant object is quite difficult. It is one thing to hear notes, but to transfer them onto an inert object is something altogether different. What is it that allows psyche to move musical ideas from the head into and through an object? Although playing seems rather commonsensical– pick up the guitar and play–it is not. Playing is a rather odd phenomenon. Thinking about the complexities of feelings and the way in which these feelings get translated and transferred from the heart into wood and steel–the matter about which the guitar is made–is not totally clear. Is it really possible to transfer feelings onto and into an inert and resistant object? For some yes, for others no.

For now, let us back up a step here and think about what a musical idea might feel like. In music, as in other forms of art, ideas and feelings are inextricably tied. Musical ideas are much like the spoken word. But music is older than speech–think about the cries of an infant. Making music might be more primal than speaking. The body has a certain pitch about it, a certain temperament, a certain aura and colour. Sound is em-bodied.

A musical imagination is complex. Sound and sight—which might be connected to the capacity to develop a musical imagination– are overlapping phenomena.

Sometimes the blind are able to develop musical capacities as an overcompensation for the loss of sight. Do the blind see musical images? If blind from birth, music is not seen but heard only. Do those with sight see music in images? Are images and sounds inextricably woven? Can we talk about musical imagery at all, or is imagery only related to the visual arts? Musical imagery becomes relevant especially if one writes music for a film score. But mostly, music hovers in the space of the vague in between sight and sound.

Playing music might not generate images at all. Music might evoke feelings only. Musical images–when they are generated by sound–tend to be rather obscure and difficult to articulate. Can psyche articulate a musical image? Are images and feelings overlapping? Are moods and images and sounds overlapping? What exactly are musical images? The Jungians tell us to *go to the image* if we want to understand our psyches and our souls. If a musician goes to the image what does that mean? I leave this an open question.

An ecological approach to music might suggest that the oral, the aural, images, sounds and feelings are all of a piece. If it is true that if everything is in everything, then the oral, aural, the visual, feeling and thinking, are interconnected. But the question is how to get all these phenomena to work to together to create sounds. Is bodily harmony a prerequisite to making music? Or might it be that a body out of whack is prerequisite to making music? What are the blues after all? Must the body be out of joint to create musical sounds?

To what use is sound put? One can hear things in one's head all day long but not be able to transfer them onto and in to an instrument. What conditions are necessary for the development of a musical capacity? A musical imagination and capacity for expression is a gift you either have or you do not have. Where the gift comes from we do not know.

A musical phenomenology– Bachelard might suggest–might be best articulated symbolically and metaphorically. What is a musical imagination attempting to express in symbols? What does the music attempt to re-present? Does music re-present anything at all? Is music a symbolic conversation in sound? When we teach music, what is the symbolic conversation we attempt to have with students? Do musicians think in symbols? Music that is original to the musician symbolizes something. Music is about something. Music is intentional. The musician must shape vibrations into patterns to make music. Music, at its most fundamental level, is about making sense of patterns. This is not unlike speaking, writing or doing scholarly work. Sound patterns are highly complex. Improvisation is built on patterns that make sense to the musician. Some musicians are better at jazz than others. Although I have listened to a lot of jazz growing up, I cannot hear jazz when I improvise. Since I was trained as a classical musician, the patterns I hear come out of a classical curriculum. The patterns that make sense to my hands are the ones I learned as a child. It is very hard for classical musicians to play jazz. We tend to play what we were taught to play at a very young age. If I listen to a guitarist play jazz, I could listen all day and never 'get it.' I might only 'get' what I already learned long ago. If Freud is right, the archaeology of the psyche guides expression. I have a classical archaeology because I was trained as a classical musician. Deep down in childhood–musical patterns get enmattered, engrained in the psyche. A rock guitarist, on the other hand, does not have the ear of the classical guitarist. A blues singer does not have the ear of an opera singer. All of these differing genres are based on intricate and complicated patterns of thought and feeling that get embedded in the psyche usually at an early age.

The more psychoanalytic question might turn on feeling states in relation to making music. What does it feel like to transfer a particular pattern of sound onto and into a particular instrument? Some things feel right and other things do not. Patterns of sound waves make up the musical imagination at an archaic level. How to capture those sound waves that resonate with the psyche. Where does the musical imagination live? In waves? Psychic waves. Yes. Waves, resonances, vibrations make up sound. But how to make sound waves intelligible? That is the question at hand. The problem is that sound waves are arbitrary. It takes an educated ear to make sense out of seemingly meaningless tones and vibrations. This is where Bachelard is useful. Think of his writings on the working of matter, what *enmatters* matter? Earth, air, fire and water. Sound waves are *enwrapped* in the basic elements. The question is how to get the basic elements to come alive and make sense musically. The will, the heart, the soul, the psyche, the living, breathing, feeling person must put into action these basic elements and work them, with them, against them and through them to create a resonant musical imagination. Recall, Bachelard talks of the importance of working matter. The musician works matter into sound as the scholar works ideas into thought.

Different instruments are capable of expressing certain kinds of things. The cello, for example, allows the musician to express that which is low, deep, sorrowful. The flute, on the other hand, allows the musician to express feelings of lightness, or buoyancy. The guitar allows the musician to express chordal sound. Violins, are always expressing the height of the sky. The psyche–in an unconscious way—draws players toward particular instruments. Unconscious stirrings drive the musician to play one instrument over against another. Is the musical imagination, then mostly unconscious? I would say yes. Ultimately, it remains a mystery why we play what we do, why we are attracted to certain instruments and not to others. Does the unconscious musical imagination flare up, like fire? Where does the conscious will come into play when talking about making music? Children who are gifted know a lot about music it seems from birth, or maybe even before birth. How to explain a musical prodigy? There is no clear explanation. It is as if the music calls the player to play and the instrument says play me because you need to play. If your psyche has some deep, archaic thing it needs to express, it will do so through an instrument.

ON NOT BEING ABLE TO PLAY: A PHENOMENOLOGICAL PROBLEM

What happens when you cannot play? What would Bachelard suggest, I wonder? Perhaps he would suggest that your basic ontological elements (fire, air, water, earth and so on) have burned out, that you have reached the bottom of the abyss, that the musical aspect of the psyche needs and demands rest. The waters have become troubled, the ground upon which you stand ontologically has become unmoored, the emotions are out of whack and musical time is out of joint. Thus, the psyche forces the musician to stop via injury. The psyche gets damaged and needs rest. Or, some physical illness prevents the musician from playing. A radical decathexis is at hand. Fighting this decathexis only makes matters worse. Forcing things only deepens the trauma.

Bachelard suggests that an attachment to and love of the object is necessary to bring that object to life. But when decathexsis from objects becomes necessary because of injury or psychic wounds, what to do with those attachments and loves psychologically? Even though the musician may not be able to play, the attachment and love of that object-instrument remains. The fire of inflamed tendons wounds the flesh. A maddening pain. The elements are out of whack. Fire overpowers water. Fluidity is stultified. The sound waves are lost in the fire of pain. The fire overpowers that which is light and airy; thoughts no longer drift as if on a cloud. Earthen matter becomes too resistant, too heavy, too hot like molten lava. To touch an object is to be overwhelmed by pain.

The elements are out of whack, musical time is out of joint. The musical imagination, however, is still there but needs a rest; the musical imagination needs a long repose or a long space of reverie in order to re-generate itself. But what if it cannot be re-generated at all? Where does the musical imagination go when it cannot be expressed? Does the musical imagination just go away, does it get lost in a vast sea of pain? Does it just burn up and burn out? Perhaps the musical imagination is in some sort of holding pattern. Perhaps it is brewing up new things, or maybe it is getting ready to die altogether. Water gets muddied, fire turns to ash, air gets polluted and the earth erodes. The body is like the earth, it is the earth and the earth has cycles of life and death. When one is not able to play a death cycle is at hand. If we are inextricably tied to the ecosphere, so too is the musical imagination. The musical imagination has its own ecology. Being enmattered is being enwrapped in the ecosphere. As we know, the ecosphere suffers from the same ailments as does the psyche. The earth suffers natural cycles of deterioration as does the body.

A paralysis of the musical imagination is both physical and psychological. Once inside of this paralysis, how to get out of it? What if the musician cannot get out of this state of inertia? What happens to an instrument that is not played over time? The strings get out of tune. Does the player get out of tune as well? Is the psyche an instrument that needs the work of tuning? The longer the strings are untouched the more out of tune they get. What are the implications for our musician?

An unplayed guitar is the saddest thing in the world for a guitarist. A piano with the lid closed is a travesty. The cello left in the case wounds. What happens to unplayed musical ideas? Do the ideas just disappear into thin air? Maybe they do. What was once resonant is now discordant. The musical imagination has to be activated in order to work. One must work on it, as Bachelard might put it. If one doesn't work on it, the resonances and vibrations die. But the question that Bachelard does not pose is what if psyche cannot work on the imagination because of natural deterioration of the body? What happens to psyche when her channels of expression are broken? A life without expression is not life at all, it is psychic death. What is to be done about it? Sometimes nothing can be done. And then we have a problem. Then we have a tragedy. The problem with studying Bachelard is that the phenomenology he fleshes out presupposes that matter is always moving in a positive direction. But what about entropy? I find Bachelard to be a little too hopeful about things. Although he does deal a bit with the negative, he does not flesh it out enough. Bachelard comes up short when talking about broken vessels, torn flesh, inflamed tendons, neurons gone mad. He is a little too cheerful for my taste. Broken matter is what is the matter. So, I hope that this study adds to the conversation a negative phenomenology, a negative psychoanalysis, a negative study of curricular matters. And part of that negative study concerns pain. Let us turn to the issue of pain and flesh out a woundedness that Bachelard misses.

A PHENOMENOLOGY OF PAIN

What can be more painful psychologically than a musician who can no longer play? What can be more tragic for a musician than not being able to express herself as she was born to do? Here I am thinking of Jacqueline du Pres. This is one of the most tragic stories in the history of classical music. Reading biographies of Jackie—as her friends called her—are terribly painful. The story of Jacqueline du Pres is certainly one of the most tragic of my generation. For those not familiar with Jackie's story, I recount here in brief that she was a child prodigy and broke ground for women in the classical music establishment by performing especially Elgar's Cello Concerto in a way no one had done before. Musicians of her era talked about how Jackie was a natural and the way in which she expressed herself on the cello wowed audiences. There are some clips on You Tube of Jackie for those of you who are too young to have remembered her. She had such a natural beauty about her playing and such an incredibly expressive nature. When she played it seemed truly that she was at one with the cello. She certainly was one of the greatest cellists of the 20th century. And then tragedy struck. Jackie was struck down by Multiple Sclerosis when she was still very young. She had to stop playing in her late twenties because of her deterioration. What a terrible tragedy not only for Jackie but for the rest of the classical music world who so loved her. Carol Easton (1989) tells us,

> Tragedy cannot be quantified, and Jacqueline's loss was incalculable. When I met her in the summer of 1981, it seemed as if she had little left to lose. . . . she had lost control of her legs, then her arms, then the rest of her body. She suffered from double vision and tremors of the head so severe that they made reading, or even watching television impossible. (p. 11)

The tragedy of Jacqueline du Pres is beyond language. There are such horrors that can happen to people and certainly this is one of the worst horrors the classical music world has known. She was so young and so gifted. That is part of the tragedy. She changed the classical music world partly because she opened doors for other women to be soloists. The cello especially was not accepted as a proper instrument for women to play before Jackie changed all of that. The classical music world is just as sexist as every other profession. But Jackie helped to open doors for women when those doors were closed before. No one can match Jackie's performance of the Elgar Cello Concerto to this day. And then tragedy struck. Elisabeth Wilson (1998) remembers when Jackie began to show signs of illness. She tells us that

> . . . attacks of laryngitis, an unaccountable unsteadiness. . . Once in Moscow (in the Spring of 1966) I saw her tumble all at once and hurtle down the Conservatoire staircase—nobody knew whether to be more anxious for her or for her precious Strad cello [which was worth $90.000]. (p. 377)

It took a long time before Jackie was diagnosed. Her health deteriorated steadily until she died in the 1980s. What a loss to the music world!! I cannot even put into words how devastating this story is to me. Classical musicians the world over loved Jackie and were heartbroken when she got ill. When you see her on You Tube you see such a happy-go-lucky, vibrant, gifted artist who enjoyed performing so much for her public. What a terrible story this is. And what words do I have to express this sadness I feel for her? I found it terribly difficult to read biographies of Jackie and to watch her on You Tube. What disturbs is that at one point early in her life, she felt that she had to " pay" in some way for being so talented. Carol Easton (1989) explains that Jackie

> . . . confided to Liz Wilson that as a child she had always been frightened of being ill. " She told us many times that she had some deep-seated fear that she couldn't have all this talent without having to pay for it—some idea of retribution. " . . . (p.183)

What a strange thing for a child to think about. Perhaps this strange idea of retribution came out of her Christian upbringing. And perhaps it is no accident that Jackie converted to Judaism after she married Daniel Barenboim. Jackie's mother who was in many ways responsible for Jackie's terrific musical education, was—according to Easton (1989)– also guilty of abandoning her when she got sick and even blaming her for her illness. Carol Easton (1989) tells us that Jackie's mother thought that because Jackie had turned her back on Christ that she got sick. It is worth noting here too that Jackie's mother was an accomplished pianist. She was a very smart woman. But what does smartness mean against this context of blame and religious intolerance?

At any rate, when we talk about not being able to play we are not just talking about an abstract idea. Phenomenology—as abstract as it might seem—can be put to use when speaking of the concrete, lived experience of people who suffer. The abstract must be made concrete if it is to have relevance in a world of suffering and pain. I wanted to talk a little about du Pres as a tribute to her life. She is a presence in my life even though she has been long gone from our world. As I took up the cello in my mid- forties, I have turned to Jackie's playing to try to learn how to play better. Jackie has been one of my teachers through listening to her recordings and watching her on You Tube.

Let us turn to a discussion of pain—generally speaking– and move on in our account of not being able to play. Pain is not just physical, it is also emotional. To separate these out makes little sense, and yet many think about pain as if it were only a physical problem. David Morris (1993) explains.

As current research both inside and outside medicine, the rigid split between mental and physical pain is beginning to look like a gigantic cultural mistake. (p. 12)

We learn from both Merleau-Ponty and Gaston Bachelard that everything is connected to everything else. The hand that works the earth is made up of the very same elements of the earth. The hand is of the earth, it is the earth. Everything is in everything else. Recall for Merleau-Ponty that that which is invisible (thinking, imagining and feeling) is inextricably tied to that which is visible (the body and the thing thought about). For Bachelard, the elements (fire, earth, air, water) tie us back to everything else. It is interesting to note that the Latin root of the word 'religion,' *Religio*, means to tie back. Bachelard, more so than Merleau-Ponty, seems to be more of the mystic. His writings sacralize the basic elements of the cosmos. The work of the hand, for Bachelard, is the work of the alchemist who turns lead into gold. The flesh, the touch and the hand allow us to express what is deep in psyche by making use of things, objects that we find in everyday existence. Bachelard was a Jungian and the Jungians often use the metaphors of the ancient alchemists, like turning things lead into gold.

If everything is in everything else, and everything affects everything else, it makes sense to think of pain in both physical and psychological terms. Thus, when the elements are out of joint, pain is twofold. When thinking about pain, thoughts are inextricably tied to emotions; emotions affect the physical body. When we think and feel, we think and feel about something. To say that I hurt my hand suggests that the physical impacts the emotional and the emotional impacts the physical. Now these relations are complex. Brooding and rumination seem to make the emotional pain worse. But how can one not brood on that which is painful? What is pained seems heavy, enlarged, enflamed. Feeling the pain and going into the pain is what is called for psychologically. It might not help the pain go away, but denying the pain sometimes makes the pain worse. When I say, 'My hand hurts' it seems that I am only talking literally about the hand. In a way, it is easier to reduce pain to its physical manifestations. But there is more to it than that. David Juan-Nasio (2004) explains.

In response to the injury the ego sends all the energy at its disposal to surround the wound in order to fill the hole and stop the massive influx of excitations. It is this reactive movement of energy–which Freud called "counter-investment" or "counter-charge"–that is opposed to the brutal eruption. . . . However, this self-bandaging is not applied to the damaged tissue, but on the psychical representation of the wound. (p. 61)

When the hand gets injured, it feels like the hand becomes large or heavy. The hand is turned to lead. A thick blanket of discomfort is at hand. The hand hurts because the psyche tells it that it is wounded. Pain comes from the brain. That is a strange thought if the site of the wound is a limb. Pain is a defense against further injury. Without feeling pain, one would probably die. The way in which the wound gets represented in the psyche, as Nasio points out, is a complex matter. How one re-presents the injury to oneself will determine how pain is felt and how one comprehends what has happened. The problem of pain is partly a problem of representation. It is not easy to articulate the way in which an injury is thought about and why it is thought about in the way that it is. The more pressing problem turns on the way in which the representation of the injury is used and how its use determines how the pain is felt. For Merleau-Ponty and Bachelard, the hand and the touch are crucial connecting points between what is inside and what is outside. But neither of these philosophers address the problem of a wounded hand that cannot touch the object. This is a profound question that must be raised. What we are dealing with here is a phenomenology of catastrophe.

For a musician, an injury to the hand is catastrophic. The injury introduces a block– both psychical and physical. The block thickens especially when the injury is chronic. Living with a chronic injury is like living in an arrested emotional state. The psyche might retreat in order to protect the ego from completely collapsing. A psychic retreat allows one to cope with the overwhelming catastrophe. Or maybe not.

If one cannot retreat in some way, there is a chance that the ego will fall apart. Psychical "disintegration" occurs, as Juan-Nasio (2004) points out, when one is not able to deal with this catastrophe. But how can anybody 'deal' with the magnitude of what Jacqueline du Pres suffered? How can one not fall to pieces? The bodymind falls apart in totality. The lifeworld is totally and utterly destroyed. The psyche is pain, pain is the psyche; the body is pain, pain is the body. The whole world, it seems, becomes pain. And it is this very pain that kills the psyche. What is a dead psyche? It is a psyche that becomes vacant. Mary-Jo Delvecchio Good (1994) explains.

> It is a world threatened by dissolution. Space and time are overwhelmed by pain, and the private world not only loses its relation to the world in which others live, its very organizing dimensions begin to break down. Pain threatens to unmake the world. (p. 42)

The only thing left is pain. And if this pain is chronic, everything gets swallowed up by the pain and life becomes meaningless. Nothing is left but pain. The self vanishes inside a black hole. Interiority is non-existent. Nobody is there anymore. Life is not life. The meaning of things just drop away. Life is pain. How to get out of the black hole? Do things escape it? How to come back up for air? For some, coming back is not possible. If one is able to come back psychologically from a catastrophic injury, one does not come back from the abyss unscathed. After the injury, one is never the same as one was before the injury. Chronic injury shifts the psyche and its relation to the world. At any rate, suffering chronic injury or illness changes you forever.

Experiencing injury tends to force one to dredge up issues from childhood (Nasio, 2004). How I handled pain in my childhood is probably how I handle pain in the here and now. This may sound commonsensical but it is not always obvious to the person who suffers pain. The pain so distorts things that the past seems obliterated. 'I have is no past.' 'The only thing that exists is the pain I feel right now.' However, remember that Freud said the past never goes away. Dream-life always already points to the past, points to the archaic structure of the psyche. If the dreamer, however, is not in tune with her dreams or dismisses them as nonsense, she will have missed the connection between the here and now and the past. How one responds to pain in the here and now is a clue to how one responded to pain in childhood. Seemingly irrational responses to pain probably stem from childhood traumas. The way in which one responds to current ailments tells us a lot about old psychic wounds. Old psychic wounds tend to fester over the years. The return of the repressed maims. Unconsciously, then, the Id may be using pain to work through old patterns of emotion.

The language used to express pain becomes problematic because pain is so private. We have a very limited vocabulary when it comes to pain. Elaine Scarry (1985) tells us that,

> Physical pain does not simply resist language but actively destroys it, bringing about an immediate reversion to a state anterior to language, to the sounds and cries a human being makes before language is learned. (p. 4)

Pain forces one to regress. The state which is "anterior" to language and the state to which one regresses– in psychoanalytic terms– is the pre-verbal. Is it "anterior" to language because it is before or behind language. The experience of pain is older than language. Pain is the most primal emotion there is. It must be painful to be born. Birth seems like such a violent act. Getting pushed out of the womb is violent. The crying infant knows the language of pain. Before one can form words, one can cry. Crying, in the case of the infant, is the only way to express pain.

The point not made by Elaine Scarry is that pain is not an encapsulated experience. The infant's pain is felt in the company of the mother or primary caregiver. More to the point, the expression of pain is always already in relation to the caregiver's response to the cry. If the mother is inattentive to the infant, the pain worsens. The way in which people in general respond to the injured person determines partly the way in which the injured person in turn feels her pain. It is not uncommon for couples to split up when one partner becomes injured or ill. The burden of taking care of someone who has been injured is almost too much for some people to cope with. The emotions overwhelm. If one's partner is loving and attentive, the pain is somehow tolerable. What destroys the injured person, may have little to do with the physical problem at hand, but may have everything to do with an already damaged relationship and already damaged archaic psychical structure of that relationship.

The not good enough mother reverberates through a whole life. When attentiveness on the part of the mother is absent especially in those early years of childhood, it matters little if – in the here and now–one's partner is attentive or not.

If the mother was absent—literally or figuratively–during those crucial years in early childhood–one may not have the coping skills necessary to deal with wounds. To suffer injury is always already relational. Doctors, caregivers, sisters and brothers, friends and colleagues may create an environment of response. But if you grew up in a non-responding household, if you grew up in a toxic environment where expression of anything negative resulted in punishment, the current wound is made even more traumatic.

How to express that which is beyond representation? How to speak the unspeakable? If going into the pain repairs—psychically– old wounds, how does one do that exactly? And what does it mean to go into the pain rather than being 'anterior' to it? Interestingly enough, Roselyne Rey (1995), tells us that

> The etymology of the verbs from which the nouns pain and suffering are derived provides another perspective on their specialized meanings: to suffer, for instance, from the Latin sufferre, means to bear, to endure to allow. . . . (p. 5)

The word that interests me here is 'allow.' How to 'allow' pain to take its course? What does that 'course' do to the psyche? In what way does a person 'allow' a working through of the pain? How to name one's pain? Or is pain nameless? How to think symbolically about pain? Are there no symbols for it? To make an experience comprehendible, symbolization is called for. But isn't pain beyond symbolization? The problem with pain is that it is inexpressible. This is THE phenomenological problem. The untranslatability of pain is frustrating and maddeningly depressing. Falling into a pit, the depressed sufferer may become immobile, inarticulate, psychically dead. But even if one is able to speak, symbolize and cry about pain, what good is it? Just because you can articulate your pain does not mean it gets better. Chronic pain is chronic no matter what. Terminal illness kills. Crying about it does not make it better. Sometimes it does not even help to talk about it. Sometimes, in fact, talking about it makes it worse. The talking cure might not cure at all. Talking about it might be pointless. The way one handles pain is symptomatic of a whole life.

Doctors treat the limb. They try to make the damaged limb better but they do not work with psyches (unless of course they are psychoanalysts or psychologists). Some doctors are sympathetic toward their patients. Some are emotionally disconnected from patients. Some are brusque and rude. In the case of women, doctors might chalk up complaints of pain to hysteria and dismiss it. We know that when Jacqueline du Pres presented symptoms to her doctors, some of them thought she was simply being hysterical and chalked her complaints up to exhaustion (Wilson, 1998). If she had been a man, I am certain that her complaints would have been taken seriously. Sexism and misogyny in medicine have been a long standing problem.

Some doctors treat pain. Others do not. The pain, remember, is a symptom of a larger problem. Perhaps the tendons are filled with fluid and the muscles weakened. Doctors are interested in the cause of the injury and the how to mend the injury. Pain is an epiphenomenon, an afterthought. Some doctors give medicine to those patients in pain, while others do not. What is doubly painful is when doctors dismiss pain. When the patient's pain is ignored or wholly discounted, psychic damage can work to further debilitate. Pain cannot be reduced to a number, but it is in the doctor's office. 'Between one and ten, where is your pain on that scale', they ask. Ten is the worst. The patient answers 'ten.' The doctor marks that in his notes but does nothing to relieve the pain. The doctor says, 'I do not treat pain.'

Sleeping can be used either to work through pain or obliterate the world. But when pain is overwhelming, pain can invade sleep. To dream about pain and be in pain—and to be cognizant of this while sleeping–is rather strange. The key word here is *invasion*. Pain is invasive. It is something that is not me, it invades my world. Pain intrudes into a life–seemingly– from nowhere. I was fine ten minutes ago but now I am in a great deal of pain. One minute fine, the next minute ill. Pain comes quickly or slowly, but when it arrives, the body serves as a host to the ugly beast called pain. If one does not deal with the beast, the beast will deal with you.

Pain can completely overtake the mind. As Delvecchio Good (1994) puts it, a world "is unmade" (p. 42) by pain. What is it like to live in an unmade world? What does one use that unmade world to do? Under what conditions does the world fall apart? How much pain can you endure before your entire world falls apart? If suffering from chronic injury what is one to do? Chronic injury is so hard to deal with because it is chronic. To make one's way in the world in a constant state of frustration is a puzzlement.

People who suffer from chronic pain might think about suicide. What is the point in living in a state of hell? And yet, for most, eros is still strong; the psyche lives on. Why bother living in an absurd and depressing condition? What is it that keeps people alive in spite of it all? This is a mystery. And this mystery is worth investigating.

For a musician, RSI (repetitive stress injury) could mean the end of a career. The human spirit is resilient of course. But what is there to do when you cannot do what you want to do? The psyche is at war with itself. The ongoing battle with the injury makes life almost intolerable. Can a musician do something else? When one cannot play, nothing can substitute for that form of expression. Writing, reading, painting, these activities are wonderful, but they are not the same as making music. Something in the soul dies when the music cannot be expressed. Jacqueline du Pres taught cello after she could not play but I do not think that the teaching made up for not being able to play.

Pretending that you are fine is the lie that begins the unravelling. Denial sets in. I am not injured. If the musician plays on top of the injury it only gets worse. To explain away the pain causes more harm than good. There are many ways to tell lies to oneself.

Chronic pain and depression go hand in hand of course. How could you not be depressed if suffering from chronic pain? If you are not depressed, one must wonder why that is? Depression is also difficult to articulate, especially when one is in the throes of it. For people who have never been depressed it is especially hard for them to imagine what that might be like. Again the phenomenological problem.

How to express depression? Using words to express depression cannot really capture feelings. Falling into a black hole, tiredness, heaviness, psychic death, slowness. These words do not capture depression as it is lived and felt. Depression and pain together make for a destructive pair. Which came first, the depression or the pain? Did depression lead to pain in the first place, did a depression cause your injury? Or did the injury make you depressed? An emotional quagmire is at hand.

What is really depressing is when people do not see your injury as real, especially if the injury is invisible. The conundrum is this: one looks healthy but is chronically ill. The chronically ill part of you is invisible to others because they cannot see your injury. Tendonitis is not something you can see. Now, if you break a leg, others can see that. Tendonitis is an invisible horror. And what makes it worse is the inability to explain to someone else how much pain you are in. Moreover, tendonitis does not 'count' as illness. People may think–oh tennis elbow– that's nothing. Well, it is something if you are a tennis player or musician!! Who defines what counts as illness? Patrick Wall (2000) talks about the problem of not acknowledging repetitive stress injury or RSI at all, or underestimating the psychic damage caused by the inability to use that limb due to injury. He states,

> If RSI is now to be awarded the honour of having a "real" cause rather than a self-inflicted psychosocial cause, why has it become more common? It could be that, in the past, complainers were simply dismissed, particularly as the majority were women but women have learned how to fight. (p.102)

Why would women be more prone to RSI than men? Women are probably more prone to it because more women are secretaries than men. Typing all the time is not good for your hands. Even if men do get hurt and suffer from RSI, the likelihood that they will seek treatment is nil because men think that running to the doctor is a sign of weakness. But in the case of musicians, I wonder whether the majority of RSI sufferers are women? I would think that both women and men equally suffer from RSI especially if they are musicians. Practicing an instrument requires a great deal of repetition and it is rather easy to over do it and get hurt. Why has RSI been only relatively recently considered a legitimate form of injury? It isn't as if this injury is new to the world. Musicians have been getting hurt– throughout history– just like athletes. But musicians are not thought of as athletes—even though playing an instrument requires great athletic skill. Blaming the victim is the most common response to an injured musician. You did it to yourself, you practiced too much. This is the most irresponsible response to someone else's injury or illness. I have often wondered whether concert grand pianos built after the turn of the 20th century are part of the problem for pianists. Concert grands are especially hard to play. The keys are harder to depress than on, say, upright pianos. The concert grand was built for large concert halls, these pianos are loud and are meant to be heard across great distances. In the 18th and 19th centuries, musicians played in more intimate settings and I wonder if their instruments were easier to play. Well, who knows? On the other hand, we do know that musicians like Clara Schumann got injured and I am sure there were others who got injured during the 18th and 19th centuries.

RILKE'S HANDS: THE PAIN OF THE ARTIST

Pain is both physical and psychological. Artists who suffer pain sometimes project pain back into their work, consciously or unconsciously. Here I would like to briefly look at the case of Rilke. He is an interesting character study because he talked about his illness and pain in his writings. In a book titled, *The Poet's Guide to Life*, Rilke (2005) makes some interesting comments about art and suffering.

> Have you never noticed that this is the magic of art and its tremendous and heroic strength: that it mistakes us for this most alien dimension and transforms it into us and us into it, and it shifts our suffering into things and reflects the unconscious and innocence of all things back into us out of rapidly turned mirrors. (p. 53)

This is a remarkably complex citation. I will try to unpack it with a view toward the larger question of pain and its uses. First off, Rilke cleverly talks about the way in which pain and suffering are introjected and projected simultaneously. As one takes pain in (introjection), pain gets transferred and projected onto and into an object (in this case a text). The psychological impacts the physical as the physical impacts the psychological. What is striking in the above passage concerns the ways in which pain and art, for Rilke, work simultaneously; art moves into the body as if it had a will of its own. Art "transforms" pain by projecting that pain into an object. It is as if the pain needs a place to dwell. Pain needs a domicile, a home. Pain gets turned into text. The text of the art object seems to have a character all its own. Rilke suggests that 'it' –the art object–turns "us into it". The object of art arrives as an "alien" and settles in the artist. Once at home in the artist (much like a parasite), pain and suffering have somewhere to go. The pain and suffering go into the "alien" object of art. It seems that the object (the piece of art) and subject (me) merge. I am the art object and it is me. I become the poem, suggests Rilke. This feeling of at-oneness with one's art is a rather uncanny event. Rilke addresses the strange fact that art comes from some other place, some "alien" place outside of psyche. This is what the mystics believe. There is a kind of depersonalization that happens when the artist is at one with his or her work. And that can feel "alien" as Rilke says, or it can feel mystical. Perhaps the mystical is alien. The alien is clearly something Other than the psyche, but somehow at one with it as well. When listening to music this phenomenon may be a little easier to grasp. Listening to a profoundly intense piece of music –say, Henryk Mikolaj Goercki's *Sinfonie Der Klagelieder*– has a strange effect on the psyche. There seems to be a con-fusion of psychological boundaries when music speaks to the soul. When the psyche feels as if it has collapsed into sound the experience bewilders. It is this becoming—at–oneness with sound that is curious. The ego seems to just disappear. The sound so moves through you that it becomes you. Perhaps this is what Rilke is trying to get at when speaking of the magic of poetry and prose. But in order for this to happen, there must be some kind of emotional connection with the text or with the music. Goercki's symphony is one of intense suffering and overwhelming sadness. I am overwhelmed when listening to this music. I identify in some way psychologically with this music. The pain of the music now becomes my pain. I am the pained music. I think this merging is what Rilke is getting at. This is a very complicated and strange phenomenon. Merging with the text of music– is similar also to merging with another person. This is done by projective identification where I become you. You are me. There is no distinction between me and you. If I am you, my ego has dissolved–temporarily. Projective identification might also be interpreted as that interchangeableness between art and the psyche. If I am my art and the art is me, there is no division between me and my work, I am my work, I am a work of art. What if I can no longer do my art if my art is me? Clearly part of the soul is diminished if my art abandons me.

Why would someone *want* to merge with a painful text –whether it be music, poetry, prose or painting–in the first place? What does experience of merging do for us or do to us? When one identifies with painful art, this identification tells us something about the person's psychic structure. One pain meets another pain. If one is familiar with painful events (like child abuse), one is drawn toward the familiar. The psyche tends to gather itself around familiar objects. The object of your affection might be a painful one because you desire to unconsciously repeat that pain in the experience of listening. This is called repetition compulsion. Unconsciously the psyche tends to seek out objects that are familiar. 'Oh yes, this piece of music speaks to me', you might say. But to what is it speaking? It speaks to you because you remember something–albeit unconsciously–that is familiar. The music speaks to you because it can articulate through sound, what you cannot articulate through language. At any rate, like gathers around like.

Rilke–an interminably sad poet–speaks to sad people. He felt burdened by his body and was ill for much of his life. Lou Andreas-Salome (2003) comments that "[for] Rilke his body became more and more the pillar of suffering" (pp. 34–35). If it is a *body* that creates a body of work–i.e. poetry–what happens when the body simply shuts down? Rilke (2005) complains that his body gets in the way of his art. Rilke says,

> But one lives in the density of one's own body, which imposes its particular measure already in purely physical terms. . . and since one lives, I think, in the awkwardness of this body and confined and imprisoned by the surrounding world in which one moves. . . one is not always as free, as loving, and as innocent as one should be. . . . (p. 32)

What is striking here is that Rilke talks about the "density" of the body. I am reminded of Merleau-Ponty's (1968) *Visible and the Invisible* when he talks about the thickness of the *flesh*. If a body is thick and the flesh dense it seems that it would hinder movement. Rilke seems to live in an abyss. When one is depressed, the body feels heavy, slow, lethargic and sluggish. Conversely, to be mobile feels light. But for Rilke, that lightness is absent. It is out of this thick and densely felt body that he creates his writings. This density–which is caused by his various illnesses– eventually prohibits Rilke from writing anything at all. Rilke (1985) talks about having a "distant hand" (p. 52) when his creative work comes to a halt. It seems as if the distant hand is a symbol for the distant psyche–the psyche that disappears. Rilke (1985), in *The Notebooks of Malte Laurids Brigge*, comments through the voice of Brigge that

> For the time being, I can still write all this down, can still say it. But the day will come when my hand will be distant, and if I tell it to write, it will write words that are not mine. The time of that other interpretation will dawn when there shall not be left one word upon another, and every meaning will dissolve like a cloud and fall down like rain. (pp. 52–53)

Falling into an abyss of nothingness, Rilke fears his productivity as an artist will cease. Art–no matter what genre–seems to come out of the psyche on its own and is driven out of the psyche and onto the object of its affection (text, canvass, instrument) for reasons of its own. Art, it seems, drives the subject, the subject does not drive the art. Creativity comes from a mysterious wellspring of emotions, intuitions, ideas. Rilke foretells his own psychic unravelling. Matthew von Umwerth (2005), in a very interesting book about Freud titled *Freud's Requiem: Mourning, Memory, and the Invisible History of a Summer Walk*, talks about Rilke and comments on this dissipating creative drive. von Umwerth (2005) tells us that,

> Rilke's anxiety during the long stretches of barrenness meant that he had lost confidence in his internal direction. Without poetic inspiration, he was thrown back on the disorienting conflict between world and feeling, and became, as he said "improbable" to himself. Reality conflicted with art because it too, could not be denied. . . . Through his need of his demanding art, Rilke remained the center of the world, and when his art abandoned him, he was set adrift. (p. 120)

It wasn't that he abandoned his art, it was that his art abandoned him. Being abandoned by the beloved object of one's affection–whether it be a lover, a father, the artistic spirit– brings about dread. To be "set adrift" means losing one's way. When the way is lost the psyche shrivels up. Giving in to a directionless life and giving up the ambitions and drives that makes the psyche move in the airy realms– as Bachelard might put it–is a tragedy for an artist. Not being able to write, paint, play is the death of the psyche. Being "set adrift" is the first step toward death. If one stays adrift long enough one loses touch with the very reality that allowed one to create in the first place. One is pushed back behind the ego. Trapped in a nowhere alters the way in which art objects get created if they get created at all. Rilke (2005) remarks, though, that sometimes he is able to use his sicknesses to help him create. He states,

> For me it is nothing but an insult whenever I get sick, and I cannot imagine except in the most extreme situation a great use of such suffering. . . . In such a state, then, there is virtually no other recourse but to cast into the soul that vastness of pain that could no longer be accommodated in the body. There pain becomes sheer force, regardless of its origins, just as in the work of art difficulty and even ugliness manifest themselves as nothing but strength. . . . (2005, p. 95)

For Rilke, then, pain moves him into work more deeply—as it did for Freud.

The question becomes—in a most Winnicottian fashion— what does one use one's pain to do? When does pain begin to unravel the psyche? Can an unravelling psyche help create works of art? At what point has the unravelling gone too far? These are questions, I think, that consumed Rilke.

Rilke wanted to hold onto his demons because he thought that they spurred on his creative drive. He did not want to be psychoanalyzed because he thought analysis would destroy his demons and hence destroy his art. This is a troubling way to think about the purpose of psychoanalysis. The point of analysis–it seems to me– is to allow the demons to speak so that one can become more authentic. Demons can be used in the service of eros. However, demons can also be used in the service of thanatos. It is only when the demons work to totally and utterly destroy the self, that the analyst might intervene. But analysis should never be about normalizing or pathologizing. The demons that analysts are interested in getting rid of are those that keep you from living the way you want to. But more often than not, those demons never go away. So, the point of analysis is to learn to use the demons in a productive way. This is exactly what Rilke did. He used his demons in the service of art. Rilke feared that getting rid of demons would mean getting rid of his art as well. Even if you could release the demons, pain remains. How to make meaning out of the pain that is already there–that is the question. More than likely, a depressed person does not get rid of the depression through psychoanalysis. Critic say, 'ah-huh, psychoanalysis is a failure, it doesn't work.' But it does work. What happens most often in analysis is that the patient learns how she can make use of the depression. The false hope some therapists have, however is that the patient can finally give up the depressions. But this rarely happens because depression is partly a biological problem. How can you give up your biology? Even if you take anti-depressants, you might still be depressed. The body tends to adjust to anti-depressants and after a while they don't work anymore. You are your depression after years of being depressed. It becomes you. Rilke feared analysis because he felt that it would destroy his character. Von Umworth (2005) tells us that Rilke "feared that the palliative effects of psychoanalysis would come at the cost of his creativity. . . . he now preferred the "self treatment" of writing to the uncertain influences of psychotherapy" (p. 115). Writing as cure. A curious concept. Can writing cure? Or is the psyche resistant to cure? Can a psyche be cured of itself? If you cure yourself are you merely erasing part of the self? Does cure mean erasure? The notion of cure is cure-ious to me.

Rilke talks about projecting pain into his work. It is the pain that drives him. Rilke–in order to write–needed to project that pain into his *hands*. Hands embody the pain about which he writes. One writes with one's hands. For a writer, the hands are crucial for the writing. Like Bachelard and Merleau-Ponty, Rilke has a certain fascination about hands. Hands seem to be personified for Rilke. Recall he talks about "the distant hand" in *The Notebooks*. The distant hand is the hand of the distant psyche which can no longer create. The hand lacks the will to create. It is as if the psyche comes through–or moves through– the hands literally. Distant hands are psychically unravelling. In a book about Rodin (2004), Rilke makes several references to hands–much like Bachelard. Rilke says of Rodin that "this young man who was working in a factory in Sevres at the time, was a dreamer whose dream got into his hands" (p. 35). A hand that dreams is a rather interesting concept. The hand dreams. The psyche/soma are absolutely collapsed here. The bodymind has a mind of its own. Rilke becomes obsessed a little later in the text on Rodin and talks about hands as if they are creatures. Rilke (2004) says,

> In Rodin's work there are hands, independent little hands which are without belonging to any single body. These are the hands that rise up, irritable and angry, and hands whose five bristling fingers seem to bark like the five heads of Cerberus. There are hands that walk, hands that sleep and hands that wake; there are criminal hands weighted with the past, and hands that want nothing more, hands that lie down in a corner like sick animals. . . (p. 45)

This is a remarkable passage. I am struck by Rilke's creature-making of the hands. It seems that the hand has a very peculiar personality. The hand can take on any emotional resonance like the psyche. Rilke seems to suggest that the psyche is the hand, the hand is the psyche. The will is the hand and the hand is the will. The work of the hand is the work of the psyche and the work of the psyche is the work of the hand. All art is created through the psyche-hand. When the hands "lie down in a corner like sick animals" creativity ceases. The ceasing of creativity was always a preoccupation for Rilke. I suppose it is for many artists. When will the flow stop? How much more do I have to say? What is left that I must express? Am I all dried up? I have no more subjects about which to paint. I have already created all the sounds I know and the music making has come to an end. How do artists keep going when there seems to be little to express?

A phenomenology of pain–for Rilke–is a phenomenology of the wounded hand. Out of the wounded hand comes art. But when the hand is too wounded–like a sick animal– art no longer comes. What is true for poets and painters is also true for musicians. When the hands can no longer sing, the music comes to a halt. Rilke did make a few comments about music throughout his writing that are interesting to explore here. In a letter to Benvenuta, Rilke claims that "music does not want anything for itself" (1987, p. 19). Music, like the hand, seems to be a creature with its own will. How can music 'want'? This is a very curious thought. In *The Poet's Guide to Life*, Rilke (2005) says,

> Music is almost like the air of higher regions: we breathe it deeply into the lungs of our spirit, and it infuses a more expansive blood into our hidden circulation. Yet how far music reaches beyond us! Yet how far it pushes on with no regard for us! (p. 143)

Like Rilke's hands, music seems to have its own personality and spirit. Music is anthropo-morphed. Music is a creature as the hands are creatures. Music, like art, moves into us, as we move into it. Music possesses us we do not possess it. We are taken over by the music it seems. Music pains–especially when one cannot make music any longer.

Rilke believed that it was his art that called him to write. Music, for Rilke, moved into the body of the listener–with little regard for that listener. Music has its own will. It is not that the musician makes the music, but rather that the music makes the musician. The music chooses a person who expresses its will. Musical prodigies are a case in point. How to explain Mozart's talents? There is no explanation for musical genius. Where does that genius come from? The music just seems to be there always already in Mozart. The vessel filled needs to be emptied. Mozart was merely the vessel of some greater force that was in need of emptying.

DESERT IMAGES: INTERIORITIES OF SAND AND SEA

The wounded artist is not able to do what he or she is called to do. This is the troubling question that runs throughout this book. What does it feel like to not be able to be the artist one was called to be? To get at these feelings, to get at deep interiority, scholars might turn to deeply interiorized images–as the Jungians teach. Exploring the landscape(s) of extremely interiorized space, might help to work through the damage done to the psyche-soma. Turning inward toward images, is one way to grapple psychically with pain. One might need to relinquish the hold that both the ego and superego have over the unconscious. That deep interiority is buried in the unconscious is problematic because it is difficult to get at that which is antithetical to logic. Logocentrism gets in the way of understanding unconscious messages. Dreams and the logos are at loggerheads. Reports back from the unconscious are dreamscapes. Dreams are made up of images. Focusing on the images clues us into what interiority is about.

On a conscious level, when thinking about being damaged or wounded, what might come to mind is a psychological desert. In the desert death is at hand. Think of Death Valley. What sentient being can survive the desert? Through study, though, we find that ironically the desert is not a place of death, but it is rather a place teeming with life. Focusing on desertscapes of the psyche might help one get back to, or tie back to (as in *religio*), a more spiritual aspect of life. Thinking on the desert may activate the unconscious imagination which is in fact a very lively place.

The wounded psychebody is like a desert. No–it is a desert. Psyche finds herself in hostile territory where the earthbody is sand, wind and heat. The body is in ruins. Commonsense suggests that the desert is barren, dangerous and inhospitable. It seems that the desert easily lends itself to thoughts of death. Yet, there is much more to the desert than death. The desert-in-the- real surprises. The desert, in fact, is full of life. First off, the desert is not deserted. Lots of life goes on in the desert. (Step back a moment and make the connection between the literal desert and the desert of the wounded psyche.) We should–to be more accurate–speak of desert(s) and not the desert. (Perhaps we have psyche(s) and not one psyche.)There are many different kinds of deserts. Gary Paul Nabban (2000) tells us that the deserts "–not the rainforests–are richest in pollinator diversity and perhaps reptile diversity" (p. 2). How fascinating this reptile diversity. The reptile is a particularly Jungian image–one that is found frequently in mythology. Psyche is ensnaked.

Some snakes are poisonous as some parts of psyche are poisonous as well. Medusa has snakes coming out of her head.

To my surprise, deserts are not always sandy. John Sowell (2001) points out that,

> Hot, Salty, Dry and Barren. Although most of us imagine the desert in this way, not all deserts share these characteristics, and defining the word desert is not easy. Its root means forsaken or abandoned, and indeed many perceive the desert as lacking something. . . . But biologists have applied the term to divergent regions of the globe. . . . The Artic and Antarctic have been called polar deserts, and the open seas have been termed oceanic deserts. (p. 2)

There are sandy deserts, polar deserts and oceanic deserts. One does not usually think of the ocean as a desert. Swimming in the ocean is dangerous primarily because of shark attacks. Think here of Bion (1991) who suggests that the psyche can in fact attack itself. The mind attacks itself. Psyche is part shark.

Let us dwell for a moment on polar deserts. Polar icecaps are not often associated with deserts. Polar bears live in icy frozen lands. A desert made of ice and snow seems a rather odd idea. The film *8 Below* turns on death and survival in a polar landscape. This is the terrifying story of life in the Antarctic. The earth opens up nearly swallowing a man whole, as the ice breaks beneath his feet. The scientist in the film studies rock formations and nearly sinks to the terrifying depths through cracks in the ice. His arrogance leads him to a place where he should not have been. In an arrogant rush, the scientist does not think that his guide needed to test every step of the way. Lo and behold, the ice broke beneath him. *8 Below* is also the story of Huskies who understand the wildness of the polar regions. But even sometimes they are fooled by Mother Nature. The polar regions are at once beautiful and violent. Scientists who do research in these frigid regions must brave the harshness of nature and the solitude of being in the middle of nowhere. How does one stay warm in the Antarctic? What must it do the psyche to do research in such alien territory?

Here again, analogies are rich. The psyche also has areas which can feel polar. Some people have a sort of coldness about them. Those who are injured psychically and physically might just get numb. Being numb is perhaps a defense mechanism that protects the psyche from overloading. But too much numbness or coldness can be terribly self-destructive. The lack of emotion–like being numbed out on Prozac–kills the inner spirit. The walking wounded are the living dead.

Bachelard teaches that when one dwells on images that relate to the basic elements (like in this case, frozen water) one populates the psyche. To make the imagination an active one, thinking on the elements opens up ways in which to articulate seemingly impenetrable areas of psychic space. Interiority is difficult to articulate without the use of such images. The frozen psyche is in a state of utter inertia. The snowy psyche ices over. Derrida (2002) suggests that although the body ages, the eyes remain as they were in childhood. Childhood scars remain in the eyes. Icy eyes look dead. People who have ice in their hearts exhibit little emotion. Having no emotions is quite strange.

Washing over. This is the state of oceanic deserts. Again an oceanic desert seems like an oxymoron—but this is the term biologists use to talk about oceans, surprisingly enough. Oceanic regions could serve as a metaphor for the fluid part of the psyche. Dreams seem to be fluid in that dream images blend together. The irony here is that although dreams seem fluid, the unconscious—as Freud teaches—is rather rigid. Repetitive dreams are symptoms of rigidity. Falling (and Bachelard writes about this throughout his work) in dreams is common. Flying (Bachelard makes much of these antithetical notions) is also common. These basic movements tend to get repeated over and over. These repetitive dreams of falling and flying are symptoms of problems that have not been worked through. The bodypsyche is oceanic in its depth, yet rigid when issues remain repressed.

The body is mostly made up of water, as is the earth. If we are of the earth, then we are an earthy bodyscape made up of rivers of blood, chemicals and electric currents. How is it that the bodily organs float around in that stuff and yet stay in place? Of course Freud famously criticized the notion of oceanic oneness that religions promote. He says the feeling of oceanic oneness is a throwback to more primal times. Oceanic oneness might be a feeling that unconsciously reminds one of a time before birth. Why would anyone want to return to that state? What would it be like to be fluid and frozen at once?

How does nothingness relate to the desert landscape? Or does it relate at all? Edward Abbey (1971) has this to say about the desert:

> The desert says nothing. Completely passive, acted upon but never acting, the desert lies there like the bare skeleton of Being, spare, sparse, austere, utterly worthless, inviting not love but contemplation. (pp. 300–301)

Perhaps the desert psyche says nothing. What if nothingness pervaded psyche? Nothing, blank, dead, empty, frozen, wasteland. Is this what it is to go into a coma? Do some people walk around as if they are in a coma? What's on your mind? Oh, nothing. Is that really the case? I'm not thinking about anything right now. How can that be? Isn't the psyche always thinking? What if it stops? I don't have anything to say, all my creativity is dried up. Tell me about yourself—there is nothing to tell. We all have moments like this. But what if this made up your whole life? How to inject meaning into a meaningless life?

Does not being able to play (whether child's play, playing an instrument, playing with ideas or words) signify the "bare skeleton of Being"? What does it mean to walk around like a skeleton? When you call someone skeleton head what are you really saying? Is the wounded psyche a mere skeleton?

Some find great solace in desert regions. There seems to be a wide-openness to desertscapes that– for some– allow for exploration of interiority. Carlo Carretto (2002), remarks that:

> The great joy in the Saharan novitiate is the solitude, and the joy of solitude– silence, true silence, which penetrates everywhere and invades one's whole being, speaking to the soul with wonderful new strength known to men to whom this silence means nothing. (p. 11)

Mystics have historically sought out the desert as a space in which to contemplate the numinous. Where there is seemingly nothing, there is everything. Where there is silence there is inner speech. Where there seems to be soulnessness (a harsh and unforgiving landscape) one can find soul. Can one find the soul in a desert psyche in a space seemingly empty? In the nothing there is something. Or is there? What is seemingly blank is actually rich. If the musical imagination seems dead, can one revive it in desert states of nothingness? In silence can a musician speak that nothing? It is a fact that music is interesting not so much for the notes but because of the rests. The pauses between notes allow for time and space to ingather. The pauses are the difference that make the difference as Gregory Bateson might put it. Differences in tone are created by resting. When one is at rest literally–in a life that seems to stand still–are there things that come out of the rest that are generative? I suppose it all boils down to what you use rests to do. If you find no use in rest then nothing comes of it. But if you find use in rest then something comes of nothing. But what is that something? If it cannot be the return to the state before the wound–because there is no going back–is that something anything at all?

Back to our desert for a moment. There is always already a remainder when talking of the desert. That is, desert landscapes are far more complex than one might imagine. For example, Mike Smith, Peter Veth, Peter Hiscock and Lynley A. Wallis (2005) explain just how complex deserts are in the following passage. Here they remark on the difference in deserts on a global scale. They suggest that

> the extreme variability in these habitats, [globally] . . . range from great continental deserts (such as the Sahara, Kalahari, and Australian deserts) to the basin-and-range or montane deserts (such as North America's Great Basin or the Puna in northwestern Argentina), coastal deserts (like Namib or Atacama), or regions where aridity is substantially increased by the rain-shadow effect of nearby mountains (such as in the central Asian deserts, or in the Patagonian deserts. (p. 3)

Imagine that your psyche is made up of this kind of complexity. And it is. And it is far more complex than even that. The desert of the psyche is enormously variable and psychic states differ radically from one person to the next; psychic states differ from one moment to the next for that matter. Perhaps there are a variety of desert(s) in the psyche. You do not have one mood, you have many. Contrarily, there are some people who seem to have only one mood, or no mood at all. Some people are windy, dry, icy, oceanic. The unconscious imagination is populated by stormy weather(s), aridity, wetlands and wastelands. The psyche is almost beyond description–and emotional states are–at the end of the day–beyond representation and that is why drawing on the landscape such as the desert is useful to try to think about what feelings might look like and how emotions get played out. Not being able to play is about turbulence as much as it is about repose, it is as much about sand as it is about the sea, it is as much about you as it is about me.

CHAPTER THREE

LISTENING

The Regressive Movement of Currere

Not being able to play forces one to listen differently. Listening without playing, for a musician, can be painful especially when the musician is no longer able to play. A choice has to be made. Either one listens to music or one does not. If the musician chooses not to listen to anything while injured an emptiness sets in, a depression, a melancholy takes over, the soul withers. Perhaps injured musicians go through various phases of dealing with injury. One phase is the refusal to listen to any music because it is too painful. But after a while, the call is heard. As Martin Buber (2002/1947) puts it ". . . living means being addressed. . ." (p. 12). Music is what addresses the musician. Not being able to listen is not being open to the address. This non-openness leaves a chasm, a hole in the heart of being. When a musician refuses the address of music, life is not worth living. The soul dies. Music is the soul of the musician.

In early phases of injury, as I said, a choice must be made. To keep soul or to throw it away. Walking around as if dead. Michael Eigen (1996) addresses "psychic deadness." He remarks that "[f]or some people, [in this case it would be musicians who are injured and cannot play and who choose not to listen to music] the sense of deadness is pervasive. They describe themselves as zombies, the walking dead, empty. . ." (p. 3). Just as a painter without a canvass might feel dead, the musician without music cannot play out the score of her life. Composing the life score, notes become surround sound; psyche is music as total immersion. No score, no compositions, no surround sound. Life deadens. The image that comes to mind here is the character in Pink Floyd's (1980) *The Wall.* . Pink, the un-hero in the film can no longer function and sits in front of a TV night and day. The TV is a symbol of his psychic death. Tim Willis (2002) suggests that Pink is partly based on Syd Barrett who headed up Pink Floyd and gradually collapsed into insanity. Willis tells us that Syd watched TV all the time. Syd was no longer able to play his guitar, he was too far gone. I will talk in depth about Barrett as an example of someone who is not able to play later. But for now, let us get back to the issue at hand. When the musician cannot play and no longer listens to music "psychic rigor mortis sets in" (Eigen, 1996, p. 97). Did psychic rigor mortis set in for Barrett? No one will ever know. For his public, he was unreachable.

69

ON NOT LISTENING TO MUSIC

Perhaps this is one of the early phases of injury. Perhaps this is the equivalent of going into shock. This state of shock may last days, months, years, or even forever. But if psyche moves through this schizoid phase and moves more toward a depressive stage whereby one accepts what has happened, perhaps listening to music once again becomes a possibility.

Our injured musician might begin to theorize about music, even though she cannot play. To theorize, listening is necessary. Theorizing through listening means that a certain distance between the musician and the music (because she is no longer able to play) might allow her to think about music differently, not better, but differently. The musician who listens but does not play might begin to ask deeply philosophical questions about music, about the nature of music and about the connections between music and soul. Ethereal, soulful questions about music are found in the writings of Heinrich Heine (1995) who had this to say about music.

> Now, what is music? The question occupied me for hours before I fell asleep last night. Music is a strange thing. I would almost say that it is a miracle. For it stands halfway between thought and phenomenon, between spirit and matter, a sort of nebulous mediator, like and unlike the things it mediates–spirit that requires manifestation in time, and matter that cannot do without space. (cited in Amis & Rose, p. 2)

I liken music to soul speaking rather than spirit. Music is everywhere if the ear is open to listening. Birds chirp outside near the grassy field down by the muddy nuclear wasted water toward a pathway into the chaotic sea. The wind is akin to music as it surrounds soul with its invisible arms. Music is that invisible something that blows colour into time and space, that evokes affective states and creates moods. But what is it to create a mood? Without music what kind of moods does one get in? Music is a driving force behind moods, especially in film. Silent films, of course, are moving, but film with music moves in deeper waters.

When the musician cannot play, the absence of playing does something to the soul. A working musician may not have time to dwell in the realm of the philosophical. The inability to play creates the time necessary to think more theoretically about music and lived experience. Speaking poignantly about music and time, Igor Stravinsky (1995) comments that,

> Music is the sole domain in which man [sic] realizes the present. By the imperfection of his nature, man is doomed to submit to the passage of time–to its categories of past and future—without ever being able to give substance, and therefore stability, to the category of the present. The Phenomenon of music is given to us with the sole purpose of establishing an order in things , including and particularly, the coordination between man and time. (Cited in Amis & Rose, p. 16.)

Stravinsky argues here that music is wrapped up in time, especially the present. I would argue that music might be the glue that holds the present together. Music is on a time continuum. Music is a life continuum. It glues life together even as life falls apart.

When you hear a symphony or piano concerto or guitar ensemble or a Rolling Stones' song, you are taken back. Those old moods emerge from the deep ruins of memory of things past. Music is the stuff of memory. I played that concerto when I was thirteen, I heard that guitar ensemble when I studied at the Aspen Music Festival, I heard the Rolling Stones for the first time on the radio when I was in the kitchen in the early 70s'. There is something uncanny about music and memory. Here I am thinking of the famous passage of Proust's (2003), in *Swann's Way,* about eating the "petites madeleines" (p. 60). The protagonist of this painfully long epic is reminded of things past through the sense of smell. Throughout the text there are many references to the connection between smells and memory. ". . . my mind became littered . . . with a mass of disparate images–the play of sunlight on a stone, a roof, the sound of a bell, the smell of fallen leaves. . ." (2003, p. 253). Notice in this passage that sounds and smells are mentioned closely together. These senses are our Other senses, the ones that get marginalized. The first sense to have gotten any attention in the Western philosophic tradition was sight. The Enlightenment is a symbol of sight. Sounds and smells are not considered serious philosophical subjects in Western philosophy. Today, ecologists like David Abram (1996) take these Other senses seriously. In his book the *Spell of the Sensuous,* Abram talks about smells and sounds as they are interwoven into the pattern of daily living. He states,

> Humans are tuned for relationships. The eyes, the skin, The tongue, ears, and nostrils—all are gates where our body receives the nourishment of otherness. This landscape of shadowed voices, these feathered bodies and antlers and tumbling streams—these breathing shapes are our family. (ix.)

Abram's ecological work connects the sensuousness of smells, sounds, touch with the larger ecosphere and with nonhuman animals. A smell is not just a smell. Smelling is done in a large, complex arena of sentient and non sentient things. Smelling and listening too are interrelated, unless of course you cannot hear or you cannot smell. But if you can hear and you can smell and you can feel what you touch, listening to music is a much more ecological experience when thought of in the context of the place in which psyche listens and the space into which psyche is thrown when listening. Sounds, smells, touch, place, space and memory are all ecologically related.

Sounds take you back. Sounds force you to regress. Mostly, sounds force psyche backwards to childhood. When I hear an old song on the radio, I am immediately taken back to where I was or what I was doing while listening to that song all those many years ago. And new music that I hear today will also form its own reference to the past in the future-to-come. Thus, music is, as Stravinsky points out, related to time. Time is related to memory. Memory is textured by smells, sounds, touches, images and sorrows.

THE PRESENT MOMENT: MAD ABOUT GUITARS

I picked up my first guitar in New Orleans in the mid 80s'. With $300.00 in hand, I strutted over to the music store (Werleins) and bought my first guitar. It was a low end (very low end) Takamine classical guitar. I taught myself some basic chord structures. But the instrument did not speak to me, so I kept picking it up and putting it down over the course of the next ten or so years. The instrument was an ongoing frustration. I never could get the sound I wanted out of that guitar. So it was an on again off again affair I was having with that Takamine. For some reason I kept coming back to it hoping that I would be able to get the sound I wanted out of it, but it just never gelled. It would be a long and winding road before I started to get serious about guitar playing. The next guitar I bought was from a pawn shop in Savannah. I was reminded of Maxine Greene's (1995) use of the poem the Blue Guitar in her *Releasing the Imagination*, when I spotted a blue electric guitar in the window of the pawn shop. I bought it on a whim and bought a small amplifier. I thought it was kind of funny. When I started playing this blue guitar it was really crazy. Every time I would hit a note the guitar would go out of tune. I would tune it and then it would sort of de-tune itself. This was a seriously crappy guitar. It was an experience so schizophrenic. I would tune it and then it would seemingly by itself de-tune itself. I stopped playing it. But something addressed me, as Buber (2002/1947) might put it. This short autobiographical tale takes us next to a real guitar shop and finally the purchasing of a real guitar. Now, it's the year 2002 or so. This guitar address had been going on and off in my psyche now for some 15 years or so.

I bought my first serious guitar, a Martin, about four years ago. Wow. Now this was a great guitar. It was kind of a low end Martin, but boy was it a good Martin. The whole world opened up to me then. And then it started. G.A.S. Everybody in the guitar world writes about this problem. The guitar acquisition syndrome. G.A. S. I bought and traded and bought and traded for the next few years. I am now up to my eleventh high end guitar and deeply in dept. What is it about the guitar? In my studies about the guitar I learned that many guitarists have many guitars. Pianists aren't like this, they only buy one Steinway, or maybe two. But not eleven. Well, maybe Van Cliburn has a lot of pianos. Most people can only afford one piano, especially if it is a Steinway.

My first Martin guitar was a revelation and epiphany. Here is the sound I've been looking for. All those years, I had no idea a guitar could sound like that!! Although I own several Martins now, several Taylors and a Lakewood as well as a Santa Cruz, I will say that I always come back to my Martins and experience that wow–this is it feeling. The guitar to lust after is the D-45 as far as I'm concerned but it is totally high end. This guitar goes for something like $6500.00 That's a bit much. I've settled for the D-42 which is nearly the same as the D-45 but for less money. Now, I've got big guitars and small guitars. My favorites are the small guitars probably because I can wrap my arms around them comfortably. The big guitars–like the one Johnny Cash used to play–are awkward to hold but have a booming great deep tone. And then there are all kinds of woods that go into making guitars, maple, koa, rosewood and all sorts of exotic woods. Every wood has a different tone, feel and shape. Some woods are dull and soft, some are warm and round, some are stiff as a board, some are metallic sounding, some are bell-like, some are deep and big. The thing I like about the guitar is the way the sound goes directly in the chest. The strings resonate and seem to flow directly into the body. There is something almost mystical about this phenomenon. The piano, on the other hands, is a more distant fellow. At arms length you depress the keys. But the guitar is held. That makes a huge difference in the relationship between the musician and the music. Interestingly enough, Brian Greene (2003) and other physicists suggest that the cosmos is made up of vibrating strings, these strings hold the universe together and calm the chaos of the movement of energy that makes up everything. This fascinating idea is termed string theory. From a musician's point of view it makes total sense. Of course, the universe is made up of guitar strings!! For me, the universe *is* made up of guitars and guitar strings. At any rate, the guitar speaks to me like no other instrument and my love affair with guitars has been steady even after hurting my hand again and not being able to play again. I re-injured my right hand practicing the guitar five hours a day. It took over a year to heal. But my hand has never been right since I hurt it twenty years ago. I am almost always in some kind of pain. When I don't play my hand sometimes hurts more.

While not playing, one can build in the time to study music differently by reading biographies of musicians or reading music theory or listening to music. When I was unable to play the guitar during the year I got hurt, I began reading what guitarists had to say about guitars. I'd to turn to the words of some of the finest guitarists of our times to hear what they had to say about their love affairs with guitars. First, let us look at the guitar acquisition syndrome or G.A.S. and see just how many guitars famous guitarists own. Chet Atkins (1992) tells us that he has owned over 100 guitars. Atkins states, "[a]ll together. I've had about 100 guitars in my career. I'm ashamed to count, but I think I have about 25 right now" (cited in Menn, 1992, p. 12). Atkins touches on an issue that rings true for many guitarists and that is shame. There is something shameful about owning so many guitars, there is something shameful about admitting that your entire house is overflowing with guitars. In our house, I've got guitars in my study, in the sunroom, in the bedroom, in my office at school. There just isn't more room. Plus, I feel kind of guilty having all these guitars. Guitar guilt is something I need to examine more closely. The salesman at one of our local music stores asked me if I was afraid to leave the house as it is occupied by all those high end guitars. I am occupied by guitars and guitars occupy my house—the house of my psyche. I said, no. I've got insurance, one pitbull/lab and two wolfish looking huskies who have mean howls. But yes, it is a worry. Walking off with a guitar is relatively easy, just pick it up and go. This is why I don't like people working on the inside of our house. I don't want people to know I've got a goldmine of guitars here. Jeff Beck (1992) speaks to this issue. He states,

I've hung on to every guitar; I never sell guitars, really. In fact, one time I remember Max Middleton saying, "You've only got one guitar, and you've lost that." I used to have one Strat because all the others got ripped off. I had other guitars at different times, but they were all stolen and I wound up with one guitar. Then I lost that somewhere and thought, "Wow, I'm supposed to be a guitarist, and I haven't got an instrument," That was back *in '72 or '73*. And then all of a sudden I looked around my front room the other day, and I've got 70 guitars. (cited in Menn, 1992. p. 23)

Jeff Beck must have a pretty big front room to house 70 guitars. Imagine owning 70 guitars! That is really kind of unbelievable–especially for people who don't play and don't understand G.A.S., guitar acquisition syndrome. Every guitar is a new world. Every guitar is a new planet, a new solar system. Different guitars evoke different colours and moods. I am on a quest for the perfect guitar. I've got to find the perfect sound. All of my guitars are more or less perfect, some less perfect than others. Some are not balanced. The low end is too boomy and covers over the high end, or the high end might be too twangy or too metallic sounding or not resonant enough. Some guitars sing, others do not. And too, all of these sounds depend upon the right playing conditions. The temperature has a lot to do with getting in touch with that right guitar at the right time. Cold weather is a dreadful problem for me. Part of the problem with my hands is poor circulation which could have been part of the problem with the injury. Cold weather and guitars just don't go together. Heat is also a problem. Guitars are living creatures and respond to changes in weather, wood expands and contracts, strings tighten or loosen or even break because of temperature changes. Wood cracks with extreme temperatures.

Back to the number of guitars owned. On and on. Before you know it you are sixty grand in debt. There is always something wrong with a guitar because it cannot be all things at all times. Different moods and different styles of playing need different guitars to do the work. My Martin Om prewar model is the perfect guitar on Tuesday but on Wednesday I might feel that the action is too high. On Thursday my favorite guitar is a bell-like 1974 small bodied Taylor. It's got easy, low action and the bell-like sound just transports you into a different zone. But then on Friday the Taylor doesn't do it for me because it lacks body and depth. So I go back to my Martin, but maybe a bigger bodied Martin like the D-42. And so on. Guitar guilt. I own too many guitars.

A rock star could probably afford to have millions of guitars, but a college professor like me can't really afford to be doing what I am doing. I've decided to stop buying guitars, even if another one addresses me. I can't stand living in debt. But the debt is worth it for the guitars. Buber (2002) talks about "being under a compulsion" (p. 107) and the ways in which this compulsion can be so damaging to a life. The compulsive personality–like me–has to struggle with the practical, the I can't afford to be doing this. Buber (2002) suggests that freedom is the opposite of compulsion and it is to freedom we should turn in our everyday lives and our every day choices. He states,

> There is a tendency to understand this freedom, which may be termed
> revolutionary freedom, as at the opposite pole from compulsion, from being
> under a compulsion. . . Compulsion is a negative reality. (pp. 107–108)

Being under a compulsion–and in this case it is the compulsion to buy a million
guitars– is like being under a spell, or being under the influence–not of alcohol, but
of the guitar- Id. What does this unconscious want from me? Is this destructive
compulsive behavior? How can I stop buying guitars? Well, I'm working on it and
my bank account will not allow for one more guitar, not even a trade. Holding a
guitar and smelling the wood is a sensual experience. I am thinking again of David
Abram's (1996) work on sensuous experience. Hearing the resonating and
vibrating strings is sensuous and marvellous. But most of all the overtones are
beautiful, lovely, wonderful. Delightful. How to express my love for this instrument.
I feel that acoustic guitars have souls. Electrics like Strats, at least for me, are
soulless. Archtops try to have souls but they just don't. Martins and Taylors are my
favorites and the two types couldn't be more different. In the guitar world people
are usually Martin people or Taylor people. But I like them both. Each serve
different purposes and resonate with different moods. And it is this thing about
moods which fascinates. Guitars create moods. Moods create guitar sounds.
Classical guitarist Eliot Fisk (2004) talks about his experience of listening to
Segovia.

> And Segovia's guitar just got to me, captured me hook, line, and sinker. . . . It
> seemed to speak of another world–a more elegant, wonderful, magical world
> than the one we inhabited in our everyday life, and I wanted to find out what
> that world was about. (p. 5)

Eliot Fisk is a classical player. He has a marvellous touch and impressive sound.
And of course Fisk is right– Segovia is the master. His playing is extraordinary. He
takes time and breathes like no other. It isn't about technique either. Segovia has a
soul and it comes through his playing. Of course the classical guitar world differs
from the pop or jazz world. Classical players are of a different breed than pop or
jazz players. And some pop and jazz players are actually "put off" by classical
training. Here I am thinking of Dominic Miller. Miller (2005) says,

> I went to Guildhall, but it was actually the low point in my musical career!! It
> kind of put me off music more than anything else. It was a strange time for
> me. I was 19 years old and I was surrounded by musicians, but I actually
> started thinking, I don't want to do this. (p. 95)

Indeed. My experience in music school was also the low point in my life. Music
schools are awful places for creative people. I don't want to sound anti-intellectual
here. I think it is important to study music theory and musical composition and
music history etc. Music school standardizes. Music juries terrify and turn music
into a test and punishment. It has taken me twenty years to recover from my
horrible experiences in music school. Part of the reason I got hurt had to do with
what Alice Miller calls a "poisonous pedagogy". In this context music school is a

poison for many musicians. Developing a tyrannical technique without paying attention to what the body can handle damages. Coming from above with straight wrist on the piano is ruinous. But the poison was about more than bad technique, it was the whole atmosphere. People fighting for practice rooms and the terrible pressure of juries. The terrible pressure of weekly lessons. Memorizing vast amounts of music to be played in front of teachers and peers is hardly a pleasant experience. Music school encourages a 7 hour a day practice routine. Now, anybody with common sense knows this is just ridiculous. No wonder musicians get hurt. Reading interviews with guitarists, long practice hours seems to be the norm also–and this goes for pop stars too. Pat Methany (Menn, 1992) tells us that he practices 8 hours a day. John McLaughlin (Menn, 1992) practices 7-8 hours a day. But the real kicker is Hose Feliciano (cited in Schroeter, 2004) who tells us about his childhood experiences with practicing guitar. He says,

> The guitar, from that point on, truly and absolutely became my better half, my consoler and my best friend. I remember I would come home from school eager to practice and literally, wouldn't stop until I'd fall asleep. On many occasions, my mother would find me with my guitar in my arms, having played it well into the night, until I'd lose consciousness. There were many times, especially during the summer, where I would practice for fourteen hours a day! (p. 209)

How does one play for fourteen hours and day and not get injured? Or, how can one practice so many hours and not get bored. There is something very boring about practicing. Mostly, the trick is playing slowly and repeating phrases to get them right. I find that terribly boring. After a while, you get to a point where there is no point in playing anymore. One has to know when to stop. But this is the life of many musicians. When I am able to play I only play for about 40 minutes and stop. I am afraid of getting hurt for the third time. I was playing 5 hours a day when I got hurt the second time. You'd think I would learn. I simply do not have the physical capacity, nor the capacity for boredom and for constant repetition.

There is playing and then there is practicing. When I am able to play, I wouldn't call it practicing. I play. I do not separate out the practice from the play as I did when I was studying as a classical pianist. My practicing days are clearly over. I just play and that is a totally different thing from practicing. I do not do gruelling repetitions, I do not play slowly for an hour, I don't care what my fingering is and I don't care if I get it right. After two injuries, I play. Playing means technique is part of the musicality not separated from it. As a child, I was taught to separate out these two things by practicing exercises and then playing pieces. But I could never seem to blend the two together in my head until I was much older. Now at 46, I think I get it. My playing is better–when I am able to play–because I don't focus on technique but rather focus on the whole of my playing. Somehow the technique just comes. One of the things I've learned over the years is not to force anything. The fingers will get it when they get it. There are all types of schools of technique. I studied with so many teachers that I became totally confused about what to do.

Wrist low, wrist high, come down from above, play from below. Keep hands close to the keys, spring up high from the keys and so on.

Today–when I can play–whether it's piano, guitar or cello, I do what I do. Teaching myself guitar and cello is a bit of a challenge, but I don't want to study with anybody anymore. Again, I don't want to sound anti-intellectual. I think that there is a time when we need to leave our teachers and become our own teachers. I studied music seriously with many teachers for most of my young life and I feel that now its time for me to be my own teacher. As far as the guitar is concerned, learning the fret board is extremely difficult because it seems to be upside down. Learning the patterns of the frets is very hard. I find the guitar infinitely more difficult than the piano because of the fret board and because of the way the fingers have to be so precise. Not that these things aren't called for on the piano, but it just seems to me learning guitar–at least for me–is much more difficult. The cello is an impossible instrument. I am drawn to its impossibility. It is fretless. Playing blindly trying to find the notes is only the beginning.

But back to the guitar. I want to talk a little bit about the mental space that is created when playing. This is not easy to articulate. But by the help of abstractions, maybe I can express what this space is like. Part of the reason I am so drawn to the guitar is that it creates a unique mental space that so resonates with me. When playing, I become totally absorbed in the instrument. Ego seems to melt into the wood. I am no longer ego, I am in a regressed state more like Id. It is almost as if I am not there when playing. I have created a space where I can disappear. And I think this is what music has always done for me, it has allowed me to disappear. What is it about disappearing that is so important? This is a feeling that is associated with what Melanie Klein (1943) would call the schizoid position. To go into a schizoid place, especially when the outer world is just too much is a necessity to survive. Music creates that safe space for many children who are victims of child abuse, say. Playing is a Houdini-ish art of disappearing, helping the psyche heal itself. I do believe that playing music is a highly psychological act. Being in tune is being at one with the instrument at hand. Now, these experiences are rare. Most of the time, the observing ego is too much present. The internal running commentary gets in the way of the playing. Relinquishing the observing ego to get to Id becomes key. And this is an act of regression. The point of regressing to a dream state is to get in touch with the vibrations of the instrument that serve to heal. The crucial thing, however, is to come back from the dream space into the ego. One doesn't want to stay regressed. That creates yet another problem. Being in a regressed state is almost beyond symbolization. Being regressed is where the concrete and symbolic blur, where the past and present merge, where the here and there no longer matter. Being at one with an instrument is the feeling of losing yourself. Listening in the losing of self is what is. The hands seems to know what to do by themselves. The sounds that are created are mystical. Playing in perfect conditions. The world is at one. A world where there is no world. Here is your private play world. Here is your secret world. Playing is an intensely private affair. This is probably why I never did like performing. With sophisticated technology, I can record at home and share my music with others without having to play live. This is ideal for me because performing is out of the question. I just cannot do it. I feel too exposed and suffer too much from nerves. This is one of the things that drove me away from my classical training. I just couldn't stand playing in front of people. Having to memorize pieces seemed like a circus act and an unnecessary one at that. I still can't stand performing. For me, the purpose of playing is deeply psychological and spiritual. I play to disappear. Do I write to disappear too? Do I read to disappear? One truly needs a room of one's own to do this and in this hustle and bustle of the busy world, it is hard to find that room. The phone rings, the doorbell rings, the dogs bark and I reappear from the deep. In this secret depth is a place where the heart, head and soul are attuned to nothingness, the very ground of being. But there is also a somethingness. The somethingness has to do with the vibration of strings. Stringed instruments are somewhat primal. They beckon the primal cry, the primal scream, the primal energy that makes us sentient creatures. Strings are living things and so too is wood, as I've mentioned earlier.

There are musicians and then there are *musicians*. Musicians who express these deep stirrings are rare. There are few guitarists who are able to express these primal overtones. My favorite guitarist is the late Michael Hedges. Now he was a *musician!* What is that sound he gets from his guitar? It's that oh-my-God-listen-to-this-guy-sound. Hedges did things with the guitar that nobody else can do. He was like the Houdini of pop/new age guitar. I just don't know how he played what he did. I have found some You Tube clips of him playing. You can watch him play and still not get it. How did he do that? He worked that guitar in very strange and unorthodox ways. For example, his right hand taps the bass and through these tappings he was able to get the richest harmonics and overtones I've ever heard on a guitar. It's hard to tell if one or two people are playing. Michael Hedges inspired me to practice seriously. When I first heard him play I just got the shivers. His guitar playing had such a deep sound, so much depth, so much amplification and balance. Something about steel and wood in the right hands. Hedges was the best of his generation. His life was cut short by a freak car accident in Houston. It is so tragic to lose him, his spirit, his marvellous playing. I listen to him all the time. I listen to him maybe too much. He has been my teacher more than any other guitarist. Hedges (2005) tells us that studying classical guitar and going to music school helped him to develop "an extra consciousness . . . an extra dimension" (p. 70). He also remarked that harmony was of great importance to his compositions. He stated, "I would also like to be somewhat of an educator of harmony and in stretching things a bit. . ." (p. 70) Indeed his harmonies were exquisite; he certainly stretched the boundaries of the guitar. In fact, one of his CDs' is entitled *Beyond Boundaries*. Even when he played relatively simple chords there was something so grand about his playing. He was truly a soulful, mystical man. A man I greatly admire. It is a tragedy that such a talent was taken from us too soon. Larry Coryell (1992), according to Dan Forte, says of Hedges: "I heard Michael Hedges' record, and I fell down. Couldn't believe it" (cited in Forte, 1992, p. 109). Hedges, in the interview with Dan Forte makes some interesting comments about his musical interests. Unlike many pop musicians, Hedges' seriously studied pieces by classical masters as well as pop stars. His vast musical education explains, in part, his command of the instrument. Yet, still how did he do it? In the interview, Hedges tells us who he was listening to in 1985. Hedges (1992) stated,

> Right now, I'm listening to a lot of Baroque music, Renaissance music, the recorder player Frans Bruggen, modern 20th century music– I just got a record by Ligeti, who composed a lot of music in 2001 [A Space Oddesy?]. I listen to John Martyn, [bassist] Eberhard Weber, Genesis [synthesist/trumpeter] Mark Isham, Cyndi Lauper, the Time, Prince. . . . Todd Rundgren. . . John Scofield. . . . (1992, p. 111)

That's what you call a healthy musical diet. Most classical musicians do not listen to pop music and most pop musicians do not listen to classical. So Hedges' ability to cross over these genres is partly what made his music so interesting. Certainly the classical composition training he had at Peabody helped him. Hedges was one of kind. There will never be another Hedges. He said that he never wanted to sound like someone else. To be an original you've got to do your own thing.

Doing scholarship is not that different from playing guitar. To be a unique scholar, a really good one, you've got to do your own thing. In the scholarly world, this is not easy because of the stuffiness of many publishing houses. And scholars are trained–much like classical musicians–to do things in a certain way. Scholarship has a certain form and feeling like music. One needs to learn those basic forms before breaking out of them. This is what Hedges taught. He indeed was a great music educator. His varied listening diet is an inspiration. Similarly, in scholarship it is important to read broadly, rather than narrowly. An eclectic diet of reading is the best. But most scholars–in more traditional disciplines–have to follow a rather narrow trajectory, even though there has been a growing tendency inside the academy toward interdisciplinarity. Hedges combined the best of both worlds, the classical world of Peabody and his own unique pop-new age sound. Music school for him did not seem to be a trauma as it was for me. Music school– for many creative people–is just too damaging. Guitarist Adrian Legg (2005) comments on the difficulty of straddling the worlds of formal training and playing popular music. Legg (2005) states,

> I think if you mix the academic and the non-academic you tend to get disasters. I think that one of the big things that has gone wrong with the electric guitar is this kind of sterility caused by learning lots of stuff and lots of methods and coming out and hitting everybody with your technique. Somewhere along the line those guys seem to have forgotten that music is essentially emotional, and that's the beginning and end of it. (cited in Menn, p. 80).

Yes indeed. Much of music school is about learning repertoire and technique. Studying formally can teach the musician to develop sound techniques so as to enable her do all sorts of things. Students from Curtis, Juilliard, Peabody and the rest have tremendous technique. Piano competitions are all about technique. Matters of the heart seem to be secondary. Being a *musician* has very little to do with technique, although you need a sound technique to build a foundation for expression. Musicianship, though, goes beyond technique. And musicianship cannot be taught. My problems were always technical. Technique can be fixed, but you cannot teach someone to have emotions. You either have them or you don't . You can express them or you cannot. You either have a musical sensibility or you do not. And I think that this sensibility is something that you are born with. Music school just ripped my heart out and killed my musicianship and nearly killed me. It took me 20 years to recover from music school and the classical music world. Not that I am not grateful that I have a classical background. I am very fortunate to have studied seriously with expert teachers for so many years. Without this classical foundation I could not play the things I do, or learn new instruments. But the emotional price of music school was just too much for me. Of course there are self taught players. Most of us need teachers, however—at least to build a musical foundation. I think the best training is the apprenticeship model. Studying privately–at least for me–is the only way to go. However, the player has to take responsibility for her playing. Self teaching after the departure of the master is when the learning really happens. The real music education comes when you are alone. Ralph Mctell follows a more "instinctive approach" as reported by the anonymous interviewer of *Guitarist Magazine* (2005). The interviewer says of Mctell

> that he doesn't read music. Having learned mainly by ear, he's developed an instinctive approach to the guitar." I've acquired some knowledge" says Ralph, "But I couldn't tell you what I'm doing. I can only tell you what sounds right. It's been a slow process. . . ." (in Guitarist Magazine, 2005, anonymous interviewer, p. 91)

It is a slow process when you don't have anybody pointing the way. You've got to figure it out for yourself. It is a huge challenge to learn by instinct and the ear. I am teaching myself guitar every day–when I can play–. And even with a classical background in piano, I find it extremely difficult to understand chord structures and simple things like scales and arpeggios. But it is not impossible to figure things out, it just takes longer when you don't study with a teacher. And not reading music is both a blessing and a curse. I was never very good at reading music, although I can do it. Sometimes I would rather not. The reading of the music takes away–at least for me–from my playing. I want to play my own stuff and there's no point to reading scores. But then I have discovered the Bach *Unaccompanied Cello Suites.* And these pieces must be read to be played. I don't mind reading music when it is music that I really want to learn.

There comes a time in one's life where you've got to let go of your teachers (which includes composer-teachers) and do your own thing. I couldn't tell you what note I'm playing on the guitar, I couldn't tell you what I'm doing either, like McTell. I play what I play and see how it comes out. I work to be in tune with the natural resonances of the guitar. I understand basic progressions, but if you were to put a guitar score in front of me I wouldn't understand it. Again, learning instinctively keeps you back in some ways. Not being able to read music doesn't help either. But being able to make it up as you go along and improvise is not something all musicians can do. In fact, many classical players don't know how to make it up. And in the classical music world improvising is hardly a respected art, although during Mozart's day it was. Making it up is a gift. The music school curriculum–in most conservatories and professional schools–is rather conservative. What is taught is the classical canon. For piano that means Bach, Beethoven, Mozart. Studying pop music is just not done in music conservatories. Pop is considered garbage. Cultural studies scholars takes pop music seriously. But as is well known, many inside the academy feel that pop is crap and belongs on the streets not in the classrooms.

When one thinks of the writings of John Dewey one is reminded of the ways in which he called for the intersection of the child and the curriculum. The curriculum needs to intersect with the child, otherwise it is of little value. What better way to study educational issues than going to the popular and finding out what is meaningful to kids. Peter Appelbaum (2008) has written extensively on the importance of the popular and the everyday in school life. It is music that shapes most kids' lives. Appelbaum calls for a "wierding" of the curriculum. What would it look like to weird a music conservatory curriculum? Well, for one thing it would never happen.

As a child, I was shaped by two competing forces of music. I started studying piano seriously at the age of eight, but mostly listened to pop music. For many years, I did not listen to classical music, especially after I got injured. But now I have returned to my classical roots with studying the cello and once again I am immersed in Bach, Beethoven and Mozart. But I also listen seriously to pop music. For many years I did not go to classical concerts because it was too painful for me. But recently I have attended many classical concerts. Misha Dichter, Gary Graffman, Philip Glass, Daniel Hope, are just some of the classical artists I've seen perform live within the last several years. It is a great thrill to be back in the audience listening to these awesome musicians. When I recently heard Rachmaninoff's third piano concerto performed live it took me back to my youth as I studied and loved Rachmaninoff's work. Music and memory are intertwined.

When I hear an old pop song from the '70s, I'm taken back to my young adult years. And it is here that I would like to understand what that means. My memories of childhood were made through the records I listened to as a child. I loved pop music as a child and still feel as strongly attached to Elton John, say, as I did when I was thirteen years old. What does it mean to take pop music seriously, as a subject worthy of study? Ann Powers (2001) remarks that studies on pop music are just not cool inside the academy. She states that,

> Rock criticism is a genre disrespected by just about everyone, considered trivial by "serious" critics of high art and literature, who think it's lowbrow, and shunned by the anti-intellectual wing of the rock world who think it's pretentious. (p. 254)

I wouldn't call myself a "rock critic" or even a "music critic." I'm not a "critic" at all. I am an education professor and musician trying to understand the meaning of music in people's lives. I am trying to better understand especially the importance of music for children and young adults and the way in which music shapes and alters their lives. And I am trying to understand what happens to the psyche when one is no longer able to make music or is no longer able to listen to it for one reason or another.

When I was about 12 years old, my musical tastes were already formed. I believe that it is important to study youth culture to better understand why these musical tastes get formed so early and why they tend to shape a life. I was a child of the late '60s and early '70s so my pop musical tastes were formed by listening to the records of Cat Stevens, the Moody Blues, Emerson, Lake and Palmer, Yes, Genesis, Jethro Tull, Carly Simon, David Bowie, Roxy Music, James Taylor and Pink Floyd. In the '80s I expanded my music curriculum to Brian Eno, Kate Bush, Laurie Anderson, The Eurhythmics, The Who. Of course, everybody has their own music curriculum. I'm sure your music curriculum differs from mine. The question I am curious about is what music changed my life and why. Of course, there are people who don't listen to music at all and there are those who didn't grow up with record players. I couldn't image a house without a stereo. I grew up with a musical father. He used to sit around and play songs like Ramblin' Rose on his Martin Ukulele. He had a great voice and could play by ear, as could my grandfather. I was astonished the time my grandfather came over to our house and just sat down at the piano and played. No music, nothing. He just played by ear. This is the way I am learning guitar.

Back to pop music criticism. There are a host of people working in this area. A good edited book in the field of education is titled *Sound Identities* (1999), co-edited by Cameron McCarthy, Glenn Hudak, Shawn Mikloucic, and Paula Saukko. Some good sources on pop music outside the field of education are David Hesmondhalgh & Keith Negus (Eds.) (1996), *Popular Music Studies*; Richard Middleton's (1990), *Studying Popular Music*; Roy Shuker (2003), *Understanding Popular Music*; Michael Azerrad's(2001) *Our Band Could Be Your Life*; Keith Negus's (1996), *Popular Music Theory: An Introduction*; Simon Frith's (1996) *Performing Rites: On the Value of Popular Music*. I think it is important to study broad theoretical issues related to pop music to be able to make connections between, say, identify formation (as McCarthy et al., 1999) and music. Some people are inextricable from the music they listen to. Thinking back to my childhood, memories are triggered not by smells (as in the case of Proust's Swann), but by music. I hear an old Cat Stevens song, for example, and I remember a time long ago that was associated with certain feelings. The memories aren't clear to me, but in some hazy way Cat Stevens brings back other times. Early *Genesis*, especially influenced my ear. One of the reasons I think I am attracted to acoustic guitar is because of the amazing acoustic guitar work in their early albums when Peter Gabriel was still with the band. There is the amazing Steve Howe of *Yes* who also influenced the way I hear music. I bought a guitar like his (an archtop), but traded it eventually for a high end acoustic Martin. I enjoyed playing the Steve Howe guitar, but it just wasn't me after all. I feel more in tune with my acoustics. One should never play to sound like somebody else, as Michael Hedges taught. I could never sound like Steve Howe even if I tried. And why would I want to anyway?

Like other socially constructed concepts discussed in curriculum studies (i.e. race, class, gender), musical meaning, as David Brackett (2000) points out, is socially constructed as well. Brackett makes the larger connection between "the impact of race, gender, and class on musical interpretation, and the importance of history and genre" (p. x). My particular background, my race/class/gender has shaped my musical interests and musical interpretations. Being a white, middle class female– who has studied classical piano and plays guitar and cello by ear and listens to everything from Bartok to the B-52s'– shapes the way I interpret music and make meaning out of it. My pop influences are of a particular genre. I have always been attracted to complicated music, especially of *Genesis* and *Yes*. These two extraordinary bands play extremely complicated music. I especially liked *The Who's* "Tommy" and *Pink Floyd's* "The Wall." I also always appreciated good musicianship and sophisticated chordal progressions. Most of the bands that I fell in love with were British. I didn't have much interest in, say, *The Allman Brothers Band*, or bands like them. I never got into hard core rock, or grunge. In fact, I totally missed the whole grunge scene. Michael Azerrad (2001), tells us that grunge is associated with Indie labels. When I first read this I thought he meant labels that came from Indiana? That's how out of it I've been in the last few decades!! How stupid can you be!! Indie labels are independent labels. The only band associated with indie labels I know is Nirvana. Most of the indie bands mentioned in Azerrad's book, I never heard of. For example, Azzerad studies groups like *Black Flag, The Minute Men, Mission of Burma, Husker Du, The Resplacements, Sonic Youth*. I never heard of any of these bands. Where was I during the '80s? Well, for one thing I was in music school, walled off from the world of the popular. What is interesting, though, is that the indie movement in the United States has always been there, it's just been underground and not as visible as more mainstream rock. Azzerad (2001) points out that,

> American Independent labels are nothing new: legendary labels like Motown, Stax, Chess, Sun, and Atlantic were all independent, but by the mid-Seventies, most of the key ones had been swallowed up by the majors. (p. 5)

Indie bands accuse *Genesis* and *Yes* as being "corporate" bands because they recorded with major record companies. I never thought of these bands as "corporate" just because they were famous. I really don't know what a corporate band is. I suppose if a band sells out to the record company and totally allows them to shape their music, then that could be considered corporate. But I certainly do not think that *Genesis* and *Yes* are corporate. If musicians only write music that they think will sell, then that is corporate.

There are always competing fields of pop music around at the same time. And of course these music (s) are always already situated in race/class/gender and country of origin. Country music, soul and bebop, swing and hip hop, rap and new age are simultaneous music (s), each with their own distinctive sounds and with their own followers. And again, race, class and gender matter when we talk of what kind of pop music we are talking about. Here, I am focusing on the music I grew up with. I grew up in the *post-Beatle* era when rock-operas were being made, when huge lighting shows were beginning to get popular. My musical tastes were also influenced by my classical training. I listened to pop music that had a classical basis to it. I never really liked jazz, and I still don't because I don't really understand it, I'm not moved by it; it does nothing for me emotionally. I can appreciate John Scofield, or Pat Methany, Ella Fitzgerald and so forth, but I never felt emotional about their music. I suppose the bands I really loved (and still do) have big symphonic sound.

Richard Middleton (2003) points out, ". . . musical meaning cannot be separated from the discursive, social and institutional frameworks which surround, mediate, and (yes) produce it" (p. 9). Music's meaning cannot be separated from the listener who is situated in a historical, cultural, raced, classed and engendered culture. The one who listens is the one who interprets. Those interpretations are highly emotional and psychological. This is the point Middleton leaves out. Music may be a way to "negotiate reality," as Andy Bennet (2003) points out, but music is primarily an emotional experience. Because of the strong emotional charge, musicians develop cultish like followings.

If someone insults your kind of music, you might take it as a personal insult or attack because the music you listen to is related to your identity-formation and psychic structure. It seems to be common sense that people will interpret music in their own ways. But perhaps this is not common sense. Some people assume that everybody likes x because they like x. Certain generations like certain types of music. So if you are a child of the sixties perhaps you– because of peer pressure– like Jim Morrison, or *The Beatles*. But what if you don't like *The Beatles*? People might look down on you and say you are a square. At any rate, people like different music for different emotional reasons. This is the point that many of the pop music critics miss. A case in point would be Keith Negus' (1996) theory on music. The way in which he describes the complex relations between musicians and listeners makes sense and is perhaps one of the more sophisticated analyses of pop music but he misses the main point. Music is emotion. And the meaning that is made out of it is charged emotionally. Negus (1996) talks of music in general. He states that,

> . . . music cannot simply reflect a society, an individual's personality or life, a nation, a city or 'the age we live in'. The word, reflection, is one that slips very easily into academic discourse and everyday conversations about popular music. But no music can be a mirror and capture events or activities in its melodies, rhythms and voices. . . . Hence, my general point is that music is created, circulated, recognized and responded to according to a range of conceptual assumptions and analytic activities that are grounded in quite particular social relationships, political processes and cultural activities. (p. 4)

I find Negus's position to be a bit sterile. Is music primarily conceptual? Do listeners listen for concepts in music? I don't think so. Of course there is music that is concept based, like *Pink Floyd's* (1980) "The Wall" which is based on WWII and insanity. But people who listen to this music do so for emotional reasons, not for conceptual ones. I do think music can re-present broadly 'the age we live in'. Just listen to John Lennon's album *Imagine* and it will take you back to the Vietnam War. Listen to the music of Tupak Shakur and you will be transported into rage and resistance to white culture. I do think these artists reflect a certain time period. But of course there is more to it than that. I still think the 'there is more to it' needs fleshing out. People respond to different music because of their psychological make ups. And I do think there is something about a type of personality that is drawn to a type of music. Negus suggests that we cannot deconstruct this because of its complexity. Well, I do think one can make–with care and qualification–connections between angry grunge kids who relate to Cobain and the overwhelmingly depressing culture of the United States. Adults fear grunge kids. Henry Giroux (2004) points out, the young are seen as enemies. Giroux (2004) states,

> . . . the United States is at war with young people. All youth are targets, especially those marginalized by class and color. This is a war waged by liberals, conservatives, corporate interests, and religious fundamentalists against those public spaces, goods, and laws that view children and youth as an important social investment, and includes a full-scale attack on children's rights. . . Youth have become the all important group onto which class and racial anxieties are projected. (xvi)

The 1990s was a terrible decade for the rise of school shootings. Since the era we now call Columbine, kids have been especially demonized. We should attempt to understand youth culture, instead of demonizing them. If adults were to seriously listen to grunge or punk or rap music, maybe they would better understand the position of youth culture (s). Music is a place where kids can turn. Music, for some kids, is a haven, a shelter, a place where like meet like. Attending a rock concert is almost a religious experience for some kids who need to know that others feel like they do. The music that kids are drawn to has a lot to do with their emotional investments and moods. Again, the missing ingredient in rock critics' commentary— generally speaking--- is that it lacks any discussion of emotion, mood, psychological issues.

The other thing that I am interested in– that most rock critics are not– concerns educational links and implications of being immersed in a music culture(s). There are as many music culture(s) as there are musicians. We should not talk of, then, popular music, but rather popular music(s). My aim in this book is to make the links between education and music. Music culture (s) are sites of education. Kids learn all sorts of things listening to music and going to concerts. Being a fan-atic means being submerged in a subculture and inside of that subculture codes, modes of address, emotions, languages, imagery are all explored. Pop music allows kids to fantasize about worlds that the music creates. For example, *Yes,* the band that I grew up with and became fan-atical about, allows listeners to travel to mystical places. Ian Anderson, the lead singer of the band, is a very mystical and spiritual person. He wears long white robes and has an angelic voice. The lyrics to many of the old *Yes* songs are more about the love of language and the mystical power of words than anything else. The words allow the listener to imagine other zones, other worlds. This music teaches about the possibilities of emotional space. More than anything, though, the music allows the listener to feel in new ways, to be more open to the universe.

Like Negus' analysis of popular music, Roy Shuker (2003), talks about pop music in a very sterile way and completely overlooks the emotional impact music has, the ways in which moods are created, the psychological aspects of listening and taking in music. Shuker (2003) states,

> The study of popular music is situated in the general field of cultural studies, which addresses the interaction between three dimensions of popular culture: lived cultures, the social being of those who consume popular cultures; the symbolic forms, or texts, that are consumed within the lived culture; the economic institutions and technological processes which create the texts. (p. 11)

Is music in fact consumed like any other item in the market place? I find this language rather strange and off the mark. Music is bought and sold of course, but the main point about music is the emotional one. How does the music make someone feel? Why is this question not addressed? Economy and technology of course are all important aspects of creating musical texts, but I think again the important point is lost. If anything, music is taken in via the psychological state of introjection and what the person then does with that introject is highly complex. It is this kind of question that is totally missing from the majority of writers on the popular.

Places where people are educated are often not in schools. This is common knowledge among pop musicians. One fascinating aspect I've experienced in the guitar culture(s) is the space of the music shop. The place to find out about the music world, to find out what new instruments are available, to find out what those instruments are about happens not in the academy, but in music shops. Learning to use, for example, recording equipment, one must consult someone at the music shop. Recording is not taught in the classical music curriculum. In fact, what is taught in the classical music curriculum has nothing to do with popular music as I've stated before. So everything one needs to learn about pop music culture, one learns at the music shop. There is a kind of familial atmosphere in some guitar shops. People gather to talk about gigs, wood tones, amplification, archtops and electrics, acoustics of all sorts. Music store personnel are the teachers of pop. If you want to learn about acoustic guitars hang out at a local guitar shop. I have learned much from just hanging out. I have learned that Martins have a deeper bass than Taylors; Lakewoods are extremely expensive but have a very warm sound and yet the top tends to be rather harsh. Archtops are for mainly jazzers or people who want to sound like Steve Howe; electric guitar people are totally different from acoustic types, (not to over generalize but there is some truth here), Santa Cruz guitars are used both by classical players and pop players. Many Windham Hill artists use Taylor guitars. McPhearsons are over the top money-wise and strange to look at and too big for small people to hold, inlay work is extremely expensive but beautiful to look at. Taylors are bell-like. Lower end guitars, forget it. Some people are Gibson people and that's all they play. Timbers, nuances, overtones, volume, and textures of sound are altered by different types of wood and steel.

Different strings produce different sounds. There are coated strings called elixers that are put on many Taylor guitars. They are very easy to play. And then there are Martin strings which are not coated and rather difficult to play but the work is worth the deep, rich sound produced. I cannot comment much on electrics, but I hear a lot about the Strats. I owned one and didn't relate to it at all, it just sounded like crap to me. My classical training somehow jars with a Strat. Some of the best guitars are made in the United States. My favorites are Martins and Taylors as I mentioned earlier.

The music shop is a place where education happens. So, the music store is a place to hang out, to learn about woods, to talk about music, to shoot the breeze, to get some company, to talk to other musicians. When you are a musician it is nice to have other musicians around just to talk to. It is a lonely world when you do not have another musician with whom you can share ideas and discoveries. Playing an instrument is about playing with ideas and making discoveries from complex patterns and complex nuances of touch and sound. The place to talk about these things is in the music shop.

Like the music shop, record stores are educative places as well. Anne Powers (2001) states,

> We use the [record store called the Planet] like a classroom and a library, opening up dozens of deep catalogue albums everyday, playing our weird favorites until the manager came screaming, terrified we'd drive all the Michael Jackson fans from the store. We were like Talmudic scholars, dedicated to our studies and outraged at the thought that any menial activity might interrupt them. Some Planet workers applied this scholarship to their own musical pursuits. . . . (p. 162)

Working in a record store, or a CD store, is like working in the archives. Music history can be learned in such places. Imagine getting a discount on your favorite albums. Of course, music schools have classes where music history is taught, but music history is usually only about classical music. Or, maybe if you go to a jazz school you learn jazz music history. But what school teaches pop music in the United States? It really is a shame that pop music is not part of the music curriculum. It should be.

The pop music curriculum finds its home in both the record store and the music shop where instruments are sold. Education happens outside of the formal walls of the academy.

Education scholars talk about arts-based inquiry, but there are very few people in curriculum studies who talk about music as an example of arts-based inquiry. Maxine Greene (1995), in *Releasing the Imagination*, talks about the importance of the arts but she says little about music. Why is this the case I wonder? Isn't music an art form? It is just curious to me that in my own field not much work has been done on the topic. It seems to me that children are affected by music more so than by any other cultural product. Music is everywhere. With the advent of MTV, VHI and XM satellite radio, ipods and increasingly more sophisticated technologies music has become accessible to all kinds of people. DVDs too add to the musical repertoire. Now you can see concerts of your favorite groups. Watching Peter Gabriel or Annie Lennox perform on a DVD is a totally different experience than just listening. DVDs open up a whole new world for many people who have never had the opportunity to see these bands play. Living in a small town is especially problematic because the famous bands tend to go to large cities. DVDs have changed all of that. One could get a pretty good musical education by watching music DVDs or by checking out You Tube. You Tube is a virtual music archive. Not only can you watch pop bands, you can also watch old film clips of, say, Pablo Casals, or other early twentieth century classical musicians. You Tube has opened an entire world to the public and has opened the historical archives for all to see. When I was growing up this was just not possible. If you didn't catch *Yes* when they were playing at the Civic Arena, you missed them, period. Today, you can see them on a DVD Or on You Tube. There is much pedagogical value to watching a cellist play and listening to many different interpretations of a piece that you are studying. I have learned much about the cello by watching the clips of Casals and others. Education happens outside the university walls and the walls of the schoolhouse.

I can now see all the concerts I missed in my youth. Now I can catch up with the music scene. Some might say why buy a DVD concert. How many times can you watch that? Well, if you are a fan-atic, you can watch that DVD concert a million times and it never gets old. Just like listening to the same song for 20 years. I've listened to albums over and over and over again. I've found a kindred spirit in Chuck Klosterman (2005) who writes,

> ANYWAY, by the time you read this sentence, the song I am referring to will be ten thousand years old. You will have heard it approximately 15,000 times, and you might hate it, and I might hate it too. But right now–today–I am living for this song. As far as I am concerned, there is nothing that matters as much as hearing it on the radio. . . . (p. 49)

Klosterman has a great sense of humor. But he is making a point about music which is complex. This point has to do with how one feels about a certain song on a certain day. Those feelings continually change. Sometimes you get sick of listening to a particular song and put the CD away for a few years, and then you find it in a pile of old stuff, put it on, and you feel sky high when listening. Sometimes the same song can make you feel annoyed, other times the song can make you feel ecstatic. How is it that we keep listening to the same songs over and over again and not get bored? David Brackett (2000) comments "[t]hat a broad range of facts influences listening attitudes implies that multiple listening positions may be available to a single listener, this suggests the existence of a kind of double–(or multiple) "eared" listener" (p. 23). I can, then listen to a song, one day and like it and the next day hate it and get totally sick of it. And then two days later love the song again.

And why is it that I love the song *America*, say, only in the rendition done by *Yes*, while you might like the rendition that was done by Paul Simon? Or why does Neil Young's voice make me cringe while some die- hard fans love his stuff? The one that really gets me is Bob Dylan. As David Bowie says in one of his songs, Dylan's voice is like "sand and glue." I don't get Dylan at all, but one of my friends is a Dylan fan-atic. Or, somebody might say, 'oh my God why do you listen to *Pink Floyd*, they are totally depressing.' Yes, and that is exactly what I like about them. That they are depressing is the reason why I am a fan-atic of *The Floyd.* I don't like bubble gum music, I don't care for country. I don't have the frame of reference to understand country music. I just don't get it. I'm not from the country, I don't even know what the country means. Country just makes me feel nervous and totally out of place.

Again, I argue that the 'why' question music raises is primordially emotional, not conceptual. Why I like this over against that is because of the way the piece of music makes me feel. This is really a question of psychology. I don't like to listen to music that gets on my nerves like heavy metal. I don't like grunge either for the same reasons. I don't like teeny bopper music. Teeny bopper bands just rub me the wrong way. Being rubbed the wrong way is an emotional state, period. Of course, emotions are never separated out from intellect and there is much about music that appeals to intellect and emotions. The two go hand in hand. But emotions drive listening pleasures.

What I would like to do now is focus more specifically on one band that has meant a lot to me especially during my youth, but has become even more important to me during times when I am unable to play. I want here to analyze *Pink Floyd* for several reasons. The first reason is that I love their music. I find the inside story of the band fascinating. I feel a certain resonance with their experimental and instrumental work. *Pink Floyd* speaks to me musically like no other group. And disturbingly a member of the *Floyd*, Syd Barrett, got to a point in his early career when he was not able to play, not because of repetitive stress injury, but because of his mental collapse. So here I will do two things. First, I want to take a look at the scholarship on the *Floyd* to understand better the conversation about the band. Then I want to talk about the *Floyd's* albums as they relate to certain emotional states. Finally, I will analyze the problem of not being able to play by drawing on psychoanalysts Otto Rank, D. W. Wnnicott, Alice Miller and Michael Eigen.

A SAUCERFUL OF INSANITY: *THE FLOYD* AND CHILDHOOD

Music that we listen to during childhood takes on special meaning as we grow older. When you hear songs you used to listen to, say, twenty years ago, it just does something to you emotionally. Is it nostalgia? It is if it is not analyzed. But once analyzed it is no longer nostalgia, although there are always nostalgic remainders from one's youth. Thinking about music from your past takes on a meaning in the present as you re-listen to old songs. Here is where movements of Currere come in handy. The past is the regressive movement and in the present moment one must deconstruct and re-construct the past to form the future-to-come. The re-construction of the past is no longer past, but is the present moment of the past.

If music serves as a sort of background for your life, you might collect records, CDs or some other kind of musical artefact. You might sing along loudly while driving, listening to music on the car radio. Chuck Klosterman (2005) talks about listening to music while driving. Klosterman says,

> Musical structures define the process of motion. There are particular words and melodies that lend themselves to transportation; often, pop songs of this nature only sound good to humans who are actively operating motorized vehicles. (p.151)

Yes. There is something about driving and listening and singing along—loudly– to music on the car radio because music is movement in time and space and the car in which you are driving is moving in time and space as well. The music playing on the car radio transports you from here to there in a sort of mythic way. Music lends itself to the imagination and while driving you listen to sounds and create images from those sounds. Images and sounds do go hand in hand. Sometimes those images are vague. Certain songs may bring up pictures, scenes or even colours. Some songs are grey, others are blue and others are black. Some songs are happy and some are sad. Different moods get evoked and so forth. Some songs bring up more concrete images, especially if the song tells a story. Or, if the songs are part of a longer epic tale, images get linked together as part of the epic. For example *Pink Floyd's* (1980) "The Wall" is an epic tale about WWII. The music you hear evokes airplanes crashing, a wall crumbling, somebody who says "are these all your guitars??... wanna take a bath??" As you drive you create images that go along with the storyline.

Music you choose at home might differ radically from what you listen to on XM radio. When you make a conscious decision to listen to a particular band, like *The Floyd,* your experience of listening deepens because you've heard this song ten million times. Why do you keep coming back to it you wonder? Repetition compulsion? Obsession? Thirty years later you are still listening to *Pigs on the Wing, Dark Side of the Moon, A Saucerful of Secrets, Wish you Were Here, Shine on Crazy Diamond.* Your room- mate gets really bent out of shape because you keep playing this stuff over and over. But you keep coming back and back to these songs. Is it nostalgia or is it something else? Why do you want those feelings to come back again and again? The familiar is comforting. Music that evokes familiar feelings-of-old comforts as it disturbs; perhaps you are comforted by what disturbs. Would Freud call this neurosis? Well, all of these questions are interesting ones. There are no answers to these questions however. Music raises the uncanny.

All of the songs I mention above are by *Pink Floyd*. This is the band that I've come back to over and over again. I never get tired of listening to this band. In fact, I've been listening to *The Floyd* for some thirty years. As drummer Nick Mason (2005) says "We're in danger of becoming a relic of the past. For some people we represent their childhood. . ." (cited in Harris, p. 128). This band certainly represents my childhood. It's funny how you can be walking down the street minding your own business when one of those old songs just sings itself in your head and you can't turn it off. There is something uncanny about music and memory. Memory is made up of pop music for those of us who are addicted to it. And those memories bring back associations from the past. These associations may be vague. Sometimes songs do bring up clear images from the past. These images and feelings are highly psychological. Why this song and not another, why now and not later, what does this song mean to me?

Back to *Pink Floyd*. I am drawn to them because of their symphonic sound, because of their musicianship (especially David Gilmour's awesome guitar playing), because of their cynicism and their wit. Most of all, I just like the sounds they put together. I especially love their acoustic guitar work. Do I hear a Martin? Or maybe a Gibson jumbo? That acoustic guitar sound just does something for me. My love of acoustic guitars goes way back to my childhood, although during childhood I didn't know what kind of guitar I was hearing, I just knew I liked the sound. These early influences eventually drove me to the acoustic guitar. Without the *Floyd* and other bands that use acoustics, I don't think I would have been driven to play guitar. It is amazing how important these childhood influences become when one gets older. This is why it becomes imperative for educators to try to understand the culture of their students, try to at least listen to some of their music to try to get it. The culture that I grew up in was the tail end of the Vietnam War and the drug culture. I grew up in a house where music was always playing, especially mine. The most important thing I had as a child was my stereo. I can't imagine a childhood without music.

During the late '60s and early '70s the members of *Pink Floyd* were "the darlings of London's underground intelligentsia" (Mason, 2004, p. 21). Why would the intelligentsia be drawn to this rock band, and not to another? What is it about *The Floyd*? Well, for one thing they are very smart. Their music is smart. They hit raw nerves and express the inexpressible in an intelligent way. Their music is thoughtful, carefully planned out, exquisite in texture and multi-variously layered. Even the most simple chord changes evoke a mood. The mood they evoke in most of their albums seems, to me, to be sort of timeless. Some bands have a very dated sound. But *The Floyd's* music does not sound dated (except for the early records which sound very dated indeed). This band seems to be larger than life. Part of this immensity has to do with the way the musicians blend with each other. Roger Waters' familiar voice (a voice I grew up with; I feel like I know him), David Gilmour's fabulous guitar playing, Nick Mason's unique way of drumming and the keyboards of Rick Wright mesh totally. The musicians fit their styles into one another like hand in glove. Early *Floyd*, say, their first couple of albums (when Syd Barret was in the band) are notably different from their work after Barrett left. And when Roger Waters split company from the rest of the band, things changed. I will talk more specifically about their albums in a bit, for now it is important to note that *The Floyd* became one of the most important bands of my generation. They became rock superstars especially with *Dark Side of the Moon*. It was this album that made them famous and for good reason. This was a ground breaking album.

The Floyd's long instrumental sections appeal to me because I am an instrumentalist. At any rate, *The Floyd* broke ground with their instrumental work. Interestingly enough, Alan Parsons (of the *Alan Parson's Project*) was *The Floyd's* sound engineer for a few of their albums. Alan Parsons' music is highly instrumental and very sophisticated. I never made the connection between Parsons and *The Floyd* before I discovered this, but I can certainly see a relationship in the genre of both. Parsons (2005) had this to say:

> The Floyd were, by their very nature, audio experimentalists . . . . And to be the engineer with that kind of outfit was a dream come true. The Beatles were the only band who had done that. Not only did the Floyd have the inclination to spend large amounts of time experimenting with sound, but they had the time, and the record company had the budget. (cited in Harris, 2005, p. 105)

Alan Parsons suggested that the Floyd had a lot in common with the Beatles. If you listen to early *Floyd* when Syd Barrett was the main man, yes you can hear Beatles' influence in their songs. But Nick Mason (2004) draws a distinction between *The Beatles* and *The Floyd* in the '60s. Mason says,

> For me that night [at a club called the UFO] was the moment that I knew I wanted to do this properly, I loved the power of it all. No need to dress in Beatle jackets and tab-collar shirts, and no need to have a good-looking singer up front. No verse- chorus-verse-solo-chorus–end structure to the songs, and the drummer wasn't at the back on a horrid little platform. . . . Syd's distinctive song writing and our improvisational style, we did have a rather rough but definitely original musical approach. . . . (pp. 52–52)

Already in the mid '60s *The Floyd* found a unique sound that distinguished them not only from *The Beatles* but from every other rock band around. Although their sound changed when Barrett left, they still were doing things no other group had done. The unique chemistry between the musicians made *The Floyd*. And the post-Barrett era brought more symphonic sounds and longer instrumental sections. The experimental parts of the songs during the Barrett years differed radically from what came later when Rogers Waters headed up the band. John Cavanaugh (2003) cites an interview with Barrett and Waters that was done in 1966 by the Canadian Broadcasting Corporation that is worth quoting in full here.

> "We didn't start out trying to get anything new, it just sort of entirely happened. We originally started out as an R&B group," Roger Waters told a reporter from the Canadian Broadcasting Corporation (CBC), around the turn of the year 1966-7. Syd Barrett continued, "Sometimes we just let loose a bit and started hitting the guitar a bit harder and not worrying quite so much about the chords. . ." Roger: "It stopped being sort of third rate academic rock and started being intuitive groove." Syd "It's free form". (cited in Cavanah, 2003, p. 50)

What totally fascinates here is that like other experimental movements (say in pop art, or avant-garde fiction writing, or avant garde intellectual movements) bold innovation in this music captured something in the culture that resonated with many people. *Pink Floyd* has fan-atical fans. Not just fans, but fan-atics. Wouldn't it be wonderful if academic intellectuals had fans?

Many people comment particularly on the sort of spacey feel to *The Floyd* (Harris, 2005; Cavanagh, 2004; Fricke, 1996). Indeed their music seems to expand space as well as time to transport listeners elsewhere. Some think their music was an attempt to transport you to outer space. But Roger Waters says this was not the band's intention. Rather, David Fricke (1996) cites Roger Waters who states, "'The space thing was a joke. . . 'None of those pieces were about outer space. They were about inner space. That's all it's ever been about–human beings and their insides, whether it was Syd's writing or mine. They both were about the same thing'" (p. 12). This is a sort of Winnicottian holding space. The music of *Pink Floyd* puts you deep inside of a container, it holds you inside of places that open up psychic space. I think one of the reasons *The Floyd* became such a huge phenomenon is the psychological aspect to their music. They just make you feel differently. Listening to *The Floyd* is a whole experience, it engulfs you in sound. I compare the music of *The Floyd* to the paintings of Mark Rothko. Rothko's paintings are about inner space. To appreciate Rothko you've got to just let go and allow his paintings to engulf you. Lawrence Weschler (2006) describes Rothko's work and as he describes it I think he could also be talking about *Pink Floyd's* music. Weschler (2006) makes the following comments.

> Doesn't just about everyone experience that same shudder of vertigo standing before one of those great paintings of Rothko's high maturity—the canvas poised neatly between self-possession and self-indulgence: it draws you in and gives nothing back. Its presence, like that of a black hole is of such density that you might lose your Self there. (p. 47)

Like Rothko, *Pink Floyd's* music draws you into an enormously disturbing black hole of sound. Like Rothko, *The Floyd's* music alters one's sense of self in relation to the world. If immersed long enough in the music, you can no longer tell where you stop and the world begins. Their music tears at the fabric of your spatial boundaries and moves you outside and inside psyche simultaneously. It is such a strange phenomenon. When listening to the music, you aren't quite so sure where you are. You just sort of float along. Rothko's paintings also make you float. The paintings create a certain sort of watery, liquidy image. So too, *Pink Floyd.* Their music is highly liquid, fluid, flowing. A listener cannot get her ground in this watery, slippery atmosphere. Listening to *The Floyd* is an experience of losing the ground underneath one's feet. It pokes holes in the ego. It moves toward what I term Id-ing. Id-ing is dreaming while contained in a symphonic sound that submerges ego. Here is a dream space.

Roger Waters led the band after Barrett left. As a sort of tribute to Barrett, Waters' songs especially in *The Wall* re-tell and make mythological the story of Barrett's psychotic break. *The Floyd's* whole project seems to be about insanity. Another lure for people who worry about their own sanity. Many psychoanalysts suggest that in each one of us there is a psychotic part. J. Allen Hobson (1999) argues– in his book titled *Dreaming as Delirium: How the Brain goes out of its Mind*– that dreams aren't like psychosis they *are* psychosis. He states, "[d]reaming, then, is not like delirium. It is delirium. Dreaming is not a model of a psychosis, it is a psychosis" (p. 44). Dreaming is being insane and I think people are really interested in this and the way these insane feelings shape the everyday. Hence, the interest in *The Floyd.*

Alongside insanity, *The Floyd's* other major theme is war. Roger Waters' father was killed in WW11 and it is this that he rehashes over and over again in his music. Waters seems to be, in fact, obsessed with his father's death and with WW II.

He states in a DVD about the making of *Dark Side of the Moon*, that some of the other major themes in their music have to do with empathy, being humane, and valuing difference. But for me, the main theme I associate with *The Floyd* is madness. Their music is mad, it is psychotic, it is dreaming and it is extremely disturbing. Of course, much of what the band sings about is autobiographic, having to do with Barrett's breakdown. John Harris, (2005) explains.

> Perhaps most interestingly, it is a record [Dark Side of the Moon] populated by ghosts–most notably, that of Syd Barrett. In seeking to address the subject of madness, and to question whether the alleged lunacy of particular individuals might be down to the warped mindset of the supposedly sane Roger Waters was undoubtedly going back to one of the most traumatic chapters in Pink Floyd's history–when their leader and chief songwriter, propelled by his prodigious drug intake, had split from the group. . . . albums such as A Saucerful of Secrets, Atom Heart Mother. . .never quite escaped his [Barrett's] shadow. . . . (p. 16)

The band has always worked under the shadow of the object of Syd Barrett. Although they certainly did their own thing once Barrett was gone, many still think of *The Floyd* as attached in some way to Barrett and his breakdown. The legend of Barrett lives on. Insanity is always a curious subject and I think many are fascinated about what happened to Barrett and why. There are many internet websites devoted to Barrett lure especially since Barrett recently died. Some die-hard fans of Barrett's' no longer followed *Pink Floyd* after his departure. Mike Watkinson and Pete Anderson (2001), in an important biography of Barrett, tell us that "Bowie was a Floyd fan during the UFO days but in a 1973 interview he said that after Syd left, "[f]or me, there was no more Pink Floyd" " (p. 113). After Barrett left, Nick Mason (2004) tells us that the band lost "credibility with the underground" (p. 107). Mason (2004) goes on to suggest that still today, some people think that the post-Barrett era *Floyd* is not worth listening to. Mason (2004) states,

> We did not, however, completely abandon our London scene, although when Syd left the band we did lose some of our credibility with 'the underground' (there was, and there still is, a school of thought that Syd's departure marked the end of the 'real' Pink Floyd. . . . (p. 107)

Ironically, for me the signature sound of The *Floyd* happened in the post-Barrett era. I dis-identify with the early work. I was too young to appreciate the early work and it did not resonate with me the way the later work did during my childhood.

Of course it is also important to note that *Pink Floyd* has always been associated with psychedelic pop and LSD. John Harris (2005) remarks,

> On The Piper at the Gate of Dawn [an early album] Pink Floyd had minted a distinct aesthetic identity, founded not only on their improvisational aspects, but also on the singular elements that Syd Barrett brought to the music– not least, the lyrics that somehow fused the hallucinatory mindset of psychedelic with the ghosts of childhood. (p. 59)

In the early albums we will find that Barrett's lyrics were childlike and–well–very strange. The lyrics were also rather menacing. Listening to Barrett's songs I was reminded of The *Beatles* Sgt. Pepper, but then this was no Sgt. Pepper. Listening to "The Piper", is extremely disturbing. I never found anything about *The Beatles* disturbing. Maybe because the lyrics were odd, people associated the band with LSD. Barrett was the only band member who did massive amounts of LSD. But still the band is associated with drugs. When I showed the DVD *The Wall* to my doctoral students (most of these students are older than me), they asked me if they had to do drugs to understand it. I was kind of taken aback by the comment. Most of my doctoral students are rather conservative school teachers and many never even heard of *The Floyd.* I am sure some were shocked by the disturbing nature of the film.

The disturbing nature of *Pink Floyd's* music has been commented on by many. For example, Tom Hibbert (1997) states, in an essay titled " Who the Hell Does Roger Waters think he is?", that "Roger Waters is thought by many to be the gloomiest man in rock" (p. 145). Brian Mulligen (1997), says of "The Wall",

> that it is truly a nasty film, relentless in its pursuit of depicting the worst excesses of human behavior, a study of madness and the corrupting effects of violence and alienation. Roger Waters' view of mankind is totally and morbidly hopeless. (p. 177)

Exactly!! My kind of guy. The message of *The Floyd* is not that different from the message of Freud. Freud-Floyd. Freud thought people were basically swines. I am thinking here of *The Floyd's* pink pig floating in the sky. Freud thought that mother's screwed up their babies. I am thinking here of some lyrics to "The Wall", "mama's gonna put all of her fears into you". Freud was the first to talk about shell shock. Pink, the main character in "The Wall", is a victim of posttraumatic stress syndrome or what Freud called shell shock. *The Floyd*, like Freud, suggests that the human condition is awful, that people kill each other, that men go to war, that people go insane, that school, church and state play a role in killing people. *The Floyd,* like Freud, teach that the idea of hope is stupid in a world riddled by war, death, disease and hatred. Alan di Perna (2002) boldly states,

> They've [Pink Floyd] created some of the most profoundly depressing music in the history of rock, but Roger Waters and Nine Inch Nails front man Trent Reznor are just tickled pink to shake hands. (p. 109)

I admire a band who writes music that tells it like it is. And here is a rock band fleshing out some pretty serious issues. These are the issues of curriculum theorists as well. The problems of war, madness, transgenerational trauma, alienation are of interest also to educationists. *Pink Floyd* –like many curricularists–address Fascism. Nine Inch Nails, well that's another story. I find that band to be disgusting for the sake of disgustingness. And in that, I find little that is admirable.

Interestingly enough, the film (The Wall) is about a character named Pink who suffers from transgenerational trauma because of the death of his father in WW11. Pink grows up to be a depressive who slips into psychosis. When he comes out of his psychosis he becomes a symbol of Fascism (which is also a trope for his abusive mother) –I am thinking of Freud's notion of identification with the aggressor. Pink who turns fascist heads up a sort of skinhead-Nazi-ish cult. But Pink wants to go home and take off his uniform. He wants to dis-identify with the aggressor but does not know how to undo his psychic damage caused both by his father's death and his mother's abuse. The story is also one in which the victim of child abuse becomes the abuser, or the victim of war becomes a perpetrator. The Wall is a symbol of psychic rigidity so often found in schizophrenics. The film is quite smart and the music very powerful. Much of the film is based on a mixture of Waters' life and Barrett's illness. I don't think in the early days the band started out making political statements through their music, but it seems to me that they became more political toward the 1980s. So The Wall is both political and psychological.

LISTENING TO THE FLOYD: A REGRESSIVE SPACE

Scholars of cultural studies who use a neo-Marxist framework tend to ignore the psychological implications of the influence of pop culture and especially of listening to music. Listening is a form of regression. One must push back the boundaries of the Ego, to get to Id. Music that immerses psyche pours into the unconscious. One lives in a dream state when listening, the outer world goes away. Now, one can use listening to music to do many things. One can use listening to music to find oneself or to escape. Here, I am mainly interested in exploring the psychic dimensions of the listening act. When one regresses to the Id, a private world emerges. The regressive movement that is made while listening may actually alter the way one becomes aware on a very basic level. The registers of sound may in fact alter an inner world by changing moods. When moods change worlds change. Music allows psyche to generate these moods. The question is how regressed one can become without cracking up the structures of the Ego. Without ego, the world is all Id, the world is psychotic. Music, more so than the other arts can crack up the structures of psyche. There is something in sound that alters the mind. This is a very curious phenomenon. Listening can put someone in a very curious mental space.

What is this mood to which one becomes drawn? Repetitive listening practices involve a continual returning to those moods which make one feel a particular way. When the listener has listened to an album, say, 50 times she knows what she is in for. There is no doubt that the unconscious calls one to listen to a mood that connects with the structure of the psyche. And if that psyche is always already damaged, the music that psyche is drawn toward will probably–through its minor tonal structure—resonate with this damage. Damaged people listen to damaged music. *Pink Floyd* is damaged music and kids who are damaged tune in. The psyche meets a kindred broken spirit. In this regressive act, the child may say, 'ah-huh! This is what I'm feeling but I couldn't articulate it before.' Music helps people to articulate their brokenness, their fragility and their own madness. Music is quite a scandal. It is the scandal of a broken self in search of another broken self. Of course, all music does not serve this purpose, Music can do a lot of things for a lot of people. Some happy people might listen to pop music, bubble gum music. Some like heavy metal, some like classic rock because It takes them back to their childhoods. Some like punk because they are angry and want to find a kindred angry spirit. Some like hip hop because the music expresses what is going on in their world.

What happens when one meets another kindred spirit through listening to music? One might become a fan-atic. Why does one become fan-atic? Probably for psychological reasons. When one goes deeper and deeper into one's psyche via the vehicle of music strange things happen. What those strange things are elude articulation. Thus, for broken kids, broken music can re-intensify the wounds created by the not good enough mother and the not good enough school. This re-intensification of past wounds is part and parcel of the psyche's need for repetition compulsion. To repeat those bad feelings is an unconscious rigidity that might serve to give solace or re-traumatize. Why does psyche find solace in trauma? Michael Eigen (2001) calls this "toxic nourishment" (p.1). If toxicity is all you know then re-living toxic experience is the only way you can "nourish" yourself. Wounds nourish, Eigen contends. Sounds crazy, but it isn't. In fact, it makes total sense.

PINK FLOYD: DAMAGED GOODS

Here I would like to explore *Pink Floyd* in some detail to uncover what it is about this band that speaks to damaged psyches. *Pink Floyd's* music reflects the damaged self regressed to Id spaces that are dreamlike or nightmarish. Phenomenologically, listening to this music merges time, space and place. First off, *Pink Floyd's* music de-presses. Depression means pushing down. This music pushes down to the bottom of a space- pit in psyche. You may ask at this point why bother listening if the music depresses? Well, it is a curious fact that *Pink Floyd* has a huge fan base and sells more CDs than many rock bands. Why are so many people drawn to such gloomy music? Well, we've got a lot of broken people walking around. The walking wounded need to find other walking wounded with whom to commune. When two walking wounded collide strange things happen. A mood emerges. Perhaps the mood, the feeling that is generated re-minds the psyche of some deep childhood trauma that has been repressed. The psyche returns again and again (repetition compulsion) to this woundedness to try and heal itself. Listening to wounded music is a way to heal the self. If the psyche can get back there, down there, in that regressive space it can get back to where it got broken and bring that repressed pain up into consciousness.

Upon examination of *Pink Floyd's* overall project, one finds a shift in the sound after Syd Barret left the band. Two early records, "The Piper at the Gates of Dawn" and "Relics" which were cut in the 1960's are of a piece listeningwise. In these two albums I hear the influence of Sgt. Pepper. I find the albums to be dated and silly– quite frankly. And yet there is something ominous and disturbing about this music. Syd Barrett's influence dominates these two albums. He seemed to be drawn to childlike imagery, fantasy imagery of an elementary school student. For their time, these albums were highly experimental. Tim Willis (2002) points out that Barrett's lyrics were the stuff of childhood lure. Willis (2002) states,

> . . . Barrett created a crystalline world–bringing alive the bookshelves of a clever middle-class schoolboy: the Alice adventures and Fenland folk tales; Grahames' riverbank sagas and Lear's nonsense; Eng Lit. texts, Tolkien sagas, comics and esoteric pamphlets. (2002, p. 22)

This interesting combination of material is what made Barrett a pop music legend. It is quite remarkable that he put to music lyrics that were so diverse and so playful. If anything, Syd Barrett was a remarkably child-like man. John Cavanagh (2004) says that "[f]or Syd there was no need to regress" (p. 114). Syd was already regressed. Syd was a child-man. It was this that drew people to him. He was just so strange, people said. From photos he was a good looking man with much charisma. Cavanagh (2004) tells us,

> 'Beautiful' is a word I've heard frequently from people I've talked to about Syd, regardless of their gender The qualities he had transgressed sexuality. Anna says, "He was a rather androgynous kind of being, Men and women found him very beautiful and attractive. (p. 115)

I will talk more in depth about Syd Barrett in a while, but for now I focus for a moment on musical trends in the Barrett days and musical trends in the post-Barrett *Floyd* era. Listening to Barrett's music today–for a trained musician like myself–is a bit of a strain. I find his music to be rather unappealing. I certainly appreciate his complexity and strangeness. His music is just downright strange. I can appreciate the strangeness and uniqueness for what it is, but I wouldn't play "The Piper at the Gates of Dawn" at a party, for example, or even for myself. If find the album *Relics* (1967) to be more of the same. Again, I can appreciate the experimental nature of Barrett's work. There is a very silly song about a bicycle, for example, on "Relics". I find the song to be rather ridiculous in fact. And maybe it is this ridiculousness that draws people in. Many commentators argue Barrett was a genius. Perhaps. Or perhaps he just had the guts to be weird. Talk about "weirding" the curriculum (Appelbaum, 2008, p. 35)! It is the case that Barrett invented the *Floyd* and was their guru in the beginning. He was their songwriter and leader. This in and of itself must be applauded. Without Barrett there would be no *Pink Floyd*. However, I do not find that his music has a lasting quality about it. The music–aside from the lyrics– is just not sophisticated and some of the songs are poorly written. I do not find the tonal progressions at all interesting, in fact, some are annoying and grating to the ear. Now I do like lyrics. I do think his lyrics interesting and playful. One of the incredible things about Barrett is that he didn't produce very much material compared to what the band accomplished after he left, but he left a lasting mark on the music community. Barrett is a legend partly because of this music and partly because of his extreme drug use and mental collapse. I will address these more closely in a while.

Now, let us turn to the post-Barrett era. In 1970s *Pink Floyd* changed. With the album "Atom Heart Mother" we hear the influence of David Gilmour, who replaced Barrett. David Gilmour, in my estimation, made the band what it is. Most people think of Roger Waters' influence too because he sort of took charge once Barrett was gone. Gilmour's musical talent stands out and becomes evident especially in this first post- Barrett record. Gilmour is a guitar genius.

Some reflections on "Atom Heart Mother" are these. The music is notably different from early records in the seriousness of the music. The pieces are better written. The harmonies are more sophisticated and better arranged than earlier work. *Atom Heart Mother* sounds a little like music of *The Alan Parson's Project* with its long instrumental interludes and the addition of a choir (The John Aldiss Choir) and the use of female background vocals, which will play a greater role later especially in "Dark Side of the Moon." The pieces are a bit lengthy in *Atom Heart Mother* and are highly complex. Here is the beginning of the *Pink Floyd* sound as I knew it as a child growing up in the 1970s. Here is the beginning of big symphonic sound that is rather depressing. A mournful and liquidy sound. Later in the *Floyd* archives, Waters' personality begins more and more to seep in to the music and we begin to hear a very different kind of singing later on as Waters' comes into his own. David Gilmour's voice gives to *Pink Floyd* that distinctively *Floyd* sound. Gilmour's smooth flowy, liquidy voice is like his Guitar playing. That vast space we feel when listening to this music is partly due to Gilmour's voice and liquidy sounding guitar.

Pink Floyd's Album "Meddle" begins that recognizable *Floyd* sound we hear in later albums. "Meddle" is the first album that breaks new ground for the band. "Meddle" is large, symphonic, moody and liquidy. One can even hear musical themes that get fleshed out later in "The Wall." " Meddle" is somehow hauntingly familiar and contemporary. This music is not dated. It seems to transcend time in its interesting harmonic structures and progressions. The songs on "Meddle" are masterfully written and recorded. Here we hear the unique chemistry between the musicians that made *The Floyd—well—The Floyd*. Waters' voice seems blended in with Gilmour's– it is hard to tell who is singing. I am not sure if they are both singing or not. Overall, "Meddle" is a great album. This is classic *Pink Floyd*.

CHAPTER THREE

In 1977 "Animals" came out. Again, this album is great; it is just fantastic musically. It is also liquidy and has that sort of spaced-out sound for which The *Floyd* is known. Here we begin to hear Roger Waters' voice which becomes, in 1980s, the dominant one in "The Wall." Waters' has a unique voice. It isn't' that he is a great singer, no it is that he just has such connection emotionally to what he sings that makes him an important rock star. I like Water's voice, no matter. He uses his voice to express such anguish. There are pieces on "Animals" that last 17 minutes. This length of time for a pop song in the '70s was considered cool. Here I am thinking of other bands like *Genesis* and *Yes* who also wrote very long songs. But a 17 minute song on the radio today? No way. The musical ideas on "Animals" are deeply psychological and intellectual. The subtle shifts from minor to major keys alter the listener's frame of reference. Mostly the work is in minor keys which is what makes the music depressing.

Following "Animals", classic *Floyd* enters the scene with "Dark Side of the Moon" (1972-1973) and "Wish You Were Here" (1975). It was "Dark Side of the Moon" that catapulted the band into fame. Perhaps the album connected with so many people because of the honesty and at-oneness of the music. Roger Waters (2004), in a DVD about making "The Dark Side", tells us that "it was always a bit about Syd." The dark side of the moon is a symbol of insanity. Isn't it curious that it was this album more so than the others that fans really hooked into? When the band begins to try to understand what happened to Syd Barrett through music, the music becomes mythic. Perhaps "Dark Side" is their most famous album and their best one. Ironically it is about the band member who was no longer there. What is it about the lure of insanity that attracts people? I find this an interestingly disturbing phenomenon. Here the musicians flow seamlessly into each other to create moodscapes, or moonscapes of the psyche cracked. The psyche is not like the moon, but is the moon. The moon is the Otherness of psyche, the other side of psyche, the underside of psyche, the Id. The psyche is outerspace inside out, it is innerspace that is akin to outerspace in its Otherness, in its strangeness. Remarkably, many commentators argue that the musicians (with the exception of Wright and Gilmour) were really not that good, that they were just sort of okay musicians. Many people say the Waters didn't have good technique and that Mason was not a great drummer. If this is so, it is even more amazing to me that the band was able to pull off these recordings. It just goes to show that technique isn't everything, in fact, it is secondary to musicality and to musical ideas. What makes *The Floyd* great is that they had something to say, something to tell us not just about the times, but about ourselves. Generation(s) of fans still listen to the band. For a band that went through so much turmoil–especially with Syd's insanity– and for a band that basically did not get along, it is amazing that their music somehow survived. It is a testament to their overall commitment to their project that the music was what it was, that the music was so solid, so well thought out and so beautifully performed. Some bands produce only one really good album. But for *Pink Floyd*, every album–even what I would consider the minor albums like the soundtrack to "More" (1969) and the record titled "Obscured by the Clouds" (1972), are of high quality and tremendous musicality and musical genius.

And then in 1980 "The Wall" came out and changed the face of rock and roll forever. This is the thing about *Pink Floyd*. Every album was absolutely groundbreaking. How could they keep doing this? How could "The Wall" be so intensely meaningful to so many generation(s) of fans? It is in "The Wall" that Roger Waters' personality really emerges. I think he really comes into his own with this record. "The Wall's themes, as I mentioned earlier, concern WW11, insanity and the dangers of Fascism and neo-Nazi-ism. The film is quite remarkable actually. Parts of it could have been edited out, but for the most part the film is awesome. What makes the film so interesting is that the character in the film, Pink, is a mixture of Syd Barrett and Roger Waters. One wonders about the ways in which Waters' so identified with Barrett's condition. He seems to suggest that he empathized with Barrett, although Waters' was the one who kicked Barrett out of the band. As I have already addressed the major themes in this album I will not belabor the point here.

NOT BEING ABLE TO PLAY: THE CASE OF SYD BARRETT

When one cannot play a choice has to be made. As I've mentioned earlier, a musician can either stop listening to music altogether or listen to music in order to educate herself about music while the injury–that prevents one from playing— heals, if one heals at all. What happens to the psyche when the body or soul becomes ill? Here's what I mean. Lawrence Weschler (2006) recounts one of Oliver Sack's case studies. Let's hear what Weschler tells us of the Sack's case called "Cold Storage". Weschler (2004) remarks that

> A few years ago, Sacks published a case study, entitled "Cold Storage", the British quarterly Granata, in which he recalled a patient he identified as Uncle Toby, whom he encountered in 1957, when he was studying at Central Middlesex Hospital, in London. A doctor there had happened upon Uncle Toby during a house call to see a sick child. While treating the child, he noticed a silent, motionless figure sitting in a corner, and when he asked about the figure the family explained matter-of-factly, "That's Uncle Toby–'e's hardly moved in seven year [sic]. (p.154)

In a broader way, Uncle Toby was unable to play—at the game of life. He was stuck in time and space. And yet, he was still alive while "motionless." Sacks learned that Uncle Toby had a thyroid condition that caused his body to shut down. The disturbing thing about the case is that when doctors finally were able to fix Uncle Toby's thyroid, he died because the speeding up of his metabolism also sped up his cancer and killed him. In his motionless state, the cancer stayed in remission—it was frozen in a way– along with the rest of the body. When the body shuts down it is for a reason and sometimes medical interference does more harm than good. Uncle Toby was better off in "cold storage."

Deleuze and Guattari (2000), argue that it is better to leave a schizophrenic in his schizoid state. There is a reason he is schizoid; the patient cannot deal with reality—they suggest. Why bring him back to a state that he doesn't want to be in?

Deleuze and Guattari suggest that it is cruel to bring someone back from a psychotic episode. They state that,

> The ego, however, is like daddy-mommy: the schizo has long since ceased to believe in it. He is somewhere else, [in Barrett's case he stated that he was nowhere] beyond, or behind or below these problems [of dealing with the Oedipus complex], rather than immersed in them. And wherever he is there are problems, insurmountable sufferings, unbearable needs. But why try to bring him back to what he has escaped from? (p. 23)

If mental health workers do try to bring a psychotic back, Deleuze and Guattari remark that the schizophrenic probably thinks, "they're fucking me over again" (p. 23). As Lacan reminds us mentally ill people are in love with their psychoses. Why tear them away? Of course, some may feel this position absurd. But one must remember what happened to Uncle Toby.

Being in the grip of psychosis, the person may just stop like Uncle Toby. Catatonia is often part of a psychotic episode. Severe cases of autism and Aspergers syndrome also effect people in ways that make them shut off and shut down in a variety of ways. Some people cannot do anything, others engage in repetitive rigid acts like walking around in a circle for hours, or playing the same chord on the guitar over and over again. This is what has been reported about Syd Barrett. Mike Watkinson and Pete Anderson (2001) report that

> The disappointment was compounded by a disastrous short tour of Holland when Syd's on-stage contribution effectively dried up completely. He had been playing less and less over the preceding months and by November would often spend an entire gig playing the same chord over and over again while staring blankly at the audience. On other nights he would freeze with his arm hanging limply over his Telecaster, or sit cross-legged at the front of the stage seemingly oblivious to the performance going on around him. (p.77)

Not being able to play—the guitar—can be a symptom of some deeper problem. Some people with mental illness tend to just psychically disappear as we can see in this passage above. Barrett's mind seems to vanish and what was left was a body without anybody 'in there'. ('Is there anybody in there' is a line from "The Wall" (1980) and of course the reference here is to Barrett.) Mason (2004), who was the drummer for the band comments on the Syd's condition. Mason (2004) states,

> At the '14-hour Technicolour Dream', Syd had been as tired as the rest of us, but his symptoms were much more severe. June Child had looked after him: 'First of all we couldn't find Syd, then I found him in the dressing room and he was so–gone. Roger Waters and I got him on his feet, we got him out to the stage. He had a white guitar and we put it around his neck. . . . The band started to play and Syd just stood there. He had his guitar around his neck and his arms just hanging down. (p. 87)

Some people assume that Syd became catatonic because of his LSD consumption. He took so much acid that, according to John Cavanagh (2004), his drug use became "the stuff of legend" (p. 41). That might be, but others suggest that Barrett's breakdown was probably due to a variety of factors. A better explanation of Syd's condition is given by Nicholas Schaffner (1991). Schaffner states that,

> Syd's year-long acid trip began to go haywire just when the Floyd's career was shifting into overdrive. Some of his friends attribute part of his deterioration to the pressures of "pop stardom" and the attitude of the rest of the Floyd; others, conversely, maintain that the personality conflicts with the band, along with Syd's inability to handle his success, essentially arose from his own acid-fueled derangement. A fair conclusion might be that all these factors–the drugs, the fame, personal and artistic differences, and some long-dormant disorder within Barrett's psyche—interacted. . . .(p.78)

Sources on Barrett differ on opinion over what went wrong with him. Some say he suffered from schizophrenia, while Tim Willis (2002) suggests that Barrett suffered from Aspergers syndrome. Whatever happened to him caused Barrett to change. If one looks at photos of Barrett from his younger days, he was a stunning looking man. Very hip and cool. A photo taken of him after he got ill, is rather shocking. Barrett, after he got ill, shaved his head and shaved his eyebrows and got really fat; in the photo he is not even recognizable. There were several clues that Barrett was getting ill along the way. Of course, the bizarre behavior I cite above was one clue, but Barrett also–in the early days of his illness-made some remarks that indicate that he was aware that something was going wrong. Tim Willis (2002) points out that Barrett wrote a song called "Vegetable Man" (p. 88). Barrett knew at some level that he was turning into a psychic vegetable. In the song, Barrett asks, 'where are you' and he replies that 'he is not anywhere at all.' A mind evacuating itself. Willis (2002) tells us that Barrett had an interview with Rolling Stone Magazine and in the interview Barrett stated: "I'm disappearing" (p, 123) and "I'm full of dust and guitars" (p. 123). It is quite amazing that Barrett was able to comment on his own condition. After he got ill, Barrett became fascinated with TV and he stated–at least in the early days of his illness- that his days consisted of watching TV and that was it. Mike Watkinson and Pete Anderson (2001) report that at one point, Barrett "had a half-a-dozen [TVs] in his flat" (p. 117). In the film "The Wall" (1980), Pink, the protagonist, blankly stares at a huge TV all day long–just like Barrett. Now, this behavior might not seem symptomatic of anything. But Barrett—before he got ill– played his guitars and wrote songs for hours and hours as reported by Nicholas Schaffner– (1991).

It is rather difficult to write about someone's illness–especially someone you do not know– and not make it into something that it isn't. If anything, one might have empathy for Barrett's condition and be aware that no amount of discussion explains it. In fact, discussion might explain it away. I have taken great care to tell the story with care. We must not romanticize his illness. In fact, David Gilmour remarks,

> It's sad that these people think that he's such a wonderful subject, that he's a living legend. He's got uncontrollable things in him that he can't deal with

and people think it's a marvelous, wonderful, romantic thing. It's just a sad, sad thing; a very nice and talented person who's just disintegrated. Syd's story is a sad story romanticized by people who don't know anything about it. They've made it fashionable but it's just not that way. (cited in Watkinson & Anderson, 2001, p. 131)

Mental illness is not genius. Mental illness is not cool. Mental illness is terrible and horrifying. To say otherwise is to be completely irresponsible. The entire career of *Pink Floyd* has been under the shadow of the object of Syd Barrett. Syd, as Alan di Perna (2002) points out, "was the unseen specter standing behind Water Rogers as he assumed leadership of Pink Floyd. . ." (p. 2). To this day, *Pink Floyd* is under the shadow of the object named Syd Barrett. It amazes me how much impact one person can make on others.

A CRISIS OF PSYCHE: ON NOT BEING ABLE TO PLAY AT LIFE

Syd Barrett's life story is partly the story of not being able to play the guitar. But on a grander scale his story is even more tragic because his mental illness destroyed his life. After he got ill, his life was forever altered. His mental illness ended his life in music. Mental illness devastates psyche. And it is to this crisis of psyche that I would like to turn here. On not being able to play—whether we are talking about an instrument or about life in general– is at root a crisis of psyche. The crisis of psyche has many causes, some physical, some chemical and biological, some genetic, some environmental and some a combination of all of these.

Psyche in crisis manifests in a variety of ways. We have to keep in mind that psyche is always already embodied in soma, so really we should be talking of the crisis of the psyche-soma or the soma-psyche. I want to talk here about some of the symptoms of psyche in crisis from a psychoanalytic perspective. First I want to think through the problem of psychic freeze or psychic immobility. Getting stuck is something that everyone experiences from time to time, especially artists who suffer from writer's block. Some people suffer from a general psychic freeze in that they have difficulty getting out of bed in the morning or difficulty getting going in the morning. A general sluggishness is at hand and this is a rather common problem for many. But when we are talking about a more severe form of psychic freeze, we enter a realm of Otherness that not everyone experiences. There is something so Other and so strange about immobility when it is caused by some form of mental illness. Rigidity is a common feature of schizophrenia for example. Catatonia is a state of utter rigidity. Take the case of Uncle Toby. His immobility was caused by a thyroid problem, an illness unrelated to schizophrenia. I'm sure that neurologists and psychiatrists could cite umpteen reasons for immobility.

Symptoms of a crisis of psyche may present as depersonalization, dissociation, compartmentalization, the collapse of the ego, psychotic breaks, exhaustion, depression, anxiety. Perhaps the question here is not what causes immobility, because nobody is really sure, but the fact that psychic immobility happens. That it happens at all is the question at hand.

In an article by Dennis Sumara (1999), he tells us that his mother loved to read. But right before she died, she told Dennis that she was not interested in reading anymore. This is a psyche in crisis. Perhaps getting bored with the thing you love is a sort of psychic death. I suppose that every day we have psychic deaths, but don't notice them. Perhaps these deaths are so repressed that we cannot access them. Brain cells are dying every day and with them so too our interests wane–but they also wax and wane. When someone goes out to sea and doesn't come back again, psychic death is complete. When people don't come back psychically where do they go? When the self gets evacuated where is it?

What internal force pushes psyche out to sea? Freud would call it the death instinct. Melanie Klein would call it the paranoid-schizoid position or the bad breast. Fairbairn would call it the negative introject. Alice Miller might term it poisonous pedagogy. Winnicott (1990; 1992; 2005) would suggest that psychic disaster is caused by the not good enough mother. People become sick because people make them sick—Winnicott argued. Some would argue that psychic illness is a combination of both inner and external forces. Regression to mental paralysis is brought on by many factors that we do not understand. Neurological melt down, as well, causes psyche to deteriorate.

Other symptoms of a psychic train wreck might be overindulgence, massive amounts of drinking, doing drugs, gambling, driving recklessly, doing dangerous things. Procrastination. Tempers out of control. Foot in mouth. Forgetting. Insulting other people. Detachment or obsession. These are all symptoms of a larger problem. A crisis of psyche has many faces.

Mania is the flip side of psychic immobility. Incessant talking masks underlying fears and overindulging in dangerous behaviors masks problems. Compulsive behavior masks deeper problems. Extremes of doing and not doing, then, are clues to psychic problems.

And then there are chemical and biological or environmental elements in a psychic crash. We know, for example, that schizophrenia, Asperger's syndrome, autism, are all in some way caused by chemical, biological and environmental factors such as exposure to pesticides or other toxins. In the case of Syd Barrett, (who suffered from a disease probably like Asperger's syndrome—although the public was not privy to his diagnosis) commentators suggest that his illness did not just happen one day, it was a gradual demise. Tim Willis (2002) says that while on stage Barrett would "tune and detune his Fender until the strings were flapping, and hit one note all night" (p. 83). Duggie Fields tells us that,

> I noticed he'd changed from the Syd I had known before moving to America. He was definitely nuttier and had become more withdrawn and moody. His deterioration was gradual until he reached the stage where he'd just lie in bed because he couldn't decide what to do. (cited in Watkinson & Anderson 2001, p. 87)

Now, many of us might have had days where we feel like we can't get out of bed for one reason or another. But for Syd, not getting out of bed was symptomatic of his mental collapse to come. On another instance, Nicky Horne tried to interview Syd and reports that,

> I knocked on the door and this huge fat man answered wearing only his pajama trousers. He'd shaved off his eyebrows and looked incredibly strange. . . . He looked down at me and said 'Syd can't talk." When I told David Gilmour he said the man had been Syd and he'd been telling the truth. He really couldn't talk anymore. (cited in Watkinson & Anderson, 2001, p. 122)

Here is a man Syd Barrett–who in his younger years was highly productive, extremely smart and creative– who now couldn't even speak. Barrett spoke in what seemed to be the third person—perhaps he was speaking from his observing ego. There was a part of him that knew he was ill and could comment on it. But it seemed as if Barrett could not speak from a first person position, from his ego. The reality principle was slipping. What does it mean to not be able to speak? Not being able to speak is a crisis of psyche. And this crisis again might have biological, chemical or environmental causes. Neurological diseases can cause this inability to speak and to function generally. But still saying this doesn't explain much. There is always a remainder, a left over issue, an unspeakable something that goes on with the human psyche that we do not understand. It is, after all, a mystery as to how the brain actually functions. Scientists know a lot but they don't know it all. We will probably never be able to figure out how a creature does what he or she does and what the chemicals and neurons in the brain are really about. But it is not only this. A person is also made up of memories, dreams, wishes, fantasies, mourning, melancholia, obsessions, secrets, feelings and so on. There is something so mysterious about the mind. If someone has a secret, or a dream, where in the brain is it located? Can a neurologist pin-point a secret? Is there a special place in the brain where secrets reside? I think not. The crisis of psyche eludes.

What about secrets? Everybody has secrets of course. Children keep secrets. Are secrets symptoms of a crisis of psyche? Are all secrets conscious? Are some repressed? What about repressed secrets? What happens when they come up from the unconscious? Can secrets precede a psychotic break? If someone has too many secrets, might they get in the way of being a person? Secrets make people become secretive. What is it to be secretive? It is to play hide and seek with truth telling. Fort/Da. It is more hiding than it is seeking. And what if a child hides too much? What if someone has too many secrets? Someone who lies a lot has a lot of secrets. Winnicott often talks about the false self and the true self. Although this dichotomy seems rather simple minded, it is not. A false self is someone who is so entangled in secrets that he doesn't even know who he is anymore. The reality principle cracks and utter confusion ensues.

PSYCHIC DEATH AND REGRESSION: A PSYCHOANALYTIC TALE

I would like to take a closer look at the ways in which some psychoanalysts discuss issues around regression. Here I am talking about major regression, when one can't get out of bed, when one can't speak, when one stops playing and when one stops playing at the game of life generally speaking. What do psychoanalysts say about conditions of stopping? I find useful here, some of the work of D.W. Winnicott, Alice Miller, Otto Rank and Michael Eigen. So it is to these analysts we will turn to venture deeper into a stopped-up psyche.

For a moment, I want to address two kinds of regression. As I said earlier there is regression and then there is regression. There is what I would call mild regression (what Balint called benign regression, in Bollas 1987) and a severe regression (what Balint called a malignant regression, in Bollas 1987). When playing music, for example, one must regress to a certain extent in order to express emotions. This is a mild regression. There is a sort of slackening of the ego. When you are really in tune with your instrument there is no outside world, you become one with instrument and you are the sound that is produced. This state is akin to a mystical one. In performance situations this is a rare happening. And it only happens after a long period of study and practice. It is as if the music plays itself and you sort of float off into the distance. Sometimes you can't even remember how on earth you did it, it just did it itself. Further when one listens to music a sort of regression also needs to take place. When one is transported by the music, psyche floats away and becomes one with the sound. This too is akin to a mystical state.

The second kind of regression I discuss here is regression that goes amuck, regression that cripples the psyche. This sort of regression is of a very different sort than the first kind I mentioned above. Not only does the outside world go away, you are swept away with it. The regression that goes too far back in time arrests being, everything comes to a stand still and your ego dissolves. Now you are in real trouble because you can't get back. You might get stuck inside of objects, in the case of psychosis. Psychoanalysts refer to this as projective identification. Some people get stuck inside of radios, TVs, or inside of another person's head. You become the radio, you are the therapist, and you are your mother. Projective identification is when you project yourself into something else in an attempt to cure your regression, in an attempt to get back to reality. Regression on this level can also work to make you get so far down inside of yourself you cannot get back. Of course what I am talking about here is having a psychotic break. Psychotic breaks are regressions that are out of hand.

Some psychotics get stuck inside of TVs and just stay there. What kind of life would that be? When psychotics are able to comment on their condition, like the famous Dr. Schreber (2000) they apparently have landed in what Alice Miller (1997) calls their "inner prison" (p. 56). When one has regressed too far the mind attacks itself—this is what Bion (1991) called "attacks on linking". It is as if the psyche is killing itself. Imagine living in a constant state of what Alice Miller (2001) calls an "unremitting internal war" (p. 48). We all suffer internal battles, but for some these internal battles completely and utterly devastate psyche. Michael

Eigen (1993; 1996) tells us that psychotics, for the most part, cannot control their psychosis and so their demise cannot be stopped unless anti-psychotic medicines can undo these attacks.

PLAYING AND REGRESSION

Let's step backwards here and look at what it means to play, what it means to be able to play and what a mild regression (the first kind of regression I mention above) might be. Recall, playing–whether this means a child at play or someone playing an instrument–requires a form of regression. Playing is regressing. But this is a limited form of regressing and this I would call a mild regression. We all experience mild regression whenever we play. The ability to play—whether we are talking about playing an instrument, a child at play or playing at life generally speaking– is also the ability to tolerate and endure a mild regression. People who cannot play cannot regress and that is a problem. Some regression is necessary in order to play. Here I would like to draw on D.W. Winnicott's (2005) book titled *Playing and Reality*. Winnicott is known for his work on object relations theory. Object relations concerns not only relations between people on a conscious level, but more importantly the ways in which unconscious relating occurs. How does one unconscious meet another one? This is the question for object-relations theorists. If the mother is not good enough–a phrase made famous by Winnicott– the child will not be able to relate to the mother, or maybe even to anybody. Now, Winnicott argues that the disconnect between mother and child is caused by something the mother did. Maybe she is not attentive to the child, maybe she has little patience with the child. She is just not good enough—as Winnicott puts it– and so the child becomes, on varying levels, disconnected not only to the mother but sometimes even to the world and even in some cases to reality. This is Winnicott's general thesis that runs through all of his work.

TO PLAY OR NOT TO PLAY

Back to the question of play. What *is* play after all? What is it that we play *with*? And a typically Winnicottian (2005) question that I especially find useful is "where are we (if anywhere at all)" when we play (p. 142). Winnicott's book turns on these basic questions and he provides provocative answers. For Winnicott play is located in a sort of in-between space. Play happens in the space between inner and outer. Winnicott (2005) explains that play happens,

> in the interweave of subjectivity and objective observation, and in an area that is intermediate between the inner reality of the individual and the shared reality of the world that is external to individuals. (p. 86)

Play, Winnicott tells us, is a sort of third space between one's inner world and the outside world. This third term–if you will- is not unlike Martin Buber's space of the between. Buber (2002) states,

I call this sphere, [the sphere between the I and the Thou] which is established with the existence of man as man but which is conceptually still uncomprehended, the sphere of the "between". Though being realized in very different degrees, it is a primal category of human reality. This is where the genuine third alternative must begin. (p. 241)

Of course Buber and Winnicott part ways on certain points, one being that Buber was a religious philosopher and Winnicott was an MD and psychoanalyst. So they come at the question of relation from two very different vantage points.

The question becomes for Winnicott what is it in that in-between space that allows the infant to connect to the outer world? What is it that one must play with to connect to reality? Winnicott tells us that the child plays with something—namely an object—in order to connect to something other than herself. Moreover, this object for Winnicott (2005) is called a "transitional object or a transitional phenomena" (p. 2) and takes on specific psychological characteristics. The transitional object or the transitional phenomena helps the child transfer her feelings away from the mother onto a surrogate kind of mother. This turning away from the mother is also a turning toward reality. The teddy bear– which Winnicott suggests may be a transitional object– gives the child comfort as a sort of substitute mother. Through the use of the teddy bear and through play with the teddy bear the child is able to then transfer her emotions onto the object at hand. This move is important because it suggests that the child is beginning to connect to other things and to other people beside the mother. If the child does not move beyond the realm of his primary relation, she will not be able to connect to other people or to reality at large. What is interesting about Winnicott— for this study—is the concept of transitional phenomena because he ties this notion to music. Winnicott argues that music is a transitional phenomenon very early on in a child's life. Winnicott (2005) declares that,

an infant's babbling and the way in which an older child goes over a repertory of songs and tunes while preparing for sleep come within the intermediate area as transitional phenomena. (p. 3)

Music–whether expressed as primal babble or the most sophisticated symphony– can serve as a transitional phenomena and by this Winnicott means that it is music that holds the glue together between one's inner and outer worlds. Interestingly enough, Martin Buber (2002) tells us that "all art is from its origin essentially of the nature of dialogue. All music calls to an ear not the musician's own" (p. 30). Again, Buber, coming from a philosophical perspective, suggests that music is what allows two people to connect. I play, you listen. The I-Thou is glued together through music. Unlike Buber, Winnicott suggests that what we are really after here is the relation between one unconscious and another unconscious. The deeper issue—for most psychoanalysts– is the way in which two beings unconsciously communicate. The infant's babbling is symbolic of a deeper relation with the absent mother. The babbling serves as the transitional phenomena that opens a world to the infant. To babble is to rely on sound to connect to something or someone other than the self. Babble is a form of primal music.

Now, Winnicott goes further and tells us that what we really should be paying attention to is not the transitional object or transitional phenomena per se, but how one uses that object or phenomena. He states that,

> It is now generally recognized, I believe, that what I am referring to in this part of my work is not the cloth or the teddy bear that the baby uses–not so much the object used as the use of the object. (2005, xvi)

This question of use is a typically Winnicottian one. What is it that you use anything to do? It's not so much what you are doing that matters (i.e. reading, writing, playing, thinking, making a cup of tea, driving your car, sitting in your room) but rather to what use you put your activity. People use that experience of playing an instrument for very different psychological reasons. Some people play for pleasure, others play to please their parents. Others still play out of a sense of rebellion. Some play to escape. Winnicott (2005) points out music or babbling or even a "tune, or a mannerism. . . becomes vitally important to the infant for use at the time of going to sleep, and is a defense against anxiety, especially anxiety of the depressive type" (p. 5). Music-as a transitional phenomena—can be used as a defense mechanism. The sound of babbling comforts and protects the ego from crumbling or deteriorating. Now, what does this mean for an adult who plays, say, guitar? What does it mean to use a guitar to protect the ego from crumbling? Is that what is really underneath someone's desire to play? The music that comes from the playing of the guitar may serve to cover over a psychic wound. Music serves to heal psychic trauma. Again, there are a many reasons why people play instruments. Some people play simply because they enjoy it. But for others there are deeper issues at hand. If regression allows one to play an instrument, is regression a defense mechanism? Well, some would say yes. Otto Rank (1993) tells us that regression is "a means of defense" (p. 47). Regression is a source of healing, as Rank points out. When a person has a psychotic break, the break actually serves as a healing mechanism. One gets sick, in other words, to get well.

If psyche plays an instrument to escape turmoil, that turmoil has got to eventually be dealt with. Once repressed issues are dealt with and brought up from the unconscious and struggled against–and with the help of what Alice Miller (2001) calls an "enlightened witness" (ix)—psyche begins the healing process. Now, Miller suggests that many people can be "enlightened witnesses" for the patient. Miller (2001) states,

> Therapists can qualify as enlightened witnesses, as can well informed and open-minded teachers, lawyers, counsellors, and writers. (xi)

Teachers can be witnesses to child abuse and trauma. They have an ethical and legal responsibility to report such things. However, teachers are not therapists. Therapists can work with patients in an intense way to help heal a damaged psyche.

But some psyches are beyond help because the damage done was too great. There comes a point when an "enlightened witness"–such as a therapist–can do little for the patient, especially if that patient is severely regressed. Winnicott (2005) tells us that when a child cannot attach himself or herself to transitional objects or transitional phenomena, she essentially experiences a form of decathexis. Symptoms of decathexis might be what Michael Eigen (1996) terms "psychic death" (p. 3). Eigen (1996) explains that,

> for some people, the sense of death is pervasive. They describe themselves as zombies, the walking dead, empty and unable to feel. (p. 3)

Recall how people referred to Syd Barrett as being 'gone', blank, not there. I am sure that there are moments when we all go elsewhere in our heads and certainly everybody experiences some form of depersonalization from time to time. But when these states overwhelm the psyche, we are talking about another sort of problem altogether. The question becomes what is underneath the decathexis, that is, what psychological mechanism causes someone to detach from objects and other people? Well, this too is another form of psychic withdrawal; this is a deeper form of regression. Complete and utter decathexsis is a form of severe regression. The psychoanalyst who best captures this disturbing state is Otto Rank (1993) in his controversial book *The Trauma of Birth*. This book so puzzled Freud that he broke off relations with Rank. Freud thought Rank was totally wrong in his thinking. Remember that for Freud the major complex is the Oedipal one, not birth, although Freud did state that birth is associated with anxiety. If one regresses to the point that she is psychically back at the birth trauma, disaster looms. People who suffer from crippling anxiety, Rank would say, are in actuality repeating in some psychic way the birth trauma. Rank (1993) says,

> the anxiety mechanism, which is repeated almost unaltered in cases of phobia (claustrophobia, fear of railways, tunnels, traveling, etc.), as the unconscious reproduction of the anxiety at birth. (p. 12)

Think about the birthing process for a moment. One pushes through unknown territory down a tunnel and out into a very anxious making place–reality. Being confined in very tight quarters as it were for nine months might be felt to be very claustrophobic. Rank suggests that many irrational fears are somehow tied to an unconscious memory of confinement in the womb and birth the process. Rank tells us that psychic problems begin "in the position of the unborn" (p. 6). Rank is referring to what he terms the "intrauterine state" (p. 6). This is about as far back as the psyche can regress. Is there an unconscious memory of the intrauterine state? Perhaps. Interestingly enough, the last stage of a patient's psychoanalysis deals with first things, with the beginnings of a life when the psychic trouble began. At the end of treatment we come to the beginning of life. This is the irony that is psychoanalytic deconstruction. Unpacking archaic and primal entanglements in analysis takes a backward movement. Patients begin talking usually about the everyday and then move backward—at the urging of the therapist—to dreams, to associations and to childhood. It takes probably at least four to five years if not more to begin undoing the early damage—if it can be undone at all—by the working through of the transference. Does transference begin when one is unborn? Perhaps.

Think about what it might be like to be unborn–this is a sort of Zen Koan. Rank makes some interesting claims about symptoms of an unborn experience gone wrong. The mother who is pregnant, that is, can alter the psychic state of the unborn child if she is herself a psychic catastrophe. This psychic catastrophe is transferred unconsciously to the unborn child. This may sound incredible, but I do think that there is something to it. According to Rank symptoms of "depression" (p. 61) and "paralysis" (p. 49) get introjected into the unborn whereby the depressed or psychically paralyzed mother's moods get transferred unconsciously. Interestingly enough, Rank says about "melancholia" that it is:

> a means of representing the primal state, but also shows the tendency to use objects [an interestingly pre-Winnicottian concept] in the outer world, as for instance, darkened rooms. . . . (p. 62)

For some severely depressed people, dark rooms comfort because they unconsciously remind psyche of some other dark places that have been repressed. Depression leads to immobility. Rank suggests that the intrauterine state is one of immobility. So when psyche suffers depression and is immobilized, she is unconsciously psychically thrown back to the time before she was born. A Zen Koan indeed. The worst form of immobility is total and utter withdrawal. In some cases this means psychosis. Rank claims that psychosis is a manifestation of a regression back to the intrauterine state. He states that:

> the psychotic delusions, the content of which so obviously strives to re-establish the primal state, have to replace the outer world, no longer compatible with libido, by the best of all worlds–namely, the intrauterine existence. (p. 63)

Thus psychosis is the traveling back in time to the place before you were born. For Rank, psychosis is a form of repetition. Rank points out that, in fact, nobody overcomes the birth experience and that is partly why we need sleep. Sleep is a sort of return to the position of the unborn. And when we sleep we dream and dreaming is psychosis.

Rank (1993) suggests that the point of therapy is to help the patient "to repeat the trauma of birth and thus partially to abreact it" (p. 11). In the repeating the trauma, and bringing it forth actually helps to put it to rest. But take the case of a severely regressed person. There are people who are so gone psychically that nothing can get them back. As Michael Eigen (1996) says:

> The truth is that one never is the same after this trip to the other side of the moon [in the case of the Floyd, the Dark Side of the Moon], to the blank side of being. (p. 121)

Eigen raises the issue of the impossibility of healing. For some, there is no healing and there is no getting back to reality. One is forever trapped in some kind of psychic hell. Not a particularly uplifting note.

My point in this rather lengthy psychoanalytic tale is that repression(s) are of differing sorts. The one to really worry about is the second sort, the sort that Otto Rank talks about. Rank addresses issues that exactly dovetail with my own thoughts on not being able to play. To play or not to play—this is a trope of psychic life and psychic death.

CHAPTER FOUR

EDUCATING MOODS

Regression, Repetition Compulsion and Minimalism

Getting in a mood and getting stuck in it could signal a kind of regressed state toward nothingness. Being stuck in a bad mood or a blank mood is not a good feeling. It is as if the mood has taken over the mind. In what ways are moods educative? Moods teach something about the self. Moods are windows into the past. The way one gets stuck in a mood in the here and now might be reminiscent of the way one got stuck in moods as a child. The more stuck one is in the mood, the harder it is to come out of it. When others say things like, 'come on lighten up'–the stuckness only becomes more pronounced. Getting stuck and getting out are two things I would like to examine in this chapter.

Music sets up moods. People are emotionally affected by music. Music creates moods. People are attracted to certain kinds of music depending on what mood feels familiar to them. If one is stuck a lot, if one experiences forms of psychic blockage, one might be attracted the the music called minimalism. Minimalism is especially relevant to this study because of the mood it induces when listening. Minimalism tends to induce regressive states–states in which someone might feel stuck–via repetition. But why would somebody want to get in a bad mood, or a stuck mood? It is only by getting stuck and examining the psychic history of that stuckness that one can get out of it. One does not want to stay stuck forever. Getting out of stuckness is what psychic movement attempts to do. Repetition compulsion is a symptom of regression and stuckness. One repeats over and over again primal object-relations–especially if they were bad–until one can get out of the detrimental pattern.

Christopher Bollas (1987) reminds us that Michael Balint thought that there were clearly two kinds of regressions. Bollas explains.

> In keeping with Balint's valuable distinction between a benign and a malignant regression (1968), I believe that a generative regression to dependence is characterized by the analysand's giving over to the analyst certain important mental functions. . . in order to bring the personality back to its childhood moments of origin and experience. (p. 269)

Here, I want to address this benign form of regression as it relates to minimal music, regression and repetition compulsion. Music that is madly repetitious (like minimalism) induces regressed states like the ones induced in the therapeutic relation. Music that sounds as if it is stuck on the same note, allows one to regress to the psychic trajectories that have gotten stuck somewhere back in childhood.

Minimal music allows one to float off in into the vast inner space of memory, image, dreamscape. Minimalism creates the "generative" kind of regression that Bollas (1987) tells us must happen in analysis. (p. 259). Bollas uses the word "capacity" in the context of regression and analysis. He suggests that the analyst develop a capacity to allow the analysand to regress. Relevant to this study, when one is not able to play, it is paradoxically necessary to go back to the thing that got one stuck in the first place. One must develop a "capacity" to get re-stuck. Being still takes patience and time. One must sit in a za- zenlike mood and follow the mood induced by the music. The capacity to sit and be still is not an easy thing to do for people who are always running, meeting deadlines, picking up the clothes from the cleaners, teaching classes, attending meetings and so forth. A space must be carved out during each day to get unstuck if psyche is blocked. Doing nothing in a za- zenlike state opens a space for memory and dreamwork to happen. Minimalist music helps one to stay still and do nothing because the music stays in one place it seems. The staying in one placeness of the music allows psyche to stay in one psychic space—perhaps in a suspension of desire–. Staying in one place psychically might open the path to the past. By sitting still and listening to minimal music, perhaps the mind drifts toward dreams of the previous night. A working through becomes possible especially as one listens to music that stays in one place. Freud (1900/1960) discusses the way in which dreams involve both a backward and forward movement.

> The only way in which we can describe what happens in hallucinatory dreams is by saying that the excitation moves in a backward direction. Instead of being transmitted towards the motor end of the apparatus it moves towards the sensory end and finally reaches the perceptual system. If we describe as 'progressive' the direction taken by the psychical processes arising from the unconscious during waking life, then we may speak of dreams as having a 'regressive' character. (p. 542)

The dream moves backwards toward childhood repressions that carry over into adult life. Once those dreams are put to work through the associative process in the analytic setting, the dreamer moves forward and finds the way out. Alice goes into Wonderland, explores all of her hallucinated characters and then she comes back out. Dreams are often not a wonderland if the dream content is nightmarish. But in some way the nightmares fascinate because they serve a pedagogical function. Repetitive nightmares are often experienced if one suffers from posttraumatic stress syndrome. This is what Freud called shell shocked. One does not have to go to war to become a victim of post traumatic stress. The war that one fights might be completely internal, between a part of the self that tries to move forward, and a part of the self that tugs backwards via nightmares. Free association around the dream dismantles and deconstructs the feelings left by the dream when the dreamer is awake. Those feelings might linger for the rest of the day. It is in the lingering that things can be found out. I am thinking here of Ted Aoki's (2005) "lingering notes" that he often writes at the end of his essays. Listening to minimal music might create the necessary space for lingering. Minimalist music allows one to drift, float, to become–for a time–suspended.

The aim of this chapter is to explore, generally, minimalist music. I argue that listening to minimalist music opens one to deep interiority as well as archaic relations with objects, whether those objects are actually things or primal others. Minimalist music serves a sort of pedagogical function through the moods that it may create. Moods are symptoms of primal responses to archaic relations. Minimalism is not new by any means. The movement swept the artistic community– (minimalist art, architecture, music, sculpture, painting, literature) as early as the late 1950s, or early 1960s. Psychoanalytic explorations of minimalism have been done already. What is new here is the connection between education, psychoanalysis and minimalism. Here I am interested is raising pedagogical questions around doing something and doing nothing. What does doing nothing teach? Why is it necessary to do nothing (while listening to minimalist music), to sit za-zen like, in order to understand why one is unable to play–to play music, to play games, to play with words, to play at life? To sit za- zen like is not the command of emptiness as Buddhists might urge. What I mean here is that to sit still while listening to repetitious music allows one to wander freely down into the ruins of archaic traces of object relations and states of interiority. Psyche welcomes all thoughts, feelings– through free association–by suspending desire. Psyche fills itself with words, images and memories that point to the problem at hand. Psyche welcomes a fullness, and crowdedness of distant voices, faces, feelings, events. When one sits still and listens to the psyche, one hears repetitious soundings not dissimilar to what we hear when we hear minimalist music. In a way, minimalism mirrors some archaic or primal repetition that goes back as far as memory can take us. When this primal repetition goes wrong (i.e. the mother does not feed the infant consistently, the mother does not pay attention to the infant consistently, the mother is psychically absent over and over) the child grows up as an adult to act out these primal disconnects through unconscious transference. This is what Andre Green (1999a; 1993) calls the dead mother syndrome. Christopher Bollas (1997; 1999) points out that the more the mother is dead to the child the more alive she becomes in the psyche of the child. The force of the negative imago of the mother dominates an entire life of psyche. The negative imago of the mother colonizes psyche. The mess is never resolved however and so repetition compulsion rules the day. You can't fix your past with someone who reminds you of somebody else. You may not be able to fix the past either by becoming aware of patterns that poisoned the past and keep re-emerging in the here and now–but you may get a better understanding of your current stuckness. Through understanding –and finding out what went wrong–one may come to a sort of peace about not being able to understand the why of primal catastrophe. Feeling at peace does not mean erasing the disaster.

There are many artists who are considered minimalists. I am not interested in surveying the whole picture here. What I am interested in, rather, is looking at the conditions between the listener and the psyche that allow for archaic disconnects to emerge. I will focus in the latter part of the chapter on two minimalist composers, Philip Glass and Steve Reich. I focus on these two composers because I think they changed the landscape of classical music. Glass and Reich were the early pioneers in experimental music, and I think they represent the most important additions to the classical canon. I am not a musicologist and will not approach these musical texts in a strict fashion by any means. I am not interested in deconstructing particular pieces in the way that musicologists do. I am a curriculum theorist and so my take on Glass and Reich comes from this perspective. Glass and Reich have things to teach and I want to find out what those things are. This study will read more like a collage or montage rather than a linear historical report on musical scores. I examine Glass and Reich specifically in order to get back to the question that drives this book. On not being able to play-- has something to do with deep psychic breakdowns and listening to minimalist music (especially Glass and Reich) allows one to get back to these breakdowns through feelings the music may invoke.

INTERIOR SPACE, MOODS AND THE EDUCATIVE NATURE OF MINIMALIST MUSIC

Why minimalism? Why now? Where did it come from and what does it mean philosophically? What does it do to the listener while listening? What does minimalism teach? What is the educative value of minimalist music? These are some of the gnawing questions that are raised in this study. It is a curious fact that minimalism is a direct reaction to Serialism. Serial music is atonal and has a rigid structure, the 12 tone structure. 20th Century music tends to get associated with the Serialism of Berg, Webern and Schoenberg. Serialism is ugly and hard to listen to. Philip Glass (cited in Potter, 2000) calls Serialism "crazy creepy music" (p. 10). I couldn't agree more. Why bother listen to something that is ugly? Serialism makes little sense to me. Berg, Webern and Schoenberg are squarely in the canon. Music history classes cover these composers. This music is not popular, it is not listened to by a general public and hardly ever played on public radio. These are the facts that make Serialism material for the traditional music canon in academe. Minimalism, on the other hand, is popular, beautiful to listen to, and has made its way into a general public. For these reasons, minimalism is not part of the music canon inside the academe. Richard Kostelanetz (1999) tells us that "university music departments regard Glass as an errant student" (p. 110). Robert Maycock (2002) says that "[p]rolific composers [like Glass] in recent times have often attracted negative criticism" (p. 145). This should come as no surprise to those of us within the academy. Most academics shy away from that which is popular, except for those of us who do cultural studies work. The more famous you get, the less other academicians respect you. Writing too many books–in some research institutions–is looked down on. Too many books suggest that not much deep thought was put into them. Publishing in non-university presses is also looked down on in the academy. The more obscure your work, the better. Yet, Glass (cited in Maycock, 2002) tells us that "[t]he less they [composers] care about the music establishment the better they do. . ." (pp. 150–151). Is it also true that the less academics care about academe, the better they do?

The music establishment is rather conservative–much like other academic disciplines. To buck those who have come before is risky in any field. The minimalists moved in the completely opposite direction from the previous generation of classical composers who wrote atonal pieces. Minimalism, conversely is tonal. The only similarity between these two types of music may be that both minimalism and Serialism are highly structured. But it is there that the similarities end. Jacques Derrida comes to mind when I think of a scholar who bucked the conservative world of philosophy. His work is not taught in philosophy departments in the United States. Yet, English departments and departments of education have embraced Derrida. He is the errant son of philosophy, much like Glass. In my own field, curriculum studies, William F. Pinar started the movement known as the Reconceptualization in the early seventies. This movement (which is now in the Post-Reconceptualization phase) is considered avant garde by most within the discipline of education. Pinar bucked the deadening behaviorist trends in the field of education; Pinar went against previous generations of education scholars who created rigid systems. Understanding curriculum, (Pinar, 1995) means doing so in broad ways drawing on the liberal arts and moving away from quantification. I make the assertion that the move toward understanding curriculum in this broad manner is a more tonal way to understand people. Behaviorists—like Serialists—quantified. Quantification, in my estimation, does not capture the richness of language or lived experience.

Kenneth Baker (1988), suggests that minimalism–of all kinds–has its roots in American traditions. He explains.

New York Minimalism had sources closer to home in the distinctly American tradition of respect for plain facts and plain speaking, manifested in Shaker furniture and the pragmatist philosophy of Charles Sanders Pierce and William James, in the precisionist painting of Charles Sheeler, in the "scientific" realism of Thomas Eakins, the photographs of Paul Strand and Walker Evans and the poetry of William Carlos Williams. (p. 13)

Steve Reich (2002), the minimalist composer, tells us that reading William Carlos Williams influenced him. When one thinks of Shaker furniture one thinks of simple designs. And in minimal music, some suggest that the structure of this music is simple (Baker, 1988). Contrarily, some suggest that minimalism is "difficult" and "indigestible" (Rose, cited in Vergine (2001, p. 132). From the perspective of a musician, I would say that Glass and Reich–two minimalists' work I have studied and listened to for many years-- write deceptively difficult music. Glass points this out in a DVD about him (*Philip Glass, Looking Glass*). The music may sound like it is going nowhere–but in that nowhere you'd better be able to count. I don't know how a musician cannot get lost when performing Glass. Musicians have to have a highly developed technique to play repeated thirds and fifths over and over again. It takes a lot of strength and technique to play Glass. I don't know how musicians performing his work can avoid getting tendonitis. The mere repetition involved in physically playing the music can result in injury.

Steve Reich's music is highly complex in that it involves phasing, tape loops, recorded sounds, every day speech recorded over music. A singer will start a few notes in a sort of canon and then another singer will start the canon a little out of sync with the first singer and so on. The result is haunting and powerful. I do not think minimalism is simple at all; it is difficult not only to play but to understand. As I stated above, Barbara Rose (cited in Vergine, 2001, p. 132)–who is an art critic–uses the word "indigestible" to describe minimalist art. Some might think of Reich or Glass as "indigestible" because of the repetitive nature of their music. Tim Page (1997) says that "[d]etractors call Glass's music] "stuck record music" (p. 5). This humorous critique goes only so far. If one seriously studies Glass or Reich, one will begin to see how the tonal structures unfold. But one must have patience for this kind of music. What is striking is how the music seems to go nowhere but it goes into a nowhere that is deep; the music is awesome and difficult to put into words. I suppose minimalism is something you either love or hate. I find it spell binding. Glass and Reich capture sound that moves a little chromatically here and a little chromatically there, swirling round and round. This music works small spaces. Moving in small ways musically opens up enormous depth that most romantic music does not capture. Moving up a half step or down a half step has enormous tonal implications psychically. There is enormity to the smallness of these moves. It is as if whole worlds are opened by moving a half step up or a half step down. The subtlety of the changes shifts emotional registers in an uncanny way.

Glass worked with Beckett in the early '60s in theatrical performances. Beckettian thought is similar to Glassian or Reichian thought. Reich was influenced not only by William Carlos Williams but also by Ludwig Wittgenstein. "How small a thought it takes to fill someone's whole life!" (Wittgenstein, 1980, p. 1e). This brief sentence, Reich put to music which he calls "Proverb." Wittgenstein's book *Culture and Value* (1980) is filled with little–proverbial–turns of thought. Wittgenstein couldn't sum it up better. A small a thought has profound implications. Something about small changes–small thoughts–that create worlds within worlds. Big leaps, on the other hand, like octave leaps do not have this kind of resonance. The unexpected in minimalist music is what is interesting. Yes, some of it does sound like the record is stuck. But if the listener just gives it time and patience she will see that the broken record moves in small, yet profound ways. How is it that a whole emotional world can be created by taking small musical steps? Perhaps in a way, minimalism mirrors the everyday. The profundity of repetition is something many do not understand or want to because it reminds them too much of their own lives. In much of the analytic setting, nothing happens. Session after session the patient says nothing. The psychic blocks are too in place. And then one day, the whole earth comes crashing down because of a slip of a memory–a colour, a smell, a shoe, a look. The small seemingly insignificant things move the psyche along. Freud reminds us that it is to the small things we need to direct our attention; we need to turn our attention to the things that seemingly do not matter.

Life is the over and over again all over again. There is something paradoxical about this fact. What seems to stay in place moves. Inertia, has its own non-rhythmic- rhythm. Edward Strickland (2000) puts it this way:

> In dance, film, sculpture, and literature, similarly, Minimalism exposes the components of its medium in skeletal form. Dance, the organization of motion and stasis, if often reduced to a modicum of elementary movements perhaps juxtaposed to episodes of immobility. (p. 13)

Minimalist music too seems to have a quality of inertia, and yet it moves in "elementary" ways by half steps up or down. What is the skeletal form of life? Movement and inertia. Life begins in movement and ends in inertia. Every day we repeat this cycle. We are inert in our sleep (unless we sleepwalk), and when we awaken and move about (mobility) we get on with the day. Robert Maycock (2002) talks about Glass' music as "about states of being. . ." (p. 45). Yes, there is something hauntingly ontological about both Glass and Reich. Not only does their music bring up questions around being, but also and most notably I think, minimalism brings up questions on a psychic level.

Music is profoundly connected to the emotions. But what emotions are we talking about here? The basics. Back to the basics of our emotional registers. The skeleton of emotions if you will. The skeleton of the psyche. What is fundamental or primary about human emotion? Freud (1900/1960; 1959; 1960) suggested that primary process thinking is what is most primal. Does minimalism speak uncannily to primary process thinking? Does minimalism, in other words, speak to that which is unconscious in us? Does it speak in our dreams, in our repressions and in our troubled emotional states? Art Lange (1999) argues that Glass' music is uncannily tied into the unconscious. Lange (1999) explains.

> Glass's use of repetition, of consistent body rhythms, strikes a responsive chord in the human unconscious, an inner voice that we carry along with us. The music sings in a manner that seemingly need never stop, and actually it never does. (p. 89)

Lange does not flesh out what that inner voice may be, nor does he go into any detail about the connection between the unconscious and Glass' music. Dreams are our inner voices. They are solely directed, produced and acted by parts of our psyche. All of these parts are of a whole, but the whole is broken up, or as Christopher Bollas (1996) puts it "cracked up" especially when attempting to articulate these dream-character- voices. The voices and characters in dreams have no sense of time, they just keep on marching on as if twenty years ago or yesterday are the same day. Repetition in dreams suggests that something in the psyche needs attention, demands attention. In the repetition, one will find out what the trouble is. But even when one figures out what the trouble is, the repetitions may continue. Dreaming the same dream over and over is rather disturbing. Why the same dream over and over again? What could it mean? You see, I am suggesting that minimalist music–whether it is Glass' or Reich's–mirrors most closely primary process of the dreamworld. In fact, listening to minimalism at a

119

stretch can put you in a dreamlike state. But you have to give it time and get beyond the "broken record" thing. I find minimalism endlessly fascinating both musically and emotionally. I've been listening to minimalism for twenty years and never tire of it. As the years go on and on–another repetition–I keep coming back to Glass and Reich. There is something uncannily familiar about this music but I just can't put my finger on it. Yes, and sometimes it does drive me crazy. But most often, it intrigues and makes me think and feel differently. How? I don't know. It just does. Like analysis. Session after session nothing and then all of a sudden something different happens and one feels and thinks differently about things. Like deep study. Book after book–another repetition familiar to scholars– citation after citation–month one, month two, month three of studying some topic–nothing happens, and then seemingly all of a sudden–when sweeping the floor, or taking a walk–something clicks–that's it. That is it. But what is it? It is something familiar yet strange. It is something one already knew perhaps but was enmeshed in cobwebs. Studying book after book may be tedious –like minimal music–but somehow something becomes striking and all the patterns of thought just sort of come together on their own. Like minimal music. The patterns have patterns of their own–worlds within worlds of patterns. The patterns are round, straight, crooked, large, small, insignificant or meaningful but all the same the patterns have a larger pattern that shapes and mis-shapes the work as a whole. This is a mirror not only of one's psyche but also of the universe. I am not a physicist and will not venture into the world of string theory, m theory, banes, membranes (see Brian Green (2003) on the *Elegant Universe*). But it seems to me that physicists, philosophers, educationists, musicologists may all be asking similar questions concerning patterns.

Music is about patterns of notes. The primary process of the unconscious involves patterns, re-presentations of images that re-appear and disappear, later to surface again, and then to fade out. If patterns have patterns of their own and then those patterns have their own patterns–then the psyche, the world, the universe will never be explained. One can never fully understand one's unconscious, even after years of analysis. The human mind is just too complex as is the world and universe(s). We are not alone–either psychically or cosmologically.

What minimalist music allows the psyche to do is to get at unspoken patterns of feeling, memory and thought. Listening seriously and attentively to minimalism changes what one feels. On each listening new patterns are opened up both within the music and within the psyche. States of reverie become possible when listening to minimalism, or states of complete and utter annoyance emerge. If you can get over the annoyance– and there is certainly more annoyance to come–and pay deep attention to the music and how it makes you feel, changes start taking place within the psyche. Tim Page (1997) calls this "musical alchemy" (p. 4). Turning lead into gold takes patience and time and the willingness to be open to the new. The lead in this case would be the annoyance brought about by the repetition. The gold would be insight into psyche. As John Richardson (1999) puts it, Glass' music in particular is "haunting" (xi). I also find Steve Reich's music haunting. As a matter of fact, I find Reich's music more haunting than Glass'. In many ways, Reich speaks to a part of me that Glass does not. There is something so strange about the way in which Reich goes about putting things slightly out of sync. But more than that, the medieval influence on his music is evident. And it is this that I really like. Singers have no vibrato and sing in very close harmonies. It is the jarring quality of the out of sync-ness that makes me lose my breath. I am breathless while listening to Reich. Breathlessness is the suspension of a sort of reverie that takes me somewhere back in psychic time. Reich's (2002) strange harmonies and what he calls "speech melodies" get me in my gut. I can't quite explain why this is so, but it is so. When I hear Reich I stop and furrow my brow and get real serious. He makes me get serious. He deals with serious subject matter (see for example *Different Trains*). I will get to more of this a little later on, but for now it is enough to offer these impressionistic comments.

Minimalism of whatever brand alters thought and emotion–if you let it. Christopher Bollas (1989) talks about the "ghostline personality." I mentioned this in another chapter, but here it seems relevant to the work at hand. If you really get into minimal music, you allow yourself to become a ghostline personality. You become haunted, that is, by yourself. You allow your ego to fade and open your mind to free associative thoughts. Minimalism, in other words, allows you to more easily free associate because of its repetitive nature. But you have to become a ghost to your ego to allow this to happen. Perhaps you need to get outside of your ego for a time, get underneath the defenses to find out what the trouble might be. Dreams are haunted by ghosts–by dead parents, or dead friends. But perhaps more importantly, dreams are haunted by your own split off ghosted parts of your personality. Music that haunts brings up the ghosts from within. Being a ghost is being in a sense not there too. Minimalism takes you to that not there part of yourself. Interestingly enough–as different as they are–both minimalism and the music of *Pink Floyd* open up these strange interior spaces. Now, in some of the other arts–like sculpture or painting– some argue that minimalist art lacks interiority (Batchelor, 1996). In the art world, minimalist painters and sculptors have a bit of a different take on the subject at hand. James Meyer (2000) explains.

> Primarily sculpture, Minimal art tends to consist of single or repeated geometric forms. Industrially produced or built by skilled workers following the artist's instructions, it removes any traces of emotion or intuitive decision making, in stark contrast to the Abstract Expressionist painting and sculpture that preceded it in the 1940s and 1950s. (p.15)

There is, indeed, something very impersonal about geometric shapes and there is something impersonal in producing art in a factory style where skilled workers do the work for you. Interestingly enough Warhol called his studio "the factory" and had others do some of the repetitive work for him. Mark Rothko—whom I consider minimalist—works in minimal colours but his paintings evoke many emotions. The paintings drip–as it were– from emotion. The pieces are profoundly moving, unlike any other art. Some of his paintings are rightly placed inside of a chapel because the pieces are numinous and collapse the sacred and profane. Some people stand in front of the paintings bewildered and shrug their shoulders–they just don't get it.

But again, if you can get over the initial 'I don't get it mode' and try to get into what Rothko expresses, the art is deeply moving. Interestingly enough, Christopher Rothko (2004), Mark Rothko's son, comments that his father's paintings were "preverbal" (xi) and he compares the paintings to music. Christopher Rothko (2004) explains.

> His work [Mark Rothko] communicates on a level that is explicitly preverbal. Indeed, it would be hard to find less-narrative painting. Like music, my father's artwork seems to express the inexpressible—we are far removed from the realm of words. (xi)

Many psychoanalytic writers comment on this— that music does spring from the preverbal just as Christopher Rothko suggests. There is something primal about these paintings, something that calls the viewer to listen to a deeper emotion. This emotion—the Jungians might argue—connects with a more collective unconscious.

Steve Reich (2002) says that his music connects to the impersonal. Is this what the Jungians call the collective unconscious? And yet his music seems so personal, especially his music about the Holocaust. Reich (2002) tells us that "[m]usical processes can give one a direct contact with the impersonal. . ." (p. 35). What that impersonal thing is, he doesn't say. Reich says that "[f]ocusing on musical processes makes possible a shift away from the he and she and you and me, outward to it" (p. 55). This is Jungian. If one moves toward an outward "it" is that not the same as an impersonal 'it' within? Isn't the unconscious impersonal? It has no sense of time, it is rigid, it repeats themes. There is an impersonal within and that is what makes up primary process thought.

PHILIP GLASS AND STEVE REICH: ON NOT BEING ABLE TO REPEAT

There is nobody like Philip Glass and **there is nobody** like Steve Reich. Nobody can repeat what they have done. Two originals. Two one-of -a -kinds. Both of their music is made up of constant repetition. Although both are considered minimalists, Glass and Reich couldn't be more different from each other. Even though both rely on repetition in the musical form, their forms of musical repetition are vastly different. Once you have heard them–whether you like them or not–"[y]ou will not be able to forget"(Maycock, 2002, p. 24). Robert Maycock talks of Glass' music as an unforgettable experience. I would add that Reich's music is also unforgettable. Both have a unique and distinctive sound. Although both are minimalists–though they might not like the label–they are worlds apart musically.

Interestingly enough Glass and Reich have made similar comments about academe worth repeating here. According to Robert Maycock (2002), Glass' academic training at Juilliard and studying with Nadia Boulanger followed the traditional route for becoming a professor of music at a university. Maycock (2002) remarks that "Glass was statistically putting himself in line for the quiet creative death of an obscure college professorship. . ." (p. 171). But, Glass did not become the "obscure" college professor probably because has no use for academe. Similarly, Steve Reich (2002) has great disdain for academe. Reich explains.

But for at least 10 years I did all kinds of things and I would certainly rather take my chances in the commercial world, as a person, than in the academic world. I think that if you have any close connection or involvement with a department–and this is a particularly American situation–then it's going to wipe you out. (p. 53)

Both Glass and Reich drove cabs for a while to make a living. This is not uncommon for artists trying to make it in New York City. The music business is tough. As far as music schools go, they are killing machines. Not only does academe kill the professors it kills the students as well. Music schools are like military training grounds. Old school music teachers worked to break the students, to see how much they could take, in order to get them ready for the tough world of competitions. American music conservatories are tough places to grow up for musicians. The curriculum in most conservatories in the United States tends toward conservatism–conservatories conserve the tradition. So along comes Steve Reich and Philip Glass–both of whom have not followed the traditional path. Inside of the music academy tenure is based on following the tradition not on bucking it. If you are under constant pressure to compose in a certain way, in the end it gets to you, as Reich says. And for some, life in academe is death. The death of the creative spirit. Music school for me was a complete mistake. If I could take back those years and do it over again, I would have never gone to a music school. Music school destroyed me in many ways. The scars are still with me. I would not like to repeat the experience. But I do each time I play. I still feel the psychic presence of the pressures of performance. You don't forget. The body does not forget. My arm does not forget. The damage done to it was partially caused by the pressure to be perfect.

What is it about the academy that makes it so difficult for people to be creative, different? It is absurd to me that Reich and Glass are not embraced by the academic culture. But that should come as no surprise really. In the field of music, suspicion of what is new might be more pronounced than in other fields. The classical music world is extremely conservative. Tim Page (1997) comments on the conservative nature of American opera houses:

Opera companies are notoriously timid, and most modern works are studiously ignored; when a composer is lucky enough to get a production, it is usually at a small house, and after the first run, the work vanishes from the repertory. (pp. 3–4)

Major American symphony orchestras are not much different from opera companies in their conservatism. Most concert programs consist of 19th century music. Occasionally you might hear a twentieth century piece. How often is an experimental work played? At music festivals, like Aspen, or at Spoleto, new works have a better chance of being heard. But the traditional fare at most symphony halls is 19th century. I am not particularly fond of 19th century music for a variety of reasons. That–of course–is neither here nor there. The point being made here is that symphony orchestras, opera companies and departments of music inside the academy are hell bent on conserving the tradition. Interestingly enough, Glass comments on the traditional opera scene. Glass (1987) explains:

> Besides, the operatic tradition seemed to me hopelessly dead, with no prospect for resurrection in the world of performance in which I worked. To me it seemed a far better idea to simply start someplace else. (p. 87)

Glass has composed many operatic-like pieces, but these are nothing like traditional operas. And he doesn't use the word 'opera' to describe them. Glass prefers to call his pieces "music theater" (p. 87). And by this he does not mean musical theater. Music theater is something altogether different.

Glass' famous trilogy Einstein *on the Beach*, *Satyagraha* and *Akhnaten* are operatic in nature but they are not like traditional operas. Whatever Glass writes– whether it is music theater or pieces for instruments only–it is not like traditional anything. Although Glass was influenced by Ravi Shankar and classical Indian music, Glass' music sounds nothing like traditional Indian music. Glass is Glass. Glass is Glass partly because he repeats himself in various ways throughout his work. He's got an unmistakable signature–like any great artist. His music is immediately recognizable. Robert Flemming (1997) says that many people consider "Glass [to be] a renegade" (vii). Glass tells us in his autobiography that his most important influences come from the theater. Maybe that is why he calls his art 'music theater'. Glass is an original. Some of his most powerful music is music for films. Koyannaisqatsi (1983) and Powaquatsi (1988) are two films that come to mind here. No words are spoken. Koyannaisqatsi is not my favorite. The music is highly repetitious to the point of annoyance. Here, as Robert Maycock (2002) might say, "the irritation factor is undeniable" (p. 44). Recently I watched the film after not seeing it for some twenty years. My impression is that the film is interesting because of the music, but the images are not gripping—we see mostly buildings and cabs. Some scenes are in fast motion, while some are in slow motion. The film tends to be boring; I felt as if I might have a seizure while watching it. The film, Powaquatsi, is my favorite. Here, Glass' music is extremely powerful. Much of this film is done in slow motion and captures people's faces and expressions as they struggle in the work-a-day world. My take on the film is that it is a critique of capitalism–although that was not the intended message of the film. The problem with the film is that it tends to exoticize third world peoples. And yet, the music makes it a haunting experience. The images are haunting.

Koyannaisqatsi means world out of balance, while Powaquatsi means world in transformation. Things change and things move very slowly over time. Interestingly enough, Glass' music is perfect for these themes. Listening to Glass' music, one experiences slow change, slow harmonic progressions. His music is an experience of being in transformation, but on a very small scale. The over and over again changes slightly from key to key, from progression to progression. Some of his music succeeds in capturing the listener's attention and heart; some of it is really annoying–I must admit. The same could be said of Steve Reich. Some of his music is just beautiful, and some of it is totally annoying. Some days listeners might not have the patience to take in the repetitions, other days they can take in the repetitions. What is the annoyance about I wonder? I suppose a psychoanalytic question is in order here. The question might be–in Winnicottian fashion–what do we do with the annoyance? Do we make use of it? Can we make use of what annoys? What is the threshold–emotionally–for annoyance? Why are different people annoyed at different times around different things?

Some of Glass' music is driven by philosophical ideals. In particular, I am thinking of his trilogy I mentioned earlier. Glass (1987) comments that the three pieces, *Einstein on the Beach, Satyagraha and Akhnaten* all deal with great figures in world history who have left indelible marks on culture. Glass (1987) explains,

> In a number of ways, my choice of Akhnaten as a subject accorded with my thinking in general. In this way, particularly, I could relate Akhnaten to Einstein and Gandhi. The key is that we know Akhnaten as a man of ideas and, to me, the entire history of humanity is a history of ideas, of culture. When I think of ancient Greece, Rome, France China, or wherever, what comes to my mind are poets, painters, writers, musicians, philosophers. I never think of the generals and politicians. (p.139)

It is admirable that Glass writes his music around ideas that have tremendous substance and content. The music is not just fluff stuff, it is a serious expression of serious, philosophical themes. Some might accuse Glass of being elitist or even sexist in his choice of subject matter. Gender is an issue for feminists who discuss the major trends in minimalist music and the larger art scene. David Batchelor (1996) tells us that minimalist art is generally associated with white men who live and work in New York City. The interesting thing here is that women–for the most part—have been the strongest supporters and innovators of minimalist art. Batchelor (1996) says that,

> it is worth noting here that the majority of the more sympathetic, insightful and interesting contemporary accounts of minimalist art were often written by women–Barbara Reise, Barbara Rose, Lucy Lippard and Rosalind Krauss; and that many of the most interesting developments or transformations of Minimalism [in the art world] have been initiated by women artists. . . . (p. 13)

Batchelor's comments have to do strictly with the art world, not the world of music. But these comments are important to understand because of the problems of gender inside of the arts as a whole. What women composers are considered minimalists? Laurie Anderson might be considered a minimalist but she calls herself a performance artist (Anderson, 1999). What women composers are even known? What women composers do you find in the classical section at Barnes and Noble? None. The music world–like most other worlds–is highly sexist. Think of who conducts symphonies? Mostly men. The music field is sexist. I've heard some classical pianists make comments about how sexist the Van Cliburn piano competition is. One doesn't usually think that gender matters when it comes to winning competitions but it does.

Steve Reich's music, like Glass', is unmistakably his own. Nobody can repeat Reich. He has an unmistakable style. Nobody writes music like Reich. We learn from Keith Potter (2000), that one of Reich's influences was Ludwig Wittgenstein. Potter tells us that Reich attended Cornell University as an undergraduate and majored in philosophy because he "felt that he was already too old to pursue music professionally" (p. 154).

Imagine. Performance majors must be highly developed even before they enter the university. A cellist auditioning at Juilliard—in order to get into the undergraduate program-- must play three different movements from the Bach *Unaccompanied Cello Suites* plus two other pieces at very high level of difficulty. Pablo Casals—world renown cellist—said that he spent ten years studying and playing the Bach Suites before he ever played them in public. Why does Juilliard set such ridiculous standards? Entrance into university music programs is based on either an audition or a sample of a composition (if one plans to study composition). Getting into conservatories is highly competitive and very difficult. In a 15 minute audition, it is determined whether the student gets into the conservatory or not. Preparation for that 15 minute audition takes years.

At any rate, Reich's interest in philosophy is crucial for any sort of understanding of his work. Potter (2000) tells us that while at Cornell, Reich became interested in Wittgenstein. Reich,

> developed a particular interest in Ludwig Wittgenstein, who had himself been at Cornell until 1950, the year before he died. While Wittgenstein's ideas were of great importance to Reich at the time, any relationship with the composer's subsequent thinking is somewhat tangential and tends to be greeted with scepticism by the composer himself. (p. 155)

This passage is rather curious to me because upon reading Wittgenstein's work on language games in general and more specifically his book called *Culture and Value* (1980) one can see a direct relation between Reich and the philosopher Wittgenstein–especially in Reich's piece titled *Proverb* which draws directly from a passage in Wittgenstein's book. It is interesting to me that when reading Wittgenstein, I understand not only Reich, but minimalism better. Wittgenstein made clear to me–perhaps ironically–what minimalism means. Let us turn only briefly then to Wittgenstein's (1980) *Culture and Value* to better understand what Reich is doing in his music. In 1929 Wittgenstein (1980) writes,

> I still find my own way of philosophizing new, and it keeps striking me so afresh; that is why I need to repeat myself so often. It will have become second nature to a new generation, to whom the repetitions will be boring. I find them necessary. (p. 1e)

Wittgenstein's use of repetitions appears already in 1929. Could we say that minimalism can be dated back to 1929? Is Wittgenstein a sort of philosophical minimalist? Maybe. Wittgenstein emphasizes that these repetitions are "necessary." But why we might ask? Do we repeat because we have bad memories? Or is it that our memories have been repressed and we unconsciously act them out compulsively? Or is repetition necessary because that is the way we get in touch with who we are? Is identity built on repetition? Or does the compulsion to repeat undo one's identity? Wittgenstein (1980) says in 1930, "[e]ach of the sentences I write is trying to say the whole thing, i.e., the same thing over and over again; it is as though they were all simply views of one object seen from different angles" (p. 7c). Isn't that what scholars do in general? Is it not the case that in writing–whether it be scholarship or music—ideas get repackaged? The author, composer and poet keep writing the same thing over and over again and there is no end to it. It is all of a piece–really. Wittgenstein suggests that we get at a certain topic in a variety of ways.

But this repeating becomes most evident when the music itself is repetitious. John Richardson (1999) tells us that Glass "has been accused, to some extent, of recycling ideas ad nauseam" (p. 3). But we all do this, don't we? We always repeat what we have already done in one way or another. In the academy, the scholar is to carve our a scholarly identity by addressing the same topics throughout her academic career. If you are too all over the place, you risk losing your scholarly identity.

Back to Wittgenstein for a moment. In 1946 Wittgenstein repeats what he already said in 1929 in a slightly different fashion. He says,

The repeat is necessary. In what respect is it necessary? Well, sing it, and you will see that only the repeat gives it its tremendous power–Don't we have an impression that a model for this theme already exists in reality and the theme only approaches it, corresponds to it, if this section is repeated? (1980, p. 52e)

What model of reality supports repetition? Think of fractals, repeating patterns. Think of storms. Storms come and go and come again but in different patterns. Think of the seasons, winter, spring, summer, fall. Think of the heartbeat. Everything is a repeat of everything else. Kind of mind boggling isn't it. Sing it, Wittgenstein says, and you will see how it all repeats again.

In 1948 Wittgenstein (1980) said, "[w]here others go on ahead, I stay in one place" (p. 66e). Relating this to music is rather interesting. When you stay in one place on the keyboard or ,say, the guitar fret board and only move just slightly up or down never straying very far from your home key, it seems that worlds are opened up. It is very strange that staying in one place and then moving ever so slightly up or down can generate such different moods and tones.

In 1946 Wittgenstein (1980) wrote, "[h]ow small a thought it takes to fill someone's whole life!" (p. 50e). This brings us back around to Reich. Reich takes this sentence and puts it to the most haunting melody that repeats over and over again. And when the melody repeats it is slightly out of sync, as if in a canon that is just a little out of balance. The voices come in at strange intervals and it is very difficult to follow what those voices are doing. Pretty soon the listener gets lost. It really is unsettling. All of Reich's music is like this. One just gets lost in it. The getting lost is part of the beauty of it. The piece Reich wrote to the words above in Wittgenstein's text is titled "Proverb" as I said earlier. Reich (2002) says that "[m]uch of Wittgenstein's work is "proverbial" in tone and in its brevity" (p. 191). I will tell you that when I first heard this piece, I nearly fell out of my chair. The piece is stunning, haunting and you will not forget it. All of Reich's music stuns. When listening to Reich, I pay attention. Reich's music is not background music, the way Glass' music can be. Reich's music makes you become attentive because of the way the voices haunt, the melodies are so awesome, so numinous. Much of Reich's work strikes me as mystical. Keith Potter (2000) tells us that,

> Reich became increasingly interested not only in Debussy, Stravinsky, and jazz but also in medieval music, especially the work of the French composer Perotin, whose use of strict structures such as cantus firmus, isorhythm and, especially, canon and augmentation has remained an influence. (p. 155)

What strikes me is the wide range of influences on Reich, but especially the medieval one. If you were to pick up a CD by Reich and play a medieval piece afterwards, it is hard to tell which piece is modern and which one is medieval. I do not hear the jazz influence at all in Reich's work. Stravinsky and Debussy– a little, but it is mostly the medieval influence that stands out.

The other interesting thing about Reich is that he uses terse sentences around which he spins an entire piece of music. "Proverb" is made up of one sentence "how small a thought it takes to fill a whole life". The sentence repeats over and over again continually slipping out of sync. It is a very peculiar listening experience. You must relinquish your ego when listening to Reich. The ego wants answers that it doesn't get. Here is the rub. Reich's music speaks to the unconscious in that it creates a dreamlike pattern of harmonies that forces the listener to regress in a way. And yet, his music is highly structured. His music is tightly organized into repeating phrases. One would think that improvised music would lead the listener into a state of regression. Maybe it does and maybe it doesn't. The paradox for Reich is that it is the highly structured nature of the piece that allows for a psychological regression to take place. Reich tells us exactly how he puts these pieces together in his book *Writings on Music* 1965-2000. Reich (2002), says that,

> Constant repetition through tape loops produces just such a rhythmic intensification. The idea of using constant repetition partially grew out of working with tape loops since 1963, but mainly through helping Terry Riley put together his performance, in 1964, of his In C, where many different repeating patterns were combined simultaneously. (p. 20)

In 1964 I was 2 years old. Minimalism has been going on for quite a long time, practically my whole life. That is hard to fathom especially since it seems so new to me.

Reich explains that he lines up the tape loops and then lets "them slowly shift out of phase with each other" (p. 20). I think that it is this slowly shifting out of phase that makes the music sound ever so slightly out of sync. You can't quite grasp what he's doing. Things do seems to slip out of other things musically, but just how it is done is impossible to say without studying the scores. At any rate, listening to Reich is sort of like seeing double: you can't get focused, things get all mixed up. Isn't this the way of the unconscious? This music seems to plug directly into my head, it is very strange indeed.

Another interesting thing that Reich does–and I think this is a most unique aspect of his work–is that he records people speaking everyday language that you might hear on a subway or at the grocery store or on the radio. He actually builds his pieces around people's everyday language. Here again we see the influence of Wittgenstein's language games. Reich builds up his music from everyday speech. One of his most remarkable pieces–where this technique is used–is called *Different Trains*. In the first section of the piece we hear short sentences spoken by his governess named Virginia and a certain Mr. Davis talking about trains. We hear the words "from New York to Los Angeles" over and over again. And we hear the sounds of real trains recorded on top of the music and voices. In the second part, (i.e. different trains) Holocaust survivors talk in very short sentences about the trains that went to the concentration camps. In the third part, after the war, we hear a woman's voice asking if the war is really over, "are you sure" is repeated over and over again. Clearly the piece is a commentary on the Holocaust and it is through the sounds of trains that Reich pulls the piece together. The piece is brilliant. Musically it is exquisite. Reich (2002) makes an interesting comment about how using everyday "speech melody" (p.194) allows people to be "witnesses to their own lives" (p. 199). What an interesting idea. Reich's work and my own are in sync here as my first book, *Curriculum and the Holocaust: Competing Sites of Memory and Representation* (2001) was written as a form of witnessing. What troubled me—as a scholar-witness-- was finding out that most historians did not include the voices of the victims in their work because they claim that memory is faulty and doesn't make for hard evidence. Who would better know what it was like to be in Auschwitz than a survivor? Historians erase the very people for whom they are trying to be witnesses.

Reich (2002) explains exactly what he means by "speech melody" in this passage.

> Since the early 1960s I have been interested in speech melody. That is, the melody that all of us unconsciously create while speaking. Sometimes this speech melody is quite pronounced (as in children) and sometimes it is almost nonexistent. (p. 194)

Not only does Reich include speech melody, he also includes everyday sounds like car horns and car alarms into his work. Reich explains that the piece *City Life*:

> not only samples of speech but also car horns, door slams, air brakes, subway chimes, pile drivers, car alarms, heartbeats, boat horns are all part of the fabric of this piece. (Reich, 2002, p. 187)

The car alarm is a bit much—especially for my dogs. Every time that car alarm goes off in the piece my dogs start barking. Reich works squarely in the everyday and yet again his music sounds very old, ancient even. And he always surprises. That's the mark of a good writer and good composer. In one piece he actually uses an electric guitar. The distortion is all there, just like in a rock band. In other pieces he uses marimbas. In other pieces voice and strings. He is infinitely interesting. I was surprised to learn that in one of his pieces that he collaborated with Pat Methany. Methany couldn't be more different from Reich. Methany is a jazz guitarist. But the Reich piece that Methany plays is hardly jazz! Reich takes Methany's playing and applies the same techniques of repetition and looping and the rest. I have been listening to Methany for twenty years or so and I didn't recognize his guitar playing on the piece until I looked in the CD booklet. I was shocked. Wow. Now that's a wow. Reich continues to surprise. Nobody can repeat Reich. He is a one of a kind.

What is interesting to me is the way in which listening to minimal music demands the same sort of floating attention that is demanded both of the analyst and patient in psychoanalysis. Sessions go by and not much happens. Patience needs to develop. Freud suggested that analysts need to develop what he called evenly hovering attention. That is exactly what is needed when listening to minimalist music. You must let the music allow you to drift along with it–even if you can't quite understand it. Nina Coltart (2000) says of Bion,

> Those who were fortunate enough to be taught by Dr. Bion value the stress which he laid the need to develop the ability to tolerate not knowing; the capacity to sit with a patient, often for long periods, without any real precision as to where we are. . . . (p. 3)

Now apply this to Reich's music especially. Where are we when tapes are looping out of sync or voices are slipping slightly out of sync? We must develop– as Bion put it– the capacity to not know where we are when listening to Reich. That capacity not to know where we are means being able to handle slippage and frustration.

CHAPTER FIVE

ON WAITING

States of Interiority and Intentionality

The dread of knowing that one is not going to heal from a serious injury troubles. But then again healing might be possible. And then again healing might not be possible. I am thinking here of pianist Gary Graffman who has made his career by playing with his left hand only. He hurt his right hand and it never healed. It is an admirable career that he has had. For people who do not heal, how to go on? We take great courage from Graffman.

I am curious about people who do not heal and what that is like psychologically. Is there always the fantasy that eventually the injury will heal, I wonder, knowing that it will not? It is to this conundrum that I would like to turn in this chapter.

The idea here is that eventually–if one *waits* long enough–one might be able to play again. Take the example of pianist Leon Fleisher. For thirty years he played only with his left hand as he suffered from a condition called dystonia. Today he is again playing with both hands with the help of botox. This new treatment has allowed Fleisher (2004) to use his right hand again. Fleisher's story is rather remarkable. Given the advances in medicine, injuries due to neurological disease or overuse might be able to be made good again. But Fleisher points out that he is not "cured." He will always be a dystonic. The botox merely "alleviates symptoms" (p.1). Still, for some, symptoms are not alleviated.

Hoping for the best–especially through one's darkest hours– seems natural enough. Everything will work out, things will be brighter at the end of the day. If one just *waits* long enough things will get better. And for Fleishman, things did get better. If one waits it out good will come of it. Unfortunately for some life is not this way. For those who never regain use of the injured limb, waiting for the messiah of cure to arrive only leads to false hope and deepens depression. False hope damages the psyche. *Waiting* for the injury to go away does not mean that it will. One *waits* in false hope. One *waits* for a future that will never come. Take the example of Ludwig Wittgenstein's brother Paul. He had his right hand blown off during the WW1. And yet, he played piano with his left hand. Concertos for the left hand were written for him. This is another remarkable story. You cannot wait for a blown off limb to come back again but I wonder if people who are victims of war injuries engage in magical thinking and believe at some level that the blown off limb will come back again?

For musicians who do not heal, I write this chapter. What does it mean to wait for cure when none is in sight? Here I explore the notion of *waiting*. The question is how to get beyond the belief that the injury will heal, when in fact it will not.

The body always remembers. Re-injury is common among musicians who try to play after waiting it out. One may feel fine for a time, but then the arm gives out again. Realizing that things are not okay daunts emotionally. To admit that all is not well pains. Deep psychic wounds never go away. The demon of hurt may disappear for a time, but it always comes back again. So the waiting game continues. The injured one waits until the pain vanishes. It may vanish for a time. When one tries to work the damaged arm it reminds through pain that something is not right. That day will never come when all is well. But how to cope? What is to be done once this difficult and unthinkable realization strikes? Can one admit that life as a professional musician is over? There is no going back to a time before the injury. What does life look life after the injury? What kind of life is possible now? Well, we must wait and see.

In this chapter I look at the notion of waiting from two positions. First, I suggest that waiting brings up different kinds of emotional experience; waiting gets experienced in various registers of interiority. What kind of emotional intensities emerge while waiting? The experience of waiting is highly psychological. I offer here a phenomenology of waiting. What does it feel like to wait? What does it mean to wait for something that will never come? Ah. This was Beckett's (1958) question in *Waiting for Godot*.

A second issue turns on the notion of intentionality. What are we waiting *for*? Intentionality addresses the 'for what'. For what does one wait? One always waits 'for' something or someone. The musician waits for the injury to heal, but it never will. This is the problem. Why does psyche continue to wait for something that will never happen? Waiting for cure, healing and reparation pains because at some level psyche knows that healing is out of the question. Still one waits for a better day; one waits to go back to a time before of the injury. Waiting and hope are interconnected ideas. Can we never give up this notion of hope?

At the end of the day, one must give up waiting. What would it mean to not wait any longer for cure? What would it mean to go on with life when one cannot do what one was called to do? I offer no consolation here.

WAITING: STATES OF INTERIORITY

The question here is, what does it feel like to wait? This is by no means easy to articulate. Everybody waits. But what does it *feel* like to wait? What kinds of emotions get evoked while waiting? The experience of waiting is deeply psychological. The experience of Waiting is so familiar that it is strange. Thinking about the experience of waiting makes it stranger and stranger. Feelings escape language. To tease out and articulate what it feels like to experience anything is a daunting task. W.R. Bion (1990), in his *Brazilian Lectures*, suggests that there are psychological states or, "psychic real[ities]" (p. 49), that are unrelated to language. Perhaps the experience of waiting–because it is primal (i.e. waiting to be born)– finds its roots somewhere behind language. How to articulate what comes before language? Let us turn to Bion (1990) for a little help here. He states,

But it seems extremely unlikely that psychic reality bears any resemblance to articulate speech. Words like 'attention', 'notation', 'inquiry', may be useful if we want to talk about it, not if we want to know about the reality. (1990, p. 49)

Waiting is a kind of 'psychic reality.' As Bion suggests, we can talk all day long about "psychic realities" but never really get at the experience at hand. How to analyze an experience that does not lend itself to explanation?

The longest and most primal experience of waiting (I am reminded here of Masud Khan's (1989), *The Long Wait*), is in the womb. What was your face before you were born? The unanswerable riddle of the Zen Koan. Waiting has its antecedent in that period before we were born. Waiting in the womb. Perhaps in our most existentially stunned moments unconscious memories of those psychic realities experienced in the womb emerge. There is a sort of 'recollection' (as Plato might put it) of something older, something deeper, more archaic, and non-verbal about waiting.

There is something archaic about the experience of waiting. There are no words for it. No language. Of course, we cannot articulate what cannot be articulated. Muddle through language in an attempt to express primal feelings. To really get at primal experience baffles. Perhaps through dreams edges of primal recollections surface. And yet getting to the heart of the matter troubles.

Waiting in *the now* harkens back to waiting in *the then*, in the time before you were born. Waiting is en-wombed. The ego as Freud pointed out is a body-ego. How to talk about primal, enwombed waiting? To talk about what cannot be talked about presents a great challenge. But what are our options? We might decide that it is useless to try to express what cannot be expressed. But where does silence get us? Nowhere. So we muddle on. Muddling is exactly what I propose to do here.

In *On Not Being Able to Paint*, Marion Milner (1957) talks about the value of "absent mindedness" (p. 163). Most think absentmindedness a bad thing. The absentminded professor is the butt of many jokes. However, the 'value'–as Milner suggests–of being absentminded could be that it saves psyche from collapse. To be not really there, not fully present but somewhere else serves as a defense mechanism against some painful memory. Absentmindedness is a sort of temporary erasing of pain and memory. Symptoms of absentmindedness present as a sudden clumsiness, saying stupid things, forgetting, or repeatedly locking the keys in the car. Freud called these parapraxis. Unconscious actions–such as these– point to some deeper psychic problem that cannot be gotten at directly because psyche overloads.

Waiting as an experience lends itself to absentmindedness. Especially when waiting goes on for a long time. Psyche is not totally there, but drifts. Psyche drifting in absentmindedness may feel like a slipping-into-nothingness. Psyche is neither here nor there. Absentminded psyche is psyche without mind. An absent mind might protect psyche from collapse. But when psyche is made absent what is left in its place? A hole in the heart of bodymind. A lack is all that is left. Psyche is probably always already filled with holes. Do these psychic holes ever go away? What is in a psychic hole? Is this a black hole like those found in outerspace? What does it mean to drift in outerspace? Being spaced out is being absentminded.

Is space made up of nothing? Or is all space filled with something? What is outer is also inner. Outerspace then is like innerspace. Are the Buddhists right in suggesting that at bottom we are nothingness? Are we not energy? And isn't it the case that energy never dies? Does that mean that some part of us never dies? Is that something, the soul? If psyche is nothing at bottom from whence does eros spring? Is desire an illusion?

Milner (1957) suggests that absent-mindedness is akin to reverie. But are these states the same? I am not sure that they are. And yet absentmindedness and reverie can be related by their opposing qualities. Reverie, at root, differs from absentmindedness. Waiting-as-reverie seems to be a dream-like, pleasant state of mind. Absentmindedness, contrarily, seems negative. Forgetting to do something is not pleasant. Losing car keys–because of absentmindedness–is not a good thing. Conversely, reverie is a state of grace, a gift. Reverie recalls clouds; absentmindedness makes thoughts stick in mud. Can these two psychic realities emerge simultaneously? Can psyche feel both reverie and absentminded at once? Can psyche be pulled in two directions at once? Yes. And that is the complication that is psychic life. I take my cue here from Gaston Bachelard (2000) who suggests that the psyche is dialectical in nature. He suggests that psychic states are hard and soft, earthy and of the clouds. Reverie is dreamy, absentmindedness muddy. Can psyche feel both dreamy and depressed at once? Yes. Bodymind trauma (like irreversibly damaging the arm) gets expressed in twos. The wish for the future is (dreamy); the reality check that cure will not come is (depression). Dream and depression simultaneously float through psychic mind. Or these psychological states might come in cycles, one after the other. In this case, manic depression might be at hand. Is it possible to experience both mania and depression at once? Yes. This might be termed insanity. No matter, psychic states are far more complex than words allow. Unconscious demons stir about even in reverie. Laughing hysterically in a moment of gravity is what Freud called reaction-formation. Wrong emotion at the wrong time. One might laugh and cry simultaneously when faced with trauma.

Reverie gets "worked", says Bachelard (2000, p. 60), by the hand, by matter, by resistance, by earthiness. Psychic realities are enmattered in the bodymind. Both reverie and absentmindedness are enmattered in the body and the body walks upon the earth. This is the lesson that Bachelard teaches throughout his writings.

The experience of waiting might be one of ecstasy *and* agony. To wait is to ride a rollercoaster of emotion. An emotional crash and burn comes eventually however. Psychic states–like the experience of waiting– might not be felt as a 'this or that', but rather as a 'this *and* that.'

When does reverie slip into absentmindedness; when does absentmindedness slip into reverie? Can they occur simultaneously? Hard to say. Yes. Anything is possible. And that is the daunting thing about psyche mind. Think of the possibilities. We cannot even imagine what these possibilities might be. So vast, as vast as the universe. Anything is possible. Is this not the lesson of the poets?

In talking about poetry, Bachelard (2002b) states,

if poetry is to reanimate the power of creation in the soul or help us to relive our natural dreams in all their intensity and all their meaning, we must come to understand that the hand [Bachelard's symbol for matter] as well as the eye [Bachelard's symbol for imagination] has its reveries and poetry. We must discover the poetry of the touch, the poetry in kneading hands. (p. 60)

The physical act of 'kneading hands', pulls dreamy states of reverie back down to the earth. For Bachelard, reveries–if one makes use of them– are reveries of the will, as the title of his book *Earth and Reveries of Will* (2002b) suggests. The work of 're-visioning' the soul–as James Hillman (1975) puts it in his book *Re-visionsing Psychology*– means putting visions to work via matter. Vision is enmattered. Whether we are speaking literally of seeing, or metaphorically of the vision of poets and seers, the body is where envisioning takes place. And to be out of one's mind with grief is still to be out of one's mind in the body.

Vision of the poet. The enmattered hand moves the pen to write the memoir; the enmattered hand moves the bow to play the cello. Music gets expressed via the hand which is part of the bodymind. Work the music by hand. To the listener it may seem that the music is of the heavens, for music can create perfect moments if it is done right. Music making seems ethereal but it is also grounded in the physical. Music making by its very nature is enmattered.

To wait in both anticipation and in despair. Ah. This is the problem at hand. To dread and anticipate what one waits for is a complicated emotional place to be. Jacques Derrida (1991), comments– in his piece titled "Plato's Pharmacy"– that for Plato the "pharmakon is both remedy and poison" (p. 127). Waiting is remedy and poison. But is remedy cure? No. Remedy might be a temporary healing, but not cure. There is clearly a difference. Reparation does not mean cure. Repair heals damage, yet the damage always remains at some level. There will always be a side effect to waiting no matter how curative the wait might seem. Waiting for the cure poisons. The more one remains hopeful– for a full recovery from injury– the more psyche gets poisoned. Psyche lies to herself for fear of the truth. Lies can sustain psyche for only so long and then everything falls apart. Psyche shatters eventually. The damaged musician looks to her hands for answers, as if the hands could speak. She looks at her wounded hands in utter disbelief and sorrow. How could this happen. What a cruel joke. Like the painter who goes blind, the musician who loses the ability to use her hands pains. The hands tell the truth that psyche cannot. Hands covering the eyes signal a gesture of unrelenting pain. Hands covering mouth in utter horror tell the hard truth of an enmattered psychic wound. Waiting is embodied. Waiting is an embodied psychic state. A heavy heart of bodymind. Wounded. The injured limb–or even the phantom limb in the case of amputees– feels heavy; the heart is heavy too in depression. Woundedness feels heavy, slow. As Maurice Merleau-Ponty (1968) suggests, the body has a sort of "thickness" (p. 135) about it. This "thickness" gets amplified when injury strikes. As the wounded limb gets thicker, depression thickens. Merleau-Ponty (1968) tells us that it is this feeling of thickness of the flesh that allows us to connect to the world. There is a certain thickness in our inter-relations with objects and with others.

The inner and outer are linked (but not meshed completely) via a feeling of thickness. Like Bachelard, Merleau-Ponty uses the 'flesh' as a symbol of the connecting point between sentient creatures and the world. Merleau-Ponty (1968) claims that the "touch [of the flesh or hand] is formed in the midst of the world. . . . and yet they do not merge into one" (p. 134). The hand, he says, is that thing which allows us to connect with the world but not blend in with the world. And yet, the world is not at loggerheads with sentient creatures either. The Cartesian dualism of us versus the world has been turned on its head by Merleau-Ponty. We do not stand against a world, but rather we are connected to a part of it, but not one with it. If we were one with the world, we would be psychotic. Psychotics cannot separate objects from themselves. They become objects, or stuck inside of objects. Clearly, then, objects and object-relations need difference, need that separation from the world to be connected to the world. This is Merleau-Ponty's point.

What kind of connection is formed with the world when the flesh is sick? Merleau-Ponty does not address sick flesh, wounded flesh. When the flesh is sick it must develop an altered relation to the world and to psyche's interior. Does the connection to the world hold at all? Can psyche unravel? When sick, injured, wounded—the psyche-soma disconnects on many levels. Psychological retreats may protect the ego from shattering. Psychic strictures grow from the injury. These are what we would call psychic scars. Psychic strictures harden, tighten, narrow inner life. Psyche suffocates. Suffocated by a mess. Everything seems a mess. Making sense of things–while psychically suffocated– becomes almost impossible. The tangled web we weave when wounded is a psychic suffocation that amplifies that mess.

The retreating psyche gets played out as a drama of gestures. A gesture of hands over eyes, or hands over mouth point to a crushed inner world. These gestures signal despair and shock. The poison of the wound is too strong. It is a question that is never answered, a death that comes too early, a melancholia that is never ending, a bodymind that no longer works. The heaviness of the world seems to be upon psyche's shoulders.

Antoine De Saint -Exupery (1992) talks of the "density" of one's "being" (p. 119). Likewise, Michael Chabon's (2000) protagonist, in his novel *The Amazing Adventures of Kavalier and Clay,* says that hard times make one seem "denser" (p. 554). The injured bodymind becomes more dense. The notion of density as a psychic state feels like the lead of depression, the heaviness of the wounded limb. Density is unspeakable doom that hangs over psyche. People who look at the ground while taking a walk have something on their minds. To have something 'on' the mind seems to make the mind denser. The head is heavy and the footsteps slow.

Thickness, retreat and density are clumsy words that poison. Waiting as a psychic state gets enthickend, poisoned, the further one retreats inward. Waiting-as-density is engestured. Eyes looking down to ground. Hands up to sky as if asking why. Waiting-as-thickness is the feeling of being fat. Enwrapped in suffocating flesh psyche gets stuck in thickness of mindbody. When suffocated by mindbody speech gets stultified. Tongue becomes enleadend. Or then there is speaking in tongues. Insane mania. Meaninglessness. The thickness cannot be spoken only babbled. Crazy words come. Nonsense. No sense can be made of manic utterances. Dense echolalia. Dense mumbling. Tripping over words. Suffocation.

Psyche might feel suffocated but it might also feel freed simultaneously. When life as we know it seems over, old trivial concerns matter no longer. The old worries of the past are washed away and a new freedom gets born. Perhaps this is what Bachelard (1994)– in his book titled *Poetics of Space*– means when he talks of "inner immensity" (p. 185). Bachelard (1994) comments that,

> it is often this inner immensity that gives their real meaning to certain expressions concerning the visible world. To take a precise example, we might make a detailed examination of what is meant by the immensity of the forest. For this "immensity" originates in a body of impressions which, in reality, have little connection with geographical information. We do not need to be long in the woods to experience the rather anxious impressions of "going deeper and deeper" into a limitless world. (p. 185)

Getting lost in inner immensity might be akin to insanity. Insanity might be– in a way–freeing. Insanity means anything is possible. Is that not freeing? Is this kind of freedom terrifying? Insanity is terrifying. We should never romanticize insanity because it is terrible. Getting lost in the immensity that is psychic space—if psyche does not lapse into insanity—could also be a visionary experience. Vision suggests immensity. Poets speak to this immensity. Small words can mean big things. Gestures are windows into a personality. Immensity might be best expressed in the smallest gestures.

"[G]oing deeper and deeper," Bachelard (1994, p. 185) says, into one's psyche-forest is going toward a no-man's land. There is no endpoint, no stopping. Deep inwardness keeps going deeper. Being trapped by deep inwardness makes a return to being-in-the-world difficult. How to get ego back from that space of deep interiority becomes the problem at hand. Non-articulateness, pre-verbal-ness is the site of inner immensity about which Bachelard speaks. Getting stuck in the pre-verbal troubles. Silence. Getting stuck in silence. Silence is not always golden. And it is not always resistance–as the psychoanalyst might argue–either. The silent patient in the psychoanalytic situation is not merely "resisting" the analyst's suggestions; the silent patient is lost in the wilder beast of a vast "immensity" where the way out cannot be found. The patient gets stuck in the middle of a nowhere and might not be able to come back. Psyche attempts to protect itself from invasion and intrusion by putting up a great wall of silence. Psychic death is at hand. Can the psychically dead be resurrected? Is there life after psychic death? When a part of the self dies, what happens to other parts of the self that do not die? Intrusions of other negativities push self deeper into a black hole of no return.

Waiting-in-a-state-of "inner immensity" can lead to vision–as I mentioned earlier– but it can also lead to psychic blindness. Because inner landscape of psyche daunts, one can no longer see. I am thinking here of snow blindness. Farley Mowat (2004), in *No Man's River*, tells a tale about experienced trappers in the Arctic who– along with their Huskies–get lost because of whiteouts. Snow blindness, in the Arctic, is a killer. Not being able to see anything but a blinding whiteness has caused many a trapper and Husky to lose their lives. Without a sense of direction, without landmarks, getting lost becomes a terrible possibility. Arctic travellers, as Mowat reports, freeze to death. Imagine, if you will, the landscape of the Arctic. Psyche is that arctic. The deeper the venture down into an inner psychic blizzard, the harder it is to find a way back to warmer climes. Frozen psyche. Rigid. Stuck. Cold. Silence is only the tip of the iceberg.

An accident on Mt. Hood means certain death. Three experienced climbers in December of 2006 lost their way. Rescue workers got faint clues as to the hikers' whereabouts. A cell phone signal, axes left in snow caves. Mt. Hood is enormous. Forbidding. The rescuers searched for days. The 'immensity' of the mountain was just too much. In the early hours of the search, journalists talked about hope. 'We are hopeful that we can find them.' Hope was dashed quickly when one body came home in a bag. The other hikers were not found. Maybe they will be found when the snow melts in springtime. We will have to wait and see. The nightmare of waiting. Do we really want to find out what happened? Can we stand it? Speculation. Avalanche? Did they fall to their deaths?

Mt. Hood could be a symbol of a psychic mountain. The higher the climb the more frozen the wasteland. We usually talk about the unconscious as a place deep down and buried under the ruins of psyche. But we could also think about the psyche as an immense snowy mountain. The sheer immensity of a psychic freeze baffles. Psychic whiteout. A perpetual winter-psyche paralyzes. A mountain of frozen waste. How to unfreeze psyche?

Inner immensity is akin to fog blindness. The fog is thick, dense. There is no exit–as Sartre might put it–from foggy psyche. The foggy psyche cannot function. Inner psychic fog colonizes.

Outer Fog –that is fog in the outer landscape– is particularly dangerous for motorcyclists. When visibility is zero and fog sets in there is a good chance of either driving off the road or of being hit by a car from the rear, side, or getting hit head on. If the motorcyclist pulls over to the side of the road, a car might drift onto the side of the road and collide with the motorcyclist. That means certain death for our motorcyclist. What choices are there? Think quickly and respond. Psychic fogginess is not dissimilar to the fog that motorcyclists battle on the road. Drifting off the road could mean death.

Dreams drift into unknown places. Foggy dreams terrify. Dreamer gets pushed off the royal road into unknown territory. If psyche is not ready to swerve from its path, collapse might ensue.

Interminable *Waiting* is like being trapped or lost in psychic fog, snow or forest. Being trapped. Being lost. An immense disastrous psychic mess. This is a frozen, fogged, enforested madness. The forests, snows and fogs of interiority alter perception. Time, space, season, height and depth become still. Is stillness what the dead are? Psychic death stills. All those who wait here– enter here. Where is here? Here is hell.

DREAMS, MEMORIES AND WAITING

One of the difficulties of exploring the notion of waiting is that it is a rather vague notion. The vagueness is always already a reminder of the remnants of archaic life. Feelings we have when we wait are both of the archaic and of the now. The archaic and the now get mixed up all the time. This is the lesson of Freud. Freud discussed the archaic nature of the psyche throughout his writings. He was fascinated by archaeology for this reason. The mind is a vast archaeological landmind. Freud teaches that psyche is, at bottom, rigid. Transference by its very nature is rigid. Psyche tends to get stuck in archaic rigidities. The more rigid psyche becomes the more likely psyche will collapse. Undoing rigid patterns is hardly simple or possible. Dreams give clues. But repetitious dreams–especially– are hard to understand. It is to the repetition that the dreamer must turn. Or she will be tormented always.

Wait it out. Repetitious dreams might stop one day. Wait it out. Images get blurred together, dreams pull material from the day before (Freud called this day residue). Concurrently, dreams pull from the deep past. Dreams seem to make sense at the time the dreamer dreams, but upon waking it is difficult to articulate dream feelings and dream images.

Dreams are vague. Jungians say, go to the image! Images are not transparent. Images are vague. Freud and Jung argued that one must freely associate around the images in the dream. The keys to the Kingdom of one's psychic past turn on free association. Free association rambles. Freely associating often surprises. Like the mark of a good writer, the good dreamer surprises. Surprises in dreams are also clues.

Memory, the root of dreams, **is vague**. One remembers things piecemeal, or not at all, or only sometimes. Memory may or may not correspond to reality. What really happened back then is not the point. There is no exact back then. Back then is embellished or made up. Memories are never clear. Old memories sometimes pop up out of nowhere. To suddenly remember something from childhood surprises. While one can remember the back then, yesterday's happenings remain fogged over by forgetfulness. Memories from the previous day cannot be articulated. If psyche constructs disturbing memories, what is one to do? Firstly, forget them. However, the more one tries to forget bad memories, the more they pop up in dreams. The disturbance must be given full weight and not pushed away. Eventually things come back, like specters. Jacques Derrida (1994) contends that "a specter is always a *revenant*. One cannot control its comings and goings because it begins by coming back" (p.11). Ghosts haunt bodyego. The worse the memory-specter the more it tries to come back. Over and over again the ghost comes back in a multitude of guises, dis-guises and utterances. Ghosts, if they are demon-ghosts make the dreamer feel awful. One feels so bad in fact that the badness cannot be expressed. The bad breast. The introjected bad internal object. Bad feeling is ultimately vague. Not only do we suffer from reminiscences, we suffer from not being able to articulate the way in which the old stuff of memory makes us feel. Badness explains little. Badness is a vague signifier. What to do in the meantime? **Wait out** the badness.

ADDRESSING VAGUENESS, VAGUELY

Vagueness springs from the unconscious and cannot be fully understood. But how to continue? How to address in language what is vague? This is the task at hand. It seems counterintuitive to attempt this. Perhaps it is. But sometimes what seems counterintuitive surprises. Andre Green (1999b) talks of "blank thought" (p.196). Is "blank" thought also vague? Are blank and vague the same things or are they different things? Is the experience of waiting both blank and vague? Green (1999b) tells us,

> . . . I have tried to understand the mechanisms involved in blank thought. I think that we would be able to understand it if we could imagine thinking, not only without images– without representation–but also without words to perceive what one thinks. (p. 196)

Is blank thought felt at the preverbal stage? Can a thought occur without an accompanying image? If there are no images is thought happening at all? If someone is blind, she may not have images but certainly has thought. Is thought ever separated out from emotions? Are emotions thoughts? Or are thoughts emotional? Madness.

Let us focus for the moment on what Green (1999b) calls 'blankness.' This is a peculiar state of being. What does it mean to be blank? What is a blank emotion? The vague feeling experienced while waiting might feel like blankness. Waiting-as-blankness? I do not know if the blankness is a form of thought exactly–as Green suggests above– perhaps it is not. Going blank. What is that? Is blankness like snow blindness, whiteouts, blanking out while performing a piece of music? What happens to the musician when she blanks out? The fingers may remember where to go–or maybe not– the mind goes blank, the image of the notes in one's head vanish. If the fingers do not remember and the mind goes blank, the musician stops; she seems frozen in mid air. She does not remember what to play. It seems that nothing works. When one goes blank it is as if memory has been sucked away. Nervousness–it seems–plays a role in blanking out on stage. What is nervousness about? Fear of performing is perhaps at root a fear of being vulnerable, a fear of revealing oneself. I am thinking here of Kevin Bazzana's (2007) fascinating biography of a child prodigy pianist named Ervin Nyiregyhazi. At one point in this pianist's career he suffered from terrible stage fright and went to great lengths to play despite his fears. Bazzana (2007) reports that

> He [Nyiregyhazi] had not had a real career for more than twenty years and had become. . . terrified of performing in public; he would give concerts only when starvation loomed. If only there were some way of presenting his art to the public without presenting himself, Nyiregyhazi mused. And so Parnes [his agent at the time] came up with a radical solution: Nyiregyhazi, billed only as Mr. X, could give a recital while wearing a black silk hangman's hood to disguise his identity. (p. 5)

This is a most bizarre way to handle stage fright. What must his audience have thought? Almost macabre. At any rate, soloists fear blanking out, forgetting the music. Soloists are supposed to perform having memorized the music. Only on occasion have I seen soloists appear while reading a score. I think it is rather ridiculous to make soloists memorize their music. It is in fact sadistic. It would be like giving a paper at a conference by heart. That is insane.

At any rate, blankness occurs for other reasons too. When the memory goes blank, neurological problems might be the cause. Blanking out is a terrible experience no matter what the cause. In blankness, time, space and place seem to be obliterated. Or–when a blank state arrives– a sort of meaninglessness may drag on and on interminably. When everyday is Sunday I would rather be dead. Sunday is the most meaningless day of the week.

A blank waiting is a dead stare. Frozen limbs. Nonfeeling, nonthinking zombification. Waiting-as-blankness can be absolutely paralyzing, like being stuck in time. Blank waiting is a blank emotionless state, a thoughtless state, a placeless and timeless state. Perhaps blankness is not thought at all, rather it is nonthought. There are moments in everyday life when psyche goes totally blank. What should I do now? Blank. Should I go to the park or continue working? Blank. Inside of this blankness is an emotional paralysis which may be a remnant of archaic psychic interference. Blankness is like stuckness. Standing in front of the refrigerator– blankly– looking in, closing the door, opening the door, closing the door. Not knowing what to eat or whether to eat at all. The mindless opening and closing of the refrigerator door serves little purpose. It is an experience of a nothing. However, turning to these seemingly nonsense experiences is where we might find out surprising things about ourselves.

Blank waiting can also feel as if psyche is not of this world anymore. Antoine De Saint-Exupery (1992) talks about his experience as a pilot as a sort of blank waiting. He states, "I remember, for my part, another of those hours in which a pilot finds suddenly that he has slipped beyond the confines of this world" (p. 14). At any moment in day to day life, the mind can sort of slip beyond the confines of the world. Is this madness? What does it mean psychically to slip into another world? Are you here or there or nowhere. What are the consequences of getting "beyond the confines" (Saint-Exupery, 1992, p. 14) of the mind? Is this a feeling of surrender or defeat? Is there no going back?

THE FROZEN TABLEAU OF GRANDMOTHER

An image that comes to mind here is one of the grandmother slowly rocking in her rocking chair. Head bent; hand holding up head. Blankly staring at the TV. She is not really watching TV at all. Off into some other space. The child calls out to her, "grandma? Are you there?" The grandmother does not answer. She does not even hear the child. Grandmother is blanked out. This disturbing state is one in which people fall all the time but probably do not pay much attention to. Falling into a black hole of psychic nowhere empties out personality. Is somebody at home? Is grandmother living? Or is this the beginning of dying, or is this the beginning of dementia? Is this symptomatic of depression? Is it nothing? Grandma is stuck in a frozen tableau. An artist could easily paint her portrait because she does not move, nor does she speak. She waits. But for what? It seems to the small child that grandmother does not want to be here, that she longs to be elsewhere. But where? What does it mean when someone falls into a sort of blankness, into a frozen tableau? Where is one falling into? How to get out of it? The grandmother is in an altered state of radical Otherness. Derrida (1988; 1992b; 1995; 2000) talks throughout his work of Otherness, differance—a deferred and delayed meaning— and alterity. If we focus for a moment on his notion of differance, we begin to understand that what we see, learn, read, think and do always already has deferred and delayed responses and consequences. The effects and affects of lived experience are not known at the time of their occurrence. Thus, the frozen tableau of the grandmother-as an example of alterity and differance—affects the child in ways we simply cannot know. Her image gets introjected into the psyche of the child and that introjection has complex meanings that might not surface for years to come.

I am not so certain that blankness is a form of 'thought' as Andre Green (1999b) suggests. Blankness is, rather, a vague feeling state without thought. Perhaps this is Bion's (1994) "thoughts without a thinker" (p. 309)? But if there is no thinker where are those thoughts to which Bion refers? Are they just floating in the air? I suggest that this thinker (who blankly waits) is not thinking at all. Rather, waiting-as-blankness is a return to an earlier primal experience before one is born– a Zen Koan. Waiting-as -blankness is like a veil coming down over one's eyes when the retina detaches; a cloud moving over vision leading to blindness. Waiting-as-blankness is felt as a cloud of unremembering. It is one thing to forget things. It is another thing entirely if one cannot remember five minutes ago, or yesterday. Short term memory seems to be shorting out. One feels surrounded, suffocated by a cloud of unremembering. The cloud of unremembering closes in on one unexpectedly. The cloud of unremembering gets bigger and bigger with each passing day. The closing in of the cloud of unremembering eventually becomes blankness, which is not thought at all. If life becomes one giant blankness, what kind of life is that? What waiting-as-blankness is, is hard to say exactly. In many respects, waiting-as-blankness just 'is'. This might be thought of as the 'isness' of waiting blankly. The Zen-like moment can become useful if one makes it so.

MORE ON THE INTER-RELATIONS OF DREAMING, WAITING AND UN-MEMORY

Waiting is inextricably tied to either the loss of memory (un-memory) or being stuck in memory. Can psyche get lost and stuck inside of a memory? Wait it out. Psyche will find her way out, or not. When one waits, things come up from the unconscious. Dreams surface especially in free association. If one is willing to wait for dream- meaning to arrive, some sense might be made of what seems to be nonsense. Meaning might be made of what is meaningless. Wait for the meaning of the dream to come. This takes time. Dreaming and waiting are inextricably tied. How does dreaming effect waiting? How does waiting effect dreaming? How do memories from the deep past work on waiting? Dreams of waiting? Is that purgatory? Did the notion of purgatory spring from a dream? Jung (1977; 1983) argued that myth and dream are of a piece. What could those dreams be teaching us? Is waiting a form of dreaming?

The grandmother is rocking in a rocking chair, head bent, hand holding up head staring at the TV but not really watching it. The child tries to rouse grandmother. Grandmother says, "Oh, I was dreaming." Daydreaming is what many do while waiting. Waiting–as–daydreaming. Daydreaming about the past can lapse into Nostalgia. Nostalgia is a frozen tableau. Nostalgia is not truth. Nostalgia is a lie. Nostalgia is a trap. Some people live inside of a sort of nostalgic waiting. We all get nostalgic from time to time, but getting stuck in nostalgia is something different. Nostalgia is like living in a time warp. It fills up the waiting. Does waiting have to be filled up with something? Maybe not. Is waiting, rather an empting out. Even blankness is something. Or is it? Is blankness nothing, is it really empty? Maybe it is. Maybe it is not. At any rate, the question here is what does one do with the waiting? When one waits in a nowhere space, where does psyche go? Nowhere? But what is this 'nowhere.' Again I turn to Andre Green (1993) who is helpful. In his book titled *On Private Madness,* Green talks about the curious problem of 'vanishing' patients. When grandmother does not answer the child, and does not even hear the child, where is she? Has she vanished psychically? What part of her has gone elsewhere? Or, has grandmother disappeared completely? Is grandmother an empty shell? Psychic vanishing occurs especially in traumatic situations. Disappearing is a psychic defense which paradoxically works to keep psyche together. But if psyche constantly vanishes disaster looms. Does there come a point when psyche disappears once and for all? Andre Green (1993) tells us,

> In many cases it appears that the ego as disinterested in itself as the object, leaving only a yearning to vanish: to be drawn towards death and nothingness. For me, this is the true expression of the death instinct. . . . (p. 13)

I would like to focus for a moment on Green's word "yearning". Green is right on the mark to suggest that the psyche–eventually– 'yearns' to stop. A yearning is a desire. Desire is movement. To desire is to want, to wish. A yearning is almost a plea, a cry in the wilderness. To *yearn* to vanish might hasten one's death. The thought of death can come as a relief to terminally ill patients who are suffering. Or thoughts of death might come as a relief to people who are just tired of it all. I am thinking here of the rather astonishing statement by Eve Sedgwick (1999), in her book called *A Dialogue of Love,* where she states that she has had "enough." She tells us that she is tired, sad and wants to stop living. Sedgwick (1999) says "[w]hen I tell you how bad it is, how hard I've worked at something, how much I've been through, there is only one phrase I want to hear 'That's enough, you can stop now.' Stop: living that is. And enough: hurting" (p. 69). Sedgwick's yearnings are –to me– shocking. One does not expect this will-to-death from a such an accomplished, successful, well respected scholar. Obviously, being accomplished and successful mean very little. In some cases–ironically–it is the very nature of success that leads to collapse.

The scholarly life is one of absurdity. Some of us feel an inward drive to read everything in the library. Being on a university campus with a great library excites. What is it about the library? What is it about the words of others? Perhaps the library holds keys to psychic archives. Reading the words of others allows us to get to know ourselves better. Do scholars always already write autobiographically? Perhaps. But coded. Many creative artists write autobiographically. Novels are really veiled autobiographies. Poems–in the case of someone like Anne Sexton–are highly autobiographical. We know from biographer Janet Malcolm (2007) that everything Gertrude Stein wrote was autobiographical. Are we always writing about ourselves?

Psyche has a passion to find out about itself. But she can only find out about herself by writing about others or thinking through others. Studying and writing allows psyche to articulate that which is unconscious. Interestingly, biographer Virginia Spencer Carr (2004) reports that Paul Bowles engaged in a sort of automatic writing. Things just sort of came to him. Is this not the work of the unconscious? Is this the unconscious wanting to know more about its own workings? Bowles had a terrible relationship with his father, Carr tells us. Did this shape Bowles' unconscious? Did he have to express what he deeply repressed because of the violent explosions he witnessed? Do creative writers have to have a demented father, a violent father, an abusive mother, or a dead mother to write? How about scholars? What are they expressing? Some unconscious hatred toward the bad breast?

BACK TO WAITING-AS-VANISHING

What is it to wait in a state when the ego dissolves? Nobody is at home. To vanish means to go away? But where is away? That is the strange thing about vanishing. Where do we go when we disappear? To what use do we put that disappearance? These are the kinds of questions that Adam Phillips (1995; 1996; 1997a; 1997b; 2000; 2001; 2002) asks throughout his work. People who are victims of abuse– both physical and emotional– develop the capacity to vanish as a way of protecting the psyche. Vanishing is a gift or it is a curse. Or maybe it is a talent. Vanishing can serve as a defense mechanism against pain. Virginia Spencer Carr (2004) tells us that Paul Bowles disappeared into his private world as a child to escape the abuse of his father. And perhaps it was this creation of the private world, the fictive world that led him to become the creative artist that he was. Vanishing into a make believe world can be made useful. Vanishing becomes an art and a profession. Writing can be used to make psyche disappear.

Playing an instrument can have the same effect. Repetition–the key to practicing– makes psyche go away. There is something about repetitive work that makes psyche vanish. Playing an instrument might be used as a protective measure against abusive parents. Musicians–like dancers–experience a sort of disappearance while performing. The performance seems to be automatic. Observing ego watches from above. This experience only comes after much waiting. And practice. If conscious ego is too present during a performance it can spoil the flow of things because it keeps getting in the way. Disappearing while playing can be spiritual. It is as if the musician is not *willing* her hands to play; the hands seem to play by themselves. The musician–some believe– is merely the channel through which music flows. And this is exactly what Paul Bowles reported to Virginia Spencer Carr (2004) about his writing. Bowles was also a composer and I wonder if his composing gifts were experienced in the same way as his writing gifts.

One must wait for the gift of musical genius to arrive. It arrives on its own and must be nurtured or else it vanishes. But what happens when the gift is unwanted? What if the music feels like more of a burden? Does one give the gift back? When one gives back a gift where does it go? A Winnicottian question. If injury occurs and the musician becomes incapable of expressing that gift, what happens? What kind of a life might it be where the innate expressions given freely must be dropped? What does it do to psyche when psyche cannot do what it is supposed to do? What does it mean to live a life without being able to allow a gift to flourish? This gift gets sublimated. Or repressed. Re-channeled. Or not. One must wait and see what psyche allows. If the gift is not re-channeled and remains buried deeply in the soul, what kind of a life would that be? Waiting for another gift to arrive. But the new gift never does arrive. The letter is never opened. The passage is not taken. The experience is not experienced. Death in life is a life not lived. When you cannot do what you were called to do, what do you do? What can you do? Wait. Wait for a sign, for a messiah, for a hero or a goddess, for a message or a handkerchief. Alas, the sign, the messiah, the hero and goddess, the message and handkerchief never arrive. Or maybe the check is in the mail. Is the new gift arriving tomorrow? Or is it all over.

When undergoing psychoanalysis, psyche must also wait. The waiting that goes on in analysis is experienced by the patient and analyst in different ways. For the patient the waiting might be the waiting-in-fear, waiting-in-anxiety, waiting-in-anticipation, waiting-in silence. Before the patient walks into the analyst's office, she must wait, in a waiting room. And then there is waiting for the transference to come. Wading through that transference. And finally waiting for the transference to be over. But do we ever get rid of transference? No, so therapy is never over. Ah, the interminable profession.

The analyst may feel some of these kinds of waiting(s) too. The analyst waits-in-a-countertransference mode. The analyst waits in-a-motherly-mode. The analyst waits-in-a-holding mode. What makes these various modes-of-waiting possible? How does the analyst shut off the outside world or her ongoing inner commentary to just BE. Waiting-as-Being is the analyst's waiting mode. Let us address here, for a moment, the nature of shutting out chatter, clatter, the outside world and inner turmoil around which the analyst must work. Talking about the work of Wilfred Bion, Gerard Bleandonu (2000), tells us that Bion insisted that the analyst must detach "memory, desire and understanding" to do good work. Is this the imperative, then, to become blank? Can going blank be productive? Bleandonu (2000) reminds us that

The suspension of memory, desire and understanding would seem not only to be in direct opposition to the established psychoanalytic technique and practice, but also to duplicate what in fact occurs in severely regressed patients. (p. 222)

Bion's imperative of shutting off basic ways of knowing the world– memory, desire and understanding– is not dissimilar from the basic tenets of Buddhism. Emptiness is the key to Buddhism. What is 'is'. Desire leads astray. Mark Epstein (1996) comes to mind here as he relates Buddhism to psychoanalysis. This is an interesting pairing. The striking thing is the way in which Epstein talks about the Buddhist idea of "bare attention" (p. 8). Is bare attention the same experience as going blank? What kind of attention is, in fact, bare? Can one pay attention but not think or feel anything? Buddhist thought suggests that there is no essential self, the self is made up of elements like the earth and stars, but the center (of the essential body) does not hold. Interestingly enough, Epstein (1996)–coming from the Buddhist perspective– explains that analysts need to "float" (p. 17). Freud talked about the importance of free floating attention. How to do this, if it can be done at all?

Thus, another kind of waiting emerges here. Waiting-as-Floating-as-bare attention-as free-floating attention. The patient might have trouble getting to the stage where she can feel free-floating. It is nearly impossible to stop internal censors that inhibit psychic freedom. Do we ever achieve psychic freedom? Is this not one of the goals of going into analysis? What would we be like if we did achieve psychic freedom? Would that be like floating? Adam Phillips (1997) asks, "[c]an one teach people to float, in their minds–" (p. 101). I do not think we can teach people to float. By the time most patients arrive in therapy, too many psychological barriers are already in place. Some psychic walls can be knocked down, if the patient waits long enough. However, most psychic walls never fall down. For those who have an overly stern superego, inner psychic life is a dictatorship. Up go the great walls of psyche. Behind the iron curtain of psyche. But we know from our history that walls do come crumbling down and iron curtains collapse. But what replaces them? I am not so sure that democracy comes easily, if at all. Psychic democracy might never come.

Talented analysts probably are able to float psychically. I would imagine that arriving at this state takes years of training and years of work with patients. The analyst who floats along with the patient's narrative is perhaps better able to freely listen, and she might even listen more intently than the preoccupied therapist. Being preoccupied prevents bare attention and floating. If both analyst and "severely regressed" patient (Bleandonu, 2000, p. 222) float together, where do they go? Adam Phillips might ask this sort of question. I am asking it too.

The underlying question of this book is about the 'maybe not.' It is easier to think that wounds will heal, that scars will go away, that diseases have cures, that sad stories have happy endings. But what if they do not? This is the question. Most people run from this question. People have a difficult time dealing with that which is irreversible and incurable. We would like to think that in the end it all works out. But for many it does not .The mistake people make is reassuring others that things always work out, that god has a divine plan. Truth of the matter is that for some, things do not work out. There is no god. And certainly no plan. And there is very little that is divine when psyche gets wrecked.

PSYCHOANALYSIS, TEACHING AND MUSICIANSHIP: THINKING BACK BEFORE INJURY

Let us take a moment to think more thoroughly about the interconnections between psychoanalysis, curriculum studies and music. Let us begin by making connections. As in any profession, the key to doing good work is to be fully there psychically. Thinking more psychoanalytically through education and through music is what I attempt to do in this book. Thinking psychoanalytically means to get out from under psychic freezes and to allow psyche to be one hundred and twenty percent present —to BE THERE in the Buddhist sense. The 'isness' of the psychoanalytic hour–the intensity of that hour–might carry over into the professions of professor or musician. The absent minded professor is not present, nor is the musician who is not focused during practice or performances. Psychoanalysis helps psyche focus and get back a basic intensity that somehow got lost. More importantly, psychoanalysis becomes most helpful to the professor or the musician whose life has been thwarted or even destroyed. Intensity can be re-channeled. Otherwise psyche dies. A psyche without intensity is as good as dead. Is it possible to get intensity back after devastating injury or psychological woundedness? Sometimes it is not possible to get intensity back. Then what? What kind of life is it when spirit has flatlined? Gertrude Stein according to Janet Malcom (2007) uttered on her deathbed "what is the question. . . If there is no question then there is no answer" (p. 172). What *is* the question? And what if there *is* no answer? The question I raise in this book has no answer. If a person is so destroyed, so wrecked psychically or physically and she cannot get her intensity back, what to do? I do not know the answer to this question. Throughout this book I struggle with this unanswered question because I want so to find an answer, to find a way out. To give up in the face of catastrophe is always a dangerous possibility. I argue that we must find a way out but also admit that for some there is–as Sartre would put it–no exit.

THE PSYCHOANALYST AND THE TEACHER: A LINGERING DEBT OF GRATITUDE

For the patient, the experience of the analyst's 'isness' can be felt. Sometimes the therapist's isness is emotionally overpowering. The isness, the thereness of the psychoanalyst is almost too much for the patient who is not used to such attention. Therapy, of course, is more than listening intently. But it begins always with the ear.

Teaching is not dissimilar to analysis. The teacher who listens–intently– to students is rare. Good teaching always begins with the ear. Teaching might even be more about listening than lecturing. Ted Aoki (2005) speaks to these issues most profoundly. A title of one of his essays is this: "The Sound of Pedagogy in the Morning Calm." A beautiful title. Brent Davis (1996) remarks that a sound pedagogy is one that takes into account sound, the ear. Interestingly enough Ted Aoki ends many of his essays with the phrase "a lingering note." Take note of the word 'note.' A note could be a footnote or it could be a musical note. And as mentioned elsewhere in this book Aoki was one of the earliest curriculum scholars to make connections between music and curriculum studies. My work can be seen, in part, as an expansion of Aoki's and Davis's thought. I owe both of these curriculum scholars a debt of gratitude.

Like the good analyst and good teacher, the good musician is able to listen intently not only to her instrument but to her emotions. Music is primarily emotional. Expression comes from the gut, heart and soul. Of course, the score must be studied–and study is primarily an intellectual act–although one can never separate out the intellect from the emotions. The musician must be aware of the sounds she produces and the actual physical strain it takes to produce the wanted sounds. Every "lingering note" –as Aoki (2005) puts it– must linger in the gut and the ear. Music is not about technique, although many think that it is. Of course, musicians must develop technique in order to be able to express the wanted sound. Getting the wanted sound means that the musician must pay close attention and not drift off.

The inattentive analyst, teacher and musician cannot express what they set out to express. Bad days are many. Depressions spill over. Too many distractions. Too split off. Too detached. Analyst, teacher and musician engage in a great deal of repetition. The analyst asks particular questions to different patients over and over again; the practice session for the musician is built on hours and hours of repetition. The teacher teaches the same book over and over or plays with the same idea in different forms throughout a career. The mundane, repetitive nature of work–whatever that work may be– can get in the way of the project at hand. Repetition can bog psyche down. But it is only through repetition that freedom comes. In any profession the long term goal is freedom. Freedom to be able to express the soul is what we are after here.

The analyst must learn also the repetitive nature of the patient's illness. Repetition compulsion can make one sick literally. Undoing repetition that thwarts internal freedom is key when doing analysis. In music, however, the musician must always repeat because the hands are stupid. One cannot simply stop repeating or technique goes down the drain. And on fretless stringed instruments–like the cello or violin– the hands forget where the notes are if they are not continually reminded. It does not matter how advanced the musician, repetition is a must. Passages must be repeated over and over again to get them right. Being a good musician also requires much patience. Waiting in the repetition until the passage becomes automatic. But not automaton. The soul of a musician must always be at work even in the repetition.

There comes a time in one's life when no more teachers are needed; there comes a time in one's life when no more analysts need be consulted; there comes a time in life–for those who get injured– when music has to be given up because of injury. There comes a time in the life of the professor– because the academy so wounds psyche–to retire. Do something else. How to do something else? Is it even possible?

THE DEAD MOTHER: THE DEAD SOUL

I am thinking of Camus' (1989) *The Stranger*. The main character in the novel is named Meursault. The name *Mersault* is most closely related to *la Mere and la Mer,* to mother and to ocean. *Mersault* murders someone on the beach with a gun *(made of metal or matter la Matiere)* and he uses his hand, *(la main)* to pull the trigger near the ocean *(la mer)*. His crime–according to the townspeople–is not so much the murder as it is the lack of tears shed at his mother's funeral. Mersault has a dead soul. The death of the soul is the absurdity and the crime. Not showing emotion at his mother's funeral makes him a criminal. Not crying becomes a criminal act. This seems *absurd,* and that is Camus' point. *The Stranger* is a very strange book. We read on the first page a most absurd passage. Mersault tells us,

> Maman died today. Or yesterday, maybe, I don't know I got a telegram from home: "Mother deceased. Funeral tomorrow. Faithfully yours." That doesn't mean anything. Maybe it was yesterday. (p. 3)

That this death of his mother means nothing to Mersault is rather strange. This is certainly a predicament worth looking into. Who are we to judge? Lack of emotion means criminality. But does it? Is it criminal to have a dead soul? Is it criminal to not care? Is it criminal to be indifferent? Is it criminal to give up? Is it criminal to be resigned to a fate that is deathlike? Is a dead soul a criminal one? We are taught in the Western tradition that giving up is bad. Giving up or being resigned is termed nihilism. I do not care whether mother died today or yesterday. What difference does it make? These are Camus' points. But throughout his work he argues that he is not a nihilist. And what if he were? Does *The Stranger* lend itself to a nihilistic interpretation. What if–after a catastrophe–psyche gives up? Is that okay? Is that a morally defensible response to trauma? In the Western tradition, the answer to this question is plainly no. Giving up is not an option. But why is it so? Do we not have the right to choose–as the existentialists point out–the way in which we want to live our lives? Were the ancient Stoics not resigned? And what is wrong with resignation? Perhaps we need to rethink this idea and rethink Camus' message. Perhaps we need to trouble the notion of resignation. Is a dead soul criminal? Or is it a choice and a right? Now, I am not arguing that this is my choice or my thesis. My own life is not built on resignation and indifference. In fact, the theme of this book is finding a way out. I am always looking for the way out. I hope that there never comes a day when I cannot find the way out. On the other hand, thinking with Camus and through Camus, I am suggesting that if someone chooses to live a dead life, that is their choice and we are not to judge that. We should not make criminal the one who has a dead soul. Is this not Camus' point? Thus, the retiring professor, the wounded musician, the teacher who has no more lessons to teach are all like Mersault. They might not cry at leaving behind their professions. And it is not for us to judge them.

WAITING AND PSYCHE: THE END AND THE BEGINNING

We end this chapter by returning to the notion of waiting. I began this chapter talking of waiting; I end the chapter going back to the beginning and once again raising the issue of waiting as it relates to psyche.

Waiting as a psychic state is much more complex than I am able to articulate here. The feelings associated with waiting are nearly beyond representation. Waiting in its most primal form cannot be articulated. There are two kinds of waiting which are impossible to articulate. I am thinking here of waiting to be born and waiting to die. We cannot know what it means to wait to be born. Otto Rank (1993), as is well known, suggested that being born is *the* crisis. Being born is the trauma of all traumas. Waiting in the womb for that trauma to happen is of course an unknowable state. Waiting to die, however, is something else. We can articulate it. But we still do not understand what exactly we are waiting for.

"Whatever waiting is, it is" –as M. Masud R. Khan (1989) points out in his book titled *The Long Wait* – a "core experience" (p. 188). Everybody waits. Of course we think of Samuel Beckett's (1958) *Waiting for Godot* or the prophet Elijah. Setting the Friday night sabbath table means setting a place for Elijah and opening the door for his arrival. But–in good Deriddean fashion–the arrivant never comes. We wait for a revenant and are haunted by the specter of Elijah. When waiting the center will not hold. Christopher Bollas (1996) –- in his book *Cracking Up: The Work of the Unconscious*– declares that sentient creatures have "millions of psychic intensities" (p. 69). And these millions of psychic intensities are also millions of psychic watings. Waiting happens in millions of ways. Waiting–as a state of being– is endless and is always already happening. We are always already waiting in one form or another. We do not give much thought to waiting because we are always waiting. We need a certain distance between waiting and exploration of what the waiting means. So, *what* are we waiting for? Let us get on with this discussion and examine the question, for what do we wait?

WHAT ARE WE WAITING FOR?

What is it that we are waiting for? Many are waiting for a god, a prophet, the end of the world, the end of school, the beginning of psychoanalysis, the mother who affirms, the father who kicks the habit, the teacher who becomes mentor, the book to be published, the month to be over, the salary that gets raised, the lover who comes back from the war. We all wait for different things. But what is the deeper meaning of the idea of 'waiting for'? I hope to explore this question as we move forward.

In F. Scott Fitzgerald's (1993) novel titled *The Crack-Up*, a character named 'F' says,

> The girl hung around under the pink sky waiting for something to happen. There were strange little lines in the trees, strange little insects, unfamiliar night cries of strange small beasts beginning. (p. 135)

Whatever we are waiting for–mostly– we wait for 'something to happen.' That 'something' may be strange, as Fitzgerald's character suggests. Sometimes the longer the wait the stranger it gets. What are F's "strange small beasts"? Thoughts get stranger and stranger as they begin to take on a life of their own. Obsessing over the what-will-come-next can be maddening. Here I am thinking of Jean-Paul Sartre's (1964) novel titled *Nausea*. Waiting for meaning to emerge may take on a dimension of the grotesque. Antoine Roquentin–the protagonist of Sartre's strange novel– describes his encounter with a chestnut tree. Antoine says,

> How long will this fascination last? I was the root of the chestnut tree. Or rather I was entirely conscious of its existence. Still detached from it–since I was conscious of it–yet lost in it, nothing but it. An uneasy conscience which, notwithstanding, let itself fall with all its weight on this piece of dead wood. Time had stopped: a small black pool at my feet . . . . I was inside; the black stump did not move, it stayed there, in my eyes, as a lump of food sticks. . . .
> (p. 131)

Encountering a tree in all its existential heaviness is a strange experience if one allows it to become strange. Most people pay little attention to trees or nature or to the wild world. We do not have time in this rush-rush society to stop and smell the roses or anything for that matter. However, if one takes the time to take in psychologically the beautiful, the absurd and the grotesque, surprises *await*. But one must wait for such an experience. William James (1998) suggested that "truth happens" (p. 97). Well, Chestnut trees–like the one in Sartre's' novel– *happen* too. Trees happen when they make an impression on the person who waits and watches. Trees happen to matter–that is, they become meaningful– when one waits for them to unveil meaning. Descriptions of raw existence–Sartre suggests–nauseate. In moments of intense waiting, objects tend to merge with psyche–as in the case of Roquentin–and when this happens nausea sets in. This is what psychoanalysts term projective-identification. Or, one might put it this way. Psychotics feel as if they get stuck in objects. Imagine being stuck–psychically–inside of a chestnut tree. I suppose if you wait long enough, and focus long enough on an object, you could get frozen inside of that object. Perhaps we should not wait too long for meaning to emerge while sitting in front of objects. They could over-take us.

WAIT A MINUTE!! THAT CLOUD LOOKS LIKE A MONKEY!!

Clouds, oceans, rivers, animals–when stared at long enough– seem to take on human characteristics. We tend to anthropomorphize things in the natural world, which some scientists say is a mistake. Nonetheless, we do it. Anthropomorphism happens. Clouds change shapes and morph into different animals. Clouds become horses, dogs, cats. Trees smile, animals smile too, especially wolves and huskies (probably because of their markings around their mouths). Staring at a cloud or a tree opens the door to strange perceptions. One might begin to see things that are not really there. Yet, hallucinations–to the one who hallucinates–seem real. Psychic reality is real. Perhaps we see in objects what we want to see. Seemingly mundane things take on a strangeness if one waits for this strangeness to emerge. That cloud looks like a monkey! Wait a minute!!

W.R. Bion (2000) tells us that: "Freud, in his obituary notice of Charcot, lays great stress on, and was enormously impressed by Charcot's idea of going on staring at an unknown situation until a pattern begins to emerge. . ." (p. 313). In the psychoanalytic sense, the analyst must wait for patterns to emerge in the patient's life story, in gestures, feelings, wishes and demands. The patient reveals patterns over time. Moreover, in psychoanalysis, dream work is all about recognizing patterns and making meaning of those patterns through free association. Free associations–although free–are still patterned. We must be patient to allow those patterns to emerge. The unconscious is highly patterned even though it seems be free floating. Dreams seem fluid but repeating themes emerge over time to suggest that the unconscious is actually quite rigid. Repetition compulsion means getting stuck in patterns that kill eros. Continually repeating destructive behavior is symptomatic of the rigidity of psyche. The death of eros–resulting from repeated destructive acts– is the death of the soul. If we wait long enough, the soul dies naturally. But if we are impatient we could inadvertently kill the soul.

One goes into analysis to recapture the meaning making that is soul work. The patterns that arise from dreams and those that get acted out in lived experience, however, are not easy to untangle. The analyst is needed so that the patient is able to make meaning from the seemingly meaningless patterns that choke off a life. It takes years of analysis–if one is lucky and has a good analyst– to understand some of the patterns that lead down the path toward destruction. The death drive is negatively patterned on destructive images, feelings and behaviors.

Waiting for patterns to emerge is also a keystone to scholarship. In scholarship patterns emerge from reading and studying. Scholarship is all about finding patterns that help make meaning across texts. Like analysis, developing good scholarship– having things to say that truly are one's own– takes years. Patterns emerge out of the notes taken, years of reading and studying. Intellectual work needs time. It just does not just happen on its own. The scholar must wait. She must be patient.

Of course music is all about patterns emerging. Playing the Bach Suites on the cello is a good case in point. Bach was particularly fond of mathematical patterns. His music fits well in the hand because of these patterns. Some composers–however–write in such a way that the music does not fit well in the hand because the patterns are too all over the place. This is why Bach is such a pleasure to play. The patterns are built for the hand. Again, the musician must wait to find these patterns. Learning the Bach Suites is about learning the patterns of the hand. Bach's Cello Suites are intense because of the tight patterns around which the phrases turn. And it is this tightness of the patterns that makes for profound listening.

Reading Paul Bowles–like playing Bach–is an intense experience. (and by the way Bowles was also a composer). Paul Bowles' (1977) character in the novel *The Sheltering Sky* , makes much of "ribbed pink canyon walls" (p. 160). Interestingly enough, much like Sartres' Roquentin, the character in Bowles' novel talks about his "intense" existential experience–not with a tree–but rather with the sky.

> He did not look up because he knew how senseless the landscape would appear. It takes energy to invest life with meaning, and at present this energy was lacking. He knew how things could stand bare, their essence having retreated on all sides to beyond the horizon, as if impelled by a sinister centrifugal force. He did not want to face the intense sky, too blue to be real, above his head, the ribbed pink canyon walls lay on all sides in the distance. . . . (p. 160)

The striking thing here –when we compare this to Sartre's (1964) novel *Nausea*– is that when nature emerges as patterns– as objects with their own "essences" and characteristics– it all becomes rather "grotesque" (as in Roquentin's encounter with the Chestnut Tree) or "sinister" (as in Bowles' (1977) *The Sheltering Sky*.) Bowles' character says the sky is too "intense." Primal nature in its starkness, in its violence and beauty, in its colourful hues and uglinesses shock. Most are not open to taking in the "bare" (Bowles, 1977, p. 160) and skeletal 'isness' of things. Dwelling on the 'isness' of things means that one must wait for the 'isness' to emerge. The isness is made up of patterns. And some of these patterns are too hard to take in psychologically. The universe is a violent place. The "too real" (p. 16) is at once everyday and surreal. There is something boring, shocking, nauseating about primal things. Experience of the primal sets off many juxtaposed and seemingly unrelated feelings. Boredom is a response one might have while staring at the sky. Boredom could turn to "energy" (Bowles, 1977) as shapes seem to appear out of nothing, colours brighten, textures deepen. As Bachelard (2002b) suggests the material world is energy and it is motion, it is not dead or static by any means. Matter needs 'work,' Bachelard declares. The hand must 'work' matter to make it take on meaning and spur imagination. The inert is–in reality–not inert at all. The inert is in motion. To feel a primal landscape is to 'work' it intellectually and emotionally. Bowles (1977) worked with images in order to make meaning of the sky. Think of all the qualities of nature Bowles 'worked' to make meaning. Pink, ribbed, too blue, sinister, intense.

Many do not see or understand the notion of a "sheltering sky." To miss what is directly perceived suggests preoccupation. To focus on the basic "isness" of life as it gets expressed as a sheltering sky or a nauseating tree means thinking in the realm of the symbolic. Nature *happens* in most peculiar ways. Nature is a symbolic representation.

Peter Matthiessen (1987), on a trip to Nepal, waited for the famed snow leopard to appear but it never did. The reader gets anxious toward the middle of the book wondering if this guy will ever find his snow leopard. Mattheissen- a Buddhist– suggests that if you are not ready to encounter a snow leopard, you will not. If you are not ready to encounter a sheltering sky or a nauseating tree you will not. If you do nothing with what you do find, you will live a meaningless, pointless life. Making use of patterns is what the soul does. What we wait for–most primordially– is a pattern to take shape so we can make sense of things.

WAITING FOR SOMETHING THAT NEVER ARRIVES

What else are we waiting for? Children wait for the school year to be over, professors wait to be tenured. We wait in airports. We wait for the newspaper to come. We wait for the concert to begin. We wait for the phone to ring. We wait for the evening news. We wait to fall asleep. Some wait longer than others. We wait to be rescued from a fire. We wait to be rescued from ourselves. We wait for the messiah. There are a million waitings-for. Most of our waitings-for happen. Or do they? The school year does come to an end, professors sometimes get tenured, our loved ones hop off of planes–god willing– to greet us, the newspaper comes, the concert does begin and the phone does ring. The evening news does come on and we eventually do fall asleep.

Bit what if what we wait for never arrives? The musician waits to heal from an injury to get back to playing music. The scholar waits until the wounded psyche heals to continue writing. But for some the wait never ends and the return back to the work of the profession never happens. The musician who waits to heal, never does. The scholar who waits to begin writing again never does. What happens then? What kind of a life is that? David Peterson (2005) in his book titled *On the Wild Edge: In Search of a Natural Life*, talks about waiting for winter to be over. He states,

> Even so, I admit to being tired of winter right now, eager to put away the snow shovel and get back to walking on nice dark dirt and rock. Happily, we haven't much longer to wait. (p. 67)

Waiting for something that will never happen is encountering the winter of the soul. We grow tired of the soul's winter–yes–because it is a season of hardship and struggle. But musicians who can no longer play can never walk again on "nice dark dirt and rock". The winter has become interminable. If psychic winter is interminable, why are we waiting for that which will never arrive? Spring will never arrive for the damaged musician. How long do we wait for winter to be over? What do we do while we wait? What happens if we wait no longer? To continue to wait for something that does not come maddens and depresses.

The most primal waiting is for the mother. But what if the mother (like the health of the musician) never comes back? If the mother is not good enough, she simply never arrives. What is the child to do? Andre Green (1999b)– in his book titled *The Work of the Negative*– tells us that Winnicott,

> suggests that the traumatic experiences which have tested the child's capacity to wait for the mother's longed-for response, lead, when this response is not forthcoming, to a state where only what is negative is felt to be real. What is more, the effect of these experiences is such that it spreads to the whole psychic structure. . . . (p. 5)

The mother freezes out the child so that her connection with the child poisons. The mother who freezes out the child is a winter mother. She will never be found on the other side in the tropics. In fact, she is found nowhere. The empty chair at the funeral. She is never there. The child continues to wait for the mother to defrost but she never does. The child utters an interminable cry, but her cry gets lost in the frozen wilderness. Even as an adult–the child in the adult–still waits interminably for her mother who never arrives. The mother will never come to the child. Still, the child waits. The dim hope that the mother will hear the child's cry is dashed repeatedly. The mother who never arrives is a specter haunting the forsaken children. This mother-specter becomes a demon–in the child's psyche. Demon colonizes psyche. The demon cannot be killed. The demon-mother who never arrives is a frozen tableau. Interminable waiting drives one mad, because at heart one knows–and yet does not believe–that these primal connections will not be fixed. One looks for the absent mother everywhere to no avail. As Andre Green (1999b) suggests, the whole of the psychic structure turns negative for the forsaken child. The problem, then, is what to do with this negative psychic structure? Forever haunted by the feeling that something is always wrong. W.R. Bion (1993) tells us that the "[i]nability to tolerate frustration can obstruct the development of thoughts and the capacity to think. . ." (p.113). How much frustration–about the missing mother– can one take? Doesn't there come a point at which psyche breaks down? Forsaken children secretly believe that one day the mother will come back and yet they know–at some level– that she will never come back. This is the unthinkable. And yet one must think it. How to think the unthinkable? Jan Abram (2000) comments on Andre's Green's work and helpfully clarifies. Abram tells us that,

> Green points out that there are two aspects of the negative. In one there is destruction and foreclosure– an attack on insight and the analytic setting–and the other, the work of the negative (which is instigated by the analytic relationship), contains the potential to bring the unthought known into consciousness . . . . (xiii)

Psyche can drown in the negative or *use it*–as Green suggests– or *work it* as Bachelard would put it–to find a way out. Recall, Bachelard (2002b) makes much use of the word 'work'. Psyche must *work* matter in order to fully express the imagination. Similarly, here with the case of Andre Green, the negative must be worked on so that one can live a better life. But how to work on the negative? What possible meanings are made while working on what is negative? Working the 'unthought known' for Andre Green means working what is known but cannot be thought. The unthought known is something that is dimly intuited. It is too hideous to think. And yet, psyche knows it at some level. The unthought known is the winter of the soul. It is only through the 'work of this negative', Green suggests, that psyche finds '*the voyage out*' as Virginia Woolf (2004) puts it.

Does working the negative always make the negative go away? Sometimes not. Working the negative can amplify the horror. W.R. Bion (1994) talks about the importance of "negative capability" (p. 304). Here, he suggests that if the patient is able to tolerate the negative–to put up with it, to let it have its way, to really experience what is horrific– psyche is better off. If psyche has little capacity for dealing with the negative, on the other hand, psyche may just crack. There is the negative and then there is the Negative. Perhaps one can deal with negatives (envy, jealousy, rage) but not the negative (horrors of an abusive childhood). Sentient creatures are only able to handle so much tragedy. One hopes that after a while– if one just *waits* long enough–time will heal all wounds. But time does not heal all wounds. Some wounds are so deeply embedded in the negative–which structures the psyche– that there is no getting out of it. For some, no amount of working through will heal psyche.

THE MOTHER WHO NEVER ARRIVES. THE MUSICIAN WHO CAN NO LONGER PLAY. THE PATTERNS.

The child's disconnect with the not good enough mother is not dissimilar to the primal disconnect the musician experiences when she can no longer play. When one's chosen lifework has been, for one reason or another, destroyed one's most basic psychic structure get destroyed. The psychic disconnect of that of the forsaken child is likened to the psychic disconnect of that of the forsaken musician.

PARABLE OF THE SNOW LEOPARD

When I began the groundwork for this study, I deliberated for some time on my title, *On Not Being Able to Play*. Firstly, I wanted to honor Marion Milner's (1957) *On Not Being Able To Paint*, for I found that her book illuminated ideas across the arts, psychoanalysis and education. Marion Milner helped me formulate my thoughts on the place of the arts in our lives. And she made me think more deeply about scholarship as an art form.

Along with Marion Milner, I owe a debt of gratitude to Peter Matthiessen (1987). In his fascinating book titled *The Snow Leopard,* he tells his readers about a journey he took to find a snow leopard in Nepal. He searches far and wide for the snow leopard. For some three hundred and twenty pages he talks about wildlife; he offers thick descriptions of awesome natural settings and the trials of the traveller through rugged terrain. All the while, he awaits the appearance of a snow leopard. Matthiessen explains that, "[t]he snow leopard is the most mysterious of the great cats; of its social system, there is nothing known" (p. 153). Matthiessen tells us that "[a]lmost always it is seen alone; it may meet over a kill, as tigers do, or it may be unsociable. . ." (p. 153). Before Matthiessen left for his search for the snow leopard, a Zen teacher told him that on his travels he should not expect to see anything. Indeed, the snow leopard never appears. We wait alongside our storyteller, Matthiessen, hoping that soon the snow leopard will appear. We are anxious as readers to get a glimpse of this great animal. We wait and wait, turning the pages in anticipation for the snow leopard. But he never finds his snow leopard. Some readers may be disappointed. The whole book is built on the hope that our storyteller would find the snow leopard. But that hope is misguided.

The Snow Leopard is as much about the landscape of Nepal as it is about Matthiessen's inner psychic landscape, the inner psychic landscape of an interminable winter where the snow leopard never arrives. The snow leopard is that symbolic thing that one wants but cannot have. The snow leopard is that healing that never comes. The snow leopard is the recovery that is never made. The snow leopard is the reparation not granted. No reparation. No recovery. No healing. No snow leopard. When does one stop waiting for that which will not come? One must stop waiting for the snow leopard. Jacques Derrida (1994) talks of the difficulties of waiting. He says, "[a]waiting without horizon of the wait, awaiting what one does not expect yet or any longer, hospitality without reserve. . . " (p. 65). Waiting but not expecting. How can this be? Waiting without anticipation? What does it feel like to wait without anticipation? To anticipate that which cannot be anticipated. Psyche torn asunder. How can one be hospitable to the thing that will never come? When does waiting become meaningless?

STOP WAITING FOR A SNOW LEOPARD

Psyche must stop waiting-for-a-snow-leopard. Knowing that healing–whether psychic or physical– will never come, disturbs. Can our traveller give up the false hope that the snow leopard will arrive? Can one give up hope? False hope is a lie. Can one face up to the lie? Perhaps Matthiessen (1987) says it best when he tells us that,

> Already the not-looking-forward, the without-hope-ness takes on a subtle attraction, as if I had glimpsed the secret of these mountains, still half understood. With the past evaporated, the future pointless, and all expectation worn away, I begin to experience the nowness that is spoken of by the great teachers. (p. 300)

I have dealt elsewhere and in some depth (Morris, 2001) with the problem of hope. The West is all about hope. In the East, this is not so. To not expect, to not anticipate, to just Be. This is the heart of Buddhism. Being able to just Be in the here and now seems a difficult task. To Be–in the Buddhist sense–means to focus on the now. This is what is and this is how it is. Things are what they are. Cure will never come. Neither will the snow leopard. Give up the notion of cure.

THE SNOW LEOPARD IS DEAD

Waiting for something that will never happen is foolish. We all want things to work out in the end, we want things to get better, we all want to get back on track and get to work and get to the bottom of it. We all want to see the snow leopard. But the snow leopard is dead. In a sense, when the musician finally realizes that she can no longer play, it is as if her inner snow leopard dies. The musical animal is dead. How to go on when your snow leopard dies? How do we go on? We just do. Or we don't.

CHAPTER SIX

ON NOT BEING ABLE TO HEAL

Dread and Nachtraglichkeit

What if the musician who is no longer able to play cannot heal. What if she slips into a deep depression and is unable to do anything at all? The injuries suffered may be a result of deeper psychological wounds. The lack of emotional inertia in adult life might point back to childhood negative objects. Depression and stultification that emerges in adulthood might be traced back to some childhood trauma. That trauma could remain repressed. The repressed emerges as depression and the inability to turn bad situations into useful ones. When a depression becomes suffocating it may be a repetition of pre-verbal trauma. How can psyche understand and articulate a pre-verbal wound? To articulate the pre-verbal is the impossible task of psychoanalysis. That articulation might not come in language but in gesture, moods. Depression and stultification might be reflective of moods of pre-verbal abuse. Massive amounts of dread might feel uncannily familiar. So the question asked here is what is the afterwardness of dread? What use can psyche make of dread, depression and stultification? If no use at all is made of these negative states, trouble looms. What comes after dread? Reparation does not come after dread. Healing does not come after dread. Nothing comes after dread. Nothing at all. Repeating, forgetting and acting out are dreadful states. If one is chronically tormented by an unremembered wound, that wound will continually manifest somatically. Trading off one injury for another one is symptomatic of the unremembered wound. Today it is the wounded hand, tomorrow it is the migraine, next year it is the wounded foot, the year after it is the stomach aches. Unremembered psychic wounds are bodily wounds. The body ego is embodied. Chronic injury that seems never to heal might be symptomatic of repetition compulsion. Christopher Bollas (1987) is helpful here. He states that,

> a person may seek a negative aesthetic experience, for such an occasion 'prints' his early ego experiences and registers the structure of the unthought known. Some borderline patients, for example, repeat traumatic situations because through the latter they remember their origins existentially. (p. 17)

The 'unthought known' is that experience that seems familiar yet is beyond articulation. The experience is known–uncannily–yet not fully understood. The psyche tends to moves toward the familiar–especially if the familiar is damaging. It is as if the psyche needs to repeat bad experiences until it rights what went wrong. Freud called this the death drive. But what went wrong will never be made right.

Freud hoped that once unconscious material was made conscious, psyche would get unblocked and be able to live more freely. Freely associated thoughts allow for freer living–to a certain extent. Yet, the dread never goes away if early wounds were too deep, or chronic. And so what to do with that dread? Some are constantly tormented emotionally by this 'negative unthought known' and keep unconsciously seeking it out and repeating it. Michael Eigen (2005) suggests that we must find "a language of intensity and injury, a language of emotional storm" (p. 4) in order to cope with life that is lived as a grave woundedness.

Perhaps we can start with the language of gesture. A patient in analysis might become tense, silent. Silence may last entire sessions or for many months. This silence might be chalked up to resistance, but perhaps it is a manifestation of the regression (which happens in the therapeutic session) to that early pre-verbal trauma. Not being able to look at another person is also I think a clue to some old psychic wound. A slow gait, a heaviness that presents in the therapeutic hour are also signs of an old wound. Unpacking gesture is a way to get at that which cannot be put into verbal language.

Of course dreams tell much about early life. The Jungians say go to the image. Images tell stories of the wounded psyche. Images in dreams are gestures offered up to consciousness for re-telling. Making use of images is key to being able to make psyche plastic and mobile again. Psychic stillness, a sort of unspoken deadness, however, is hard to undo. James Hillman (2004) tells us that

> when there was nothing else to hold to, Jung turned to the personified images of interior vision. He entered into an interior drama, took himself into an imaginative fiction and then, perhaps, began his healing–even if it has been called his breakdown. (pp. 53–54).

Hillman suggests something very important here. When attempting to get back to the primary psychic wound or to that chronic woundedness, looking for facts and getting it right is not what is important. Jung fictionalized his wounds, turned them into myth, story. Because we fictionalize about the inarticulate does not make that inarticulate any less real or less important. Nobody can get back to that pre-verbal time through words, since there were no words to express things to begin with. Memory never corresponds in a clear relation with the past. Memory is foggy and unclear. But all the memories are there, stored in the brain forever. That is Freud's teaching. It is all there, every bit of it. And that is the terrifying thing. How much do trauma victims really want to remember? And if they remembered it all, how would they cope with it? Psychic life, though, is fiction. Memories are embellished or half told. Memory is fantasy, dreamlike, mythic. Everything is perceived through psychic myths. Yet these psychic myths—as embellished or dreamlike as they are—are real and are our truth. Repetitive nightmares are clues that the ghost in the machine is not happy. Some would call this post-traumatic stress syndrome. The unconscious is sending a signal that psyche must take note and deal with what is incomprehensible and unspeakable. Adam Phillips (2002) asks what it would mean if one "legitimated conflict, and refused to suppress it." (p. 13). Some people cannot do this. To admit that something is wrong is not an easy thing to do.

Suppressing emotional conflict only worsens it. If the conflict–whatever it may be– is legitimated, in what way should talk of it proceed? Michael Eigen (2004) suggests that one should not "regularize disaster, wish it away, or tone it down. . . " (p. 8). We "regularize disaster" by saying things like: 'everybody had an awful childhood, or it wasn't so bad after all. I turned out okay so it must not have been that bad.' One can rationalize away a horrific childhood by saying things like 'my parents didn't know any better, or they did the best that they could.' That may be all well and true, but the point is that the old wound(s) happened, that the childhood was horrific and the nightmares persist. Stephen Mitchell (1993) suggests that the real problem is that even if we do begin to understand what is going on psychically, understanding it does not make it go away. Mitchell (1993) says, "understanding does not provide much solace for, among other things, real loss, grief over lost opportunities, irreconcilable conflicts, and, ultimately death" (p. 213). However, if there is **no** attempt to understand, the crisis only grows and worsens. Being stuck in blockage and inertia calls for a breakdown–this was Jung's teaching. Breaking down the blockage and inertia is key to some sort of recovery. Michael Eigen (2004) suggests that we must "integrate" the negative into our lived experience. Eigen says,

> It would be a crazy idealization of life to think that we can do away with what deforms us. What psychoanalysis does is incorporate block, shock, and disability into the larger rhythm of decimation and flow. (p. 19)

The incorporation of psychic blocks is a hard thing to conceptualize because as children we are usually taught to not think bad thoughts. If you've got enough bad thoughts in your head, though, you get blocked. Bad thoughts are connected to bad objects or negative introjects. How to integrate negative introjects into a life? How to integrate blocks? Is undoing a block different from integrating it? By *not* making the negative positive is a way to integrate the bad into the good. If you attempt to make the negative positive, the negative comes back twofold. The negative is negative and that is how it must be thought of. As Ruth Riesenberg-Malcom's (2000) book title suggests what is needed is *Bearing Unbearable States of Mind*. Likewise, Michael Parsons (2000) says that psyche must have "the capacity to bear loss wholeheartedly, without pushing it away. . ." (p. 4). The capacity to embrace dread becomes key. How does one get that capacity to begin with? Adam Phillips (1997a) asks us to think about "what is unbearable about oneself and where is one going to put it?" (p. 25) Where does psyche "put" unbearable thoughts? What an interesting question Phillips raises. What is unbearable might be beyond articulation. Where do inarticulate feelings go if they are inexpressible? What are these inarticulate feelings about anyway? This is the conundrum. Sometimes forcing articulation makes things worse. The more psyche attempts to articulate what went wrong, the more inarticulate things become. And this is dreadful. Wilfred Bion (1994) writes on what he calls "nameless dread." In his book titled *Cogitations* Bion writes,

> If the dream-work capacity is destroyed, the patient feels dread which is peculiarly terrifying because it is nameless, and because the namelessness itself springs from the destruction of the patients' capacity for dreaming which is the mechanism responsible for naming. (p. 45)

Not dreaming, then, could be connected to inertia, depression and stultification. When the dreaming stops so too does all psychic mobility. When dreams die so too does psyche. Bion argues that many schizophrenics do not dream and even if they do they cannot make use of the dreams. The dream-work is cut off from the dreamer. If you cannot do dream-work, you cannot undo or integrate psychic blocks. This is dreadful.

What is it that comes after dread, what is the afterwardness of dread, the *nachtraglichkeit* of dread? Martin Stanton (1997) teaches that *nachtraglichkeit*–for Ferenczi–had to do with the,

> complex temporal connection between (aspects of) different events in the past through which unprocessed traumatic material persistently re-emerged in different contexts for reprocessing. Hence the 'persistently present' quality of the 'past' trauma (its "afterwardness"), and its residual reverberation, repetition, and reemergence. . . (p. 74)

That the past is too much in the present is the problem at hand. The shadow of the object of the past petrifies the subject's interiority. All psychic clocks have stopped in childhood. The child is too much in the adult. As Serge Leclaire (1998) suggests–one must kill the child within finally–once and for all. Getting the psychic clocks ticking again means leaving childhood behind. But again, it seems we come up short–one cannot once and for all kill the child within. The ghosts of childhood continue to haunt and torment. One can go through years of analysis, self-medicate, try to forget or–as Bion puts it "make the best of a bad job"–but at the end of the day, that dreadful feeling and that urge toward stasis is always already there. Thanatos is stronger than eros. Freud witnessed this as Austria was going to Hell in the 1930s.

Unconscious archaic states rule the day. I talked a little about the ways in which some psychoanalysts described these states earlier in the book. I drew on such analysts as Otto Rank but I did not get deeply enough into the meat of the subject. Here I would like to try to get at the ways in which psychoanalysts describe this dreadful state. Here I would like to get the rhythm of the next section going by listing phrases that come up when talking about psychic disconnects between m(other) and child. Dread of course is the key feeling but it gets articulated by different analysts in different ways.

THE DREADFUL DISCONNECT: A PHENOMENOLOGY

The connection (between not being able to play and complete inertia) could be symptomatic of an archaic disconnect between m(other) and child. Psychic inertia in adulthood could be a repetition of a deep unravelling in early object relations.

The naming of that disconnect is a way to articulate the inarticulate. Here I will examine feeling states that might be symptomatic of disconnect(s) between the child and the (m)other. I will also explore on a deeper level what psychic structures undergird these feeling states. Although feelings may be fleeting, some feeling-states remain steady and become part of the psychic structure especially when too much trauma has occurred during the pre-verbal phase. Feeling states require a phenomenological exploration. That is what I plan to explore here.

Freud reminds us that we do not forget the pre-verbal, it is always already part and parcel of our psychic makeup. The pre-verbal is there in the ruins of the psyche, even if we can't access it directly. Irrational feelings states–feelings that seem inappropriate or disproportionate to the situation at hand– might be traces of archaic experiences that the infant had before being able to talk. If the infant is abused or neglected these negativities return twofold in adulthood. This is the root of dread. When we say that one is under a compulsion, actions seem controlled as if by some alien force. These compulsions, which might become obsessions, (hence the phrase obsessive– compulsive) are symptoms of some emotional issues that have yet to be worked through. When the past (even if it is not consciously remembered) overwhelms the present, psychic structures may be irreparably damaged. Martin Stanton (1997) reminds us that Freud had a word for this: *Nachtraglichkeit*. Stanton explains,

> Particularly important to him [Freud] was the temporal form of 'afterwardness.' (Nachtraglichkeit), by which he understood the complex temporal connection between (aspects of) different events in the past through which unprocessed traumatic material persistently re-emerged in different contexts for reprocessing. Hence the 'persistently present' quality of the 'past' trauma (its afterwardness). . . . (p. 74)

There is always already a trace of the past in the present. But for those who have suffered child abuse–either emotional or physical or both–that trace becomes more negatively pronounced. The pain from the damage is chronic. Most have had difficulties in childhood. But psychic pain does not heal when children are continually beaten, constantly belittled or sexually abused. A day in and day out struggle with depression might signal some psychic scar that goes back far and deep in time within the psyche. For children who have been wounded permanently, the past becomes all, either consciously or unconsciously. Julia Kristeva (1989) suggests that damaged psyches become "[r]iveted to the past" (p. 60). Being riveted to the past is being stuck in the past–being devoured by the past. The past may not present itself in conscious awareness, but through depressions and inertias the past certainly presents itself in uncanny emotional states. The past may present as vague feelings of anxiety. Something is anxiety making, but what it is, is yet unknown. Steven Mitchell (1999) puts it this way: "we are what we have been" (xvi). More often than not, we do not know what we have been–at least on a conscious level. We are always in relation to another, to a mother or other primary figures. So our psychic make up has been shaped–partially– by that primary other. What we have been in early childhood, may, moreover, work to undo us as adults.

163

The undoing or unravelling of the self probably started in an archaic phase of childhood and continues through adulthood until the self breaks down by the weight of the past. We are victims of our pasts. In trying to recall the past, blanks or vague impressions are all that is available to memory. James Hillman (2004) remarks that it is "[p]oetic, dramatic fictions [that]. . .actually people our psychic life" (p. 56). Memories are constructions. This idea is not new. Freud talked of this. We invent the bulk of our past. There is the real mother and then there is the fantasized mother. The mother in psyche is constructed out of what is real and out of what is fantasized. And then there are unconscious constructs of the mother as well. This is what analysts call phantasy. Reality and phantasy blur. Now, just because our pasts are fictions or constructions does not make them any less real. Is it to childhood we should turn? Is that not what psychoanalysis is all about? Since we cannot get back to childhood, the only way to get at old wounds is through dreams. Dream a little dream for me. Dreaming and freely associated thoughts lead back and down into psyche. Dreaming gives clues to buried pasts. What comes up in the free associative process are fragments of archaic psychic states.

Ignoring dreams might result in the past returning with a vengeance. Acting out without remembering is what Freud called repetition compulsion. If a patient rattles off early childhood traumas for secondary gain nothing is really worked through–the depression gets romanticized and justified. Giving up the connection to the traumas means giving up the depressions that go along with the memories of those traumas. This is the idea behind going into therapy. However, depression is partly biological and chemical and giving it up is like saying give up your chemistry and biology. How do you give up your chemistry and biology? Impossible. Some patients are wedded to their traumas and know no other way of living other than in a depressed state. The depression is all they know. Take away the depression and what do you have? Some patients are lost without their depression. The psyche might feel that part of its interior structure becomes deflated or erased if the depression goes away. Without the depression, the patient feels less real. The patient might also feel that taking away the depression– by working through trauma– is a way to forget the trauma. Forgetting the trauma means forgetting the victim(s) who suffered the trauma and this is anathema especially for those who have suffered a collective trauma, like the Holocaust. People cling to the memories of collective traumas as a way to keep alive the memory of the victims. Or, patients might use their traumatic past as an excuse for ongoing psychic retreat. Martin Bergmann (1999) states,

> In my own work I have found analysands who have decathected their relationship to their inner bad objects . . . . They gracefully permit us to uncover one trauma after another because every trauma justifies their withdrawal from life; but they do not make use of this knowledge. They fail to integrate their biography. . . . (p. 197)

Making use of the knowledge of the past means putting the past back in the past. The past is not the now. As the Buddhists say, the now is all we have. And if the now is polluted with the bad objects of the past, the now is not the now at all. The now is too much the tragic past. Putting things back in place—putting the past back where it belongs– in the past that is past is what analysis is about. Childhood must be put to rest. When things are out of place, childhood becomes the adult's preoccupation, the negative mother becomes the all, and life in the now becomes obliterated. When psychic things are out of place irrational behavior signals the inability to work through. We act out when we are psychically out of place. Getting psychic things back in place also means integrating–not repressing–those bad objects that overwhelm. The psyche can eventually dis-integrate if bad objects swallow good ones. The unravelling of the self is an ego that disintegrates.

And yet, no matter how much analysis one has, no matter how much time one studies psychoanalytic theory and integrates it into the psyche, the repressed still returns. Abusive childhoods can never fully go away. We repeat what we cannot remember. And this repeating can come in many forms.

Now, repeating can be a bad thing, but there are repetitions that are good as well. And this is something that the psychoanalytic community does not address. Robert Fink (2005) examines repeating in the world of music. Fink (2005) writes on minimalism. Minimalism, which we have examined in a previous chapter, is an art form that is all about repeating. Repeating notes, repeating phrases, repeating structures—minimally—this is what minimalism is. Four notes repeated four hundred times. This is what is underneath much minimal music and this is what drives people crazy about minimal music. It can be either annoying or enlightening. You either love it or hate it. There is something about minimalist music that reflects the structures of the psyche and its drive toward repetition. Why do we keep repeating ourselves, asks Robert Fink (2005)? Repetition is what life is about. The heart beat. Repetition is basic to the human condition. Repetition is probably basic to all creatures. Evolution is a series of twists on repetitions. Fink (2005) makes an interesting connection between minimalist music and Freud's notion of repetition compulsion. He states that

> [c]ritics of repetitive music have not forgotten that Freud invented the death instinct to explain a particular war neurosis, the compulsion to repeat traumatic events [Freud called this shell shocked; today we would call this posttraumatic stress syndrome]. . . . [some psychoanalysts] assume repetition structures in music are unequivocal marks of regression. . . that precede ego differentiation. (p. 5)

Fink is unfriendly to psychoanalytic analogies between minimalism and Freudian principles however. He thinks these analogies too reductive. As against Fink, I think the psychoanalytic analogies to minimal music are right on the mark. Music is pre-verbal and on one level reflects basic psychic structures. Fink does a sort of Marxist analysis of minimalism–which I find rather unconvincing. For Fink minimalism is a reflection of consumer repetition. I do not buy this interpretation. Minimalism–I think–is a reflection of the human psyche at its most basic workings–repetitions. Think about how many times you think about something that bothers you. Do we not think about the past over and over again. Think about how life seems to move in very small repetitive ways. This compulsion to repeat becomes magnified when one suffers a traumatic event or a series of traumatic events. The worse the memory the more we come back to it. Adam Phillips (2001), reminds us of Marion Milner's insistence on the complexity of psychic phenomena. Phillips says,

> Milner counsels us to be wary of the pre-emptive imposition of pattern, of the compulsive sanity of reassuring recognitions. Of what we might be doing when we are too keen to clear up clutter. Clutter, that is to say, may be a way of describing either the deferral that is a form of waiting, or the waiting that is a form of deferral. Our eagerness for recognition can be a self-blinding. (p. 71)

We must approach the study of psychic states with a sense of caution and uncertainty. Describing feelings seems easy enough, but in reality it is not so easy to do. What does it mean, for instance, to say that you are embarrassed? If I say I am depressed, how do I capture that in language? Is depression worse than boredom or anger or anxiety? And what is anxiety anyway? Anxiety is one of most elusive terms and I think Freud knew this because he based his entire psychoanalytic framework around the problem of anxiety. We can use words to express feelings but somehow there is always a remainder, a left over, something unacknowledged or misinterpreted. On the other hand, there is a need to call things something. Words are useful if they are used with care. Words are useful when they are qualified, and perhaps admit of their unsteadiness. Words are useful if they are nuanced. To articulate what is impossible to articulate. This is the task at hand. We have to name things with care and qualification and uncertainty and understand that when we think we know it too well we are probably on the wrong track. What depression means for one person is not the same for another. Does the signifier depression reflect what it signifies? How to capture the mood of depression in language is nearly impossible because depression is beyond language. However, the task is at hand and we must articulate what is inarticulate if we are to carry on at all. Yet psyche is a big mess. The mess is what the postmoderns try to get at by writing in a messy style that is hard to read and hard to understand. Lacan and Deleuze are good examples of messy writers. The problem with reading both Lacan and Deleuze is that their writing tends to be so obscure that it becomes difficult to make use of.

Most emotional states are a mess and messy to describe. Describing inertia is very difficult because while in a state of inertia one cannot describe it. This is the problem of language use. Getting stuck in a state of inertia means language stops. Speaking of an unspeakable silence while in a state of silence is impossible. When one comes out of such a state, retrospection does not clarify. How to speak of inertia after the fact? Does speaking of inertia– after the fact– really get at what it felt like at the time it occurred? No. It is like Monday morning quarterbacking. And yet, if the only way of articulating inertia is after the fact, then we have to take what we can get. We have to work with what language can capture even if it is belated.

Pain is another example of something impossible to capture in language. The body has a pain memory. Phantom pain. A limb no longer there still hurts. The body is a memory body. An injured limb has a memory. Old injuries remember. The body–memory surprises and disturbs. Once out of pain, we forget what that pain felt like until it pains us again. Memory and forgetting are part and parcel of the experience of pain. Perhaps forgetting what pain felt like serves to protect the ego from shattering.

Martin Stanton (1997), like Marion Milner, suggests that symptoms (of emotional distress) are highly complex and should never be reduced to a simple formula. He states that:

> the symptom is residually complex. Its complexity is marked by its resistance to interpretation, and its irreducibility to fixed diagnosis or prognosis. The symptom therefore remains 'other,' it does not disappear or suddenly 'resolve' in one or other narrative of experience. It is complex, in so far as it is assumed that multiple inscriptions are not 'bound' (Bindung, to use Freud's term) or processed in a fixed way. There is no core or nucleus to a complex, but multiple and shifting connections. (p. 26)

Stanton's position is rather postmodern with its emphasis on fluidity and complexity. This fluidity of symptoms is particularly problematic when attempting to say what something is. If I say that you suffer from what Andre Green (1993) calls 'dead mother syndrome' does that mean that all of your problems can be reduced to this? Can one be reduced to a syndrome? And even if it is the case that all of your problems are connected to your psychically dead mother, does that knowledge clear things up? Well, probably not. But still, it does help to name the problem at hand, if only to get a tentative handle on things. If one goes to an analyst and expresses psychic despair, one wants to know why the despair continues and what to do about it and what to call it. What's wrong with me? The analyst might answer I don't know, why don't you tell me what's wrong with you? And on and on. The patient might ask, why do I feel so depressed all the time? The analyst answers, why do you think you feel depressed all the time? How maddening is that!! Sometimes calling an emotional symptom a syndrome –like the dead mother syndrome–helps the patient to articulate what is wrong. Not that all can be reduced to this syndrome, but naming the syndrome helps the patient understand that there is something about a psychically dead mother that has made her chronically depressed.

Feelings we have as adults can often be traced back to feelings we had in early childhood. The complexity here is that a feeling is a repeat of another earlier feeling–especially if one is the victim of a trauma. Julia Kristeva (1989) puts it this way:

> Nevertheless, the power of the events that create my depression is often out of proportion to the disaster that suddenly overwhelms me. What is more, the disenchantment that I experience in the here and now, cruel as it may be, appears under scrutiny, to awaken echoes of old traumas . . . . (pp. 4–5)

The key to Kristeva's passage is the problem of experiencing things out of proportion to what they are. This out of proportion phenomenon is a clue to a repetition of an archaic traumatic event. For example, feeling rage when clearly the situation does not call for rage is a clue. This out of proportion rage is a memory rage. And this memory rage gets entangled in the here and now-ness of the current emotional problem. This issue creeps up especially in transference situations. For example, if my teacher reminds me of my mother and my mother was a horrible, mean person I will believe that my teacher is also a horrible mean person–even if reality does not bare that out. I get the same feeling in my gut toward my teacher as I did with my mother. This is the feeling of dread and terror. In reality, the teacher has done nothing to provoke the student to feel this way. Why is that student so visibly upset about getting a C? Why doesn't that student confront the teacher? The student says, I am terrified to confront the teacher–she is terrifying. But in reality there is nothing to be terrified of. The teacher is pleasant enough, she is approachable and the rest. But the student experiences only dread going to class. Feelings are often repetitions of archaic experiences with the mother that get transferred to the here and now in a completely irrational fashion. A feeling may, therefore, be a memory of another feeling that has little to do with the here and now. This is why Milner and Stanton argue that emotional states are highly complex. If it is the case that the way in which someone responds to another is a repeat of some other unconscious relationship, then what is the emotion about? How can we trace the origins of that emotion? What do we do with the old feelings once we find them? Or do we find them at all? If they are buried in the ruins of forgetting and repression, how can we access them and what would we do if we could access them? Does accessing them mean that we can now act in such a way that the emotion felt is in proportion to the event at hand? Maybe and maybe not. The older the injury the harder it is to get rid of it psychically. If we cannot get rid of our bad objects will we always act in bizarre ways? Who knows. Everything is really very much up in the air when we are talking about emotions.

Feelings that have memory–that is–feelings that are archaic and that get dredged up out of the unconscious– are always already beyond representation and explanation. Here we are concerned with archaic feelings that precede language and that is a particular problem since we can only speculate what might be the case. Melanie Klein has often been criticized for her wild speculations about the phantasy world of children. Interestingly enough, these speculations were based on empirically based studies of the children she analyzed. Empiricism is highly problematic because it is based on the assumption that it gets to the truth of the matter because the observer can see with her own eyes what is going on. But seeing something does not mean understanding what it is that you are seeing. For Freud, the real child was not his concern. What we see with our eyes can deceive. Turning to dreams and images– as the Jungians teach–means turning to the metaphorical, not the literal to find out what associations mean that emerge in the dreamwork. The meaning of associations, however, is always belated and delayed. What is felt is only a remainder and there is always an after-feeling, an after the fact feeling, and a memory of feeling or feeling memory. Any phenomenology of feeling must complexify what we think we mean when we say we feel something. That is what I am trying to accomplish here.

Thus feelings are feelings–about feelings—yet we cannot get at the feelings that were experienced long ago. Feelings are bodies of memory, fields of memory. And memory is partly fantasy. Feelings that are re-membered through the members (the limbs) are vague and hard to get at through words. But the mood of the situation prevails. The mood that is felt in transference situations is uncanny–we've felt it before but cannot say exactly how. When past moods are too much in the present and out of step with the present–dreams and free association might help get at what is underneath the mood. When overtaken by a mood, it is nearly impossible to get out of it. Moods created by the unconscious relation between mother and child are complex. First off, the child is in relation to the mother and the mother is in relation not only to the child but to her mother as well. Emotional problems become, then, transgenerational. This transgenerational phenomena further complicates things. The disconnect between mother and child could be a repetition of the mother's relation with her mother. And it probably is. And what of her mother's mother's mother? And so on. Disconnections between mother and child, therefore, are generational. And if they are generational we have a better understanding of why they are so hard to undo. Dysfunction has a history and histories are not easy to change.

Generally speaking, disconnections do not feel good. The most primal connection is between the infant and the mother simply because the infant comes out of the mother's body. This is a rather strange thing when you get to thinking about it. What one takes from one's mother–psychically and emotionally–is very different from that which one takes from one's father. We are not born of our fathers–fathers are always at a distance. We are born of our mothers and their mothers. It is curious to me that Freud spent more time thinking about King Oedipus and the son killing the father than thinking about the mother and her relationship with the child. Here, Melanie Klein and the object relations theorists after her took up where Freud left off–with the mother child relation.

The way back to primal disconnection is as Kristeva teaches. Paying attention to our bizarre out of proportionateness of emotions to the situation at hand; this is a key to the past. There are feelings and then there are feelings. When feelings are more or less fleeting, we tend not to pay to much attention to them. On the other hand, when feelings overwhelm and get in the way of one's life, it is time to take heed. Drawing on the work of various psychoanalysts, I will discuss some of the more troubling feelings that may occur out of proportion to the event at hand that may give clues to primal disconnects. The primal disconnect gets repeated over and over as an adult with new mother-figures or new mother imagos who get tangled up in transference.

Julia Kristeva (1989) argues that the generalized feeling of sadness is a clue that something has gone wrong in early childhood. She states that:

sadness would point to a primitive self –wounded, incomplete, empty. Persons thus afflicted do not consider themselves wronged but afflicted with a fundamental flaw. . . . Their sadness would be rather the most archaic expression of an unsymbolizable unnameable narcissistic wound. . . . (p. 12)

The key point Kristeva makes here is that an ongoing sadness in adulthood can be traced back to an archaic condition. It is an uncanny feeling because it was felt long ago somewhere deep in the psyche, perhaps even during the pre-verbal period. This is what I call the primal disconnect. The primal disconnect manifests itself in awful feelings that just do not go away and have little relation to the current situation. The difficulty with the primal disconnect is that the feelings that emerge are vague and as Kristeva points out "unsymbolizable." A bad feeling that cannot be symbolized, cannot be articulated because it is beyond articulation. There are no words to describe something that occurred before language. What happened became somatized rather than articulated in language. The pervasive feeling of a vague sadness overwhelms a life. This condition is what some would call melancholic. Something is structurally wrong with the psyche. Structural damage does not go away because it is part of the undergirding of psyche. Kristeva calls this a "fundamental flaw" in the psyche. Something is always already wrong all the time. Those who have not suffered early psychic injury do not know this feeling. Of course everyone knows sadness, but not this kind of sadness. It is Michael Balint (1992) who does much work with this fundamental flaw. He calls this basic structural mishap the "basic fault." Balint tells us that this idea is a "geologic analogy" (p. 21). I think this is a helpful metaphor. Fault lines in the earth suggest structural gaps that could become earthquakes if the earth shifts. The "basic fault" is the potential earthquake of the psyche. There is no undoing the basic fault, it is there and it is there for the duration. Again, people who have not suffered early psychic injury do not feel that they have a basic fault. Many have little understanding of what this might feel like. But for the melancholic, the basic fault is all. Again, a basic fault is the feeling that there is something wrong structurally with the psyche. The basic fault, Balint tells us, colors all object relations throughout life. Balint (1992) puts it this way:

> Since the basic fault, as long as it is active, determines the forms of object relationship available to any individual, a necessary task of the [psychoanalytic] treatment is to inactivate the basic fault by creating conditions in which it can heal off. . . . Only after that can a patient can 'begin anew' , that is develop new patterns of object relationship to replace those given up. (p. 166)

The point of the analytic situation is to undo damage. But can the basic fault ever go away? And can psychoanalysis really undo the damage? Maybe not. Can the basic fault be "healed off?" I wonder. After transference is worked through enough, the analyst might be able to help the patient integrate a good imago into the psychic structure. This is what Balint means by beginning 'anew.' The replacement of one imago (the bad breast) for another (the good breast) is difficult to do psychically. The unconscious is rigid. Too much damage might have already occurred for any significant changes in psyche to take place. There are many who cannot incorporate this new (good enough imago) into the psyche because the basic fault is just too deep. Balint (1992) points out, in fact, that the "after-effects [of the basic fault] appear to be only partly reversible" (p. 22). As Michael Eigen (1993;

1996; 2001a; 2001b; 2004; 2005) points out throughout much of his work, there are psychic wounds that will never heal. For some, "toxic nourishment" (the title of one of Eigen's (2001b) books) is all one knows. If savage wounds will never heal how does psyche move on? Maybe psyche does not move on. Perhaps this is what melancholia is: not moving on, being stuck somewhere back in time, back in the primal disconnect. Psyche goes through the motions of living, but it is always out of whack. Psyche can turn on itself and become steeped in hate. Hatred gets projected out onto the other but what is really hated is the self. Or hate serves other purposes. Christopher Bollas (1987) remarks that:

> in some cases a person hates an object not in order to destroy it, but to do precisely the opposite: to conserve the object. . . . its aim may be to act out of an unconscious form of love. I am inclined to term this 'loving hate'. (p. 118)

Bollas argues that the stronger the hate the stronger the unconscious love. Maybe sometimes this is the case, but sometimes it is not the case. Regardless, the hated mother–the mother who was abusive–becomes an imago, a fantasized image and this image gets embedded deeply into ruins of a broken psyche. It takes much energy and time to hate. To hate one's mother can consume a life. The devouring mother is the image that comes to mind here. Being devoured by her means also being devoured by hatred. Everything then becomes hateful. Work, play and other forms of experience are hateful. Internal life is hateful. I hate everything about myself. I hate my hate as well–the person who is devoured might say. The mother imago becomes, as Eigen (2001b) would put it, 'toxic nourishment.' Bollas (1987) terms this paradox "loving hate" (p. 5). We learn how to relate to others primarily through our primal relation with our mothers. So if our relations with our mothers were hateful, do we only love the people we hate and hate the people we love? Bollas remarks in this respect that "only in hating the other can certain people discover a true relation to the object. . ." (p. 5). Analysts comment on this buried hated mother imago–when hatred overrides everything– in various manners. Kristeva (1989) suggests that the image of the mother in the psyche gets convoluted with other transferential objects throughout life. Mother figures, or mother substitutes or people who remind one of the mother whether consciously or unconsciously, then, become objects of one's hate. And this hate is kept in the psyche as a permanent feeling, as a way of being. Kristeva argues that "the negative mother imago becomes en [tombed] within the psyche" (p. 61). Kristeva (1989) puts it this way.

> When I say that the object of my grief is less the Villain, the mother, or the lover that I miss in the here and now than the blurred representation that I keep and put together in the darkroom of what thus becomes my psychic tomb. (p. 61).

The psychic tomb keeps hatred going. The "blurred representation" is the work of generalized transference. And in this generalized transference others become blurred with the hated mother imago. To whom does one speak? To this blurred representation, to this ghost, this phantom of mother in the other. There is always already an object to hate because hate is the only way psyche can operate. Andre Green (1993) suggests that for some, even though the object that is internalized is bad, "it is good that it exists even though it does not exist as a good object" (p. 55). The internalized bad object structures psyche. Without the bad object, psyche feels as if she just might unravel. So it is better to hold onto the bad than give it up. To give up the "hydra with its multiple heads" (Green, p. 55) is akin to giving up part of the self. The fear of relinquishing the bad mother is also the fear of relinquishing parts of the self. Being full of hate is better than being full of nothing and being nothing. Being nothing is psychic death. This battle that continues throughout the life of someone who has "entombed"–as Kristeva (1989) puts it– psychic hate accounts for what Bion (1993) calls "nameless dread" (p. 116). This feeling of nameless dread is not new to the personality, but rather is formed in the primal disconnect between mother and child. Bion (1993) puts it this way:

> Normal development follows if the relationship between infant and breast permits the infant to project a feeling, say, that it is dying into the mother and to reintroject it after its sojourn in the breast has made it tolerable to the infant psyche. If the projection is not accepted by the mother the infant feels that its feeling it is dying is stripped of such meaning as it has. It therefore reintrojects, not a fear of dying made tolerable, but nameless dread. (p. 116)

What is striking about the above citation is that psyche must be allowed to die into the mother imago. Psyche–at an early age–must feel that she has a place to go, a place to give up things, a place to find refuge in the mother. Finding refuge in the mother feels as if dying is a letting go, but that letting go has a place to go. If there is no place to go, if the mother is not a container for the child's needs, psyche turns that experience of dying into the mother into a fear of dying. This fear of dying later in life may become overwhelming and even irrational at times. The overwhelming fear of dying might manifest in vague feelings like dread. And yet dread does not have a direct object–it is that vague feeling that something is wrong. Nameless dread is like anxiety because anxiety does not have an object to which it is directed. It seems to be free floating like dread.

The mother who disconnects herself from her infant causes the infant to feel tormented by dread because the mother has not been there psychically for the infant. That not being there feeling, then, gets transferred onto other people in adult life. Even if one is surrounded by people, one might feel always already abandoned and existentially alone. Or psyche may feel disconnected, detached and even dissociated in adulthood. Perpetual abandonment is a way of life. Bion (1993) states that if the mother does not leave space for "reverie" onto which the infant can project, the infant will be consumed with nameless dread. Let us stop for a moment and consider this notion of reverie. Reverie is a kind of dreamlike state where the mother floats between the conscious and the unconscious. The mother, in other words, is able to just *be*. In this just being state, the infant is allowed to die into the mother. If the mother does not allow the infant to die into the mother, the infant holds onto this fear of annihilation rather than putting it inside of the mother.

Putting things psychically inside of the mother releases fears, dreads, hates and allows the psyche to move on. Without a place for release, psyche becomes burdened and life becomes intolerable.

Andre Green (1993) talks of the dead mother syndrome. The mother is not literally dead, but she is dead for the child psychically. Green (1993) tells us that,

> to avoid all misunderstanding, I wish to make clear that I shall not be discussing here the psychical consequences of the real death of the mother, but rather that of an imago which has been constituted in the child's mind, following maternal depression, brutally transforming a living object . . . into a distant figure, practically inanimate, deeply impregnating the cathexis of certain patients. . . . Thus, the dead mother, contrary to what one might think, is a mother who remains alive but who is, so to speak, psychically dead. . . . (p. 142)

Again we have the mother–dead–walled--up inside the mind of the child for the duration of a life. The psychic death of the mother becomes part of the psychic death of the child. Green (1993) talks about patients who are always depressed, patients who "go beyond the normal depressive reaction that periodically affects everyone" (p. 143). Being always depressed suggests that something inside of psyche has been permanently damaged. Something is in there that can't get out. The dead mother is always part and parcel of the child if the mother was depressed during the early years of her child's life. The dead mother is, as Julia Kristeva might put it, entombed.

The "toxic nourishment" (Eigen, 2001b) the "loving hate" (Bollas, 1987) the "dead mother" (Green, 1993). Three conundrums, three aporias, three inexpressible traumas create a life of torment. To be tormented by the mother is a lifelong vocation. I am thinking here of Jamaica Kincaid's novels as they she seems to struggle with the torment–and the colonization– that is the mother. The torment keeps coming back again in various guises, in new object relations that are heavily saturated with transference. The re-introduction of torment by every new transferential figure only makes the dead mother grow stronger and further devour the psyche. It is as if the mind continually attacks itself–as Bion (1991) might suggest. Psyche continually seeks out environments that are damaging. Repetition compulsion here is clear. The more psyche tries to extricate herself from the monster-mother, the worse she becomes, the stronger the bad feelings persist. Of course, depression that is ongoing is a symptom of something gone wrong. Depersonalization is another mechanism that is left over from some primal disconnect. Depersonalization is a coping mechanism when the self is attacked by, say, a primary figure. This attack of course does not have to be physical only. Emotional attacks do not go away. The attack is re-played and re-played like a broken record and gets stuck in the psyche. Depersonalization is way for the ego to get distance from itself, to protect itself against ongoing attacks. Certain things might trigger feelings of depersonalization, certain memories, smells, places, people. The adult who feels depersonalized may be repeating depersonalized states that served to protect during childhood. A continuing state of depersonalization–

one that is unremitting for years–is a clue to early childhood disconnects. As an adult if the depersonalization goes on long enough, the psyche disappears. Self gets evacuated. What once served to protect, destroys. To continually live in a state of depersonalization is like being dead while alive. Being psychically off into the distance-- not paying attention, not being there, floating above the event at hand-- becomes a way of life, not some intermittent fleeting feeling. It is as if the person lives in two separate worlds. One part of psyche is split off from another part. In dissociation the personality splits in different directions. Cases of dissociation can result in multiple personalities. This extreme form of spitting serves as protective mechanism especially in cases of sexual molestation in childhood. Dissociation in childhood– which once served as a protective measure against the attacker–now cripples the adult.

And then there is emptiness. The empting out of the psyche might be a good thing when practicing some sort of meditation. But when the psyche is chronically empty–this is totally different. Christopher Bollas (1989) suggests that when a patient "is clearly 'elsewhere', and the voice speaking is on automatic pilot, the person is quite gone. The analyst is, then, left with a ghost" (p. 130). Of course, everybody has moments of being elsewhere psychically, but when this state of mind becomes the dominant one life becomes a tragic situation. Bollas talks about the "ghostline personality" who can no longer relate to objects. Living with a ghost is like living with a corpse. The primal disconnect between mother and child may result in the complete and utter disintegration of the psyche.

Michael Parsons (2000) points out that the inability to play, to fantasize and to symbolize are symptoms of a disintegrated psyche. We return to the thesis of this book–the inability to play. Is this problem at root caused by a disintegrated psyche? If so, it is much more serious than just not being able to do something. There are deeper, historical reasons for not being able to function. These historical roots of dysfunction are not easily fixed if they go back to the primal disconnect. The ghostline personality is the musician who can no longer play or the scholar who can no longer write. These people may simply turn into ghosts.

Playing and writing involve fantasy and symbolization and when these are damaged psyche deteriorates. Parsons points out that when talking about playing, he means more than children at play. Parsons (2000) reminds that, "Freud conceived of thinking as playing with possibilities" (p. 129). The inability to think is the inability to craft a future. One cannot engage in the work of scholarship without the capacity to think or the capacity to play. And these capacities might have been lost long ago in the archaic psyche. For a time they might be revived but then they tend to revert back to the way things were in primal times. Not being able to function as an adult might be a repeat of not being able to connect to the mother in early childhood. For some, not being able to play, not being able to think and not being able to write, at bottom, might be more fundamentally about not being able to connect to the mother.

Christopher Bollas (1987) talks about repetition compulsion–the unconscious force that pulls us toward disaster–in the form of what he calls the "negative aesthetic experience" (p. 17) or the negative "unthought known" (pp.16–17). Bollas says

> that a person may seek a negative aesthetic experience, for such an occasion 'prints' his early ego experiences and registers the structure of the unthought known. Some borderline patients, for example, repeat traumatic situations because through the latter they remember their origins existentially. (p. 17).

Now, the unthought known is that uncanny feeling –a familiar feeling–that cannot, however, be articulated. It is known but unthought–or not articulated. It is a feeling that cannot be put into language and yet it is familiar. Transferential relations are unthought knowns. To be attracted to someone who is toxic makes little sense. But if toxin is all that is known by psyche toxin is what is sought out. The toxic is known but perhaps unthought. Being caught of in a web of toxic transference is difficult to untangle because it is mostly unconscious and yet there is part of the consciousness that knows that this is wrong but familiar. And because it is familiar it does not seem to matter that it feels wrong. Or, psyche feels resigned to its situation because engaging in toxic relations is all that it knows. Seeking unconsciously the "negative aesthetic"–as Bollas (1987) puts it– means living destructively. Addictive behaviors could be part and parcel of living in a "negative aesthetic." Addiction is a way of life, it is a form of compulsivity that works to undo the self. The primal disconnect is the negative aesthetic. Bad object relations continue in adult life by way of disastrous compulsions and destructive addictions. Strangely enough, the addiction feels good even though at some level psyche knows that it is bad. The abusive partner may feel like the right one even though at some level psyche knows otherwise, and the undoing of the self feels good even though psyche knows it works toward its own demise. Again, this is what Eigen (2001b) means by "toxic nourishment." This is a very powerful metaphor. Eigen has captured in two words what some take a lifetime to figure out.

Some can only be in relation to an abusive partner because it is psychically familiar. When the person with the "basic fault" (Balint, 1992) comes into contact with people who are good and loving psyche gets strangely pulled in rigid ways backward to the negative. The good person is not attractive to the person suffering from the basic fault because the only thing that feels good is feeling bad. Bad people, then, are unconsciously sought out so that the damaged psyche can continue to feel damaged. Being *possessed* by this "negative aesthetic"–as Bollas (1987) puts it– is nearly impossible to change. When psyche is driven by old conflicts–archaic conflicts–possession is an apt term to describe the pull toward the negative. It is as if psyche has little control–consciously–over anything. Something else drives psyche toward self destruction. And yet that something else is psyche, not some alien being. We are clearly the creators of our own destructions. The mother is not to blame, she is long dead. The mother imago that gets embedded in psyche is simply an imago. But this imago is a force with which to be reckoned. Images–as the Jungians teach– are not benign. Images–especially as they appear in dreams give clues to deeper psychological struggles that remain troubling. How to get rid of these bad images? Perhaps we should admit that there is no getting rid of bad images, especially if they are early ones. The brain keeps everything locked away in a vault. Can we outsmart psyche? Can we use Hermes, the trickster, to outfox these negative imagos? Can we outfox our own internalized badness?

Ella Freeman Sharpe (1968) reminds us that Freud insisted that the past remains always somewhere in memory, even if we can't consciously recall the past. Sharpe (1968) tells us that "Freud has said that the scars of what has been remain. We cannot obliterate the past" (p. 16). The primal disconnect is a scar. Some scars never heal. No matter how much therapy, or how many anti-depressants one takes, the ruins of memory continually undo the self. To educate oneself about the conditions in which the scars occurred might help to get an understanding, but still the understanding does not guarantee that psyche will be free of neurosis or suffering. However, educating the self does bring some relief. But studying psyche does not mean being able to obliterate what is bad about her. The more one tries to "obliterate" the past–as Freud puts it–the more meanly it returns. In fact, it returns in the form of a monster. The monster unleashes "a vengeance. . . from within" (Sekoff, 1999, p. 112). If you do not deal with the monstrousness of psyche, she will deal with you. Again, one way of dealing with serious emotional distress is through study. It's not enough to go through the therapeutic process with an analyst. It is also not enough to only study. I believe you must do both. Educating psyche is key to freeing up rigidities. Freeing up rigidities is not the same as getting rid of them. But still, freeing up psyche gives you openings to make choices. Education is the key to a sustainable future. Education is the key to surviving a brutal childhood. To educate psyche is the most important life-saving endeavor in which one can engage. To educate means to live better, to make a better life. What could be more important than a good education? What could be more important than an education that teaches people how to educate themselves? Educating the self means understanding that the self needs others in order to understand. We need to study others in order to better understand ourselves. I am not offering a simple solution to complex emotional problems, however. Growing up in an abusive household leaves traces in the psyche that are irreversibly damaging. No amount of education can get rid of that damage. And yet, education helps. Education is not only about the intellect, it is also about emotions and understanding emotions. This is why reading fiction is so crucial to the health of psyche. Fiction is the best place to learn about the emotional lives of others. Think of Virginia Woolf's (1993) *Mrs. Dalloway*. We learn of the emptiness of the broken woman. So many women are broken. Woolf's own tragic life reflects this brokenness. Suicide is the option for many women living broken lives. And in some cases, women's lives may have been broken not by the mother, but by the father. Living in a patriarchal culture damages women. Adrienne Rich (2001) the political poet has been writing about the damaging effects of patriarchy for years. So we also need to talk about the damage of the Father, Lacan's law of the father. The Rat Man's father, Dr. Schreber's father, Kafka's father. Three damaging fathers. The mother is not the only negative imago. The father too–as Freud knew– can be toxic. Psychic damage is also engendered damage. Fathers and mothers damage people. And then children can also turn on their parents. Children occasionally kill their parents. And so we have Greek tragedy. Patricide, matricide, infanticide, suicide. All the icides. The child must kill the father within–Freud; the child must kill the mother within–Klein; the adult must kill the child within–Leclaire. The father-daughter relation is fraught; the mother-daughter relation is fraught. The father-son relation is fraught.

Borderline mothers present a particular problem because they swing so much this way and that, that the child cannot get a grasp on what's coming next. Alcoholic parents present another problem of interminable instability. The depressed mother is not there psychically for the child. How is a child able to survive? How do any of us survive our parents? Emotional instability on the part of a parent leads to real confusion for the child. The parent is there and not there, good and bad, more bad than good, pays attention and then doesn't, beats the child and then doesn't, wants to be both friend and foe, kills the child emotionally but also nourishes the child. This ongoing uncertainty makes for a very difficult emotional ride for the child. Children from unstable families introject the unpredictable and groundlessness. Feeling groundless is perhaps what Andre Green (1993) means by "vertiginous falling" (p. 155). The child feels that she is falling into the pit of hell. The disturbed mother might give the child things and then take them away. The disturbed father might beat the child but play games with the child. Enid Balint (1993) talks of "teddy bears" with "sawdust" in them (p. 40). Every good thing is filled with badness for the child. At every turn, the disturbed primal figure ruins what could have been a good thing. Every possible nurturing experience is destroyed. It is no wonder that abused children associate badness with goodness, repeating these patterns by later unconsciously seeking out an abusive partner. Enid Balint (1993) talks of being "filled with rubbish" (p. 40). The rubbish of emotional and physical abuse does not go away; the rubbish is always there at some level. Andre Lussier (2001) talks about "the mother as terror" (p. 149). Indeed. The shadow of the mother's brutality always remains. The car pulling into the driveway gets associated with the terror to come for the child who awaits his mother's unpredictable and potentially violent behavior. Profound issues of trust are disturbed for the child. Trust no one. Keep a distance. Look out, here she comes. The rage, the hostility and the violence gets mixed in with baking cakes. This is a very confusing way for a child to grow up. School, for children of abuse, is a refuge. Teachers are gods and saints. It is no wonder that abused children tend to cling to their teachers. Abused Children look to other people–especially teachers–for comfort and support. Getting good grades, then, has very little to do with subject mastery. Rather, getting good grades– especially for children who have been abused– is a way to attach to a good enough mother substitute. Andre Green (1993) talks about the "frantic need for play" (p. 152) for children who suffer from the primal disconnect. The frantic need for connection to objects serves as a survival mechanism. Green suggests that overachievers may be attempting to compensate for what they lack in their relations with primal figures. Green (1993) explains:

> Finally, and more particularly, the quest for lost meaning structures the early
> ego. The development of a frantic need for play which does not come about

as in the freedom for playing, but under the compulsion to imagine, just as intellectual development is inscribed in a compulsion to think. (p. 152)

Becoming a scholar or artist might be a way of compensating for a damaged psyche. These activities might be a way of working through an interminable torment. Perhaps the madness of playing is the pursuit of being seen, of being recognized. So if the adult who was abused as a child is not recognized for her accomplishments as an adult, she gets re-traumatized. The issue of recognition is a profoundly psychological one. Since the primal figures did not seem to see the child, but only beat or abuse the child, the child in the adult needs to be seen and recognized to heal old wounds. But who sees whom? Is it madness to want others to see us? Or at heart, do we–those of us who are damaged–really want our primal figures to finally see us? But we know they never will, and yet we keep wanting to fix those primal bonds. For whom do you write if not for the mother who cannot love you? Maybe this time mother will see me. If the mother is dead, do you still write so that she might see you? Clearly, this is madness. But is this not the tragedy of the melancholic who is unable to give up the lost object? To what mother imagos do you express yourself through artistic pursuits? Green (1993) suggests that people who frantically produce things (whether playing with ideas or with artistic objects) do so "in an attempt to master the traumatic situation" (p. 153). But psyche cannot master an unmasterable past. Andre Green (1993) points out "there is no end to the dying mother" (p. 152). If there is no end to the dying mother, or the dead mother, there is no end to frantic production. Sekoff (2001) concurs with Green and puts it this way "the deepest secret of the dead mother is that she never dies" (p. 115). Do we, then, owe to our dead mothers our productivity, or artistic genius? Perhaps. This would be my take on what Derrida (1992a) calls 'the gift of death.' Think of Kafka's disconnect with his father. Was his writing a way of mastering the trauma of a cruel father? Did Kafka write to be seen, to be recognized? Did he want to get his father's approval? Did he want to fix his bad relation with his father? Think of Schreber (2000). He too suffered at the hands of a wicked father. Did he write to somehow cure his relation with his father? And then there are our troubling mothers. We mustn't romanticize the cruelty of the dead mother or abusive father. That is not what I am doing here. But it does seem to be a fact that many creative artists had terrible relations with one or the other parent. Out of the terrible comes the creative. Creativity is a search for cure even when no cure is in sight.

Falling ill is another response to primal injury. Illness serves to heal ironically. Neurosis serves to heal the wounds. In his book titled *The Doctor, His Patient and the Ilness*, Michael Balint (2000) explains:

We think that some people who, for some reason or other, find it difficult to cope with the problems of their lives resort to becoming ill. If the doctor has the opportunity of seeing them in the first phases of their becoming ill, i.e. before they settle down to a definite "organized" illness, he may observe that these patients, offer or propose various illnesses, and then they have to go on offering new illnesses. . . . (p. 18)

Depression is a way of healing the wounded psyche. Anxiety is a signal that psyche needs healing. Mania is a defense. All of these various illnesses may present at once in an attempt to heal the damage. Or, psychic disconnect may manifest itself in physical ailments. Migraines. Stomach problems. The somatization of psychic upheaval is a way to express what is beyond and perhaps before language. The body and the embodied mind work together as one to express what cannot be expressed only in words. However, some people get ill not because it is an expression of some psychic trauma but because the body breaks down for organic reasons; the body breaks down because of being exposed to chemicals or pesticides. Some physical illnesses are simply idiopathic. But there are some illnesses that are a direct result of child abuse. And these illnesses may not manifest until later in life. In a classic text on psychoanalysis and somatization, Georg Groddeck (1977) talks about possible "meanings of illness" (see *The Meaning of Illness: Selected Psychoanalytic Writings*). Groddeck's main thesis in this text is that illness serves a purpose. Illness serves "a protective measure" (p. 128). Groddeck argues that getting ill protects one from greater dangers. Migraines that occur after binge drinking serve to protect. Migraines associated with heavy drinking are a message sent to the drinker to stop drinking. If the drinker continues, worse illnesses might manifest. Korsakov's syndrome being one of the worst.

The body never heals from early psychic or physical injury which takes a toll on the immune system. In adult life injuries or sicknesses are more likely to occur. Why people get ill is a vastly complex issue. It is simply reprehensible to blame the victim. But this is one of the most common responses to illnesses. The point I am trying to make here, however, is that some people are more vulnerable to illnesses because their defense systems have broken down at some archaic, primal level— especially if they were abused. Michael Eigen (2005) tells us that for some people "catastrophe links personality together" (p. 60). If all you know is catastrophe than all you will unconsciously seek is more catastrophic. The familiar likes like.

The inability to heal and its afterwardness or *Nachtraglichkeit* scars an entire life. The child in the adult does not heal if badly beaten. The primal disconnect works on in the future to keep disconnecting new relations and new objects. Psyche is always already under the shadow of the primal disconnect. The question then is how to go on, how to live with so much pain and torment? Is there no solace? Is there no peace? Maybe and maybe not. It is the maybe not that troubles. If the past is too much in the present, the future is just more of the same. However, even if the future is just more of the same, the need to overcome trauma may drive one to become an artist or scholar, as Green points out. So it is an irony that out of the bad comes the good. Writing under a troubling compulsion may– in some ways– get out the "rubbish" that Enid Balint talked about. Playing, also is a form of expelling bad objects–at least temporarily. Diane Waller (2002) tells us that:

> Killick, drawing on Bion (1957), suggests that the art [i.e. playing an instrument] is: "used by the patient experiencing catastrophic anxiety as a means of intrusive identification i.e. as a way of forcibly evacuating unbearable anxieties into the art object [or instrument]. . . . (p. 6)

"Forcibly evacuating unbearable" imagos and pushing them into the instrument or the mystic writing pad—as Freud called it– is an interesting defense mechanism. Playing is also a way of forgetting. So too is writing. Sometimes forgetting is a blessing. Other times it is a curse. What do we use forgetting to do psychically? The specter of Adam Phillips again. Unbearable psychic thoughts get put into objects. How is this different from what psychotics do with their internal demons? By use of projective identification they move parts of themselves inside objects in order to get rid of them or better control them. When playing an instrument do we not do the same thing, do we not projectively identify with the object?

The thing about moving bad-mother-imago feelings into an art object or into a musical instrument is that you never get rid of her. She keeps coming back and back. She is always going to come back. If the dead mother actually died to psyche would the writing or playing stop? Do we dare give up our neuroses? The gift of the dead mother is the gift of creativity. Torment gives us something to write about, some reason to play. Again, I'm not saying that torments are good and I am not trying to romanticize torments. All I am suggesting here is that we can make use of those torments through artistic or scholarly endeavors and make use of them we should. Otherwise our lives are futile. To make useful that which has harmed us is the only way to work through an otherwise intolerable situation.

PART TWO

CHAPTER SEVEN

ON NOT BEING ABLE TO WORK

The Scholar's Dilemma

In part one of this book I argued that the musician who is no longer able to play might become a scholar of music. Studying music and writing about it might serve to heal the pain of not being able to play. In the second part of this book I talk about the scholar who is no longer able to work. When scholarly work becomes impossible due to psychic stress, the scholar might consider immersing herself in music to heal her psychic wounds. Psychic wounds can heal and the scholar must heal these wounds so as to get back to work. My argument here is that we must not let our critics get the best of us and we not let institutions so damage us that we are no longer able to do our work. Thus, I examine problems of institutions (in this case the university) and how the very nature of institutions can serve to destroy scholars. The larger question for this book is how to prevent inner collapse. When one cannot do what one wants in life, one must go on, but how? You cannot fight Tammany Hall. So what to do? When the scholar sees that it is a losing battle, how does she avoid psychic crisis? This is the scholar's dilemma.

During the crisis of industrialization in the United States, unions were born. New forms of scholarship emerge during times of great social stress. New religious movements are born during times of social stress. 1969 was a turning point in American history. Vietnam, Kent State. The Weather Collective and the Reconceptualization of curriculum studies. Radical political movements, radical new social movements and radical scholarly movements came into being at this historical juncture. It is no accident that the Reconceptualization came into being when it did. As I see it, The Reconceptualization emerged when it did partly because of the social stress of the times. The Reconceptualization changed the face of education despite its opposition. Today we enter into what is termed the post-Reconceptualization and we are going strong despite pressure from our critics and detractors.

DEATH IN A TENURED POSITION REVISITED: A TRIBUTE TO WILLIAM F. PINAR

The impetus for writing this book comes from reading William Pinar's (1984) groundbreaking essay titled *"Death in a Tenured Position."* I see my work as an extension of this essay and I take my lead from Pinar's haunting piece. What depresses is that it seems that nothing has changed since 1984; academe has only gotten worse. In 1984 Pinar notes:

> Within curriculum departments, "back to basics" conservatives assert power; graduates of "cognate" or "parent" disciplines are hired. Deans and department chairpersons become obsessed with (not just watchful of) full time student numbers, and collegial relations deteriorate as competition, suspicion fear and resentment, never absent from the academic scene, intensify. Tenured faculty even drink a little more and retire aggressively into personal lives. (p. 194).

Although Pinar wrote these words in 1984, they are still relevant today. In colleges of education across the country curriculum studies scholars struggle against conservative critics who would like nothing more than to get rid of us. Conservative educationists see no point to scholarship that is remotely theoretical, philosophical or historical. Curriculum studies is intensely theoretical, historical and philosophical. Our conservative colleagues argue that what we are doing is irrelevant. We are resented because of our strong research record (curriculum studies scholarship has grown exponentially over the last twenty years). And yet scholarship is valued little in anti-intellectual, right wing colleges of education. We are far outnumbered by our right wing colleagues and so we have an uphill battle to fight. The American curriculum studies field is under attack by the right wing–as it has been for the past twenty some years. A vast number of American curriculum scholars have fled to Canada for good reason. The conservative climate in the United States has made a significant and negative impact on all public institutions. And colleges of education are no exception. The future of curriculum studies in the United States looks bleak. It looked bleak to Bill Pinar in the 1980s. And yet, here we are. Somehow we survive. The younger scholars carry the torch. And they carry the burden. Young scholars in the field of curriculum studies have a tremendous responsibility to not give in to the older, more conservative generations of critics who would like nothing more than to destroy us and destroy what we stand for. After the older generation of conservative scholars retire, the battle is ours to win or lose. This book is written so that we might win this battle.

The younger generation of curriculum scholars carry the torch through academic landmines. Pinar (1984) laments that during the early days of curriculum studies, "our arrival brought no applause, only an occasionally broken hostility which expressed itself not always directly, but often obliquely in a myriad of ways that made professional life difficult and discouraging" (p. 196). Some twenty years later, little has changed. No applause still. We are not welcomed still. Our scholarship is not recognized as legitimate by number crunchers. We arrive at tenure in a state of psychic death. We get tenure and then sing the song, *"Is that all there is?"* Ours is a torch song. Even after tenure our critics want to bring us down, humiliate us.

Psychic death is at hand. The institution shuts psyche down. The introjected bad object suffocates. Shutting down may be momentary or it may be periodic or it may be for good. For the scholar, psychic death means no more thoughts. I am thinking here of Bartelby's *The Scrivener*. 'I prefer not to.' I prefer not to think any more thoughts. I have had enough!! I have nothing more to say about the matter.

I am interested in academic breakdown. Academic crackup.

Is there a way out? This is what I call the scholar's dilemma and it goes something like this: The academy has killed me psychically. What do I do now? Can I get back? How can I get back to my thoughts, to my writing and to my studying? What if I cannot?

The scholar who can no longer work, who can no longer think, write or study might take the lead from our damaged musician. Perhaps the scholar might move onto a different psychic register. If the intellect gets blocked, travelling to another psychic place becomes necessary for survival. The scholar might turn toward the more artistic part of her personality, she might sit back for a while and listen to music. Music heals psychic wounds. Of that I am convinced.

The message of this book comes in the shape of a Parabola. Here is the parabola: The musician who can no longer play might become a scholar of music or a scholar of anything for that matter. The scholar who can no longer think might become a musician or listen to music to heal psychic wounds. The scholar might begin to dwell in a world without words—for a time– to heal the psychic damage.

Music may serve to heal the damaged intellect. Perhaps if one allows the psyche to expand in the realm of music the intellect may begin to heal and thoughts might come back again. The choice is yours. Move on or die. Which will it be? The scholar's dilemma is finding a way out. I am not the first person to talk of this. William Pinar (1994) talked of this years ago. However, my ideas on that way out differ from Pinar's in that I suggest that that way out might be found in the healing aspects of music.

THE GREAT INTRUSION: THE SCHOLAR'S BREAKDOWN

The scholar who suffers from an inability to work suffers from a form of psychic breakdown. I dealt with psychic struggles in the first part of the book in relation to the musician who can no longer play. The scholar who can no longer think is in a bad state no doubt. The scholar who can no longer work has reached a state of psychic crisis. This is the crisis of scholarly breakdown. Linda Hopkins (2006) tells us of Masud Khan's ongoing struggles with breakdown. Khan became a raging alcoholic as a way of not dealing with his "false self", as Hopkins puts it. He went through many periods during his career of not being able to write or even get out of bed. Although he was an analysand of Winnicott's and a well known analyst himself, his psychic trouble wrecked his life. His turn to alcohol might have caused his psychotic breaks late in his life. He began to believe that he was a character in a Dostoyevsky novel. Although Khan had many personal troubles he did offer to the psychoanalytic community some important theories of self that might have had something to do with his own problems. One such theory was rather postmodern. Hopkins (2006) explains:

... he [Khan] was firmly convinced that people have multiple incompatible selves that are all real. The way to understand a person, he said, was to "explicate the paradox," not to try to resolve it. ... (xxiv)

Certainly, his personality—as reported by Hopkins–seemed to bear out this theory. He was a complex man who did many good things in his life but also engaged in some questionable behavior—like sleeping with his patients and fabricating stories about other analysts. He also talked about what he called "cumulative trauma" (p. 166, Hopkins). Hopkins explains:

... [in] Khan's article "The Concept of Cumulative Trauma," [here he suggests] ... that a person can be severely traumatized by an accumulation of small disruptions that add up. (p. 166)

This adding up of "small disruptions" is what child abuse is about, except that abuse is not in any way small. The adding up of the inattentive mother, abuse, neglect and the rest can catch up to a person later in life. If in later life a person gets injured or sick, the way in which she deals with it has a lot to do with the effect of cumulative trauma as Khan puts it. For people who are not victims of child abuse or neglect, the idea of cumulative trauma means little. But for those who already suffer from post traumatic stress from an old injury, a new trauma makes life simply intolerable. This intolerable state can lead to breakdowns. On a related note, Julia Segal (1985) suggests that phantasies we have in adult life might be repetitions of phantasies we had as children. She tells us that:

Since we already understand something in terms of what we already know, my present-day adult phantasies must be related, however distantly, to phantasies that I developed not only in childhood but also in earliest infancy when perception began. (p. 29)

What is astonishing in Segal's remark is that psyche has a very old unconscious memory. We cannot remember consciously "earliest infancy" but still, the unconscious memory of everything is there, somewhere in our psyche. If as the Kleinians put it, our phantasy of the murderous mother is encrypted in psyche from earliest infancy—whether the actual mother did anything to cause these feelings or not—and psyche has not worked through these murderous phantasies (what Kleinians call the paranoid-schizoid position), these feelings still linger into adult life. Paranoia can undo psyche. Certainly paranoia can cause a breakdown. At any rate, the point I am trying to drive home here is that psyche is incredibly repetitious. We feel now what we felt then, we act now as we acted then, we respond to things as we responded then. We do what we have always done. The only way to break these cycles is of course to go into analysis and work through what gets in the way of living a life. Acting out, as Freud teaches, is a form of repeating something we do not remember. And it seems that most of us act out more than we know. A breakdown is a disconnect between the memory, the now and the acting out. Perhaps a breakdown is yet another form of acting out.

There are all kinds of breakdowns. We have little ones every day. If the mother–university insists on intruding and intruding and intruding on scholarly work, how much intrusion can the psyche take? We know that an intrusive mother can cause the child all sorts of psychological damage. Being colonized psychologically by the mother arrests emotional growth. Being colonized by the university can arrest intellectual growth. Let us look at some useful metaphors of psychic distress in order to better understand what it feels like to be continuously intruded upon.

Let us look at William Pinar's (1984) *"Death in a Tenured Position."* I return to Pinar's piece in order to get a more historical sense of the problem at hand. I return to Pinar's piece also to honor the work that he has done on the problem of psychic damage and its relation to the larger culture and the university. At the end of his 1984 essay he states:

> . . . autobiography, however practiced, supplies no insulation from the pain of living in bad times, times when the forces of what is dead-and-past triumph, when what is ugly mars the landscape, when death fouls the air, and we the living cringe, and despair. (p. 198)

Curriculum studies was built on the idea that scholarship must be a working out of the self (i.e. autobiography), of going inward in order to understand what Pinar terms the psychosocial. Pinar was the first in the field of education to take this turn. Early on, Reconceptualization–as Pinar envisioned it–meant studying historically and theoretically educational issues via psychoanalysis and phenomenology. Yet, even in the 1980s when the Reconceptualization was well under way, the *"dead-and-past"* still *"triumphed."* The quest for standardization, assessments, outcomes reign still today. It seems as if nothing has changed–the dead and what is past is present still. We progressives keep fighting the fight but it seems as if our conservative colleagues are always on the winning side. Quantification, standardization and assessments rule the day. The specters of Thorndike and Ralph Tyler.

The more disturbing point Pinar (1984) makes is that if one practices autobiographical scholarship (i.e. via psychoanalysis or phenomenology), there is little guarantee that this kind of intellectual labor will shield the scholar against the psychic onslaught. However, working out of the self—as Pinar urges us to do—is the best way to get at psychic issues in scholarly work. What we curriculum studies scholars do is still considered suspect. And indeed as Pinar points out, it is painful to know that our work is not valued or supported by our conservative colleagues and that these colleagues look at us as rogues or even worse, as kooks.

Curriculum studies scholars are trying to carry out Dewey's progressive educative project. But as we know since 1957 with Sputnik, curriculum scholars have had little say in what goes on in public school curriculum. Generally speaking, the public schools have never been progressive; in fact public schools have never even been a site of education. Rather, public schooling has always been a place of mis-education, under-education and factory training. Public education in this country is a tragedy. Teachers have to do what they are told on what day and what time, teach to the tests (the standardized tests), teach books they have not chosen, and fear for their jobs if the test scores are not high enough. No child left behind is every child left behind and every teacher left behind. Children are traumatized by the constant intrusion of testing nightmares and teachers have little power to stop this testing mania. Teachers and Education professors get blamed for our failing public schools.

So what do we do? *"We return to the self"*—as Pinar urges. A return to the self is part and parcel of the progressive project. However, the progressive dream is simply not considered a legitimate research agenda at some universities. Some conservative critics tell us that, for example, curriculum studies journals are not research journals. Our critics believe that real research is found in crunching numbers, doing statistics and empirical studies. Theoretical work that broadly draws on the humanities and the social sciences-like curriculum theory—remains suspect by many inside of the larger field of education. This realization, for the younger generation of curriculum scholars, is shocking.

Marxists who do curriculum studies work focus mostly on politics and power inside of public schools and universities. This work is needed and important. But those of us in the curriculum studies field on the psychoanalytic wing can work to uncover what psychic ruins are left after conservatives try politically to demolish us and our work. My task here is to undertake the psychoanalytic work that is needed to better understand what happens as a result of this political battle at hand.

Professors, like schoolteachers, have little power. Working in oppressive institutions like the university or the schoolhouse takes its toll. The psyche dies under enough pressure. How to avoid utter collapse working under oppressive conditions? I think these are the major questions that Pinar (1984) asks in his groundbreaking essay *"Death in a Tenured Position."* But what is this death? What is psychic death? What does it feel like to be psychically dead? As Pinar points out, "pain is a key element of psychic death." But what is pain? Earlier in this book I worked to explore a phenomenology of pain and the upshot of my discussion was that pain is hard to articulate because it is intensely private. The problem with 'pain' is that it is hard to put in words what it means or what it feels like. Psychic pain is especially troublesome to articulate. Pain is an intensely private affair. There certainly is ongoing psychic pain for the scholar who is not recognized or who feels degraded by her peers. Progressive knowledge(s) trouble the academy because the purpose of the university is to conserve tradition, conserve the past. The new is not welcomed. Now, curriculum studies is no longer a new discipline. It has been around for over thirty years. But it is still not welcomed. It is painful for the scholar to work in such a hostile environment.

There is a constant ongoing pain that the progressive scholar experiences on a daily basis–especially in American institutions. American colleges of education are notoriously conservative. Progressives who are housed in conservative colleges have an uphill battle to fight daily. And this is painful. That pain might be felt as a tightness in the chest, as a furrow of the brow, as a cloud hovering. That pain is felt in the bowels and in the stomach as knots. Being all tied up. Feeling sick to the stomach. Nauseated. The pain of denial. This is not happening. Yes it is. This is not happening. Yes it is.

If the mother dismisses the child enough, the child becomes dissociated. Dissociation serves, however, as a defense mechanism against trauma. The death of the psyche begins in a dismissal. Your work does not count. It matters not what you do, it will never count. It will never be worth anything. These dismissals translate into: You are worthless. And this is what it feels like to be a progressive scholar in reactionary times. We often overlook these dismissals and pretend that it does not really matter. But then physical illness strikes. The psyche and soma are not disconnected. What you do not acknowledge psychically will emerge somatically. The body has a way of speaking trauma. Living in unhealthy places can literally make us sick. Imagine the mother constantly berating the child, making fun of the child, denigrating the child. The child eventually gets sick. The disintegrating child. The academy–as mother to the scholar—causes psychic disintegration. Carl Jung (1977) suggests that universities are indeed "mother symbols." He states:

> Many things arousing devotion or feelings of awe, as for instance the Church, university, city or country, heaven, earth, the woods, sea or any still waters, matter even, the underworld and the moon, can be mother symbols. (p. 81)

As against Jung, the university—though it may be a mother symbol—does not arouse awe but dread. The university is the bad breast, the not good enough mother, the dead mother. She pays not a wit of attention to the child. Psyche withers. Working in hostile conditions is like living with an abusive mother.

The university is a place that arouses not awe but what is awful. It is a place that fosters conservative thinking or no thinking at all; it is a place that, ironically, does not value the intellectual. It is Kafka's Castle. Conformity, mediocrity and conservatism. These are the things that the university values.

Mother likes her children to be obedient. The symbol of the mother can also be an "evil" one, Jung (1977) contends. Evil symbols–Jung teaches– accordingly are these: "the witch, the dragon (or any devouring and entwining animal. . . deep water, death, nightmares and bogies Empusa, Lilith, etc.)" (p. 82). The university is devouring, a nightmare, full of bogie men. The university is the devouring mother. In nightmares, one often dreams of water (a symbol of the unconscious) and of drowning. One can drown in the poison waters of university politics. Edgar Allan Poe (2006), in his short story titled *"A Descent into the Maelstrom"* describes being pulled into a raging vortex (a symbol of psychic death). He describes the descent of a large boat that sinks violently into the depths of the sea as if pulled under by a black hole. The narrator of Poe's story states:

> . . . the noise being heard several leagues off, and the vortices or pits are of such an extent and depth, that if a ship [the ship of the ego] comes within its attraction [the intrusion of the mother into the unconscious] it is inevitably absorbed and carried down to the bottom, and there beat to pieces against the rocks. (p. 30)

The university is an Edgar Allan Poe world where scholars–especially progressive ones– descend into the maelstrom. The maelstrom that is the university can cause psychic death. The maelstrom that is the university *"beats to pieces"* our psyches against the rock of ruin.

As Jung (1977) teaches deep water can symbolize evil. On a conscious level, the scholar may be able to stay above ground and keep going more or less, but she might be tormented by nightmares of drowning. Drowning is a symbol of psychic going under of losing the ego, of disintegration. Getting *"beaten against the rocks"* as Poe's narrator puts it, is what the scholar may feel walking through the negative space that is the university. A child is being beaten– a well known piece by Freud– could be a trope for the scholar who gets beaten down. The university beats the scholar down day in and day out. Thomas Moore (2004) – a Jungian psychoanalyst– talks about the experience of being *"battered."* "Enter a dark night of the soul." Moore (2004) states:

> A dark night of the soul doesn't merely plunge you into darkness, it also batters you, so that you may well feel emotionally beaten and lacerated. The alchemists described this process as mortification, emotional suffering that leaves you destroyed. As the word implies (mors, mortis means death), mortification entails dying to your will and ego. (p. 77)

We might connect Moore's dark night of soul with Pinar's (1984) *"Death in a Tenured Position."* Death in a tenured position is a dark night of the soul indeed. That psychic death is felt as being "beaten and lacerated", "battered." Head down to the ground, stomach in knots, chest tightened. Derrick Jensen (2006), drawing on the work of Judith Herman suggests that the abused suffer an ongoing "cringe" (p. 726). Herman argues–according to Jensen–that some people who suffer from long time 'captivity' [captivity inside of the university?] suffer from perpetual trauma. Herman explains that:

> Prolonged captivity [of childhood or working in the university] . . . undermines or destroys the ordinary sense of a relatively safe sphere of initiative, in which there is tolerance for trial and error [experimental scholarship]. To the chronically traumatized person [the wounded scholar] . . .any action has potentially dire consequences. There is no room for mistakes [there is no room for progressive thought]. (Herman qtd. in Jensen, pp. 725–726)

To speak one's mind, to have dissenting opinions, to push intellectual boundaries are all potential pitfalls for the wounded scholar who lives in the house of Usher. It feels–after a while–that the university is not a safe space for open ended and progressive intellectual work. The 'House of Usher' (Poe, 2006) produces what Herman calls "chronically traumatized person [s]". The chronically traumatized person has got to become paranoid, always looking over her shoulder, looking out for any pitfalls for fear of falling into any 'pits' with swinging deadly 'pendulums' (Poe, 2006). The continual fear– of working in the House of Usher, where any situation can turn psychically deadly– causes the structures of one's psychic house to deteriorate. Poe's (2006) narrator in the *"Fall of the House of Usher"* describes a gloomy place:

... a sense of insufferable gloom pervaded my spirit. . . . I looked upon the scene before me—upon the mere house. . . upon the bleak walls–upon the vacant eye-like windows–upon a few rank sedges–and upon a few white trunks of decayed trees. . . . (p. 109)

If the university is the House of Usher and the scholar internalizes this scene of horror and paranoia, her own psychic house will eventually collapse under the weight of "*decayed trees.*" Decayed trees eventually fall. The body is made limb by limb of matter not unlike that matter that makes up trees.

 If you tell a child over and over again that he or she is bad, the child will eventually internalized this. The scholar who is continuously belittled is like the child who is told of her badness. Like Poe, Dickens (2005) talks about a "Bleak House" in his novel by this name. The Bleak House of the soul is a house of decay and ruin. For Dickens the bleak house is industrial 19th century London. A character in Dickens's novel comments:

I asked whether there was a great fire anywhere? For the streets were so full of dense brown smoke that scarcely anything was to be seen. . . . Everything was so strange–the stranger from its being night in the day-time. . . . (p. 42)

Bleak House reminds me of the creepy Sweeny Todd (which was a Broadway musical) who was the 'demon barber of Fleet Street.' This demon barber symbolizes industrial 19th century London in all of is killing aspects. The working class in London paid a terrible price for technological advance and industrial progress. Industry always comes at a price. Coal—a common source of energy in the 19th and early 20th century– produces soot which turns the sky black. It turns buildings black. It turns lungs black. People died of black lung disease in droves. In my own lifetime, I can recall the fallout from industrial waste as I could see the soot from the steel mills on buildings. You could smell the stench. And the skies were always overcast with a sort of grey-black hue. Like London, many people report that Pittsburgh was so full of soot from the mills—especially at the turn of the 20th century– that it was dark during the day. Samuel Schreiner (1995) reports that work in the mills turned:

Pittsburgh into a restless, clangorous, noxious place that was loud at midnight and dark at noon. . . . black smoke . . . would lie like a pall over the whole area. . . . Anthony Trollope described it as "the blackest place I ever saw". . . . British philosopher Herbert Spencer said that a month in Pittsburgh would justify suicide. (p. 8)

I grew up in Pittsburgh and know from first hand experience that this is one of the most depressing cities in the country. It still gets dark at noon especially in winter. It is always overcast there, it is always gloomy. The soot of the mills can still be found in traces on buildings in the university area of Pittsburgh. Some of the buildings are still blackened. Soot leaves a literal and psychic trace. What is psychic soot? The psyche internalizes soot. A soot like-psyche dies unto itself.

Soot needs to be cleaned off, pressure washed. But after a while, the soot stains so deeply that no amount of cleaning will fix the ruins of the soul.

It surprises me that more professors do not commit suicide. Jungian analyst James Hillman (1997) has written one of the most important books on suicide called *Suicide and the Soul*. This is a must read for scholars who suffer from working under oppressive conditions. Suicide of the soul means the symbolic death of psyche. To be the wounded scholar is to have a dead psyche. Autobiography and the talking cure might help to bring alive a dead psyche, but as Pinar (1984) points out, working on autobiography is no guarantee that one will be "*insulated*" from the horrors of an oppressive institution. There is no "*insulation*" against soot. It gets on your clothes, on your shoes, in your lungs, in your hair, on your fingers. Soot seeps in no matter what you try to do to keep it out. We know what happened to the steel city–Pittsburgh– during the 1970s. The mills collapsed. The industry began dying. Many people lost their livelihoods. Industry dried up. I do not think that Pittsburgh has ever recovered from the collapse of industry there; the city remains dead even today. A visit to Pittsburgh today—at least for me– is disappointing. Nothing is going on in the steel city. Downtown is completely dead. All the old time stores are gone, family run bakeries are gone, the big department stores that were once milling about with people in the downtown area are no longer there. Today Pittsburgh has one of the largest elderly populations in the United States. There is little to attract young people to move to this city, little goes on there. Don't get me wrong, I love Pittsburgh—symbolically it is a very important city for me, it is the city where my family is from, it is the city where I was born, it is the city where I went to elementary school and college, it is the city of my ancestors. But it is always depressing to visit because most of my family from Pittsburgh are now dead and gone. When I get off the plane in the airport in Pittsburgh my father is no longer there to greet me. It is like stepping into the void. No matter how much clean up was done after the mills closed, the mess remains. The soul that gets polluted by the mess of psychic soot remains.

In a book titled "The Inhuman" [an appropriate symbol for the university], Jean-Francois Lyotard (1991) remarks that one day, "[w]e wake up and we are not happy" (p. 197). Unlike experiencing "A Happy Death" as Albert Camus (1995) puts it, we in the academy who cannot psychically function because of being beaten down experience an "*unhappy death*." We progressive scholars on the left are profoundly unhappy. We keep fighting what seems to be a losing battle. We are the myth of Sisyphus. As Winnicott (1992) might put it, "we are forever falling." The oppressive nature of any institution forces the psyche to fall forever down the mountain.

Why is it that institutions are such inhuman places? We have created them! We can destroy them, or at least reform them. But we know that pubic schools, for example, have been under 'reform' since they were invented. We hear politicians talk about fiscal reform but nothing ever gets reformed.

Wounds can heal but they take time to heal. Perhaps these unhappy death[s] are plural. We die everyday. Perhaps like perennial flowers we can regenerate. Is there enough regenerative power in psyche to keep going despite the toxic atmosphere of the university-mill? Such psychic toxicity. The feeling of heaviness, of being weighed down. And then there is the dread. Unspeakable dread.

Emerson (2003) comments on the hostility that scholars have to continually face. He remarks:

> In the long period of his [sic] preparation, he must betray often an ignorance and shiftlessness in popular arts, incurring the disdain of the able who shoulder him aside. Long he must stammer in his speech; often forego the living for the dead. . . . and the state of virtual hostility in which he seems to stand to society, and especially to educated society. (pp. 236–237)

To 'stammer' takes courage. The scholar works long and hard to make her way through ideas. Ideas do not come over night, and sometimes do not come at all. Crafting papers or books is all consuming. The scholar must be submerged in her studies which means that the outside world comes second. A life in text means world is second. Everything that makes the difference in thinking centers on texts. To say anything remotely unique one must spend a great deal of time with ideas. Books are the lifeblood of the scholar. Getting inside of texts-- and internalizing that which is studied-- takes a certain psychological disposition that not everyone has. Firstly, patience. One must be patient with ideas and let them come of their own accord. Forcing things will not work. Ideas come in their own time and space. America, though, is not a culture of ideas. It is a culture of sports and movie stars. Those of us who work with ideas are shunned and belittled. Certainly our salaries tell the tale.

There is an inordinate amount of mystery that goes along with working on ideas and working on texts. What happens between the reading of a text and the writing around that text cannot be rationally explained. The awe with which the scholar must approach a text must be kept alive. But much '*stammering*' as Emerson puts it, is at hand. To be able to acknowledge a certain tentativeness about ideas takes maturity. Never sure which way the wind will blow our thinking, we press on. It is this intellectual labor–as tentative as it may be– that gives life meaning. And yet there are those who would like to bring the scholar down. Jacques Barzun (2002) comments on the "house of intellect" as being a "divided [h]ouse" (p. 13). There is something wrong with the place in which scholars are housed. We are indeed a house divided. Those who are hostile to scholarly work are anti-intellectuals housed in universities themselves. Barzun (2002) comments that "[i]ntellect is despised and neglected. . . . the recrimination begins and ends with intellectuals themselves. It is they who find one another corrupt..." (p. 2). What disturbs is that some scholars enter into the House of Intellect [the university] only to give up their intellectual life. Scholars who no longer produce scholarship should not be called scholars. What is it about the very conditions of that house of the intellect that make it rather uninhabitable? Somebody has made that house of intellect uninhabitable. But who are these people? When did this house of intellect become a house of usher and not a house that ushers in a new age of thought? I do not know the answer to this question. Perhaps looking for the root of the problem leads only to a dead end. We know that the problems of the university are not new. The question haunts because no answers come forth. This makes for a certain frustration.

Killing the psyche–or attempts at killing the psyche– are felt early on in an academic career. What does this feel like? To continually feel assaulted. I want to return to some metaphors that may help describe these negatives. Aldous Huxley (1954/2004) talks about what he calls "the negatively transfigured world. . ." (p. 135). When one feels pressed by ongoing hostility–by an invisible hand of oppression–things turn ugly. Huxley talks about one Renee–a schizophrenic–who described the world as a living hell. The description of Renee's world could be also what scholars feel inside the house of the university of usher. Huxley (1954/2004) reports that for Renee:

> The summer sunshine is malignant; the gleam of polished surfaces is suggestive not of gems, but of machinery and enameled tin; the intensity of existence which animates every object. . . is felt as a menace. (p. 134)

The house of the university of usher is this very "negatively" transfixed description. Renee's world is our world in the university of the house of usher. One does not have to be schizophrenic to experience the world in this way. The house of the university of usher is a site of 'menace.' There is something menacing when others are out to bring you down through humiliation, back stabbing, ridicule, and glaring looks in the hallway. And then there are those who pretend you are not there at all. Not acknowledged as existing–as other faculty turn their heads and do not acknowledge your presence at all– could be symptomatic of homophobia, racism, sexism. Or maybe this non-acknowledgment is political. They don't like our politics, a friend on the faculty tells me. But even still, whatever happened to the notion of collegiality? Maybe it's worse when they smile in your face and stab you in the back.

At any rate, making someone feel invisible is to kill symbolically. Entering into the most beautiful of surroundings–brand new offices, mahogany desks and bookshelves–matters little when one is treated as the despised. We are the untouchables—left leaning, experimental curriculum theorists. This may sound unbelievable and exaggerated but it is not. The young professor just coming out of graduate school has high hopes for a university position. But then when she gets that position those hopes are dashed because what she thought the university would be turns out to be pure and utter fantasy. The university is not what it seems. All that is potentially beautiful turns ugly and menacing– and as Poe's Renee tells us. What is outside of that office door is a creeping crawling anger, a negativity that is so thick that one cannot cut through it. Houses of higher education are haunted houses. I am reminded of Poe's (1976) *The System of Dr Tarr and Professor Fether* where the narrator arrives at a famous madhouse called the *Maison de Sante*. The narrator tells us that:

> It was a fantastic chateau, much dilapidated, and scarcely tenantable through age and neglect. Its aspect inspired me with absolute dread, and, checking my horse, I half resolved to turn back. (pp. 175–176)

Inside of the most beautiful building—and this could be a college of education—one feels as Poe describes above–that the place is "*scarcely tenantable*" because it is psychically "*neglected.*" A certain pathology hovers in the air. Everything that one touches turns monstrous. Living in a psychically "*dilapidated*" house is like being on a bad acid trip. Many join ranks with the monsters and turn on new professors coming into the system of Dr. Tarr and Professor Fether. This is a system (a university system) like Tarr's madhouse run by the inmates. In my last book (Morris, 2006) I suggested, indeed, that the university is a madhouse and one has to do the best one can to survive in it or get out. The university is the only house for intellectuals and so we have to make our beds there. But we cannot hide under the covers or we die. We must meet the monsters head on. This is where the intellectual deals with the hand it has been given and goes forward. Progressive intellectuals–those of us inheritors of Dewey's dream–are the ones who suffer most from the monstrous treatment. When we turn to our writings we do so in order to deal with these monsters. We do not write in well lit rooms, but in rooms of darkness. We do not write in a room of our own, but in rooms inhabited by monsters. Richard Mabey (2005) comments about Annie Dillard's writing of *Pilgrim at Tinker Creek.* He tells us that:

> When Annie Dillard was writing her extraordinary odyssey into the meaning of evolution, Pilgrim at Tinker Creek, she worked in a second-floor carrel in Hollins College Library overlooking a tar-and-gravel roof [shades of Prof. Tar] 'One wants a room with no view,' she wrote, 'so imagination can meet memory in the dark.' (p. 33)

One "meets" the dark through and in the dark. One meets monsters by welcoming them into one's study. 'Come in, sit down, have a cup of coffee, talk to me monsters, what do you want?' Trying to re-imagine those harsh feelings that one confronts at the university of the house of usher is a way to begin to cope with them. Giving them names and turning them into images helps to cope. We must not let the monsters win. The 'tar-and-gravel roof' of the psyche is that place that makes our feet stick. Perhaps we need to get stuck and fall in order to get unstuck and not fall. Jung (1977) teaches that *going into* images helps us to *get out of* situations that make us feel stuck. He states:

> The symbolic process is an experience in images and of images. Its development usually shows an enantiodromian structure like the text of the I Ching, and so presents a rhythm of negative and positive, loss and gain, dark and light. Its beginning is almost invariably characterized by one's getting stuck in a blind alley or in some impossible situation; and its goal is, broadly speaking, illumination or higher consciousness by means of which the initial situation is overcome. . . . (pp. 38–39)

The way out is found through going into images, especially the negative images. The scholar's dilemma is about finding a way out through exploring negative images. A way out is made by finding a way through images and study. Studying in the dark.

Huxley (1954/2004), in his book *Doors of Perception: Heaven and Hell*, talks about images that get synthetically produced when taking drugs. Some drug trips are heavenly, others hellish. Ah–here is what Jung talks about with enantiodramian images! Huxley was in a better state of mind to do drugs since he could play with both sides of the psyche, the good and the bad. Some drugs can at once make psyche feel higher than a cloud and simultaneously paranoid. Some drugs are just awful. Hallucinations can terrify.

A scholar pushed to brink hallucinates. Hallucinated giant gingerbread men about to attack. The gingerbread men are the school people who obey and follow orders without question. They follow the marching orders in the army of academe. Huxley (1954/2004) talks of living in "a visionary hell" (p. 133). But what is 'visionary' about living in hell? Huxley (1954/2004) comments that Dante's world is a world where people get stuck inside things. He states:

> Dante's sinners are buried in the mud, shut up in the trunks of trees, frozen solid in blocks of ice, crushed beneath stone. (p. 136)

To get unburied, to get outside of tree trunks, to get unfrozen and uncrushed –this is the task at hand. To find the way out of being frozen in blocks of ice—psyche must fight. To be stuck inside of the ice block that is the university is to be utterly frozen, buried, crushed. This is what depression feels like. It is a frozen immobility, it is that frozen stare, it is the vacant look, it is the head downcast, it is that slow walk. Being stuck inside of a tree trunk or a rock or even a radio is a pretty depressing proposition. This is called projective identification. Schizophrenics experience getting psychically stuck inside of objects and sometimes they do not come back. I do not think you have to be schizophrenic to have such experiences– I think we all have them–in small doses–. Living in bad circumstances forces psyche to take refuge inside of objects. A self evacuated. But that psychic refuge can also become a psychic prison. Gwyn Thomas (1946/2006), in his novel *The Dark Philosophers* talks about the depressing life of coal miners in Wales. Coal miners not only suffer from black lung disease but they also suffer from disease of the psyche from working in such horrid situations. The miners' families suffer alongside them and in some instances sink beyond repair. A character in Thomas' story tells us:

> I made some tea. I poured a strong cup for my mother and took it upstairs. I knocked on her bedroom door. There was no answer. She slept well. I remembered that there was nothing in my mother's world worth getting up at a quarter of seven for. The distant look she wore showed that. She was elsewhere all the time. (p. 38)

The fall of the house of the university mining company kills psyche. The scholar has nothing to get up for when she feels as if her work does not matter, when her work is dismissed, when her words are meaningless, when she is made to feel invisible. The invisible scholar suffers from black lung disease of the soul. A soul blackened is never coming back. A dead soul. Can a soul be dead? Yes. When the scholar can no longer get out of bed the soul is a dead soul. When the scholar can no longer open a book and do her work, she is as good as dead. When the scholar no longer wants to study, her scholarly life is over, finished, done once and for all. Can they get away with this? Can the monsters do this? Can they so get into one's psyche as to annihilate it? Is this what the famous Dr. Schreber (2000) in, his book *Memoirs of my Nervous Illness*, called soul murder? We hope not, but for some the pressure of the house of usher to conform is too great and the psyche folds. The face tells the story. The down turned mouth. Pacing. Or not moving at all. Staying in bed all day. Are these breakdowns? Can the wardens in the house of usher break down our psyches? If we let them they can and they will.

THE WAY OUT

Psyches are prone to breaking. The psyche breaks down every day in small ways. Small breaks are probably good. Small breaks might prevent major ones. Mark Epstein (1999) suggests that we can "go to pieces without falling apart" as the title of his book suggests. Going to pieces is an interesting metaphor. What does it mean to go to pieces? Does psyche split in a million fragments like shattered glass? When a rock is thrown through a window, it may shatter but it could still be intact. The rock thrown through the window of psyche shatters and yet psyche can still maintain its integrity. A shattered self is melancholic. The melancholic self allows the shattering to occur. Psyche must attend to the broken shards with care. If not, the psyche can disappear into a black hole. This is a case of going to pieces AND falling apart. (see Epstein, 1999). Humpty Dumpty cannot be put back together again. So the question is how to go to pieces and not fall apart completely. Withstanding ugliness means going through the psychic "*garbage*", as Hillman suggests (see Moore (2004) on Hillman).

To find a way out of the scholar's dilemma, paying attention to emotional states becomes key. The intellect is often blinded by its own psychic censors. But the intellect can find ways into the emotional wreckage. What gets tough is mulling around in the emotional mess especially for scholars who for the most part are not used to working through emotions. Emotions, for many who rely on intellect, may be split off and hard to reach. This is the trick for the scholar. She must find a way around and through the intellect down under into the emotional wreckage. She must use both the emotions and the intellect to understand emotions. One must not intellectualize emotions away. From dark to dark. Emotions often overpower intellect though and scholars might be at a loss as to how to proceed.

Understanding is a faculty of the intellect. Understanding emotions means going into these emotions, not splitting them off. To intellectualize emotions is highly problematic. To intellectualize emotions is to avoid emotions altogether. Intellect can cover over emotions. And if intellect covers over emotions completely, no amount of searching or attempting to understand what has gone wrong will fix the problem at hand.

What has gone wrong in the scholar's life? The scholar's non-relation to the house of usher university is certainly part of the problem. There will never be any kind of healthy relation to such a pathological institution. The relation must be a dis-connected one. A divorce is called for. One must divorce oneself from that which harms the self. Otherwise, one becomes meshed with the crushing force of power. One must never become symbiotic with the house of usher. So, first and foremost one must fight symbiosis. The scholar is not her institution. Her work will not be remembered by what institution she gets attached to (like a para-site). What gets remembered are the scholar's texts that are left behind. The scholar must psychologically detach herself from what pathology abounds. Albert Camus (1956) tells us that we must rebel against an *"intrusion"* (in this case the rebellion is against the intrusive house of Usher). Camus (1956) teaches:

> Thus, the movement of rebellion is founded simultaneously on the categorical rejection of an intrusion that is considered intolerable and on the confused conviction of an absolute right which, in the rebel's mind, is more precisely the impression that he "has the right to. . ." Rebellion cannot exist without the feeling that, somewhere and somehow, one is right. (p. 13)

When the toxic mother intrudes psychologically, the child has two choices, give in or fight. If the child gives in, her psyche will become merged with the mother's. What toxins the mother projects into the child, the child will internalize for the rest of her life. If the child, however, refuses to allow the intrusive mother in psychically and fights the intrusion by drawing on her own psychological defences, the mother will not be able to colonize the child's psyche. If those lines between the mother and child are blurred because the mechanism of symbiosis is too strong, big problems wait in the wings. If the scholar blurs the lines between her own scholarly identity and the identity of the institution in which she is housed, big problems wait in the wings.

Sometimes people only fight back when things become intolerable. When does a psychic intrusion become intolerable? This question is not so easy to answer. But if one is going to pieces all the time the intrusion has become intolerable. Standing one's ground for what one believes in takes courage and strength. And as Camus tells us, psyche must believe that at bottom *"somewhere and somehow, one is right"*. Maybe the rebellion is single handed. Single handedly taking on the mother university is a tall order. A price will be paid for taking on the fight. Others–who are like characters out of Sinclair Lewis' (2005a) Babbitt–will try to persuade junior faculty to merely give in and go along. Tenure is at stake. It's not worth it they say, just play the game and get by and forget it. Institutions destroy. Senior professors are beaten down and just plain beaten. Some have no more thoughts and walk around defeated. It's hard to say what happens to people once they enter into a community for life. Think of the brotherhood of monks. What happens to people who enter these institutions forever. They never leave. They grow old together. The intellectual community is not that different from a monastic community. Intellectual labor requires a certain monkishness. One must step away from the world to study the world, one must dwell in the world of texts. Reading texts is a monkish occupation.

Back to the question of psychic intrusion. How to keep out unwanted toxins? That is the question. How does the scholar put up enough emotional barricades to keep out toxic forces? The mother can be very toxic. So too can the university. Jung (1977) has a suggestion:

> Again, resistance to the mother can sometimes result in a spontaneous development of the intellect for the purpose of creating a sphere of interest in which the mother has no place. . . . Its real purpose is to break the mother's power by intellectual criticism and superior knowledge, so as to enumerate all of her stupidities, mistakes in logic, and educational shortcomings. (p. 91)

The more the university–negative mother– tries to intrude into the psyche of the scholar, the more the scholar becomes, ironically, more scholarly and goes deeper into the wreck work. Psyche pushed towards psychic death tends to live more intensely. The way out of intrusive encounters with the mother usher is to focus more deeply on work that helps you understand and find a way out of problems at hand. The more they make trouble for you the harder you work. Jung teaches a very important lesson to struggling scholars. Keep working. The work will keep you sane. If you stop working, you lose. You will die psychically. You will have nothing to live for and won't be able to get out of bed and you just might go and lose your mind altogether. Don't let them win.

The progressive scholar's world is a difficult one because of the onslaught of conservative culture. Clearly we are outnumbered–especially in America. But being in the minority allows one to have a different kind of vision. This is the vision of difference and critique. A place at the margins opens up the doors of perception. These doors should open to a sacred world. The scholar's world is a sacred world where no intrusions are allowed. It takes work, though, to keep the doors of psyche closed off from dangerous toxins.

The scholar's world is a place that is–in a way–cut off from the everyday because–ironically–it analyzes the everyday. It is almost an impossible task to analyze what is directly in front of you unless you get some distance from it. Hence, the problem of phenomenology. What is right in front of you is the hardest thing to get at. And if what you are trying to get at is painful, how to express what is so painfully private to others? Can we let the secret of our pain out of the bag?

Children have secrets and usually want to keep them from their parents. Do we scholars want to keep our painful secrets away from our parent university? Perhaps. Children's' secret worlds are sacred. Are our secret worlds sacred too? Maybe children have make believe friends or fairy castles in the sky or space ships that take them to mars. We scholars—where are our space ships? Inventing secret worlds are ways that the child protects herself from the intrusive mother. Mother will never know about my space ship and when she tries to beat me I will fly away in my space ship and she won't be able to hurt me. Hence, the defence mechanism of dissociation is born. A scholar's secret world is not dissimilar. The secret world of ideas are meant to code reality in order to better decode it. Turning reality into hermetic codes and turning pain into metaphors are ways in which the scholar engages her secret pain. Coded and decoded texts, secrets, hermetic worlds, private pain–all of these are the scholar's tools. Here I am reminded of Mark Epstein's (1999) remarks on his secret room. Epstein tells us that:

> I had a recurring dream during that time of suddenly discovering, through a variety of means, a secret room in my house that was my one special place. I can still picture, or rather, feel, that room today. It was hidden behind a fake wall and was reached through a secret corridor or back staircase. Every time I came upon it in my dreams I felt relieved. (p. 4)

The secret room of the psychic house is the one safe room into which psyche can retreat. The scholar's secret room is the psychic house of intellect where ideas are sacred. Ideas are secret codes for unlocking pain and unlocking understanding. The secret room of the psyche– where the intellect does its work– is protected by defensive barriers where no one can come in. Here, like the alchemists of old, the scholar mixes up chemicals to turn lead into gold in order to release the bonds of psychic colonization. As Epstein (1999) puts it, one feels a sense of relief in houses of psychic retreat. Being totally and utterly alone with psyche without the intrusion of Medusa is where scholarly ideas begin to congeal. Once the ideas are out there on paper, of course, they are no longer secret. But the production of them is done in secret. When the secret is out it's out. And working through secret codes is a way out of the scholar's dilemma.

Hannah Arendt (1976) tells us that the first step toward "bearing the burden" of our bad situation is to understand it–or at least to try to understand it. Arendt declares:

> Comprehension, however, does not mean denying the outrageous . . . or explaining phenomena by such analogies and generalities that the impact of reality and the shock of experience are no longer felt. It means, rather examining and bearing consciously the burden that events have placed on us– neither denying their existence nor submitting weakly to their weight as though everything that in fact happened could not have happened otherwise. Comprehension, in short, means the unpremeditated, attentive facing up to. . . . (xiv)

Writing about psychic decay and psychic death, writing about what Pinar (1984) called *"Death in a Tenured Position"*, is a way to begin to comprehend things and fight back–even if it is a losing battle. Even still, writing cannot explain fully what it means to psychically die–even just a little bit– under the weight of oppressive institutions. Arendt and Pinar argue that we must not succumb, we must not submit to the powers, to the invisible crushing hand. If we do submit or succumb, they win. We mustn't let them win. But how to fight back? The unthinkable cruelty of institutions is hard to comprehend. Arendt's (1976) masterpiece on totalitarian regimes was an attempt to understand the institutions of Nazi Germany, Fascist Italy. Let us learn from Arendt and take courage from her.

Universities –which were created by intellectuals– are places that have always already been sites of brokenness. Is the house of the scholar broken? Brokenness, fear and paranoia. The tenure system is highly problematic for psyche. Scholars jump, cannot speak their minds, worry that their colleagues will vote against them based on personality and not intellectual matters; scholars worry that their work will not be valued. The constant worry for some six years is enough to do any psyche in. Worry every year that one could get sacked is enough to kill the psyche. Of course, tenure or not, there is no job security really. If they want to get rid of tenured faculty they get rid of entire departments. Even after tenure, dissenting opinions are not permitted at many institutions. If one does dissent, there will be hell to pay. Feeling more and more hemmed in psyche collapses. One retreats, drinks a little more as Pinar (1984) says. Parts of the psyche just fall off the face of the earth. Bits and pieces of the self get lost in an *Eraserhead* (Lynch, 2000) kind of world where nothing makes sense, all is a black and white nightmare where radiators drip bleeding non-human embryos and Fats Waller sings "In heaven everything is fine." Is it all just a bad dream? Too many books on the university blame corporations. But is the corporatization of the university too simple an idea? The problems inside of universities are not only ones of power as I have made clear in this chapter.

Is the university an *Eraserhead* (Lynch, 2000) world ? Watch *Eraserhead* and you will wish that you were back in the real world because this psychotic nightmare reminds you too much of your own world, of your own psychic disturbances. Watch *Eraserhead* and you will long to turn it off because it is the most disturbing film you have ever seen. Be relieved when you are back in the real world. Escape from Eraserhead world. But how can you escape from an Eraserhead psyche? The question at hand is this: Was your psyche made this way by working at an Eraserhead university? Eraserhead is the kind of film that reminds you of the bleak scenery that your see while riding on the metrolink from downtown St. Louis to the West End. Here you see broken down trains, graffiti, mounds of dirt, canisters of toxic waste left on the side of the train tracks, smoke rising, radiators steaming, broken glass, abandoned buildings and squalor. The metrolink is the way the poor get to work everyday. This is an Eraserhead journey that the poor have to take every day. Taking in that broken down world has got to do psychic damage. It will take you days to recover from watching the Eraserhead world pass by. The university is a kind of Eraserhead world because it creates psyches filled with toxic canisters and squalor, broken down train tracks and mounds of psychic dirt. Carl Jung (1977) tells us that we must "interpret" what we cannot. Jung states:

> Interpretations are only for those who don't understand; it is only the things we don't understand that have any meaning. Man [sic] woke up in a world he did not understand, and that is why he tries to interpret it. (p. 31)

What is striking here is that Jung argues that we interpret not what is understood but that which is not understood. Why interpret something we have already figured out? Interpret Eraserhead university. This is an ongoing project. It seems that there is no stopping the interpreting. Words keep coming. Eraserhead university is a bottomless pit of words.

The world is a strange place and we are part of that strange place. The deeper we get inside of that world the stranger it gets. The deeper we get inside of an oppressive institution the stranger it gets and the stranger we become because of it. Our surroundings have to impact the psyche in ways we do not understand. I say we must keep the toxins out, but at the end of the day we do not because we cannot. The psyche has holes in it and toxins are bound to leak into the holes. We do not really know what happens when the continual assault batters. We know about trauma and what happens to victims of ongoing trauma–or we think we know. But do we? We have our theories, but chronic trauma defies reason. Living in an atmosphere where we feel that we are chronically traumatized has got to ruin the structures of the psyche. Do ruins collapse? They can.

What about those missing pieces? The life of the scholar is one of missing pieces. Bits of psyche turn up missing. But where do these missing pieces go? Putting pieces together again is the job of the intellectual. One of the lessons of psychoanalysis is that instead of ignoring our psychic woundedness we must go into that woundedness and explore it. We must go down under; we must go into Hades and dwell there for a while. If we repress the ruins or pretend that they are not there, bigger trouble is ahead. If one does not pay attention to psychic wounds the repressed returns in monstrous ways. Thomas Moore (2004) talks about James Hillman's idea on psychic "*garbage*." He states:

> In his writings on dreams James Hillman stresses the association between Hekate and garbage. He equates this garbage with the day-residues Freud said were the stuff of dreams. But Hillman sees this garbage redeemed in the dream and Hekate as "the Goddess who makes sacred the waste of life, so that it all counts, it all matters." (p. 83)

Garbage is profound. This is Hillman's message. Most of us would rather throw out our garbage. Instead, we must keep it around– at least for a while– in order to try to understand it, to go down into it, to get into it, to get sooty, dirty. Steel workers of the soul, go back into the mills and get sooty. But we must go into that which is disgusting to make anything out of it. Waste not the waste. Break down feelings–freely associated– before they break psyche down. Take care of things before they take care of us. Do we explore our own lunacy or let the lunacy destroy us? The garbage of the university is profound garbage because it is the house of our intellect, it is the place where we live, we inhabit this place and the place can kill us if we let it. One way not to let it kill us is by going deeper into the pit and allowing the pendulum to swing ever closer. In a book titled *On Bearing Unbearable States of Mind*, Ruth Riesenberg-Malcolm (2000), like Jung, tells us that:

> To progress into a further and more consolidated use of the depressive mode of functioning, a much greater capacity to tolerate psychic pain is indispensable. The anxieties brought forward by depressive-position functioning are felt both for one's self and for one's objects, internal and external. (p. 154)

Riesenberg-Malcolm's main point here turns on the ability to tolerate psychic pain. Many people cannot tolerate psychic pain so they shut it off or shut it down. They simply cannot go into the garbage. Putting up with the pain of feeling insulted, belittled, dismissed and angered takes work. The question is how much can you put up with? How much should you put up with? Day in day out, year in year out insult is just too much. Shouldn't the garbage finally be emptied? The full weight of the garbage of psychic pain must be felt deeply. Otherwise, the garbage will back up and clog the drain.

William Pinar (1984) argues that curriculum studies scholars–who are progressives fighting against a reactionary climate–must not "*succumb*" (p. 197). Pinar states:

> I regard as most intense that struggle not to succumb to the routinization of life, and to the attendant freezing over of the fluidity of individual life, the struggle not to succumb to role, to the robotic, to witness and by so witnessing to amplify our withering capacities to live outside the bureaucratic mainstream. . . . (p. 197)

Old timers who are hangdog in the hallways of academe have succumbed. You can see them going through the motions of teaching classes, going to meetings and going home. They produce little or no scholarship. And what they do produce is not worthy of the name 'scholarship.' They have clearly let the institution kill them. They have become robots and dupes. They are the Babbitts (Lewis, 2005a) of the world. To grow tired of the fight is in essence to give up. Our ideas are our battlegrounds and we must continue to guard them in our secret scholarly rooms. And then one day let loose on the world dangerous, progressive ideas. Marx was a dangerous man. Arendt too. Dangerously progressive. Let us be dangerously progressive. Pinar talks of our "withering capacities." Psyche gets withered after a while. Despite that withering, that flagging, we fight on. Curriculum studies is here to stay whether or not the reactionaries like it. Curriculum studies marks its third decade. We have survived our darkest hour. But our work is yet to be done.

INSTITUTION AS INTRUSIVE MOTHER

A School for Scandal

There are reasons why the scholar gets in trouble. The inability to work-- as a scholar-- is due to many competing pressures. One large problem is that the conditions under which the progressive scholar works are unbearable. These conditions cause a trauma in the life of a scholar. Robert Stolorow (2007) says that trauma is "an experience of unbearable affect" (p. 9). The institution so works against the creative spirit. Everything about the institution gets in the way of the scholarly life. The institution serves as a continual interruption to scholarly productivity. The university is lost amidst the cries for higher numbers and accountability. I would like to focus on the image of the institution as an intrusive mother and a school for scandal. The scandal is that the intrusive mother (the university) can eventually squash her child (the scholar). Scholarly productivity can come to a screeching halt if the scholar has little protection against the ongoing intrusions of the institution. This discussion leads us to the crisis of American education that we face as scholars and what can be done about it, if anything. This is the crisis of psyche. Can scholars find a way out of psychic paralysis? We know that the psyche has a great capacity for plasticity. How can we make use of that plasticity when it seems that the life of thought gets blocked? Parts of the psyche die when conditions are simply intolerable but out of this intolerableness new life might emerge. How to psychically push out the intrusive mother? We must never submit to the whims of an abusive mother. Rather, finding a way out of the abuse means digging deeper into the ways and whys of intrusion. We must carefully examine the intrusion in order to get out from underneath it. We must get out from under the killing force. The term crisis is key in this chapter. We have reached a crisis point in American education. I want to look at other crises in American culture to show how people have used these crises to create new kinds of work and argue that the field of curriculum studies can advance even as we are up against the crisis that is American education. In this chapter, I briefly talk about the some of the artists of the WPA (The Works Progress Administration) and how these people made use of bad times to create and express those bad times. The WPA artists found a way out of a crisis and so too can scholars.

The schoolhouse–which is a scandal– has long been known to be troublesome. The school is a fraught institution It is a scandal because it has never really been about educating young people. What *are* schools for? They are holding cells, not places of education. Schools kill psyche and soul. Young people get squashed in the classroom. School is partly to blame for the destruction of creativity in young people. We really need to reconsider what it means to get a public education in this country. The social structures and psychic fallout of the schoolhouse get repeated in the university. The university is more of the same. Students live under the sign of fear and testing, fear and testing. They learn to hate reading, they learn to hate study and they learn to hate themselves. Rote memory, test taking and pointless repetition create a society of wounded souls. We have created a university in which the conditions under which university professors work are troubling because we are asked to repeat what was done to us as children. We continue to kill each other (psychically) as we were killed (psychically) as children. Schooling erases personalities that are eccentric. Standardized knowledges standardizes personalities. Jung (1983) addresses these issues as he talks about the herd mentality. Jung points out that:

> the development of personality from the germ-state to full consciousness is at once a charisma and a curse, because its first fruit is the conscious and unavoidable segregation of the single individual from the undifferentiated and unconscious herd. This means isolation, and there is no more comforting word for it. (p. 197)

Real personalities are eccentrics, Jung suggests. But as Jung points out it is risky to become eccentric. To be eccentric means to be alone. It is much easier to simply be like everybody else. School teaches that we should be like everybody else. Standardized knowledges means standardized personalities. So if you are going to develop an eccentric personality you have to do it outside of school and on the margins of society. What would it be to embrace eccentric knowledges? Reading on the margins. The scandal of the schoolhouse is clonehood. As it is now, in public schools it is thought that every child in each grade should be learning the same thing and be able to recite the same boring, useless, detached and frivolous 'knowledge.' Teachers are taught to be on the same page on the same day at the same time. And this is called education? If teachers are on the wrong page they get in trouble. Is this not Kafkaesque? Test taking is mind numbing and soul killing. What kind of standardized test is there for life?

Ironically, developmental psychology has always been about not developing a real personality but developing a standardized personality which is no personality at all. Development should follow a pacing chart. On this year the child should be here, on that year the child should be here. The scandal is that the schoolhouse does not allow children to become eccentrics. Perhaps they could start by allowing children to talk freely about what matters to them, like their dreams, their nightmares, their wishes and desires, their fears and their worries. Freely associating, however, might be dangerous. Freely associated thoughts do not follow a logical pattern. There is no pacing chart for freely associated thought.

Maybe we should ask children what interests them. Of course this is not a new idea. Progressive educators asked this question in the early 20th century. But maybe we need to ask the question again. The mandates that teachers have to follow are completely and utterly intrusive and have little to do with educating the child. Many graduate school students have difficulty finding intellectual interests because they have never really been allowed to have them since elementary school. They have been told what to do since early childhood. The state decides what is best for children. Memorizing rote facts and taking standardized tests is for the good of the child–the state tells teachers. Alice Miller (2005) knows that what we do to people "for their own good" is usually abusive and mean. Derrick Jensen (2006) comments generally on the abusive culture which is America. He states:

> Given the near-ubiquity of abuse within our culture–and I'm talking not only about deformations of child abuse, but of coercive schooling, the wage economy requiring people to waste lives working jobs they'd rather not do, the trauma of living in a world that is being destroyed before our eyes. . . what causes or allows resilience? (p. 714)

Jensen points out that abuse is a larger cultural problem in America. Abuse is not just a family affair or school affair it is a cultural affair. Because the problem is cultural it is nearly impossible to undo. And because abuse is an historical problem, it will take generations to undo what has been done to our children in the name of education. Schooling is abusive when it does not allow the child to become eccentric. Do children collapse psychically at a young age? I am beginning to wonder about school shootings. If children learn to hate learning and learn to fear learning and learn to hate themselves would it then not make sense that they retaliate against the very institution that damaged them? I am not the first to make this point. Julie Webber (2003) has written a very important book on Columbine and other school shootings and tells us that the school is certainly not a holding environment in the Winnicottian sense. The school makes children violent because it is a violent place. Henry Giroux (2004) and Alan Block (1997) both make similar points about the violence that is done to children in the name of education. But why the guns? Aren't there are other ways to get even? Whatever happened to writing letters? Or, children could engage in creative activities like painting and playing music for example to express their frustration. But it seems that guns seem to be weapon of choice. Most children who are angry at a terrible school system do not retaliate but we have to worry about the rising number of school shootings. Last year was Virginia Tech. This year was Northern Illinois.

People do bounce back from abusive situations. Scholars can bounce back from working under intolerable conditions. Musicians can bounce back from injury. If the injury means the end of a career, then musicians can still bounce back by going into other disciplines and channelling their creativity into something else. Derrick Jensen (2006) knows all about resilience. He was the victim of child molestation and abuse and yet he has done remarkable things with his life. Jensen has written very important books on ecology and politics and has given talks around the country about our dire ecological crisis. He sees the ecological crisis as yet another symptom of abuse. Somehow he got out of the abusive cycle and I think he did this partly through his writing. Repetition compulsion is not the fate for everyone. How to get beyond repetition compulsion?

Getting beyond repetition compulsion means working on damaged parts of the psyche. Psychological paralysis is caused in part by living under abusive conditions. Institutions by their very nature are abusive. Efficiency, the bottom line, accountability all erase the human. And institutions are driven by the bottom line and accountability. But what does the bottom line have to do with the soul? If the institution damages the part of the psyche that produces thought, play might be in order. Play. Play an instrument. If you can't play, think. Work on playing with ideas rather than with notes. A psychic Parabola is at hand. If one can internalize Parabolas psychically there is always already a way out of abusive situations. Turn things on their head, turn things upside down, start again or start somewhere else, move to different emotional and intellectual registers. Institutions, because they are intolerable and abusive, are of necessity violent. Is there a way to not repeat the violence? It amazes how many commentators refer to school as a troubled place. Wendell Berry (1981) remarks:

> And, as I think about it now, school was a distraction. Although I have become, among other things now, a teacher, I am skeptical of education. . . . There is an incredible waste and clumsiness in most efforts to prepare the young. (p. 34)

Berry and other poet-ecologists might call for a more poetic education. School is certainly not poetic. College is no different. And this is the scandal and the crime. The 'incredible waste' to which Berry refers is the waste of mind and soul. Childrens' minds are wasted as they sit in classrooms filling in bubbles on scantron tests. This is not education. This is death. Education means digging into life and trying to understand what is unfathomable. Education should be endlessly exhilarating because life is endlessly exhilarating. School–from the very start–should engage young people in the wonders and awe of life. If the mind is not used in such a way as to fully engage it, it withers and even turns violent. Children who come to school expecting exciting things to happen are soon shocked to find that they have to live instead in a world of fear and anxiety. The schoolhouse is built on fear just as the university is built on fear. Children develop, then, fearful personalities. Public school in America is a tragedy.

Being schooled means being drilled and skilled to death. Being schooled means being disciplined. The school for scandal is one in which young people are actually mis-educated. The scandal is that schooling has nothing to do with education. Education happens when one seriously studies texts and works with them, on them and through them. Working on texts is also work of the soul. Studying the work of others is studying the workings of the soul. Serious study of texts rarely happens in school. Serious study means grappling, working over, thinking through and making soul connections. Studying in this sense is mystical. Studying has nothing to do with memorizing for its own sake or fill in the blank tests. Studying is an art form that has been lost in the scandal of the schoolhouse. We have lost touch with our own capacity for wonder and curiosity. And it is this that we pass down to our children? This is an outrage and a scandal. Theologian Matthew Fox (2006) remarks that an education should be a "mindful" one. He teaches that:

A mindful education would, for example, increase our capacities for silence, for stillness and contemplation. It would enhance our capacity for grappling with chaos and for living with stress; our capacity for letting go, for letting be, and for forgiveness. It would grow out of our capacity for creativity. . . [it would grow out of] our love of the earth, and our capacity for compassion. (p. 28)

Elementary school students learn none of this. Fox's Buddhist meditation might serve as the groundwork not only for the elementary school curriculum but also for the college curriculum. Education–if it is soulful– is about the spiritual and mystical that is life. But our schools are not driven by Eros, they are driven by Thanatos. The death drive is repetition without meaning, of drilling 'facts.' Our children grow up, go to college and the mess starts all over again. Then they become public school administrators or university professors or administrators and start this mess all over again. Repetition compulsion becomes institutionalized. This is indeed the root of our problem. How to break the cycle of repetition compulsion on a cultural level? On and on. Fox (2006) says schools, as they are today, are nothing more than "vile medicine" (p. 15). David Jardine (2000) remarks that schools are "pernicious" (p. 1). Jardine, like Fox, tells us that the disciplines have been sucked dry of all life. Jardine (2000) aims to inject life back into the curriculum. Jardine has some interesting ideas on what education should be. He says that education

is an attempt to find ways in which ecologically rich images of ancestry, sustainability, interrelatedness, interdependence, kinship, and topography can help revitalize our understanding of all of the living disciplines in our care. (p. 3)

Jardine, like Fox, speaks in a different, more mystical language. The language of the schoolhouse is not at all like this. The language of the schoolhouse is a dead language. The aim of education should be spiritual or mystical; our aim should be related to our place in the world (topography). But as it stands now schooling is unrelated to anything remotely interesting or life giving. The most basic ontological principles around which Jardine speaks should ground all elementary and college curricula. These lively principles could be life giving and even life saving. If education were life giving, students could become eccentric and find interesting things to do with their lives. Why universities model themselves after businesses has always been a conundrum to me. The business model is life denying. We are not in the business of making profits. We are in the business of making souls. Education should be the lifeblood of our culture. If our young people were educated with a sense of the mystical and the love of life, maybe we could better prevent school shootings. Things need to change now.

The schoolhouse is a scandal because it does not educate. Education–if it is grounded in earthly, loving, caring, mindful attentiveness—as both Fox and Jardine point out– is not a scandal but a gift. Education should be a gift that allows people to follow their own paths and find out who they are and what they can do for others while on this earth. We can no longer afford to destroy the lives of our children because that is what schooling does. Schooling is abusive and mean. There is something altogether morbid about the schoolhouse.

THE INTRUSIVE MOTHER AND HIGHER EDUCATION

The university is an intrusive mother. The university does not have a soulful ontology or topology. The university does not have an earthly grounding, it is not a place of wonder, but a place of fear both for the students and professors. The university is the intrusive mother, the devouring mother, the mother medusa. We have learned well from our primary and secondary schools how to set the wheels of fear and intimidation in motion. If an institution of learning is built on the dual foundation of fear and intimidation what do we expect as a result of this pathology? The university should be a place of wide opened exploration, a place where no core curriculum exists, a place where students can study whatever they want and choose from a much more varied and experimental curriculum. But as it stands now, most universities have core curricula which limit students to only a certain kind of knowledge, majors are strictly designed with few electives. The curriculum isn't the only problem either. The way in which material is treated at universities is not unlike the way it is treated in elementary school. Scantrons win the day. Students continue to memorize 'facts' for a test. The university is built around exams and more exams. But again, life is not an exam. Scholars could take students under their wings to teach them the crafts of scholarship early on. Scholars could tutor students and teach them what it means to live a life of erudition and study. Learning the ways of the disciplines means learning about what scholars do in those disciplines. Undergraduates and even masters candidates still have no idea what it is that scholars do and so are miseducated to think that learning means memorizing things for a test or writings papers that merely summarize the thoughts of others and that have little connection to the student. Students are not really taught the meaning of writing scholarly papers. They are given topics and told to write by quoting other people but have no idea why they are doing that. They do not understand the idea of honoring intellectual ancestors. They do not understand how to generate their own thoughts because they were never allowed to have their own thoughts. Standardized knowledges disallow thought. The university life could be so much better for students if the curriculum would be opened up, broadened and made more meaningful. Forcing students to take Core curricula means that somebody else has decided what knowledge is of most worth for all students. But that is just ridiculous. Scholars do not have a core curriculum. Their work is the whole world. The idea that doing scholarship means (symbolically) studying the whole world is unfathomable to doctoral candidates who get into a program thinking that their professors will tell them what to do, how to do it and what to write on. They are horrified when professors say write what you want, it's your work now. How to do one's work when that was never an option before? Doctoral work can be a bewildering experience. Intellectual freedom can be dizzying. Tightly woven curricula, programs that allow for few electives, course syllabi that are departmentally restrictive are all symptoms of a larger problem of the university: the intrusive mother. This intrusive mother is abusive. Is it not abusive to always tell someone else what is in their best interest? Is it not abuse to tell someone else what they should study and how they should study and how they should think?

The institution by its very nature is intrusive. What are the undergirdings of this intrusive mother from another angle? We have talked here mostly about the problems of schooling and the university from the perspective of the student, but now let us turn to the problems that face our bewildered scholar and return to the question at hand. What is it that kills the spirit of the scholar? We are all victims of public schooling (if we attended public school, that is) so we start off on the wrong foot. Scholars have created a highly restrictive place where rules and codes dictate whose knowledge is of most worth.

Here I want to talk about intrusions from above and what these intrusions do to the psyche of our scholar. Of course, our Marxist friends have done work on these issues for years and we thank them for paving the way. My interest though is not the abuse of power per se but what that abuse does to the psyche and the dangers it creates for the human soul. Here I will turn the conversation, more specifically, towards power, violence, and interference as a crisis of the psyche.

ALMA MATER: MOMMY DEAREST

Alma Mater suggests *"nourishing"* or *"dear"* (Webster's). What happened to our nourishing mother? Where is our dear mother? The academy is a far cry from a nourishing or dear mother. Something has gone terribly wrong with our beloved institution of higher learning. Our dear mother is more like mommy dearest than a dear mother. Oh dear what can the matter be, mommy's not home from the fair. The institution as intrusive mother batters. The intrusive Medusa Mother spits you out when she has no more use for you. The institution is a dead place where the dead mother hands out death sentences. In the novel *Death in a Tenured Position* (the book around which William Pinar wrote his 1984 essay with the same name), Amanda Cross' (1981) narrator remarks that

> I've always had a morbid fascination with institutions, the army, the church, the prestigious universities, they are so implacable. I can't take my eyes off of them, as though they were a grotesque sideshow. And I want terribly to be present at the moment they begin to shake and change, if they ever do. (p. 70)

The problem is that institutions rarely seem to change. And if institutions do change, the change is usually for the worse. Institutions of higher education might be *"grotesque sideshows"* but they are not nearly as interesting. They are grotesque in the way they treat people, in the way they give out orders like the military, in the way that they have little regard for real intellectual work. Institutions are indeed *"morbid."* They are dead places that offer little nourishment and no love. Herbert Marcuse (1991) calls institutions "total administrations" (p. 104). A totalizing institution is the site of what Marcuse (1991) calls the *"one-dimensional man"* (same title as Marcuse's book). The one-dimensional institution is totally flat, dissenting opinions are not allowed, everyone is the same and everyone is administered. Heavy handed administrations allow little in the way of innovation on the part of its workers. One must fall in line, get aligned with the standardized mentality, the standardized curriculum and the standardized behavior. Bertrand Russell (2002a) tells us that the university is all about interference. He states:

> A few great historic universities, by the weight of their prestige, have secured virtual self-determination, but the immense majority of educational institutions are hampered and controlled by men who do not understand the work with which they are interfering. The only way to prevent totalitarianism in our highly organized world is to secure a certain degree of independence for bodies performing useful public work, and among such bodies teachers deserve a foremost place. (p. 135)

The total administration–not unlike a totalitarian government–attempts to control all aspects of that which it governs. Most universities are totalitarian universes, especially the mediocre ones. Like sheep to slaughter. The intrusive mother pushes her way inside of disciplines where she has no business meddling. Since she knows what is best for her children–see Alice Miller (2005) on poisonous pedagogy–she controls what faculty can and cannot do, what they can and cannot say. The bulk of American universities are mediocre, they are not great by any means. And as Bertrand Russell points out it is in the mediocre institutions where the reigns are pulled ever tighter; the noose is tightly tied around the necks of intellectual workers. It is of note that this problem of totalizing institutions is not new and not limited to American institutions. Intellectuals who become part of the total administration have turned on each other. So who is to blame? Upton Sinclair (1922), in an alarming book titled *The Goose Step: A Study of American Education,* points out the similarities between goose stepping and educating. Of course what immediately comes to mind is Nazi Germany, legs kicking up high, in unison; or today, North Korea, legs kicking up high ready for the kill. In the academy who kicks up their legs? Sinclair (1922) states that teachers (both public school teachers and university professors) are "*browbeaten*" and "*downcast.*" Sinclair puts it like this:

> American university teachers are greatly underpaid; there is no first class man who could not get more money if he turned his energies to other pursuits. If he stays as a teacher it is because he loves the work, and is willing to accept his reward in other forms– in the respect of his fellow men. But if he finds that he has no standing and no power; if he sees himself and his colleagues browbeaten and insulted by commercial persons; then the dignity of the academic life is gone. . . . (pp. 49–50)

It is astonishing that Sinclair wrote these words in 1922. Nothing has changed. Much to our chagrin and horror, bus drivers up north make more money than college professors down south. This unfair pay scale across the country tells us something about how little professors are valued. Neither public school teachers nor professors—especially professors of education– have any standing in the

United States as Sinclair (1922) points out. Professors of education are considered the bottom of the barrel by the rest of the university community. The stereotypes of professors of education run deep. People across campus think that all we do is teach students how to make lesson plans. Of course, the discipline of education has had a long history of anti-intellectualism so, in part, the discipline is to blame for its bad reputation. But there are those of us, especially in curriculum studies, who do theoretical work. Our subject matter and field is difficult and complex. And yet, some of our more scientific colleagues accuse our scholarship of being soft. What a ridiculous critique. Our focus is on the complexity of curriculum. There is nothing soft about this. These are tough issues because we are dealing with human beings, with souls, with life and death in the classroom. Thinking through school violence is not soft, it is tough and it is painful. Thinking through the problems of anti-intellectualism is not soft, it is tough. Thinking through the problems of racism, anti-Semitism, homophobia, classism is not soft, it is tough. Thinking through the loss of dignity suffered by both school teachers and university professors is not soft, it is tough. The question Sinclair (1922) raises about dignity is a large one. Teachers who are seriously underpaid do lose their sense of dignity. Money in American culture is tied to one's worth. But those of us committed to public education and the discipline of curriculum studies feel that we need to fight the good fight even though everything seems to go against us as it did in Dewey's day.

Education as a field has had a long history of conservatism. Curriculum studies, however is a field that is not conservative; most of us in this field are progressive educators and we are to the left politically. Our right wing colleagues in the broader field of education dislike our politics. The progressive movement in education has clearly lost out to the reactionary strand in education generally speaking. Curriculum theorists are outsiders in their own field. We have lost to the powers of behaviorists, cognitive psychologists, and anti-intellectuals. Standardized testing is a direct outcome of Thorndike's behaviorism and Tyler's Rationale. Dewey was never on the side of Thorndike. Neither are we curriculum theorists. Progressive education is at loggerheads with the largely conservative Christian right in this country. Imagine a presidential candidate arguing for creationism and adding an amendment to the constitution that would discriminate against all non heterosexuals? They say it couldn't happen here, but it is happening. There is clearly a fascist strain in the Christian right and they already have too much power in government and they are dictating what it is that our children should and shouldn't be learning.

We know ours is a losing battle—we progressives— but we continue to fight. The fact that there still is a progressive wing in the field of education is an astonishing. Curriculum studies is that progressive wing. We fight to hold on during these turbulent and right wing times. The Thorndikes of the field have clearly won as assessment movements have completely and utterly colonized our fields. Education is not about assessing outcomes. Education is about nurturing the soul. How can one measure the soul? The scary thing is, is that they've got us at every turn, they've got us by the throat. School teachers have it worse than we do, but we too are feeling the strain of the goose step. Russell Jacoby (2000) states that "the institutions are winning" (p.190). The institutions are winning because they are on the side of assessments, outcomes, measurements and standardizations. These Tylerian (1959) Rationales are morbid. So much energy, time and focus is put into accreditation that the university has lost its focus on the intellectual work at hand. At some point, one feels like throwing up one's hands and saying '*the hell with it.*' When professors try to raise objections they are not heard or they are punished because the institution is controlled by what Herbert Marcuse (1991) calls as "closed language" (p. 101). Marcuse (1991) states:

> The closed language does not demonstrate and explain–it communicates decision, dictum, command. Where it defines, the definition becomes of "separation of good from evil"; it establishes unquestionable rights and wrongs, and one value as justification of another value. It moves in tautologies. (p. 101)

Mandates are dictated from above in a contradictory and crazy fashion. Administrators assure us that they will not interfere with the curriculum decisions of faculty and then they interfere. The administrators say that faculty has say in all curricular decisions, but clearly faculty has no say. Administrators say that faculty has the right to speak its mind, but clearly faculty do not have that right.

The state has begun to intrude even into colleges as they now are telling us what courses to teach and even how to teach them. Most universities–even if they have a governance structure—are not democratic institutions. Everything is already decided from above. The intrusive Mother Medea moves in a "closed language" where nothing is permitted. Public or private, mediocre or great, large or small– universities are places where dictatorial control rules the day. And American universities are not the worst. These problems are international in scope and historically old. Like meat packing factories, universities are institutions of "brute power" (Sinclair 1906/2006, p. 261). Jurgis, the meat packing factory worker in Sinclair's novel *The Jungle*, tells us of his disgust for the so-called American dream. Our narrator of Sinclair's novel states:

> He saw the world of civilization [meat packing factories, or in our case university packing factories] then more plainly than ever he had seen it before; a world in which nothing counted but brutal might, an order devised by those who possessed it for the subjugation of those who did not. He was one of the latter; and all outdoors, all life, was to him a colossal prison, which he paced like a pent-up tiger, trying one bar after another, and finding them all beyond his power. (p. 261)

Push as hard as you like but whatever you do–if you are not part of the power structure of any institution–whether it be a university, a church or a corporation– you lose. The Boss Tweeds of academe control everything. In our own little universes, the power structures are quite clear. Professors–no matter where they teach–have no power. Think what you would like but do not delude yourself like Jurgis did when he first came to Chicago. When young professors first come to the university they are very much like our young Jurgis. Jurgis thought things would be great until he saw what actually went on inside of the meat packing factory. *The Jungle* (1906/2006) should be bed time reading not only for students but also for all university professors. It is a real eye opener to the dog-eat-dog world we have inherited. *However,* our intellectual work remains. The written text, the document, the testament to the truth will remain in our (public) libraries for the public at large to read. We remember women and men of letters, not institutions. Institutions are forgettable places. Do we know where great scholars were housed? Do any of us remember, for example, where William James was housed? Or even if we do know the answer to this question, does it even matter? No. It doesn't matter because we read his texts and care little that he was housed at Harvard. It makes little difference where a scholar is housed if she is doing intellectual work; it is the work that remains, not the affiliation with the institution.

THE ALMA MATER AND SCHOOL VIOLENCE

The school and university have been of late places of incredible violence. We have witnessed the Columbines. Why have the schoolhouse and university been a site for such violence? This is where we really need scholars to focus. The end of the age of enchantment has come. The meat packing factory university is a killing ground for her children, by her children. Julie Webber (2003) blames school violence on the school itself. She suggests that kids act out because schools are prisons and students are feared as enemies. Many have made this claim. But is it so simple? The culture of testing fear adds fire to the flame she suggests. That is true, but why does that lead to murder, to mass murder? Or are these violent outbreaks much more complex that this? I have studied violence for many years in the context of the Holocaust (see Morris, 2001) and yet questions remain about why people do such horrific things. In the case of Virginia Tech, many psychiatrists on TV are telling us that the shooter was a paranoid schizophrenic. How they can diagnose after the fact and from afar is a mystery to me. But what to do about it? As I sit here revising this chapter another episode of school violence occurred just last week at Northern Illinois University. The shooter walked into a lecture hall and opened fire killing five and wounding many others. The shooter was a student. And people said he was just a normal guy. They said he was the nicest person you would ever want to meet. We have reached a crisis point in American education. Things must change. They simply must. We have got to be kinder and more loving to both our students and our professors. Perhaps it is naïve to say that love will cure all and this problem will be solved. That is certainly not what I am saying. However, I do think that if we begin to treat people as human beings and treat people in ways that they feel cared for, nurtured and respected things might be a bit better. Still, there is much more to do.

Of course, it is not so simple to know who will crack and kill and who won't. One begins to wonder if institutions are natural places for killing grounds. Institutions are not human by their very nature. They are alienating places. Antonio Gramsci (1919/2000) commented years ago that institutions were "*lethal*" places. Gramsci states, " traditional institutions are impoverished and become inadequate to their task, obstructive and lethal" (p. 86). Institutions are lethal because they are not human. They are power apparatuses. Hannah Arendt talks about an invisible hand of totalitarian power. Arendt (1976) states:

> In governments [I would add universities and public schools] by bureaucracy decrees appear in their naked purity as though they were the incarnation of power itself and the administrator only its accidental agent. There are no general principles which simple reason can understand behind the decree, but ever changing circumstances which only an expert can know in detail. People ruled by decree never know what rules them because of the impossibility of understanding decrees in themselves. . . . (p. 244)

Universities are run –as Arendt puts it –by decrees which no one understands. When a rule is handed down and faculty must obey, no one knows where it comes from so that no one knows how to stop it . Speaking out against a totalitarian state is suicide. But speak out we must. Yet, the powers that be are just too strong. It has become a Foucauldian world of complicated networks of unstoppable powers. Like Arendt says, it is as if the power is an incarnation of power itself. Power has birthed itself and keeps re-birthing itself by itself. Power is always already associated with violence. There are all kinds of violence(s). There are metaphorical violences and then there are psychic and physical violences. And then there is the violence that is the university. Allen Ginsberg (2000) talked about the link between violence and the university in 1959. Ginsberg states:

> And violence. By police, by customs officials, post-office employees, by trustees of great universities. By anyone whose love of power has led him to a position where he can push people around over a difference of opinion—or vision. (p. 5)

When the university encounters a counter-culture (such as the Beats, ala Ginsberg) it tends to react in a violent way. The university is not about what is counter to culture but rather it is about holding onto a tradition and conserving that tradition. By its very nature the university is a conservative institution because its main purpose is to maintain control over a certain tradition. Disciplines that run counter to tradition are considered rogue. Counter-disciplines run the risk of being ostracized from the university. The Reconceptualization, not unlike the Beats, has been a counter-cultural movement since the early 1970s as William Pinar points out (1995). To be part of a counter culture means butting up against the guardians of traditional culture. Traditional institutions always exhibit resistance to the new. Sometimes this resistance to the new borders on violence. Douglas Brinkley (2000), commenting on the work of Edward Abbey, tells us that Abbey (who was a pioneer in ecological activism)

> fancied himself an old-fashioned American moralist, a Menckenesque maverick who kowtowed to no one in his quest to expose others' treachery, hypocrisy, and greed. It was the "moral duty" of the writer, [and I would add

of the scholar], Abbey insisted, to act as a social critic of one's country and culture, and as such to speak for the voiceless. (xvi)

It is the duty of the scholar to speak with the voiceless, not for them. It is the duty of the scholar to tell us what is wrong with our culture and what is wrong with us! To confront the violence of power with the power of writing. Antonio Gramsci was imprisoned for years but managed to write some 2,000 pages of text. (Hoare & Smith, 2005). This text has been handed down to us in what is called *The Prison Notebooks*. We must write our prison notebooks and keep our wits about us no matter how bad things get. Gramsci set the example for all of us. Quintin Hoare and Geoffrey Nowell Smith (2005) comment on Gramsci's situation. They state that:

> He was 35 years old. At his trial in 1928 , the official [fascist] prosecutor ended his peroration with the famous demand to the judge: "We must stop this brain working for twenty years!" But, although Gramsci was to be dead long before those twenty years were up. . . . his health broken, ... his jailers did not succeed in stopping his brain from working. The product of those years of slow death in prison were the 2,848 pages of handwritten notes which he left to be smuggled out of the clinic, and out of Italy. . . . (xviii)

Let this be a lesson to all of us who are imprisoned metaphorically by the schoolhouse or university. We can smuggle out our dissenting counter-cultural thoughts through writing. Let Gramsci be our guide and our model for courage in hard times. This is still what we fight for: freedom. But we do not fight for freedom by dropping bombs on people. We do not bomb people into democracy. The stakes in the university are not as high as they are in war, but we are fighting a war of words whose implications and ramifications affect culture. We must never submit to any form of totalitarian governance. As Albert Camus (1956) famously said, it is " [b]etter to die on one's feet than live on one's knees" (p. 15). One must never submit to the wheels of power, to those invisible hands of power. One must never submit to the violence of the state, or the violence of any institution. If we allow institutions to kill us, shame on us. Camus knew a better way. Gramsci knew a better way and so too can we.

Why Columbine? Why Virginia Tech and all the others? Who is to blame? The problem of school violence is highly complex and simply cannot be reduced to one cause. American society is violent, period. We learn violence at home, we learn it on TV, we hear about it on the evening news and then we send our young people off to war. What has gone wrong? We better start thinking more seriously about the fate of our young people and how we are all partly to blame for the mess that is America. The conditions under which children grow up in this country are violent. A violent culture produces violent people. However, only the individual who pulls the trigger is guilty of the crime. But the conditions under which children learn and live in America do not help the situation any. Thousands of books on the problems of the university and problems of public education have been written and written again. But we still are not at the heart of the problem. School violence is a symptom of a larger cultural problem. Drug use and alcoholism are also symptoms of a disturbed culture.

Violence is done to people in all sorts of metaphoric ways. Perhaps it is to the metaphors that we should turn. Maybe here we will find some answers. Why one person kills another one, or why we have mass murderers is a question that is beyond human understanding. We cannot change what has been done, we cannot change paranoid psychosis, it is what it is. But what we can change are the conditions under which we raise our children and we can change the conditions under which children are educated and we can change the conditions in which teachers and university professors work. We have reached a crisis point in American education. A crisis alters one's psyche for good. The crisis of psyche is the crisis of American education. What psychic work must we do to work through this crisis? Under what conditions would we rather educate children? Educating children first and foremost means allowing them to explore ideas that otherwise they would not have. And this means introducing them to interesting books. If children had interesting things to read, they would stay focused and want to learn more. But the way that school is set up now testing and standards take precedence over intellectual discovery. I could not imagine a life without interesting books. Books that have been meaningful to me range from fiction to science fiction, from history to psychoanalysis, from curriculum studies to cultural studies. If children were excited about what they read, maybe things would be different. To not allow children to freely explore a world of books is criminal. This point is eloquently addressed by Umberto Eco (2004a) who states:

> . . . the wretches who roam around aimlessly in gangs and kill people by throwing stones from a highway bridge or setting fire to a child—whoever these people are—turn out this way not because they have been corrupted by computer "new-speak" (they don't even have a computer) but rather because they are excluded from the universe of literature and from those places where, through education and discussion, they might be reached. . . . (p. 4)

The problem with public schooling in America is that first of all it is not a place where education happens and second of all it is not a place where books can be freely chosen, read and discussed by children. If children do read books, they get "*tested*" on them. Children, if they do read great literature, get punished by having to take multiple choice exams. If children do get to read books they get quizzed on the plot, the characters and who said what to whom. And this is what spoils reading for children. They feel that they get punished for reading because they have to memorize characters and the rest. This is part of the reason why, if children do get to read books, they don't want to read books after they leave school. This testing mania lends itself to post traumatic stress syndrome. This is the shame of the American educational system. The testing does not stop at grade 12, it continues on into college. Children who grow up being tested on books, go to college and get tested on more books and then become professors who give students tests on books. We must work to stop this madness!! Can we please be a little more experimental and allow our children to read for the sheer pleasure of reading? But then there is another problem at hand. After watching the film called "The Reader," Mary Aswell Doll (personal communication) suggests that the tragedy of it all is that perhaps---and this might have been one of the points of the film—great literature might not, in fact, humanize. No matter how educated people are, still some will always already be vile and violent. This is what we find out when we study the history of Nazi Germany (Morris, 2001). And yet, on the other hand reading great literature can change people for the better. And we hope that more people are good than bad. But Freud teaches that more people are bad than good. And here is the trouble.

SCHOLARSHIP AS MURAL: THE GREAT EXPERIMENT

The scholar's dilemma. What path to take?
Here, I want to talk about what we learn from WPA Murals, public education and the discipline of curriculum studies. WPA Murals teach that experimental work can in fact be done during times of great crisis and social stress. The WPA murals are metaphors. Scholars take note. Scholarship is a sort of mural. The mural of scholarship tells a story–like the WPA murals. Struggling in bad times. The 21st century has not gotten off to a good start. 9-11, the Iraq War, the Virginia Tech massacre. We are in crisis.

Murals tell stories. Scholars need to tell their stories. Stories can be told by painting visual images. Jung teaches that turning to the dream image helps unpack what is going on psychically. When the psychic weight of things (i.e. working in a university or public school) gets to be too much, it is easy to lose natural rhythms. Antoine De Saint-Exupery (1986) states:

How difficult it is to advance one's own internal rhythm, when one is constantly fighting against the inertia of the material world. Everything is always on the verge of stopping. How vigilant one has to be to preserve life and movement in a world on the verge of breaking down. . . . (p. 10)

Inertia becomes heaviness and thickness when working under an iron fist. Scholars inside of the university suffocate from the massive weight of oppression. The rhythm of work can easily be thrown off in a place that runs counter to thought and reflection. Continual interruptions keep the scholar from doing her real work, the work of the intellect. Interruptions keep the scholar from finding her own scholarly rhythm. And if she has a scholarly rhythm the university gets in the way of that rhythm by interfering with it. If there is enough interference the scholar will stop producing work. It is inevitable. Or maybe it isn't. As De Exupery suggests, "everything is always on the verge of stopping" (p. 10). The university interferes with the scholar's writerly life by continually being in a state of crisis. Everything is always already on high alert. Everything seems to be a high stakes game. Public school teachers know all too well what it is to live in a high stakes world. They are threatened with losing their jobs if the standardized test scores do not get raised. Living in a high stakes world creates an oppressive and overwhelmingly negative atmosphere. When one works in an atmosphere that has already crumbled it is hard not to crumble psychically.

Part of the problem is that scholars' lives are continually interfered with and nothing the scholar has to say seems to have any real meaning. This is part of the reason the psyche tends toward dissolution. Scholars "feel that they live in a time of big decisions; they know they are not making any" (2000, Mills, p. 5). The university makes big decisions and asks the scholar to participate but this participation seems to be false. In a totalitarian regime only the "power elite," as C. Wright Mills (2000) suggests, make real decisions. Scholars are not part of this power elite. School teachers are certainly not part of a power elite. Psychic energy gets wasted when "big decisions" –as Mills puts it- run counter to the productivity of the scholar. In a factory, workers' complaints are not heard unless they are unionized. In a state where there are no unions, scholars basically have no rights. The hand of power wields the executioners' sword. I am reminded here of Theodore Dreiser's (1914/1965) novel *The Titan*. Describing Mr. Cowperwood, the narrator tells us that "[m]en must swing around him as planets around the sun" (p. 32). The Mr. Cowperwood of the university is that "power elite" (Mills, 1965/2000). Scholars must "*swing around*" that power elite "*as planets around the sun*." The power elite is not a Mr. Cowperwood, though, it is a conglomerate, a network, a power apparatus, an invisible hand. Scholars know that they swing around the power network. Industry–especially at the turn of the 20th century–was bleak, abusive, oppressive, mean, dirty, chaotic. University as *Bleak House* (Dickens, 2005). A Dickensian world indeed.'*Teaching first'* institutions tend to be high on interfering with scholarly production, since scholarship counts little. Perhaps the notion of interference should become part of the scholarly investigation. The psychoanalytic question would be this: To what psychic use does one put interference? A question Adam Phillips might ask. Interference can be used as a way to get into the bleak aspects of psyche herself. How does it feel to be continually interfered with? Interference is a form of psychic intrusion. A psychic intrusion impinges upon the psyche, it sort of breaks into it and dents it or even damages it. Can that damage be repaired? Or does that damage become a permanent part of the psyche? If interference goes on and on year in and year out, the psyche cannot withstand continual intrusion. In this case, damage becomes part of the psychic package. Pushing the human psyche to a crisis point, to that place of possible break down, might allow the scholar to take certain risks that otherwise would not be taken. Also, a sense of urgency is felt when scholarly work feels threatened. The urgency comes out of a deep psychological need to right what is wrong. Eros is on the move. Those of us with a strong life drive will find a way out of the scholar's dilemma, but the weaker ones will be left behind and simply become–as Gramsci (1919/2000) would put it, "absorbed" (p. 85) by their situations. Gramsci (1919/2000) talks about the failings of some socialists to resist oppressive and authoritarian situations. He states:

> The gravest error of the socialist movement was akin to that of the syndicalists. Participating in the general activity of human society within the

state, the socialists forgot that their role had to be essentially one of criticism, of antithesis. Instead of mastering reality, they allowed themselves to be absorbed by it. (p. 85)

Being absorbed by reality is a lapse into psychic symbiosis .The intrusive mother devours her children– scholars. To introject deeply the alien force of the intrusion damages. Being absorbed by the mother means being crushed by her. Once devoured, the psyche ultimately dissolves. The rise of fascism is in part due to peoples' getting absorbed by the state. This absorption produces indifference. Here I am reminded of Sinclair Lewis's (2005b) novel titled *It Can't Happen Here*. My reply is, Oh Yes It Can happen Here!! And it already has!! This is the point of the novel. Don't think that fascist Italy, Nazi Germany or Stalinist Russia are far away and out of sight. Today fascism(s) abound. People are arrested without trial, they disappear and are tortured and murdered. The government spies on her citizens. We are under tight surveillance. Our phones are bugged, our university halls have cameras in them to keep a watchful eye over subversive faculty.

The President of the United States goes to war based on a lie. Congress seems powerless to stop him. Congress seems utterly powerless. Nobody is able to stop this president from destroying the world. Disagree with the President and disappear. The firing of the US Attorneys is a good case in point. Troop surge is a one man idea; nobody wants troop surge. We are reminded of Vietnam every day as the numbers of dead rise. When will the country start rioting? Where are the activists? Where are our demonstrators? Sinclair Lewis' narrator points out when people do nothing to stop fascism we've got real problems. In Lewis's (2005b) *It Can't Happen Here*, the narrator says:

The tyranny of the dictatorship isn't primarily the fault of Big Business, nor the demagogues who do their dirty work. It's the fault of Doremus Jessup! Of all the conscientious, respectable, lazy-minded Doremus Jessups who have let the demagogues wriggle in, without fierce enough protest. (p. 186)

Doremus deconstructed is door mouse. A door mouse is a doormat. There are too many door mice and doormats in this world!! It is the door mice who should be blamed for our current state of affairs, says Lewis. We know that during Nazi Germany many people turned their heads and pretended that nothing was going on.

Lewis (2005a) makes the same point in his novel titled *Babbitt*. The narrator here tells us that industry is not the problem, but rather it is the "Family Man" who is at fault:

The real villains of the piece are the clean, kind, industrious Family Men who use every known brand of trickery and cruelty to insure the prosperity of their cubs. The worst thing about these fellows is that they're so good and, in their work at least, so intelligent. You can't hate them properly, and their standardized minds are the enemy. (p. 92)

The Babbitts of the world are like the Doremice of the world. The Babbitts of the world are wedded to the status quo. Babbitt is indeed a family man who sees that something is lacking in his suburban boredom, but he is resigned to stay inside of a dull lackluster life. The Babbitts of the world are like Fred Flintstone, cave men in mentality. Babbitt represents all that is reactionary. Babbitt is so blinded by his privilege that he cannot see that just down the street from him the workers in the factories are committing suicide, nor does he care. He will do nothing to buck the system because he is the system. He will do nothing to help others because as far as he is concerned others can help themselves. Industry works to "standardize minds" (p. 92). Industry works to kill the spirit and soul as it ruthlessly works the workmen to death. I am thinking here of the Robber Barons of the world who do not give a tinkers' damn if workers die in a coal mine. Les Standiford (2006) reports a famous incident between Frick and Carnegie when Carnegie–after a falling out with Frick– wanted to mend fences. Frick's reply was this: "Yes, you can tell Carnegie I'll meet him. . . . "I'll meet him in Hell, where we both are going" (p. 15). The Robber Barons were nothing short of criminal in the way they treated their workers. Both Carnegie and Frick, though, were philanthropists—leaving behind libraries, concert halls and museums. But these gifts do not right what wrong was done to mistreated workers. It was because of this gross mistreatment and abuse of workers that labor laws and unions came into being. The Robber Barons made billions of dollars off of the backs of the poor, struggling underclass. If a worker got hurt in an accident in the steel mills, the families were not compensated in any way. (Standiford, 2006). They lived as indentured servants as they had to buy foodstuffs at the company stores affiliated with Carnegie's steel mills in Pittsburgh. They lived in company houses that were contaminated with toxic waste. Carnegie and Frick kept their workers poor enough so that they had no choice but to work without complaint. Many workers were brought over from Eastern Europe and could not speak the language even if they wanted to complain (Standiford, 2006). Sinclair Lewis suggests that although the Fricks and Carnegies of the world were blameworthy, the Babbitts of the world who allowed the Fricks to get away with gross mistreatment were also at fault. The middle class turned their heads away from the sufferings of workers in the steel mills and for Sinclair Lewis this was the biggest sin of all. The middle class do-nothings were part of the problem because in no way did they attempt to right what was wrong. To allow the Robber Barons to rob working people of their dignity, to rob them of a decent life and earning a decent wage is nothing short of criminal.

If we turn our heads or are fearful of raising objections when terrible wrongs are committed we are contributing to the population of the Babbitts of the world, we are contributing to the overpopulation of doormice. To hide in the suburbs and not fight for social justice is a way "to protect one's cubs" at any cost (p. 92, Lewis, 2005a).

Left leaning scholars are under attack from all sides. Scholars are under attack from the right especially. The right wing in this country has grown so strong as to resemble the social fabric of Germany during the 1930s. The Christian Right is a very disturbing phenomenon. Students in the deep South–many of whom are of the Christian Right–think that curriculum studies scholars are evil. I can recall a particular incident in class when I said that curriculum studies scholars are mostly to the left and the students ganged up on me after class and went into a tirade. I was taken aback. One pays a price for being honest about politics in the classroom. The progressive wing of education has always been under attack. For young professors of curriculum studies this hostility from those students who are right wing, comes as a surprise and a wound. Florence Krall (1994), a pioneer curriculum studies and ecology scholar, reminds us that "James Hillman explains our need to return repeatedly to "deep hurts" " (p. 14). Paying attention to wounded psyches is a must. The classroom can be a wounding place. Professors of the experimental— like those of us in curriculum studies—are considered rogues by the administration. It becomes very difficult to deal with pressures from both students and from administrators. Teaching is a tightrope act. Many professors in academe are not in good psychic shape as a result. The downcast are many, the bitter are many, the wounded are many. I am reminded of Thoreau (2000) who declares, " [l]et your life be a counter friction to stop the machine" (p. 25). Being a counter friction in academe is a struggle indeed. This fight is fought in words and deeds, in speech and in writing, in being and doing. That counter friction will grind against the wheels of the status quo. Sparks will fly. Let those sparks be bright.

Halting the machine of the intrusive mother—mother academy– is no easy task. Mother academy has closed her eyes and ears to her children, she pays little mind to her children. Inattention on the part of the mother is nothing short of neglect and abuse. This abuse must be stopped. The university is a crisis of psyche. Those of us who engage in the experimental, in work that is left leaning, pay a price psychically. Our work is not taken seriously, we are not rewarded or even recognized for what we do—especially because what we do has little to do with the market. We are punished. And some of us are silenced. The intrusive mother does not listen, she operates with brute force; she pushes her way into the psyche. This is called projective identification. The mother pushes herself into the child's psyche to make room for her own bad objects. But how does one halt the damage? There comes a crisis point in these sorts of interfering relationships when something must be done to protect psyche. Writing is what must be done, for writing is resistance and it is protest. Perhaps writing is one of the best forms of protest because words travel. Publishing is a form of dissent. Thoreau's (2000) *Civil Disobedience* is a hallmark of resistance. Antonio Gramsci's (2005) *Prison Notebooks* are a testament to resistance. We can take great courage from both Thoreau and Gramsci. Quintin Hoare and Geoffrey Nowell Smith (2005) tell us that when Fascist Italy emerged on the scene

> All remaining opposition organisations and their publications were banned, and a new, massive series of arrests was launched throughout the country. Among those arrested was Antonio Gramsci. (xviii)

Faculty watchdog organizations such as the AAUP are supposed to prevent the "*banning of publications*". But the AAUP cannot stop the train wreck at hand because there are many ways of banning publications. One way is to deny tenure. Then there are more subtle ways of banning a professor's writings, by simply ignoring the importance of her work. This is a negative symbolic gesture on the part of the mother university. Mother university makes her children feel insignificant. Here I am thinking of Freud. At the university in Vienna he was considered a nobody and he was denied promotion early on in his career not because he was not worthy of it, but because he was Jewish (Morris, 2006) and also because the work that he was doing was considered experimental.

I am thinking here of Upton Sinclair's (1922) diatribe against many major American universities who in the 1920s were in cahoots with the J.P. Morgan's of the world. What Lewis uncovers is really quite shocking. Sinclair's chapter titles give pause: The University Goose, The University of the House of Morgan, The Dean of Imperialism, The University of Lumber Trust, The Mining Camp University, The University of Standard Oil, The University of the Steel Trust, The University of Jabbergrab. Corruption starts with industries' alignment with the university. When monies are given by industry to the university, the university, in turn, must kowtow to industry. Pretty soon industry dictates curriculum. Upton Sinclair (1922) talks about what he calls interlocking directorates between universities and industry and explains how these work. Lewis states:

> The president of the university is a director of one of Mr. Morgan's life insurance companies, and is interlocked with Mr. Morgan's bishop, and Mr. Morgan's physician, and Mr. Morgan's newspaper. If the president of the university writes a book, telling American people to be good and humble servants of the plutocracy, this book may be published by a concern in which Mr. Morgan (or a partner) is a director, and the paper may be bought from the International Paper Company, in which Mr. Morgan has a director through the Guaranty Trust Company. (p. 21)

The corporatization of the university has a long history. This example, while rather humorous and farfetched is neither. We know that the Ivy Leagues also have a sort of interlocking directorate when it comes to hiring new faculty. Frankly, they hire their own. Just look briefly through the credentials of an Ivy League faculty and you will soon find that most faculty come from Ivy League Institutions. Terminal degrees from state schools do not cut it for the big leagues. The Ivy League locks out potentially good candidates from non-Ivy League schools. Ivy Leagues have an interlocking network and unspoken rule that prevents outsiders from coming in. How to fight Tammany Hall? It seems an impossible battle. The machine is just too strong. But one can fight back through the printed word, through writing. We learn this lesson from Gramsci. We must work to get our writings smuggled out. We must follow in the footsteps of John Reed (1919/1977) who wrote the famous socialist documentary: *Ten Days that Shook the World*. Professors might write their own '*ten days that shook the world*' as an act of defiance, as an act of resistance, as a "counter friction to the machine" (Thoreau, 2000, p. 25) of Tammany Hall University.

In times of social crisis great works of art and literature do get produced. This is a great testament to the resilience of the human spirit. Social stress—ironically–opens up avenues for doing edgy work. Freud said that he did his best work when he was in some kind of discomfort. Living during times of social stress produces a sense of great discomfort. And this discomfort in turn causes anger. Some of us write best out of anger. Some of us write out of an ethical imperative to right what is wrong. An ethical sensibility drives writing when one sees social injustices all around. This book is one of protest and has been written out of a sense of ethical responsibility.

WHAT WE LEARN FROM THE WPA

During the Great Depression, the amazing story is the WPA. The United States government paid artists, supported artists and encouraged them to work. Of course they were not free to do whatever they wanted, they were not free to do highly subversive works, or produce work with a Communist overtone. So they were in some ways under surveillance. However, they could make a small living using their creative talents. I certainly do not see the government today supporting artists in any way.

Try being a professional painter or musician today. See how far you get. In many cities across the country symphony orchestras have gone belly up. The government does not step in to save them. In public schools the first thing to go when budget cuts occur are art and music programs— it is as if these programs are merely superfluous. The arts are not superfluous but integral to the human condition. Being human means being expressive. What could be more fundamental than the expression of music and art? Music and art are the breath and bone of culture. Without music and art we cut off the breath of a culture and bones of a culture. Music and art can serve to "cure" the university as Matthew Fox (2006, p. 29) might say. Likewise, music and art might serve to "cure" the public schools. Without art and music our institutions suffer from soullessness. Playing music is soul work. Without soul work, one is as good as dead. Writing is also soul work. Scholarly writing is soul work. When the scholar is unable to write, she is as good as dead. But we must not let them win!! To get clues on how to not let them win, we turn here to the lessons of the artists of the WPA.

The WPA artists teach us that art is possible to do in hard times; one can produce important work even if times are really tough. We see this in the famous WPA murals. The murals are astounding and historically important works of art that nearly got lost in the dustbin of history. Heather Becker's (2002) remarkable book on the history of the WPA and its connection to the Chicago Pubic Schools is a testament to the importance of art in connection with education, art in connection with our own cultural history and art in connection with our memories. Many of these murals were "rediscovered" as Becker puts it because they were either painted over or covered over and hidden–on purpose– because their subject matter seemed too controversial and too left leaning. Many of the murals were painted over because right wing educators and politicians thought the subject matter too leftist, too working class, too much oriented toward the plight of women and African-Americans. Flora Doody (2002) tells us what she discovered while uncovering a painted over mural in a Chicago public school. Doody (2002) states:

> Newspaper articles from the 1940s refer to an all-male committee from the Board of Education describing the mural as "depressing and misery laden" in addition to "subversive." The articles mentioned that the school had requested lighting for the foyer because the room was too dark. So the school board sent a representative to investigate. In 1941 it was decided to paint over the "dark" mural. (p. 22)

Conservatives banned together to get rid of the murals as Doody tells us because they thought the murals too liberal. What message would these murals send to school children? They might teach school children the story of the struggles of the poor, African Americans and women. Reactionaries thought these murals to be subversive. Conservative educators actually believed that the murals expressed dangerous messages. So in a word, they got rid of most of them that were in the Chicago Pubic Schools. But—eventually many of these murals were unearthed and recovered. Chicago has had a long history of racial tension and so it is not surprising that these murals disappeared especially during the 1950s. Racism, sexism and homophobia are usually of a piece and so too it is no surprise that depictions of women, African-Americans or homosexuals were erased from public view. The WPA was not by any means a liberal institution but it seems that what they allowed often slipped past their conservative members.

How is it that the right has had so much power in this country? What else does the right try to cover up in public education today? Well, a quick look at elementary or high school textbooks will tell the story of what else is covered up or whitewashed especially in history texts. Slavery is given little space, Native Americans are virtually ignored. The Holocaust is given two paragraphs or it is treated in a way that whitewashes it. America has had a long history of whitewashing history and it starts in elementary school. Georgia history begins—as the State mandates—after Columbus. How can this be?

It really is rather shocking and appalling that many of the WPA murals were ruined, painted over or hidden from public view for decades. Surprisingly, as Harry Sternberg (2002) points out "[t]he dominant public attitude toward the WPA was negative" (p. 80). This is just astounding to me! But then again why am I surprised? What does this suggest about the fabric of American culture? The WPA was seen by the right wing as a social program (read socialist program, read Communist) meant to help minorities, the underclass and women. But public education is a social program isn't it? Is public education Communist? You see how these arguments make little sense. Health care in this country is a total disaster because the right wing insists that medicine made available to all is socialized and socialized medicine means Communism. What sense does that make? None. The rich do not want to help the poor. Let them eat cake. Conservatives think that the underclass can pull itself up by its own bootstraps and to hell with them.

Barry Bauman (2002) speaks to the importance of preserving the WPA murals. He states that

> The murals speak for the masses during the early decades of the 1900s, representing their cultural, ideological, and political concerns. Despite the

enormous suffering caused by the Depression, it was a time of extraordinary innovation and social consciousness. (p. 40)

What kinds of artwork speak for us now? What will be preserved and what will be covered over? What kinds of artful scholarship will be preserved and what will disappear from the archives? What experimental movements today will be squashed? I worry about the post-Reconceptualization—I worry about my own field of curriculum studies. I see the way in which we are incorporated forcefully inside of teaching and learning programs. I see the way in which our programs are altered by outsiders-against our will— and I see the ways in which government is encroaching on scholarly freedom inside of the university. What are we to do? We are powerless as faculty members. The only power left to us is writing. The scholarly murals we paint are political. These scholarly murals are forms of resistance. These scholarly murals serve to undo social oppressions of all sorts. We are interested in unpacking intersections between public education and oppression and undoing this oppression. But sometimes it seems like a losing battle. And yet. And yet we learn from our history that the WPA murals survived—despite being covered over or hidden for many years. Books outlive people and so too shall our scholarship.

What is to become of John Dewey's progressive dream? This too is our dream. We are also the inheritors of that progressive philosophical movement to which Dewey belonged: American Pragmatism. American Pragmatism is a distant relation of ours. In order to get a better historical understanding on progressive thought in America, it will become imperative to understand the way in which the Pragmatic philosophers thought about their work in the academy. I will deal with this in the next chapter, but for now I will just say that Dewey was not the only one interested in the progressive dream. Josiah Royce, C.S. Peirce, George Santayana, William James, A. N. Whitehead, Jane Addams and others like Dewey developed progressive philosophies that shaped American thought. Curriculum studies scholars are also related-even if tangentially-to these progressive intellectuals.

What we learn from the history of the WPA is that art can be done in bad times. Artfully done scholarship that cuts edges and pushes boundaries can be done in times of social strain as well. The Reconceptualization burst on the scene during the Kent State disaster (personal communication, William F. Pinar). It was no accident that curriculum studies arrived on the scene when it did. Curriculum studies has survived the right wing onslaught in the United States and is now an international movement with the development of IAACS (The International Association for the Advancement of Curriculum Studies). Still, there may be attempts to cover over or hide what we do in the more conservative wing of the field of education. There may be attempts to whitewash or erase what we say by the right wing in the larger field of education. But like the rediscovered WPA murals, our work will continually be rediscovered for generations to come. Nobody can stop the presses. As long as we keep writing nobody can stop us.

It is astonishing that the WPA murals were rediscovered and restored. Imagine being an elementary school student in Chicago and being surrounded by such tremendous beauty and history. Public memory is instantiated in those murals.

Memory gets passed down from generation to generation via works of art, science, scholarship. And yet reactionary segments of culture attempt to stem the tide of progressivism—but they just do not succeed in silencing us!! Eventually the good news gets out. You can't stop the printing press.

IF WE LET THEM, THEY WILL WIN.

We must not let them win.

On the psychic front there are reasons why a progressive scholar might stop working. Like the musician who can no longer play, the scholar who can no longer write has lost the battle against mother. The scholar who cannot psychologically manage the force of the intrusive mother (the academy) loses the battle. If we let them, they will win. We must never let them win.

But the negative atmosphere of the academe is a powerful force. Struggling under this force may result in psychic paralysis or catatonia. Sometimes psychic meltdown is inevitable. It is just a matter of time before the return of the repressed takes revenge on psyche. Psychic meltdowns might even be transgenerational. Does one scholarly generation pass down to another their psychic meltdown? Jung (1963) points out that:

> Our souls as well as our bodies are composed of individual elements which were already present in the ranks of our ancestors. The "newness" of the individual psyche is an endlessly varied combination of age-old components. Body and soul therefore have an intensely historical character. . . . (p. 235)

What has been "present in the ranks of our [scholarly] ancestors"? The university is a place where one scholarly generation comes after the next. These generations affect one another. If our scholarly ancestors have had psychic damage done to them, do we then symbolically inherit that damage? What can we do to stem the tide of this transgenerational trauma?

Study. Work through. Talking cure. Writing it out. Not giving in.

Scholarship is soul work and is our only solace after being beaten up by the university. Soul work may lead the damaged scholar out of her psychic crisis. The intrusive mother academy must not win.

THE SCHOLAR AND MUSICIAN

On Not Being Able to Work or Play

I begin this chapter with a quote by Ted Aoki who was one of the first people in curriculum studies to talk about music. He states,"[t]he time is ripe for us to call upon sonare to dwell juxtaposed with videre" (Aoki, 2005, p. 373). Ted Aoki (2005) calls for a more "sonorous" curriculum (p. 369). He turns to the ear to suggest that too much thought has been influenced by the eye, by visual metaphor. The Enlightenment is about light; to see the light is to understand. But turning toward the ear, obscurity reigns. Brent Davis (1996) also calls for a turn toward the ear as he comments that:

> Listening, rather, is more toward an imaginative and conscientious particip-
> ation in the unfolding of the world. Immediate, intimate, implicating, and
> interactive, listening is more an interrogation of one's perceptions than the
> mere sensory capacity. (xxvi)

Davis (1996) and Aoki (2005) have opened up a space for curriculum theorists to think through the ear rather than through the eye. How does one think through the ear? Teaching is the art of listening is it not? And scholarly writing demands a certain rhythm. I am not the first person to suggest that teaching demands a certain artistry. Tom Barone, William F. Pinar (2007) reports, calls for the educator to be a *"strong poet."* Educator as poet. Nice. Educational researchers have historically been thought to be social scientists. But with the advent of the Reconceptualization William Pinar (1994), Ted Aoki (2005), James Macdonald (1995), Maxine Greene (1995), Dwayne Heubner (2002) and Mary Aswell Doll (1995)—to name a few-- turned toward the humanities to do curriculum theorizing. The humanities inform curriculum theorizing. The social scientific paradigm has been turned on its ear!

Turning toward the ear, my interest here is making connections between the musician and the scholar. Aoki (2005) already does this–in a sense– when he talks about bringing the jazz trumpeter Bobby Shew into one of his seminars. Curriculum as jazz, Aoki (2005) suggests, is a sort of improvisation. Curriculum work might be, in other words, more like the improvisational work of a musician. Unlike Aoki, my work turns on the parallels between musicians and scholars when they are no longer able to play–either with notes or with words.

The scholar who is not able to work is kin to the musician who is no longer able to play. "Family likenesses "(Wittgenstein, 1965, p. 17). On not being able to play. On not being able to work. Family problems. Familiar problems to both musician and scholar. To play and to work. Not being able to do either. The curious interrelation between work and play brought Marion Milner (1987, p. 2) into psychoanalysis. She says:

> In fact the question of what is the creative relation between work and play was to become an interest that finally landed me in the psychoanalytic consulting room. . . . (p. 2)

This work is in part a tribute to Marion Milner. She opened the door for me to be able to think about the problem of not being able to do something. When playing and working are interrupted how to think through the catastrophe?

In this chapter I would like to do two things. The first large section of this chapter is devoted to unpacking complex relationships between language, music and thought. My aim here is to show that at an ontological and epistemological level, language, music and thought are inter-related. I do this so as to make the case for arguing that there are connections—at both an ontological and epistemological level– between the musician and the scholar.

The second part of this chapter is devoted to the main thesis of this book. Recall, in the early chapters of the book we examined music and musicians who were not able to play. Here, I look at particular scholars who–at one time or another—had struggles inside of the academy. I want to show here that these intellectuals struggled with emotional upheavals during their careers and yet were able to produce important scholarly work. These scholars did not have to give up their academic careers because they suffered from set backs of sorts. They could have, however. But the point is that they did not.

LANGUAGE, MUSIC, THOUGHT: THINKING TOGETHER SCHOLARS AND MUSICIANS

Let us turn first to the uncanny connections between language, music and thought to connect musicians and scholars. Both musicians and scholars live inside of language and thought. It is the unconscious that binds these realms together. The psyche drives itself and perhaps we are just the channel for some kind of mystic energy. There is something uncanny about the way in which music can be used in the service of thought—as both are driven, at bottom, by unconscious properties. Here I am thinking of an interesting biography of Einstein written by Walter Isaacson (2007). Isaacson tells us that Einstein—who played the violin—used music to help him think. Isaacson (2007) explains:

> Music was no mere diversion [for Einstein]. It helped him think. . . . "He would often play his violin in his kitchen late at night, improvising melodies while he pondered complicated problems," a friend recalled. "Then, suddenly, in the middle of playing, he would announce excitedly, 'I've got it!' As if by inspiration, the answer to the problem would have come to him in the midst of music." (p.14)

The inspiration could have come up from the unconscious. Playing music puts the musician in a sort of psychic zone or space that frees up the conscious mind and allows it to undo itself and slide into regression. In a state of regression, what comes up from the unconscious might just be new ideas. Sometimes ideas come through music. Music works, in this case, in the service of thought. So there is some uncanny connection between these two realms. Music allows the thinker to freely associate—and this is what I think Einstein did when playing the violin.

If language is freely associated, there is no telling where it is going or where it has been. Freely associated language goes in its own direction. How to get a handle on what is beyond our understanding? Martin Gliserman (1996) says, "[t]he sentence has depth, reaching back into unconscious processes, into histories" (p. 7). Whose histories? Object relations theorists teach that unconscious links between the mother and child ensue. Not only this, transgenerationally from the grandmother to the mother to the grandchild unconscious links exist. So who is it that is doing the talking when all is said and done? There are certainly transgenerational properties to language. And this complicates. How do children learn to form words? At the end of the day, we really do not know. Linguists and scientists can give reasons, but when it all comes down to it, language is a mystery. Language forms sounds; sounds are the root of music. The language of music and the music of language are interrelated.

Music springs from the unconscious. When a composer writes a piece, from whence does it spring? Can we really say? Why can some people write music and others cannot? How could Mozart have imagined entire symphonies in his head before writing them down? Did his musical ability come from nowhere? How did Bach write what he did with such mathematical perfection, with such intense emotion and beauty? How is such profundity possible? Marshall Edelson (1975) tells us that

> language, music, and dreams as systems are significantly alike. The theories
> that account for linguistic utterances, musical compositions, dreams . . . shall
> be significantly alike. (pp. 14–15)

What kind of dreams did Bach and Mozart have? Did they dream music into existence?

The symbolic order of language, music and dreams blend, blur. Dreams are of the unconscious, they are made of what is called primary process thinking. This is the thinking of dreams, where contradictions abound, where time has no meaning. And yet music is of time, it is written in time, it is measured in bars, in notes with durations. But in dreams, time is of a different order. Dreams operate in parallel time(s); dreams operate in the time of childhood alongside the time of the present. Is music written in these parallel times? Dreaming forms the basis of all language and music; dreaming forms the basis of the language of music. What drives rational thought is, at bottom, irrational, dreamlike, fantastic. Even the most structured piece of music springs from a more primal place, the unconscious, the dreamworld. And yet, Freud had no truck with music. But music is a language. There are detractors of course. I am thinking here of Suzanne Langer who suggests that music is not a language. G. L. Hagberg (1995) tells us that:

> Langer claims that art picks up where language leaves off. This would seem
> to suggest a radical disanalogy between art and language. (p. 9)

Langer's claim does not convince. Language and art are of a piece. Music, as a
kind of art, is the touchstone of language. The language I am thinking of here is a
symbolic one. We are not talking about a literal note for note, word for word
correlation between language and music. Music is a symbolic language. Splitting
off music from language is a basic category error. The splitting of music from
language is akin to the splitting of speech from writing. These activities are
interconnected–as I will show in more detail later. Psyche is made of the many
complications of interconnections. The human mind is a fluid enterprise as we
know from dreams and dreams require thought, image, symbol–the symbolic order
is a language.

Nietzsche–like Langer–felt that music was not a language. Vladimir
Jankelevitch (2003) points out that

> Nietzsche no doubt wanted to say the following: music is not proper to
> dialogue, whose nature rests in exchange, the analysis of ideas, amicable
> collaboration that takes place mutually and equitably. Music does not allow
> the discursive, reciprocal communication of meaning but rather an immediate
> and ineffable communication. . . . (p. 9)

As against Nietzsche, I suggest that music is not immediate. Like other forms of
expression, it is a form of mediation that must be processed through the ear and
through thought. For some people this processing fails and they suffer from tone
deafness. Musical expression is mediated by the brain and by the ear. And the ear
is a strange organ. What is it to hear music? What is it to express something
musically? If anything it is vague. William James (1890/1950) comments on the
nature of the mind as being vague. So too the ear of the mind. James says:

> It is, in short, the re-instatement of the vague to its proper place in our mental
> life which I am so anxious to press on the attention. (p. 254)

If one were to speak of a phenomenology of listening to music one might speak in
terms of the vague. The experience of listening to music is a vague one. Listening
to music creates moods. How to describe moods? Are moods not vague? I am
moved. What does that mean? This meaning is vague because it is beyond words.
To be engaged in musical expression is to speak in vague terms–because sound is
vague. Notation might be precise but when music gets played its hearers are rapt in
sound and can only speak vaguely about that experience. I was swept away. What
does that mean? The music makes me feel melancholy. What does that mean? We
really cannot say. Music is the language of vague melancholy. Then there is some
music that is beyond any understanding. Here I am thinking of serial music. It
might be highly structured but when played it sounds crazy. I can make little sense
of serial music. It is a mystery to me. No matter what kind of music we are talking
about it remains a mystery.

Igor Stravinsky (2002) is another person who feels that there is little relation between language and music. He states that music

> . . . is at any rate far closer to mathematics, to something like mathematical thinking and mathematical relationships, than to literature. How misleading are most verbal descriptions of musical forms! (p. 266)

I would agree with Stravinsky that music is mathematical but it is also a language and it is related to that which is literary. Why can't it be both a form of math and language? Isn't math a language of sorts? Speech expresses the experience of listening but speaking about it somehow diminishes that experience—this is, I think, Stravinsky's point. But this does not mean that one cannot put into words what one has heard.

Yes, music is mysterious but so too is language. Lacan suggests that people never really communicate. What happens when three parties are engaged in a discussion? The musical trialogue—which you might think of as a musical discussion– is between composer, player and listener. What does this trialogue reveal? The incommunicable. Feelings are evoked. But attempting to explain feelings and their connection to what is heard proves impossible. St. Anselm in his proof for the existence of God said that the fool did not understand what he had heard. Perhaps we are all fools.

The language(s) of the unconscious are many. The unconscious is where interconnections and criss-crossings are made. Music is language and language is music–these two are inseparable. These criss-crossings are rooted in the unconscious. Ben Ami-Scharfstein (1993) comments on the connections between words and musicality:

> the various forms of ineffability are relevant to one another. There is something unformulated and perhaps unformable and finally mysterious in the prosaic, everyday successes and failures of words; and the musicality of music itself is echoed in the less concentrated but inescapable musicality of our speech. . . . (xvii)

Perhaps words and music fail to communicate. We only understand bits and pieces of notes, sentences, phrases, pauses, rests and so forth. We take in psychologically what we can. The rest we ignore, or let go or forget. What is forgotten is of the utmost importance and it is perhaps the most ineffable. Perhaps it is to the forgotten we should turn.

Music, speech and language are all fleeting. All are based on sounds. From whence the sounds come we do not know. And the sounds have a certain rhythm, a certain cadence and lilt. Ludwig Wittgenstein (1958), throughout his later writings often suggests that music, language, speech and thought are interconnected. In his *Philosophical Investigations*, Wittgenstein (1958) claims:

> I can imagine such a use of words (of a series of sounds). (Uttering a word is like striking a note on the keyboard of sound. (p. 4e)

Words. Sounds. Music. Words are spoken, written. Words are sounds, words make sounds. Further on in the text, Wittgenstein (1958) says, "[r]eading the written sentence loud or soft is indeed comparable with singing from a musical score" (p. 11e). As we read further along in this text Wittgenstein again drives home the same point. He states:

> Understanding a sentence is much more akin to understanding a theme in music than one may think. . . . Why is just this the pattern in variation and tempo? (p. 143e)

Wittgenstein's point couldn't be clearer. The implications are many. When thinking about the musician who plays a piece of music, one can also think about the scholar who writes a piece of scholarship. The composer and scholar especially parallel each other. To write a piece of music is not dissimilar from writing a piece of scholarship. Both work in symbolic languages of sorts. Both deal with phrasing, timing, sounds, melodies, cadences, rests, pauses and so forth. The composer and the scholar have many things in common. What fascinates about Wittgenstein is that he grew up around many musicians. His mother and brothers were musicians (Janik & Toulmin, 1996). In fact, Allan Janik and Stephen Toulmin (1996) tell us that his father, Karl Wittgenstein

> was a great patron of the musical arts, to whose home such musicians as Brahms and Joachim, Mahler, Walter, and the youthful Pablo Casals were no strangers. (p.169)

Imagine growing up in such a household! Childhood influences like these make a difference when choosing a career later in life. Imagine this. Guess who's coming to dinner? Pablo Casals. Wow. No wonder Wittgenstein wrote so much about music. It does help to read biographies because intellectual labor happens in the context of life experiences. If I hadn't read some of the biographies of Wittgenstein I would not have had a context against which to understand why he wrote about music. Scholarly work or musical work is highly related to the biographic situation.

Early on in Wittgenstein's career he focused mostly on the structures of sentences, the logic of language and for this he is often–interestingly enough– compared to the well known serial composer Arnold Schoenberg (see for instance, Le Rider, 1993; Johnston, 1972; Janik & Toulmin, 1996). Serial music is about structure and logic. The composer follows strict rules for notation. I talked about serial music early on in this book and stated that I am not much of a fan. I don't like the way most of this music sounds. It is as if the composer works backwards. And it is here that I think serial music failed. Musical expression is not about rules, but emotional expression. For both early Wittgenstein and Schoenberg, what mattered was structure and logic. But, as is also well known, Wittgenstein changed. The older he got the less he believed that the rules of logic outweighed the expression of an idea. Later in life, he became interested in the ineffable and the mysterious. Wittgenstein became more interested in exploring the mystical and the ways in which language participates in the mystical. And part of the ineffable and mysterious concern the overlaps of language, music, speech and thought.

Wittgenstein says, for instance, "[h]earing a word in a particular sense. How queer that there should be such a thing!" (1958, p. 144e). The keys to this sentence are the words '*queer*' and '*hearing*.' What does it mean to hear a word queerly? When I hear the word melancholy—I think to myself what a queer word. This word is at once poetic and queer. What does it mean to feel melancholy? What kind of a feeling does that word take on? How can a word evoke a vague sensation like melancholy?

Back to Wittgenstein for a moment. Most strange in his *Philosophical Investigations* (1958) is what he calls "the dawning of an aspect" (p. 194e). This dawning is what I would consider part and parcel of the ineffable and mysterious. All of a sudden a perception of someone or something changes. This is the famous duck-rabbit figure found in Wittgenstein's text. The drawing is at once perceived as a duck *and* a rabbit, or perceived variously as a duck *or* a rabbit. How and why perceptions shift remains a question. This is the question for Wittgenstein. And this question is rather queer.

For me, the "*dawning of an aspect*" is a particularly useful idea when thinking of the musician-scholar relationship. This too is the duck-rabbit problem. It '*dawned*' on me that these two professions are similar. The problem of the musician who can no longer play and the problem of the scholar who can no longer work is the problem of the duck-rabbit. Again, not that the scholar is a musician. A duck is not a rabbit. But turning a duck on his head shifts perception to become rabbit. Wittgenstein's work is of the utmost importance to my project because he ties together the links between music and language. If language is a kind of music and music is a kind of language then the musician and scholar suffer similar problems ontologically and epistemologically. Paralysis. The case of both musician and scholar is at once an ontological and epistemological problem.

We can get at this problem from another angle. From the musician's side, Leonard Bernstein (1976), in his well known book called *The Unanswered Question: Six Talks at Harvard,* suggests throughout the text that music is kin to language. For example, Bernstein refers to music as a "grammar" (p. 27), as "linguistics" (p. 9), as "heightened speech" (p. 16), as "prose" (p. 81), as "metaphor" (p. 133), as "poetry" (p. 424) and finally as "language" (p. 424). Bernstein's message couldn't be clearer. How unlike Langer, Nietzsche and Stravinsky he is.

The scholar who can not work is like the artist who suffers breakdown. Is it taboo for an academic to talk of scholarly breakdown, of scholarly paralysis? There are not many books on this problem. The scholar who is broken. Who has written on that? It is common knowledge, on the other hand, that artists– creative writers and poets especially– are often subject to breakdown. Much has been written on this front. As I stated earlier in this book, Adam Kirsch (2005), in his book *The Wounded Surgeon: Confession and Transformation in six American Poets*, discusses the likes of Robert Lowell, Elizabeth Bishop, John Berryman and Randall Jarrell who all suffered from some sort of psychic paralysis during their careers. All of these artists had some kind of emotional turmoil that prevented them–at one time or another–from working artistically. What I am adding to this discussion is that scholars can also suffer from the same kinds of problems as do poets and creative writers but no one to date–as far as I know–has written extensively on this issue. However, Ralph Waldo Emerson (2003), in his famous work on *The American Scholar*, briefly comments on troubled scholars. Emerson states:

> When the artist has exhausted his materials, when the fancy no longer paints, when thoughts are no longer apprehended, and books are a weariness–he always has the resource to live. . . . Does he lack organ or medium to impart his truths? He can still fall back on this elemental force of living them. (p. 235)

What I am interested in here is the scholar for whom "books become a weariness." This troubles. What to do when books no longer fill the void? What to do when writing becomes a chore? What to do when the writing won't come any longer? What to do when the intellectual life dies? These are questions that scholars do not raise often perhaps because they cannot afford to. Is it suicidal career-wise to admit to problems such as these? Paralysis is a serious problem for academics but it is not discussed openly. Here I want to crack open this taboo.

MORE ON THE INTERCONNECTIONS BETWEEN THOUGHT, LANGUAGE, MUSIC

The connections between thought, language and music are quite complex and could be the subject matter of an entire book. My aim here is to briefly touch on some issues relevant to my project at hand. I am not a linguist and I am not interested in semiotics but I am interested in language and the idea of language and the way in which language is connected to both musical and scholarly composition. Perhaps the scope of this discussion is too large and too complex. If we just took two of these three domains, thought and language we might write volumes on the complexities of these. Jean Piaget (2007) says that the question we are asking is "vexed" (p. 3). Piaget (2007) explains that

> This is not the place to raise the vexed question of the relation between thought and language, but we may note in passing that the very existence of such questions shows how complex are the functions of language, and how futile the attempt to reduce all to one—that of communicating thought. (p. 3)

Interestingly Piaget tells us that language should not be reduced to thought. Language, that is, is not always used to think. That is a curious thought indeed. If language is not used to think what is it used to do? Well, Piaget tells us that language has different functions especially for children.

SPEECH AND NONSENSE

Piaget (2007) talks of echolalia. The child talks nonsense–Piaget points out– just to hear herself talk. Babble without meaning is common among children, he suggests. Or, then there is the child's monologue. Here, Piaget (2007) contends that

The child does not ask questions and expects no answers, neither does he attempt to give any definite information to his mother who is present. He does not ask himself whether she is listening or not. He speaks for himself. . . . (p. 247)

Piaget's passage above concerns children, but perhaps adults engage in meaningless monologues as well. Here I am thinking of Samuel Beckett's characters who go on and on speaking meaningless monologues. What does it mean to speak to no one? Do we speak only to hear ourselves speak? Certainly, students in doctoral seminars often engage in monologues just to hear themselves speak. Conference attendees do the same thing. Off they go on a monologue as if speaking to no one. And often two people engage not in dialogue but in dual monologues. Sometimes we speak just to get it out and care little if anybody hears or understands. Sometimes we do not even know what we are saying.

ON NOT BEING ABLE TO SPEAK

Aphasia is the term used by neurologists when one loses the capacity to speak. We learn much about the complex way speech is connected to other modes of address like thought, imagination, sight and sound when the capacity to speak is impaired. Interestingly enough some people, according to Oliver Sacks (2007), who lose the capacity to speak–usually due to some sort of brain injury—"can sing" (p. 215). And yet singing and speaking spring from different parts of the brain. Sacks (2007) points out that "there are major differences (and sometimes overlaps) in the processing of speech and song in the brain" (p. 216). Anthony Storr (1992) talks of the strange brain relation between words and song. He states:

> Music and speech are separately represented in the two hemispheres of the brain. Although there is considerable overlap. . . . language is predominantly processed in the left hemisphere, whilst music is chiefly scanned and appreciated in the right hemisphere. The division of function is not so much between words and music as between logic and emotion. (p. 35)

This seems rather queer! When one sings a song, the vocal cords are used, melody carries the singer along and the singer uses words to sing a song. But sometimes the words to the song can impair the singer who suffers from a brain injury. Some people who suffer aphasia can only hum, but not use words when singing. If they try to use words, the melody evades. Henry Head (1963) – the famed neurologist— says:

> Most of the soldiers who came under my care had been accustomed to sing popular songs of the day by ear, although few possessed any knowledge of music. . . . But as soon as he tried to say the words, he usually broke down. (p. 379).

Here, it is as if the words get in the way of the music. But do we not use words to sing? So what is it about words that interfere with song? And yet it is a well known fact that languages can be learned by children by singing songs. The words to the song help children master a language especially if the conventional way of learning language fails.

But again we have a counter example – reported by Anthony Storr (1992)– of a composer who suffered from aphasia and yet could write fantastic symphonies and even teach music!! He could not use words yet he was able to compose music. Notation is a kind of language and one wonders why his notation skills were not impaired. At any rate, Storr (1992) tells us that:

> . . . Luria studied a composer named Vissarim Shebalin who, following a stroke, suffered from severe sensory aphasia; that is, he was unable to understand the meaning of words. Yet he continued to teach music and composed his fifth symphony which Shostakovich said was brilliant. (p. 35)

How can you teach music without understanding words? How to speak about music without using words? How to speak about music when the capacity to speak eludes? Can music speak for itself?

Some who lose the capacity for words cannot notate. Here we have yet another case of aphasia that offers a counter example. Henry Head (1963) tells us about a musician who suffered from "nominal aphasia" who

> was a professional performer on the double bass and the cornet. He lost the power of understanding not only printed words, but also musical notation– [he] became entirely unable to play either instrument. (p. 380)

In this case there is a tight relation between writing down words, writing down music and playing music. All of these functions were lost. These examples and counter examples could go on endlessly. The interconnections and disconnections between speech, language, music and thought are endlessly mind boggling. The connections and disconnections of these functions may seem to have a universal structure but on an individual level, each person can suffer differently from the same kind of brain injury.

Some describe their experience of aphasia as also *not being able to think*. Take for example the case of Mrs. K . reported by Karen Kaplan-Solms and Mark Solms (2002). Although Solms & Solms (2002) point out that Mrs. K. was not literally unable to think, she felt–at some level– that she was unable to think because she kept losing her words. Solms & Solms (2002) point out that "she was far from being truly able to think. Rather. . . she suffered from an inability to attach words to her thoughts, resulting in an inability to bring her thoughts to consciousness (and keep them there)" (p. 108). Mrs. K.'s words kept slipping away and so too her thought, so she thought. Her thought was continually interrupted by not being able to articulate in words what she thought. More disturbingly, "her ongoing awareness of her own self . . . kept disappearing. . ." (Solms & Solms, 2002, p. 98). Here, the felt experience of loss of self troubles. Slipping away–self evacuated, self vanishing!! We recall the case of Syd Barrett who some believe suffered from Asperger's syndrome. He reported– as his condition worsened– that he felt as if he were disappearing. In the film titled *Away From Her*, the main character–who suffers from Alzheimer's disease, tells her husband (much like Mrs. K. and Syd Barrett) that she feels as if she is disappearing. This must be a terrifying feeling. When the brain begins to shut down so too does the sense of self. What must that be like? The feeling of not being able to think because of brain injury is very different from the feeling of not being able to think because of depression. In depression, the thoughts are arrested because of an emotional weight and mental paralysis. I think this difference important to point out. Aphasia caused by brain injury is an altogether different kind of '*not being able to think.*'

It is worth re-stating that there are differing kinds of not being able to think. And that needs to be thought through. There is a huge spectrum on which people become incapacitated. People who are literally not able to speak–who have literally lost all capacity to speak due to brain injury or coma–fall into an entirely different category than what I am trying to get at in this book. When I talk of not being able to think, I am concerned about mental paralysis due to depression, anguish, anxiety. But I thought it necessary to look at brain injuries to point out that this problem is highly complex.

Henry Head (1963) talks much of the work of another famed neurologist Hughlings Jackson who suggested that when speech gets damaged, so too does writing. Here, I am thinking of Derrida's (1976) pronouncement-- in his book titled *Of Grammatology*-- that writing is in speech and speech is in writing. Although Derrida's (1976) argument might sound poetical and philosophical, at the neurological level his position is probably more true than not. Writing is inextricably connected to speaking and speaking is inextricably tied to writing. And we understand this better when we study impaired speech. In many cases when this impairment is caused by brain injury so too is the capacity to write. In the well known document archived by A.R Luria (2002) called *The Man with the Shattered World*, the patient who suffers brain injury–from being shot in the head– is encouraged to keep a journal. He loses the capacity to remember but is determined to write about not remembering. Like victims of Korsakov's syndrome (a condition whereby short term memory is severely damaged), this patient can barely remember what he thought two minutes ago or what he wrote two minutes ago. Remarkably over years and years of struggling he does leave behind a fascinating document about not remembering. Here, he re-writes sentences over and over again because he cannot remember what he had written only seconds ago. Indeed, his world was shattered–and yet he made the best of it. The book is a remarkable testimony to determination and will when a world is shattered. Brain injuries shatter a world. Depressions too can shatter a world–but in a different way. Not being able to work because of depression again is a very different problem from not being able to work because you were shot in the head!!

Many tend to dismiss depression as nothing or '*oh you will get over it.*' But depression is a deadly serious problem. In fact, many people who suffer from chronic depression commit suicide as we know from our poets and creative writers. Think of the list: Anne Sexton, Sylvia Plath, Virginia Woolf, Ernest Hemingway, for starters. But what of academics who jump out of windows? Think of Giles Deleuze. Lines of flight indeed. Not enough thought is given to troubled academics. I hope this book can contribute to the conversation of the problem of academe.

Hughlings Jackson points out–Head (1963) tells us–that loss of speech, curiously enough, does not necessarily mean loss of words. How can this be? Is this not queer? Head tells us that Hughlings Jackson talks of a particular patient who

> cannot speak, he cannot write, he cannot read, not because he has lost "images" or "memories" of words, but because he cannot propositionise. (p. 48)

Not being able to utter propositions but being able to understand words must be extremely frustrating. We have little access to others' interior worlds. And when those interior worlds shut down can we –at any level– understand what it is like to not be able to "*propositionise*"? How limited is our understanding of anything. Some who suffer with brain injuries–like this patient above–have lost what most take for granted–the automatic nature of speaking, imagining and putting words into thought.

Luria (2002) makes a connection between writing and music. Luria (2002) says that "writing is an automatic skill, a series of built-in movements which I call "kinetic melodies" (p. 72). It is interesting to note here that Luria uses musical imagery to describe the process of writing; musicality and writing are interconnected. When inner melody and rhythm are lost– what Bergson called duration– so too is the writing. Time is experienced like a melody. Music is written in meters. Music is highly mathematical as fluid as it sounds; it is broken up by the ways in which notes are measured. The kinetic nature of writing, as Luria puts it, is built on our internal feeling of time, duration. What is it like when one can no longer feel a sense of time? Words are felt in time, because cadence, phrase, pause, happen in time.

Like the inability to write due to a loss of one's inner melody, Oliver Sacks (2007) reports that there is a neurological condition called "*amelodia*". Here the patient cannot understand music; she cannot hear a melody or recognize that a melody is, in fact, a melody. For these people music sounds only like noise. This is the ultimate nightmare for a musician. Imagine the musician who can no longer hear a melody or recognize that a melody is a melody. A nightmare indeed. Again, Sacks (2007) states that this condition is called "*amelodia*."

> [A]melodia [is] analogous to the losing of sentence structure or meaning. . . . Such a person hears a sequence of notes, but the sequence seems arbitrary, seems to have no logic or purpose. (p. 110)

What strikes me here is that Sacks compares losing the understanding of a melody to losing the capacity to understand a sentence. The connection between music and language becomes clearer when we study the loss of either of these functions. And yet one must finally admit of differences between music and language. Differences, however, do not negate the fact that they are interconnected. Music and language part ways–most superficially– when it comes to structure. Aniruddh Patel (2008) points out what he considers to be "important differences" in music and language. He states:

> Important differences do, of course, exist. Take a few examples, music organizes pitch and rhythm in ways that speech does not, and lacks the specificity of language in terms of semantic meaning. Language grammar is built from categories that are absent in music (such as nouns and verbs), whereas music appears to have much deeper power over emotions than does ordinary speech. (p. 4)

I think the problem here is that when people attempt to make a literal connection between music and language we run into problems because obviously they are not the same things. Yet, as I have pointed out earlier, if we think of music as a symbolic language, then we can certainly see the interconnections.

Musical idioms and complex musical scores might be understood by someone but words might elude them. Or a person might have a great understanding of words but be tone deaf!! Or a person might be highly musical and highly literate. There are people who can compose symphonies as well as write complex pieces of scholarship. Here, clearly the musical and the linguistic overlap. And yet there are those who have little understanding of words–because of brain injury–and yet understand expression. A curious thought. One can understand gestures and emotional expressions without understanding language or the spoken word. Gesture is a wordless language–another symbolic language– but speaks volumes. Oliver Sacks (1998) explains that some people might be unable to decipher your speech but

> they have an infallible ear for every vocal nuance, the tone, the rhythm, the cadences, the music, the subtlest modulations, inflections, intonations. . . . (p. 82)

Sacks reminds us that some animals are this way. Dogs especially are attuned to human emotions. Dogs know when people do not like them and they know when people intend harm. How do they know this? They just do. Some dogs are incredibly intuitive, whereas some humans are not intuitive at all.

The upshot of this discussion, once more, is that music, thought, and language are all complexly interrelated and this becomes even clearer when we explore the ways in which various impairments point to these interconnections. Neurologists are most familiar with the varieties of symptoms that get presented in brain injuries. And it is the variety of presentations that point to the complex interconnection between these various cognitive functions. Thus, when one asks the question about whether music and language are connected or if music is a language the question becomes complicated. What underlies this question are a series of other related questions because the functions of music, speech, symbol, melody, language, notation, writing and reading are webbed together. Music, speech, writing, symbol, notation, words, melodies seem to be nested inside of one another. There seems to be no untangling this weave.

When one part of the brain gets injured, another part tends to compensate. Again this points to the interrelation of brain functions. Speaking of compensation, it is well known that the blind can develop a strong capacity for music. Sacks (2007) says that, "[b]lind children are often precociously verbal and develop unusual verbal memories; many of them are similarly drawn to music. . ." (pp. 161–162). The brain compensates for losses. When sight is gone, the ear gets developed. When the ear is gone, the painter is born. When serious illness strikes, the sense of smell gets heightened. This is what neurologists refer to as plasticity. The brain's plasticity is remarkable.

Back to the question of the relation between music, thought and language for a moment. I am thinking of the quirky response of Noam Chomsky (2000) which is certainly worth noting here:

. . . [D]oes it follow that music is a language? That is not a meaningful question because the notion of what is a language is not a meaningful notion.
. . . Is it like human language? Well, sure, in some ways, but then the question is: how 'like' do you mean? (pp. 44–45)

Maybe the question ' is music a language' too simplistic. Or, in a way, it is too complex!! Perhaps the question should be how are music, language, and thought altered when one of these functions breaks down? Even if you say that music is not a language, still music is tied–at least on some level–to words. If words get in the way of humming an old war song–as in the case that Henry Head (1963) reported– the very fact of words interrupting the capacity to sing a song suggests a connection between words and song. Both words and wordless songs are symbolic languages.

Similarly, composing and storytelling have similar roots, Robert Jourdain (1998) tells us that:

[c]omposers can navigate the hierarchy of categories, plucking ideas and combining them into musical phrases, cadences and whole compositions. This is no different from the way a storyteller scans his hierarchy of knowledge about the world for ideas. (pp. 165–166)

Composing a piece of music is akin to writing a novel or writing a piece of scholarship. To say that music is not a language, therefore, seems to me counterintuitive. All the evidence points otherwise.

QUEER THOUGHTS

Is a thought only a thought in language? Wittgenstein (1958) says:

When I think in language, there aren't 'meanings'going through my mind in addition to the verbal expressions: the language is itself the vehicle of thought. (p. 107e)

Wittgenstein suggests that language is thought. But there are other ways of thinking.

Can one think without language? Can one have language without thought? Of course. There are thoughts without language. Those who are born deaf certainly are thinkers without hearing a language. Hans G. Furth (1966) is critical of the

> ready made association of thinking and language. . . . The history of the deaf stands out as one exceptionally glaring instance of man's [sic] inability to see beyond the confines of his own theoretical assumptions. (p. 212)

It is profoundly difficult for people who can hear and verbalize in grammatical structure to understand that thought is possible without language. Sign language–is symbolic thought—so there are languages that are visual. Thought can occur without hearing. Think about a child who is born deaf and never hears a sentence uttered. This child clearly thinks. But she thinks without hearing language. Thinking in images is another way of thinking. Images without language are possibilities. What must it be like to never hear a word? Or what must it be like to have never heard music? These are difficult thoughts for those who hear but this is reality for people who are born deaf. What must it be like for people who are born with the capacity to hear and then lose their hearing later in life? Here I am thinking of Beethoven. What must that have been like? Oliver Sacks (2007) reports that people who become deaf later in life or who have chronic ringing in the ears or some kind of hearing impediment often hallucinate music!! I suppose this is like the phantom limb syndrome. How does one feel pain in a limb that is no longer there? How does one hear music when one cannot hear? Does the painter who loses her sight hallucinate paintings I wonder? Are hallucinations compensations? And if they are compensations should we get rid of them? If medicine gets rid of hallucinations does it damage the brain's plasticity? Are all hallucinations bad? What if you like your hallucinations and want to keep them? Well, so be it.

MORE QUEER THOUGHTS

Autistic thought comes to mind. Jean Piaget (2007), drawing on the work of Bleuler, talks of "autistic thought" (p. 43). He states that autistic thought

> creates for itself a dream world of imagination. it tends, not to establish truths, but so to satisfy desires, and it remains strictly individual and incommunicable as such by means of language.

> Or on the contrary, it works chiefly by images. . . symbols and myths. . . .
> (p. 44)

Piaget points out that Blueler argued that autistic thought is unconscious. How do you know unconscious thoughts? Well, you cannot. That is why you go into psychoanalysis to make that which is unconscious conscious. Much autistic thought is indeed "incommunicable." If it is indeed incommunicable how do we know about it at all? I have no answer to this. But because we dream strange thoughts, we might by analogy suggest that autistic thought and dream thought are on a continuum. We can get our dream thoughts back, at least somewhat. Yet, dreams often cannot be put into language. They leave a residue (what Freud called day residue) of feeling. We might be left with fleeting imagery but as we try to articulate that imagery it slips from our grasp. The world of dreams is strange and rather mad at times. The dream world is the Other. Images occur as if on their own, disconnected from language and difficult to articulate in thought. Can images occur without thought? How can an image be an image if it is unthought? How does one call up an image if one cannot think it?

EXTREMELY QUEER THOUGHTS

And then there is thought that is wrong thought, mad thought. Is impaired thought thought at all? There is thought that is totally disconnected from reality. Is this called psychosis? In some cases yes. But here I am thinking of people who suffer from brain injury–and perhaps this injury does not result in psychosis but in extremely queer thoughts. In particular, I am interested here in what neurologists term anosognosia. Karen Kaplan-Solms and Mark Solms (2002) talk about this as a "disavowal of illness" (p. 150). It is one thing to deny the severity of an illness, but it is another thing to suffer from anosognosia. Solms & Solms (2002) tell of bizarre reports from the case notes of Babinski and Anton. Solms and Solms (2002) report this "*disavowal of illness*"

> such as in Babinski's (1914) seminal collection of cases in which densely hemiplegic patients insisted that they could walk without difficulty, or in Anton's (1899) classical study in which cortically blind patients insisted that they could see normally. (p. 150)

How strange this is. What is it about the brain that allows one to think that one can do what one clearly cannot do? These cases are certainly more than denial. The thought that walking is possible when it is not or that seeing is possible when it is not is extremely queer to say the least. These thoughts are simply bizarre. Brain injuries can cause some of the strangest thoughts. In academe we make much of the notion of the Other at an abstract level. When studying brain injured cases, Otherness is made eerily concrete. Here I am thinking of more strange cases of thought gone extremely queer, one in particular that is called capgras syndrome. V. S. Ramachandran and Sandra Blakeslee (1998) report the case of a man who thought he had "*duplicate parents*" (p. 2) A patient named Arthur

> sustained a terrible head injury in an automobile crash and soon afterward claimed that his father and mother had been replaced by duplicates who looked exactly like his real parents. (p. 2)

This is so strange as to be unreal but it is very real for these people. And it is a catastrophe. The human mind is stranger than we think indeed. These very strange cases point to the fact that the brain is very strange. This is thought out of whack. Another weird case is what is called somatoparaphrenia, or "the denial of ownership of one's body parts" (Ramachandran & Blakeslee, 1998, p. 131). I have heard of 'this is not a pipe'–by the famous painter Magritte–but I have never heard of–this is not my leg!! Take the case of the schoolteacher reported below:

> A schoolteacher suffered a stroke that paralyzed the left side of her body, but she insists that her left arm is not paralyzed. Once, when I asked her whose arm was lying in the bed next to her, she explained that the limb belonged to her brother. (Ramachandran & Blakeslee, 1998, p. 2)

My leg is my brother's leg? Extremely queer thoughts. Why are they generated? What are thoughts when thoughts are wrong? A thought might represent the thing thought about, but in these cases the thought represents fantasies about what is thought to be there, but is not. This drives home the notion that fantasies are reality. Are these thoughts psychotic or are they simply an extreme version of denial? Or is denial a form of psychosis? Knowing that thoughts are psychotic does not make them any less real. Are all thoughts fantasies? Freud suggested that certainly fantasy life makes up much of our thought. To what extent do we fantasize? When can we tell whether our fantasies match reality or not? When asking the question about what is thought, the answer becomes spookier and spookier. It is not so clear what thought is. How different is thought from fantasy? In academe we talk about the social construction of knowledge. But if someone believes that their leg belongs to their brother, is this the same thing as a social construction? If thoughts are socially constructed does that mean that they are all made up? What does it mean to make things up? How made up is made up and when do we step over the line into madness? How far we have moved away from Descartes! His dreamer was wrong–so he thought. But I think his dreamer was right and Descartes got it all wrong.

Take paranoia or envy for example–are these social constructions or are they madness? Are these thoughts projections? Paranoia might be justified if one is living in a totalitarian situation. But people who are always looking over their shoulder, no matter what the situation, are living on the brink of madness. The nightmare world that paranoid-schizophrenics create is mad. Likewise, envy might be justified in some cases, but envy might also border on the psychotic.

What does it mean to think? I do not think I know anymore!! What does it mean, this thinking queerly? Thinking crazy thoughts is still thought but thought that is crazy. Is that being unable to think? Well, yes and no.

Thought that is "incommunicable" is not just autistic or psychotic– sometimes it is also scholarly! Here I am thinking of Noam Chomsky's remarks about Jacques Lacan. Chomsky (2000) states:

> I knew Lacan personally and I never understood a word he was talking about.
> . . . In fact, I have a rather strong feeling that he was playing jokes, that he was trying to see how crazy he could be and still get people to take him seriously. (p. 47)

A remarkable admission in light of the fact that people do indeed take Lacan seriously. I do not know whether or not he was playing jokes on people but I do know that I cannot understand him either. I have tried on several occasions to read

Lacan but come away only frustrated and feeling rather stupid. What does it mean when scholarship borders on the incommunicable? I am not sure how to answer to this question. There may be deep meaning in the incommunicable–it is just a matter of decoding it. Perhaps what is incommunicable to one is totally understandable to someone else. I do not understand chaos theory because of the mathematics behind it and I cannot–with any depth–get at its meaning. But there are people who can unpack the mathematics behind it and make much sense of it and get the depth of the meaning of it. Scholarship should push the boundaries of thought and when it pushes into the extremely abstract it can become incommunicable and perhaps it is in the incommunicable that we find the ultimate in queer thoughts because life is queer. There are scholars who do understand Lacan and do have a better grasp on the incommunicable than do I. Perhaps Lacan was really a poet of the psyche. Poets are hard to understand.

Poetic thought. What must that be? Where do poets come from? Who gets to claim that she is a poet? When does one become a poet? The language that is truly Other to itself must be poetic. I wonder if mathematicians and physicists perceive their work as a form of poetics? Here, I concur with Heidegger (1971) that deep language is always already poetic. Heidegger says that the poetic calls us; It calls us from some beyond. Heidegger is a mystic. He states:

> But the responding in which man [sic] authentically listens to the appeal of language is that which speaks in the element of poetry. (p. 216)

Listening to the "appeal of language" means hearing the call of the poetic. Those who cannot hear the call of the poetic are not living queerly enough. The poetic is necessarily queer because much of it is beyond understanding. Language calls and the calling is poetic. Language calls from elsewhere and writes its way into psyche, if only psyche can hear the call. If language comes from some other place, that place is Other to us, it is some beyond, some mysterious beyond. And it is this that I think Wittgenstein attempted to get at in his later writings. Logician turned mystic. What a queer turn. Thought, he says, is "*queer.*" Wittgenstein (1958) says:

> This queer thing, thought–but it does not strike us as queer when we are thinking, but only when we say, as it were retrospectively: "How was that possible?". . . . We feel as if by means of it we had caught reality in our net. (p. 127e)

Queering thought. How is it possible to even think a thought? Wittgenstein thinks queerly on queer thoughts. And can one think a thought of one's own? The postmoderns would of course say no. My thoughts are all the thoughts I've come across. Thoughts get combined and mixed up with the thoughts of others. And then they take on their own life. My thoughts are never purely my thoughts, they are the thoughts of others worked on. And so they are Other to me as I work on them and make them more Other through queering them even more. Thought is personal and thought is cultural and thought is of a time and of a certain inheritance of which we are not fully conscious. Thinking is like spinning, spinning a wheel through time.

The wheel spins without stopping. Thought is like fabric, fiber. Thought has textures. What happens when no thoughts come?

Queering thought again. Here I am reminded of William James (1890/1950) and Wilfred Bion (1994) who talk of "thoughts without thinkers". This is very queer indeed. James (1890/1950) remarks:

> Whether anywhere in the room there be a mere thought, which is nobody's thought, we have no means of ascertaining, for we have no experience of the like. (p. 226)

Is James saying that thoughts float around the room by themselves as if the thinker projected them outside of her head into the atmosphere? Is this impossible? Maybe. Maybe not. We do not know where consciousness ends, we do not even know how it begins. We have little understanding of the unconscious and we have little understanding of the brain. Even though scientists might suggest that thoughts are distributed over varying parts of the brain, they do not know—at root—where thoughts come from or how they come to be at all. Richard Selzer (1996) eloquently states, "[t]he surgeon knows the landscape of the brain, yet does not know how a thought is made" (p. 30). This is a rather profound admission. We know nothing. And that fact is queer! Bion (1994), who is strangely like James on this point, says:

> I shall suppose a mental multi-dimensional space of unthought and unthinkable extent and characteristics. Within this I shall suppose there to be a domain of thoughts without a thinker. (p. 313.)

This puzzles. Do these thoughts go on as if no conscious part of the mind picks them up? Are these thoughts generated on their own without the conscious part of the mind? But where are they? And who generates them? Can thoughts exist as if on their own? Is there no access to these self generating thoughts? Whose thoughts are they if they are not the thinker's? Are there thoughts in my mind that are not created by me, are they mine? Are these thoughts created by something in the brain that is not me part of me? Well, one might suggest that these thoughts are those that are deeply unconscious or the thoughts that we are not aware of that allow us to do basic things like move, talk, walk, feel, see, smell. But are these thoughts at all? Or are they something else? Or does Bion mean that there are thoughts floating around out there without thinkers like James suggests? If they are floating around outside of the head where are they and what are they saying? Whose thoughts? This is rather queer. Schizophrenics say that thoughts are put into their heads by alien forces, by God, by the devil. Or psychotics engage in what is called projective identification whereby objects seem to take on animate characteristics. Minds get stuck inside of shoes or radios. I am stuck in the toaster. I am the toaster. I am my mother? To hear the thoughts of mother in our heads is intrusive. The intrusive mother is the psychically colonizing force that we hear always. Is this introjective identification? Is this insanity? Am I becoming my mother? Oh my God, I sound just like my mother! That I am like my mother is a different sort of psychological issue than believing that I am my mother or that I am Christ. Christ speaks through me, my mother speaks through me. What does this mean? Christopher Bollas (2000) speaks to this point. He states:

> To be found in Freud, much as Lacan indicated, is a subject who speaks to no one, not even to himself; indeed, where to speak is to be spoken through, interrupted by this unconscious that slips us up as it expresses unconscious psychic reality. (p. 13)

Who speaks to whom? Being spoken through? Who is speaking? There is conscious speech and unconscious speech. Speech. Talking is speech. But does one speak in one's own voice or in the voice of our mothers? This is sounding more and more like a Beckett monologue!!

And then there is the notion of inner speech. What is that if it is conscious? What is that ongoing inner monologue? What is the observing ego? But what if the speaker has no observing ego? What kind of inner speech do schizophrenics have? Or what about the inner speech of those with multiple personalities? Who is doing the speaking and who hears the speech? Lev Vygotsky (1981) comments on inner speech. He states:

> Inner speech is not the interior aspect of external speech–it is a function in itself. It still remains speech, i.e., thought connected with words. But while external speech thought is embodied in words, in inner speech words die as they bring forth thought. Inner speech is to a large extent thinking in pure meanings. It is a dynamic, shifting, unstable thing, fluttering between word and thought. . . . (p. 149)

What, I wonder, does Vygotsky mean by 'pure meaning?' What is pure meaning? Is pure meaning something without words? Is pure meaning symbols, images? Or is it raw feeling? Sometimes meaning is felt stronger in emotions than in words. We are left after viewing an intense film with very strong feelings that are hard to articulate. The taking in of the film–this introjection–is the taking in of feeling, of meaning that lacks any clear articulation in words. Is this pure meaning? Or is there anything that is pure? This I doubt. All the senses are mixed up. If inner speech "flutters" between word and thought–as Vygotsky says–where is it fluttering? What is between word and thought? A gap no doubt exists between word and thought. Does inner speech happen in a gap? A void? Is inner speech speech at all? Here I am thinking of Chomsky's comments about the deaf in relation to inner speech. Chomsky (2000) remarks, " [p]eople lacking exposure to spoken language may or may not have something that resembles "inner speech" " (p. 46). If you never heard anyone speak, how could you have inner speech? But perhaps if you became deaf later in life, you would have inner speech. If you were born deaf you may not have inner speech, but you may have inner imagery. Does inner imagery speak? It speaks, not in sound, but in symbol and sign. Martin Halliwell (1999) commenting on Paul Ricoeur, tells us that for Ricoeur some "bypass" language [I would add inner speech] altogether. Ricoeur (1999) says that there is the existence of an opaque subjectivity which expresses itself through the detour of countless mediations–signs, symbols, texts and human praxis itself." Ricoeur's use of 'detour' may suggest a way of bypassing language. . . . (Ricoeur qtd. in Halliwell pp. 7–8)

What strikes me here is the notion of an "*opaque subjectivity.*" Indeed the mind is opaque; our very existence is opaque. The way in which we experience the world is always already mediated. Mediated experience is highly opaque. There is no direct experience of the world. It is experienced through the mediations of language, sound, sight, text, and images. We have no direct access to things in themselves. Mediated experience may have very little to do with language–if anything at all. Mediating the world is sensory, emotive, bodily, fleshy. Merleau- Ponty (1968) had it right when he said that it is the flesh that allows us to be in the world; it is the hand that touches that which is out there to be touched. The hand is Merleau-Ponty's symbol of mediated experience. The flesh is not a language, it is something much more primal. Flesh is that '*opaque subjectivity*' around which Ricoeur speaks. However, some might think that the flesh is its own language. Bodies do speak illness. The body tells a story of disease. The flesh is somehow more primal than language and speaks otherwise. To reduce the body to language is not enough. The body is far too complex to be reduced to this one thing.

Primal language is flesh. But thought is enfleshed and also primal. Communicating thoughts takes talent. Some simply cannot communicate what they feel. And then there are those who want to think and write but have no talent to do so. Wittgenstein (1980) addresses this. He states, "[w]anting to think is one thing; having a talent for thinking another" (1980, p. 44e). And so you have scholars and then you have "*dullards,*" as A.N. Whitehead (1967) puts it. Whitehead (1967) remarks:

it is quite easy to produce a faculty entirely unfit–a faculty of very efficient pedants and dullards. The general public will only detect the difference after the university has stunted the promise of youth for scores of years. (p. 99)

As against Whitehead, I do not think the public would detect much of anything at all--if their children are being undereducated that is– because education in this country is a non-issue. This is a country where business rules. If money were involved, people might take notice of second rate professors. Those of us who have been victims of public education in this country have to learn anew. We have to start our education all over again. Some of us were lucky. I studied with very talented people. I studied with people who were truly intellectuals. And this is rare in the United States. Part of the problem is the state of the university. The bottom line–money– is the only line of thought in the university. It is a sad day in the history of the American university when talented professors are asked to dumb down their curricula by competing with for-profits where open admissions and 100% graduation rates for doctoral students are the rule, not the exception. American intellectuals are clearly not respected nor are they honored. American intellectuals swim in a sea of anti-intellectualism and pedantry. To be asked to

compete with the lowest common denominator–the for-profit schools for scandal–
is not only detrimental to the health of the university at large but it ultimately
harms the students. Let them all in and let them all out. Spoon feed them and lead
them on choke chains. Teach them only obedience and non thought. Get them in
and out of the mills quickly to make more money. It is a sad day in American
education.

Back to thinking. Thought as it gets mediated through language can be poetic.
Language can address the Other via poesis. And poesis is musical. Julia Kristeva
(1984) points this out in her work titled *Revolution in Poetic Language.* What is
revolutionary about poesis? Can a revolutionary speak in poetic form? Can we
revolutionize the academy through poesis? And is this revolution musical? Are
poesis, language, music and revolution related? Is thought at bottom musical or is
the musical at bottom thought? Wittgenstein says that there is such a thing as a
"musical thought" (1965, p. 166). This could be read in several ways. Music is
thought or thought is musical. To think music is to think thoughts. Music cannot be
music without thought. Thought is musical. Thought is not thought without musical
cadence, time, rhythm. Poesis, music, thought, language. All are related. The
academy however wants to cut off thought from its roots. The academy wants to
rid the scholar of her poetic and musical unconscious. Poesis and musicality come
from the unconscious. In fact, Cooke (2001) states that, "the most articulate
language of the unconscious is music" (x). Music is addressed through the
unconscious. Music, like language, addresses us. Some people are called, others
are not. Some people want to play music but have no gift for it. The gift is
necessary in music just as it is in writing, in poetry and in thought. Not all
scholarship counts as thought either. Most of it is wretched. Most scholarship is
done out of pressure to survive a tenure system. Most people inside the academy do
not like to think or write but must do so to survive. If one only writes out of a sense
of fear, the kind of work generated is not good. Where are the Kristeva (s) or
Derrida (s) of American culture? Where have Americans gone wrong? We clearly
do not produce the intellectuals that France does. Can we take a lesson from the
French? They are doing something we are not. Thinkers write because they are
called, not because they are fearful. Writing out of a sense of fear is not writing at
all because it is not thinking at all, it is forced, imitative and unoriginal. So much
scholarship is rooted in this fearful imitation, jargon and unthought. Thinking
requires risk, it requires queering thoughts as Wittgenstein remarks. How many
American scholars are willing to risk and to queer thoughts, to make real changes
in thinking, to make real progress in their fields? Perhaps at elite institutions
scholars are doing this. But most of us who get stuck inside of state apparatuses are
not so lucky. The state apparatus insures pedantry because it is run on fear. Not
getting tenure. Lines getting cut. Programs being eliminated. Entire colleges
closing. We live in a climate of economic uncertainty with rising gas prices and the
threat of recession, more war, more war and more war. Graduate students worry
about getting jobs and once they have them they worry about keeping them. The
bottom line is the bottom line. So in this climate taking risks could mean losing
your job. Once tenured, more threats of losing lines and losing departments and

losing programs continue. Numbers, number, numbers. The bottom line is the bottom line. In this climate how can one be an intellectual? How can one risk becoming an intellectual? Do we ever stop being afraid? We should covet and revere intellectual work and do this work without fear no matter what our precarious positions, otherwise we have sold out.

Thinking thoughts in dreadful times. How is it done? How can it be done and why should it be done? Because we are called, we are responsible for educating the next generation. The next generation is what comes next. And if we want nextness to come we must educate for the future and not for the safety of the past. Emerson (2003) addressed this very issue in his famous work on the American scholar. He states:

> The book, the college, the school of art, the institution of any kind, stop with some past utterance of genius. That is good say they–let us hold by this. They pin me down. They look backward and not forward. But genius looks forward. . . . (p. 230)

What is there to look forward to in state apparatuses of higher learning? One must find some way to fight the machine of the bottom line. I have been writing about this issue for some time (Morris, 2006). And I cannot stop writing about it because of the gravity of the state of higher education in this country. Looking forward–as Emerson puts it–also means carving out new ground, making way for the next generation and allowing people to think thoughts that are truly otherwise. Thinking thoughts means taking risks, and risking the other of language is that about which Derrida (1976) speaks. We must move toward the future of the other of language to carve out a space for the other. The other of language is found most deeply, I believe, in unconscious, transferential relations psyche has with musical and poetic utterance. These most primal undercurrents of thought must be gotten at. We must get back to primality in order to move forward into the future of thought. Institutions are sluggish and are resistant to change. But somehow we must move on, move forward and write more primal thoughts to make advances in our respective fields. Great thinkers carve out new landscapes by changing language. New language like new music has new rhythm. There is always new music. Musical possibilities are infinite as are the possibilities of language and thought. It is amazing how the same structures of music, the tonic, the dominant, fifth and the third can be rearranged endlessly to make new and different sounds. So too with language. The same words written and spoken can go off in radically different trajectories if only we are willing to give up the old. Upon first hearing new music, there is a certain specialness about it that cannot be put into words. When I really like something I hear for the first time, the feeling I get is indescribable. The feeling gets deep down under and into psyche and inspires in ways that cannot be put into words. This is what Whitehead referred to as "romance." Whitehead (1967) remarks that

> The stage of romance is the stage of first apprehension. The subject-matter has the vividness of novelty; it holds within itself unexpected connexions

[sic] with possibilities half-disclosed by glimpses and half-concealed by the wealth of the material. (p. 17)

The romance with an intellectual idea is not dissimilar to the romance of a musical idea. On first hearing music that one really likes, there is just something there, something queer about the experience that cannot be described. Can we not get that back again with ideas? Or are ideas dead? For most pedants, as Whitehead points out, ideas are "mental dry rot" (p. 2). Institutions of higher learning are full of people who think thought that is mental dry rot. They cannot get beyond their own rottedness, their own complicity with the bottom line. Academe is full of people who should not be there. We all know this. But what is to be done? How to inspire the next generation of scholars to not become full of mental dry rot and resentment? How to get beyond resentment and bitterness? How to get back to the romance of intellectual life? This is the task of the scholar of today. Many have lost the romance or have never had it at all. Where is inspiration generated? Not inside the academy, but outside it. One must turn outside of the state apparatus to find the spark of intellectual romance. And this spark can be found of course in books but it can also be found on the internet and on You Tube. Here one can see streaming video of Derrida, Hillman, Kristeva, Lacan, Freud and so forth. Here is where we find our romance; we find our romance in books and on You Tube. You Tube changes our entire notion of archivization and history because now we have access to live and moving images of the people we could never see or hear before. This is where the romance with intellectual life can be re-kindled. But the danger persists. Getting bogged down in the state apparatus of dry rot University can kill. And it does kill. The university can be a killing ground, it can kill psyche once and for all. My utmost concern is this killing ground and what it does to scholars.

Wittgenstein (1980) talks about taking "wrong turns" in language, and these wrong turns are many and treacherous. He states:

Language sets everyone the same traps; it is an immense network of easily accessible wrong turns. . . . What I have to do then is erect signposts at all the junctions where there are wrong turnings so as to help people past the danger points. (p. 18e)

We live inside of language and that language shapes how we see the world. The world also shapes how we articulate things in language. If our world happens to be an oppressive one, an oppressive state apparatus, how to move beyond the oppressive language used to kill those of us who want to have an ongoing romance with language, who want to break open new grounds of thought? When do we know that we have taken a wrong turn, as Wittgenstein points out? A wrong turn is so easy to take. Turning the wrong way is selling out and playing into the game of fear. Taking this wrong turn means the end of one's intellectual career. Writing textbooks to make money, being complicit with the powers that squash, these are the wrong turns taken by many inside of the academy. Money, power and greed are all wrong turns. Language reflects these wrong turns. Outcomes, assessments, the bottom line, competition, the market, standardization, management, coming to consensus–all wrong turns. Jumping on the publishing band wagon of whatever is hot and sure to get published– these are wrong turns. Wrong turns in language means going against the gut and the intuition. Going in the wrong direction is the death of the scholar and the birth of the pedant. It is so easy to get caught up in the game when one is offered power, money and prestige.

THE ART OF LANGUAGE. THE ART OF THE SCHOLAR

Thinking on the scholarly life is thinking about thought and language. The problem with much scholarship is that there is not much thought given to the language used to express ideas. But great thinkers think through language and in language and that language becomes an art. Language as art, language as artfully crafted. A. N. Whitehead (1967) tells us that "the art of thought" (p. 52) is just that– an art. That art gets expressed in words and the words signify ideas. Ideas written without an artful sense cannot express what they were meant to. This expression, of course, is not transparent by any means. In fact, it is layered. Artfully crafted words must create a condition to layer ideas. Packed ideas are packed in language. Language that is packed must be artfully packed, colourful. Plain or flowery. Poetic. Can scholarship afford to be poetic? At what price? Taking chances with language the scholar takes a chance at publication. The public prefers poesis but the academy prefers propositions, neat and tidy. But if we look at late Wittgenstein or Freud or James or Arendt for example, what we find is art. Great thought is artfully done. How can it be otherwise? Heidegger (1971) tells us that "[i]n any case, language belongs to the closest neighborhood of man's being" (p. 189). If this is the case, being must be thought of as art. The body is art. Art is the body. I prefer the word body to being here to point out that one's language is not just em-beinged, if you will, but embodied. If it is embodied, it is physical. Martin Gliserman (1996) addresses this issue. He states:

> Language, when exercised, is physical–it puts things into motion and draws energy; it displaces (e.g., air), consumes, organizes, creates new pockets of chaos, stirs up resonances. (p. 2)

Language is physical, it is embodied. Language is not merely a floating signifier. Language is embedded in our very bodies and so too are our thoughts. Speaking takes breath, sound, movement. To speak, to write, to think require an artfulness. Scholarly life is an artful life.

The scholar as artist. The scholar who is also a teacher is also an artist. But how does an artist see the world of the classroom? Is there a different vision? What kind of teaching vision informs scholarly work? What kind of scholarly work informs teaching? Care with words in the classroom, crafting of words, creating the conditions in which students can listen to artfully crafted words–this is teacher as artist. The musician as artist crafts her work in sounds. Sounds must be crafted artfully to make any impact on the listener. A musician who is a technician only does not move the listener. A teacher who teaches technique moves no one and teaches little about the complexities of the teaching life. Tolstoy (1995) tells us that for Fichte, the scholar's work is the work of the artist. Art for Fichte:

> is located not in the world but in the beautiful soul, not only of the mind, which is the work of the scholar. . . . [but] of the whole man. (p. 21)

The scholar is not merely a mind. Not a talking head behind a podium. Not a writing mind without hands to work the words. Rather, she uses mind and soul and emotions and fantasies to ground ideas, to embody ideas, she uses abstractions to ground the concrete and the particular. The everyday life of the scholar must be made artful. The surroundings in which the scholar works might speak to this issue. An aesthetic space in which to do the work might help draw out deeply buried encrypted messages from the unconscious. This is where scholarship is born. Deep in the deep. Deep in the underneath. Deep in the unknown. And that unknown, if it truly comes from the embodied soul, is artful. The body is a work of art crafted from an unknown source. This unknown source has created an entire world into which the scholar is thrown. This entire world is also artfully crafted. The scholar works in words in an artfully crafted world. But she must be open to this. Words embodied in an artful world open out only if the scholar experiences time and space in new ways. Time and space draw thought into depths unknown, depths that deepen space, that open out space that give space, that breathe in space. Taking time to think, opens up this space. This space, however, is not some distant horizon. It is all deeply found inside. Space is in the head, in the body, in the soul. Inner space is psyche. Open space is the place where thought is artfully crafted. In place, the scholar faces this openness and the sublimity of this openness. This depth is not altogether pleasant, rather it terrifies.

Creating music also opens space and goes down deeply. The primality of sounds and words crisscross. The primality of this very basic experience of space in and out of time, in and out of place is both captured in music and in language. The musician and the scholar work in primal places, work down deep into primal spaces. How could it be otherwise? This is why writing takes time and it takes space. One needs space away from the academy to write because the academy kills the writing spirit. The academy has no room for space. The academy is a mill, a factory of thought. Real thought is not milled, it is not drilled out in a factory. Space away from the academy is a must. The academy as killing grounds. These killing grounds can kill the scholar, her spirit, her soul. The scholars that I comment on like Royce, Wittgenstein and James could not get away from the academy fast enough. Their service to the academy got in the way of their real work.

Studying is art. Studying should be artfully done. Studying, the scholar explores new regions, new times and new spaces. She attempts to carve out paths not carved previously. This can only be done alone in the space away from the academy. While one is alone with one's thoughts, the thoughts of others always hover. Our teachers, our books, our students all inform our work. We are a community of voices that speak and are spoken through. And yet, scholarship is done alone, in private, in seclusion. Some need more seclusion than others. Wittgenstein claims that he did his best work in a hut. Jacques Le Rider (1993) says of Wittgenstein that he was an ascetic:

> The life and thought of the young Wittgenstein showed a distinct ascetic tendency. . . . his admiration for the ageing Tolstoy, his penitential sessions working in a monastery and as a village school teacher, his refusal of the family fortune. . . . (pp. 116–117)

The life of the scholar is monkish. For Wittgenstein this was certainly true. Artfully crafted words and ideas can only be written under the sign of solitude. But how scarce is solitude in the businesslike academy where attending meaningless meetings count more than thought or writing. The meetings are Kafkaesque and rather pointless because everything is already done, everything is already fixed before the meeting begins. This too our Pragmatists comment on (i.e. James and Royce especially). Getting away from the killing grounds of the academy, the devouring mother, the bad breast, becomes more and more important as one grows older and time is ticking, time is forever running out. The clock of life does not go on forever. Freud felt the press of time. He feared that at any moment he would die. And it was this mentality that kept him at his mystic writing pad. Would there be writing without any sense of urgency? But there is an urgency to the scholarly life, if one is truly engaged in the project of artful scholarship. There is never enough time to write and think and read. Everything seems an interruption. And certainly the academy is nothing but an interruption. There is little that is artful about the academy. The scholar fights to keep that artful sensibility and not drown in the drudgery of academic bureaucracy. Reading, understanding, thinking and writing are all artforms. In fact, R.G. Collingwood (1958) tells us that:

> Ars in medieval Latin, like 'art' in early modern English. . . meant any special form of book–learning, such as grammar or logic, magic or astrology. (p. 6)

To study grammar is to study an art form. Grammar is not drudgery. There is a certain beauty to it. Like logic. Logic for most philosophy students is drudgery. But like grammar (and logic is the grammar of philosophy) logic is art. There is a certain beauty to the symbols. These symbols are artfully crafted and are beautifully and carefully etched on the page. These symbols, as Wittgenstein points out in his late work, are road maps or games but we never get where we really want to go because the symbols are in fact not complex enough to capture the meaning of language. Language obscures meaning and meaning obscures language. Beautifully crafted language sometimes surprises. Symbolic meaning, struggle, insight, courage, and vision can all be crafted through words, through the speaking body, through the heart. Here I am thinking of the beautifully crafted pathography by Anatole Broyard (1992). He talks about the ways in his terminal cancer shaped his views on being an intellectual. He says, "nature is a terrific editor" (p. 6). Death as editor. Writing becomes urgent under the sign of an impending death. The stunning quality of Broyard's piece is that he surprises at every turn. His erudition, his wit, humor, and insight make one curious. Is that not the mark of a good writer, a good scholar? For example, Broyard (1992) says that patients—when they tell stories about their illnesses– are like fiction writers. He says, "[a] hospital is full of wonderful and terrible stories, and if I were a doctor I would read them as one reads good fiction" (p. 50). Not only are patient's stories like fiction, so too is scholarship. Scholarship is like fiction. Scholarship is an art form; the scholar tells stories through theory. The way in which a scholar puts material together is akin to the way in which a fiction writer puts material together. Putting material together is arbitrary. One never knows where thoughts will take the mind. Can the hands keep up with the mind? The mind is a wonderful and terrible thing. For some–like Wittgenstein–it never shut off. Some have suggested that philosophers and schizophrenics have this in common. Words keep coming, thoughts keep coming. Thoughts and words never stop. Pages and pages get filled. If we look at the memoirs of Artaud and Schreber and compare them to the writings of, say, Wittgenstein or James, or even Freud, we will see that the thoughts keep coming; these writers wrote pages and pages and pages of words and thoughts. For a writer, there is a great need to express these thoughts through words, whether or not they make any sense. What gets written becomes rather curious. A.N. Whitehead (1967) suggests that scholarship is "a process of becoming used to curious thoughts" (p. 32). Broyard's (1992) book is one full of curious thoughts. It is a most curious pathography. There is something about knowing that one is going to die that makes you free. What do you have to lose? No longer is one afraid of what people might think. Can scholars live as if they are about to die every day? Is there an artfulness to this mentality? Yes. Living unto death, living as if death is right around the corner does free up thought. Words will come if urgency is there. Broyard (1992), upon learning of his terminal cancer, said "'[t]ime is no longer innocuous, nothing was casual anymore. I understood that living itself had a deadline. . . ." (p. 4). What a curious thought. Life has a deadline. What drove Freud was death. He was very superstitious and many commentators point out that he feared that he would die at every turn. How could it be otherwise? Why get anything done at all if one does not dwell on the end? It is this that philosophy teaches. Philosophy is mostly about death, it is a preparation for death. What a curious thought. Is the scholarly life generally speaking a preparation for death? If it is not, should it be? And what could this mean? Derrida (1992) addresses this issue:

> Philosophy [or curriculum studies] isn't something that comes to the soul by accident, for it is nothing other than this vigil over death that watches out for death and watches over death, as if over the very life of the soul. (p. 15)

Vigil is the root of the word vigilance. To be vigilant about writing, working, and doing scholarship. This task is an ethical one. Vigilance means writing with more care and more craft, caring more deeply for ideas and for the language used to form ideas. Vigilant ideas are those that are thought through with great deliberation. The deliberation is made more curious in the face of death. To think and write deliberately in the face of death is to know that time is running out and whatever must be said must be said now and not tomorrow, for there may be no tomorrow. This is the lesson of the Greek philosophers. It is not a new lesson by any means.

It becomes easy to forget what the scholar's task is when mired in the net of university politics. Derrida (1992a) reminds us that we must always already be reminded of death–even in the midst of oppressive institutions. Death becomes the horizon against which scholarship must be done. Derrida says, "[t]his concern for death, the awakening that keeps vigil over death, this conscience that looks death in the face is another name for freedom" (p. 15). Working in the university is like living with a terminal illness. The place is deadly. It is a dead end. There is no out. As the scholar realizes this, she is forced into a position of "freedom." Weber's phrase, *'the iron cage'* is useful here. The iron cage of the university creates a space for–ironically–the freedom to write as one pleases. What does the scholar have to lose, if everything else is lost always already? All is lost. All ye who enter here, lose hope! When hope is lost, freedom to write begins. Intellectuals who work in such conditions must find a way out. The way out is through writing. No one can stop the flood gates of writing and thinking. Thought is freedom. No one can stop my thoughts. No one can stop the way in which those thoughts get put on paper. How curious. Is this not how revolutions begin, in thought and in text? Marx's text came before the revolution. As Derrida (1992a) points out in *The Gift of Death*, Jan Patocka, Vaclav Havel and Jiri Hajek all were involved in the famed Charta 77 which was the text that came before the democratization of the Czech Republic. Words, text, speech and writing change the world–even in the face of extremely oppressive, tyrannical situations. Nobody could stop Havel. They tried and they failed.

How to make sense of this curious thought. The final word. What would that be? What kind of legacy to leave? Do scholars think about legacy? I certainly do. As much as I love teaching, it is the writing that sustains me because it is in the books that I will leave my mark. My books are meant to teach. I follow Bertrand Russell (2002a) here as he re-marks that "[a]ny man who has the genuine impulse of a teacher will be more anxious to survive in his books than in the flesh" (p. 124). Books outlive us. Books mark thought. Books are archives of thought. The archive of a scholar's thought is best found in text. Keeping thoughts contained in books is a way to archive more fully the scholar's ideas. How can it be otherwise?

Books are things that can be held. Books are to be held in the hand. Books feel good in the hand. Books are pretty to look at. Books are inviting. Books are not elitist, they are cultural objects found in the public domain. Books are found in public libraries. They are written for a public. Books are democratic. Books are art objects. Books are loves. Books are art. Books tell the tale. Books allow the writer to write with a sense of space. Language, speech, writing, reading, holding, all turn on the idea of a book. The idea of the book is the idea of legacy. I am Intoxicated—not by illness, as Broyard (1992) would have it– but by books. I am thinking here of a fascinating novel by Umberto Eco (2004b) titled *The Mysterious Flame of Queen Loana*. There is much talk in the book about reading books. In a chapter called "Eight Days in an Attic", the main character talks of a reading marathon he had while up in the attic. He tells us that

> For eight days, I rose early to take advantage of the light, went upstairs, and remained there until sundown. Around noon, Amalia, who was alarmed the first time she could not find me, would bring me a plate with bread, salami or cheese, two apples, and a bottle of wine. ("Lordy, Lordy, he'll get himself sick again and then what will I tell Signora Paola,. . . stop or you'll go blind!") Then she would leave me in tears, and I would drink down nearly all the wine and keep turning the pages. . . . (p. 118)

This book marked my consciousness and I have come back to it time and time again because of passages like these about the voracious appetite of the reader. I can identify so with Eco's character. The character goes on to say, "[s]ometimes I would go downstairs with an armful of books to hole up elsewhere. . . ." (p. 118). How can anyone kill this kind of spirit? The university can kill the love to read and write and think. Somehow we must find a way out. But what if we cannot? This is the problem I address throughout this book. Find a way out, find a way out. But what if there is no way out and what if they do win in the end? Certainly there is little inspiration to be found in the hallways of standardized U. But they cannot take the love of reading away we say. And yet–the frightening thing is–they can.

Reading a book is a sensuous experience. I would not say this about reading a journal article, although certainly journal articles are of the utmost importance. Reading a book is sensuous because the book fits into the hand nicely–if it is not too big. As one turns the pages, curious thoughts travel. Placing a book on the shelf in one's personal library is satisfying. Coming back to that book, picking it up, re-reading it and holding it again is a very personal and satisfying experience. A book can be loved anew, every time it is read. I cherish, for example, Anatole Broyard's (1992) *Intoxicated by My Illness*. I love this book. This book is filled with curious thoughts. This book was written by a man true to his heart. I love this book. This book makes me think differently. This book moves me, it speaks to me. Books can speak to us and they can change us. Scholarly life is about reading life changing books and then writing them! But how to write life changers? And what if you are not able to do your work, what if the writing stops? This is the struggle.

Books allow scholars to delve deeply into a certain eloquence. Part of the allure of books is that they allow the reader to take time with the writer. It takes time to read a book. Sometimes it takes a few hours, sometimes a few days. Sometimes it takes three months. Derrida, Bachelard, late Wittgenstein, Anne Sexton and Freud. I want to spend time with these writers. In fact, I come back to them time and time again. Open the books, hold the books, study the books. Come to new meaning, or missed meaning. We read for different reasons at different times in our lives. When our reasons change, so too do our reading practices. When life changes, so does our reading. We read what we must to survive. The scholar reads to survive. How could it be otherwise? Anne Fadiman (1998) talks about the "heart of reading" (x). She asks

> how we maintain our connections with our old books, the ones we have lived with for years, the ones whose textures, colors and smells have become as familiar to us as our children's skin. (x)

To re-read an old book, a beloved book, alters perceptions yet again. On a new reading of an old book new thoughts emerge. Perhaps the pieces come together a little easier or new avenues of thought open up. Dennis Sumara (1996) talks about the importance of re-reading books. Re-reading books can change a life. It is important for the scholar to have a private library because it is in the private library that life changing experiences can happen. Borrowing books is like borrowing experiences. A personal library makes these experiences more accessible. Isn't university life about reading books and sharing them with students? Maybe not.

Upon doing my research on William James, Bertrand Russell, Ludwig Wittgenstein, Josiah Royce, Ruth Benedict and Native Americans, I was surprised to find that all struggle in the halls of academe for one reason or another. It seems as if nothing in the academy has changed, it has only gotten worse. We live in a market driven society that cares little for intellectual work. I have written extensively on the anti-intellectual nature of the institution (Morris, 2006). Mary Catherine Bateson (1989) talks about the way in which people's careers can evaporate. She says, "[m]any of society's casualties are men and women who assumed they had chosen a certain path in life and found that it disappeared in the underbrush" (pp. 6–7). We must not let the oppressive nature of the institution push us under the underbrush. But I fear that underbrush of despair that the university causes. Some days I feel as if they have won. How can the very institution that is supposed to promote the scholarly life kill it? Marion Milner (1987) reminds us that "William Blake said, without contraries there is no progression" (p. 10). Is the university that contrary? Would I have been so productive if I felt at home inside the university? Maybe not.

Anne Hunsaker Hawkins (1993) tells us that there are different kinds of archetypal narratives about illness .There are quest narratives, religious narratives, journey narratives. I suppose there are also archetypal narratives about working inside of universities. There are narratives of the corporate university. There are narratives of the university as business. There are narratives by professors about how to survive inside of universities. Hawkins also tells us that there are pathographies that are "didactic" and then there are pathographies that are "*angry.*" (p. 11) Like these pathographies, I am interested in the angry narratives If the university does not make us angry, we are not paying attention. These feelings of despair and frustration were not unfamiliar to Wittgenstein or James or Benedict as I will talk about in more detail momentarily. The reason why some scholars are not able to think is because living inside of a pathological institution makes them sick with despair. The institution can kill the scholarly spirit. But we must not let these inhuman places kill us. Yet, I worry about a time when the words will no longer come because thought is dead. W.Van Dusen (1999) says that "[i]t is extremely important to know what people do when faced with encroaching blankness" (p. 54). The blank page is the scholar's worst nightmare. The blank mind startles to say the least. James Hillman (1997) talks of a "still-hungering soul. . ." (p. 73). But what if the soul hungers no more? What if the hunger for reading and writing vanish, dry up? I am sure many of my colleagues have experienced this but no one dares to talk about it. But what if the hunger never comes back? There are those who walk around like corpses, heads hung low, without any expression, totally demoralized. There are those who haven't read a book in years. The dead.

THE KILLING GROUNDS OF THE ACADEMY

Troubles in the academy are not new. I have done much work on the problems of the academy in my book *Jewish Intellectuals and the University* (2006). But in that book I focused on the life of Jewish scholars inside of academe. The work I am doing here differs in that I am looking more generally at the ways in which the academy has worked to kill the spirit of thinkers, especially and most surprisingly some of the most well known Native American scholars, philosophers and anthropologists of the 20th century. The fragility of thinkers like William James surprises because from the output of work and the importance of his work, readers would not suspect that he had a nervous breakdown and felt extremely frustrated with the university. His breakdown stuns. And yet he was still able to write volumes of work. How did he do it despite having a nervous breakdown? It surprises that there were times in his career that he could not write at all!! The same for Wittgenstein. And for others. At any rate, there is a certain solace in finding these things out. I find company in my own struggles, for when I have my moments and feel utterly crushed by the academy I turn to the archives to find other souls who have been crushed–and yet survived to tell the tale. Not only that, the books written by these scholars changed the face of philosophy and anthropology in the 20th century. How did they do it being under such an enormous burden?

Richard Selzer (1996) comments on the "companionship" of the suffering. He states:

> True it is that we cannot bear our lives, our work, our pain without the companionship of the past. It helps the deaf man to know that Beethoven could not hear his own glory, the blind that Milton too dwelt in darkness. That Keats and Chopin endured the fevers and the bloody cough of tuberculosis is Balaam in Gilead to those more recently afflicted. (p. 89)

The thinkers upon which I draw–like the musicians we have discussed earlier in the book— suffered perhaps from organic psychic deterioration but also suffered the degradation that is the life of academe. The already fragile health of James or Wittgenstein or Benedict probably worsened because of the pressures of working in the academy. The academy is a stultifying atmosphere that encourages psychic death. Again I am certainly not the first one to point this out. I owe a debt of gratitude to the work of William F. Pinar (1995) who brought these issues to our attention in the field of curriculum studies. Pinar's work differs from the work done by the neo-Marxists on the university because his main interest is in the social-psychological. I follow in Pinar's footsteps and argue that the problem that we need to pay more attention to is psychological fallout from working in oppressive institutions. The neo-Marxists like Henry Giroux, Peter McLaren, and John Weaver are not so much interested in issues on psyche as they are on issues of power and politics.

INTERIORS: THE WINDOWS OF FRAGILITY

An already fragile interior. Those who dare to create. The thinkers and artists. Creativity can be born out of that very fragility. Thinking and artistic creation spring from the taproot of vulnerability and a deep sensitivity to surroundings. Music conservatories are brutal places. There is no room for error in the world of classical music. Practicing an instrument ten hours a day is brutal and it is expected in music conservatories. Conservatories are not good places for the vulnerable because there is no room for mistakes.

The academy can also destroy the most vulnerable thinkers. External pressures may not be the cause of a damaged psyche, but external pressures can push an already fragile soul over the edge. The killing grounds. The inability to play music and the inability to work thought begins in a strange feeling of inertia. What does it feel like to be a victim of the killing grounds of the academy? A strange sense of being stuck, immobile, frozen in space. No words come. A psychic death. An impressionistic nightmare. A psychic wasteland around which no return is possible. How to avoid this disaster?

There are people who are literally frozen in time for years, people who are psychically stuck because of disease. In his book *Awakenings*, Oliver Sacks (1999) describes those who suffered from an epidemic that stole the lives of many people in the 1930s–this was called the sleeping sickness or encephalitis lethargica. It is as if these people got frozen in time and space–for years. Sacks (1999) explains:

> States of immobility and arrest had been distinctly uncommon in the early 1920s, but from 1930 onwards started to roll in a great sluggish, torpid tide over many of the survivors [of the sleeping sickness], enveloping them in metaphorical (if not physiological) equivalents of sleep and death. Parkinsonism, catatonia, melancholia, trance passivity, immobility, frigidity, apathy: this was the quality of the decades–long 'sleep.' (p. 23)

Sacks goes on to state that these patients were like "living statues–totally motionless, for hours, days, weeks, or years on end" (p. 15). One should not compare this kind of disease with mental paralysis like depression but there are people who become so depressed as to be totally immobile, catatonic. Or course, the sleeping sickness was not a form of depression but still there are some uncanny similarities. Upon reading first hand accounts of the scholars who suffered the inability to work [Wittgenstein and James in particular], uncanny parallels haunt. Wittgenstein and James suffered from a sort of psychic paralysis. The cause of this paralysis was not sleeping sickness or Parkinsonism. And I want to make that clear. But the symptoms of depressive breakdowns have strange overlaps.

Oliver Sacks (1995) points out, during the early days of talk about autism, mothers were blamed. Clearly this is how sexism works. The real cause of mental illness is neurobiological Sacks says. And yet–there is always an environmental factor that can make things worse. The autistic child who is put in an institution will not do as well as one who is cared for at home, Sacks tells us (1995). Institutions are inhuman places and the lack of nurturing and individual attention takes its toll. I am thinking here of music conservatories and universities. These are tough places to survive not only for professors but for students as well. My advice to a young musician is to study privately with someone and major in something else in college. Too, it is better to be an independent scholar. But who can afford to do either? Musicians need to be credentialed, but at what cost?

NATIVE AMERICAN STRUGGLES WITH AMERICAN EDUCATIONAL INSTITUTIONS

The pressure of working inside of an institution unfriendly to change can feel so oppressive that it is likely to cause one to stop working altogether. Such struggles we hear about from our Native American friends. Native American scholar Sidner Larson (2000) talks about Native American scholars or what he calls "ethnic scholars" and their "burnout." Larson states:

> ... the most complex aspects of intercultural relations provides only a glimpse of what it takes to survive as an ethnic professor, and has taken years to develop. . . . . The burnout of ethnic educators discussed in Shattering the Silences [a PBS special] becomes more understandable when one considers the usual situation of near complete cultural and personal isolation. . . . (p. 15)

To work under the shadow of an oppressive institution is extremely difficult especially if you are a minority. If you are the only person in your department doing work on Native American studies, you are indeed isolated. And then you do not know which of your colleagues is racist. Along with racism comes the attitude that Native American studies has little worth as an academic subject. I am sure that there are academics—our conservative colleagues– who believe these things. It is appalling that racism is underneath curricular decisions. And it is racism that is underneath decisions of tenure and promotion. Nobody says it, but it is true. Racism gets cloaked in other terms but whose knowledge is of most worth is also a question of whiteness and white privilege and the privilege that white knowledge has in the academy.

These pressures can make you want to quit teaching altogether or even quit writing. What happens when the scholar wakes up one day and feels as if she has nothing left to say? This is an ongoing worry. Fiction writers, like academics, suffer from similar worries. N. Scott Momaday (1990) says:

> I can imagine myself coming to a point where I must work–I love my work, I'm compelled to work—and can't. That frightens me. Last night, trying to sort things out, I thought: I have come to a dangerous place in my life. Something threatens me—middle age, sickness, what? (p. 138)

Momaday—perhaps one of the most well known and well respected Native American fiction writers—worries, as do I—about not being able to work. He is well published and well known and yet he worries about his creativity drying up. When we talk of Native American writers, it has been pointed out by some Native American academics, that white people and people in the academy in general do not even think of Native American scholars as intellectuals. Native American scholar Donald Fixico (2003) addresses these problems in the academy. He states:

Indian intellectualism has been grossly neglected by mainstream academia, and how the American public does not consider Indian peoples to be intellectuals. (xiii)

One of the problems about talking about 'scholars' is the question of who counts as a scholar or who is imagined to be capable of being a scholar. Historically, women have never been seen as scholars—as we will learn more when I talk about the problems women anthropologists had in the 1930s in the United States. But here too is another problem of Native Americans trying to find their voice in a place— the academy– that does not validate or recognize what they do as scholarship. Taiaiake Alfred (1998) addresses these issues concerning the academy:

Universities are to turn to an old anti-imperial phrase "the heart of whiteness." They accomplish the acceptance and normalization of Western ideas, the glorification of Western societies as the highest form of human Organization . . . (p. 96)

What counts when going up for tenure is—as Native American scholars know— knowledge and expertise of the center. Some more conservative—and frankly racist—academics might not publicly say to a Native American colleague that they think the work of Native Americans of having less worth than the work of white scholars. But when voting for tenure, these racist sentiments do come into play. Devon Mihesuah (1998) tells us that:

After only seven years as a history professor I can attest to the reality that Indian scholars still endure accusations that courses on Indians are not important, that our lectures are "too politically correct," and that we obtained jobs because of our race. (p.16)

These same sorts of accusations get launched against women's and gender studies programs especially by more conservative scholars who argue that gender issues are not relevant and that women's issues are beside the point. Queer theorists also get the cold shoulder by conservative scholars who have little patience for issues around sexuality and alterity. The climate of the academy has always been a conservative one and it has always been a hard place for minorities and women. I do not mean to suggest that all minorities suffer the same oppressions inside of the academy, however. Native Americans have a different struggle, than say, queer theorists, because of their specific history and culture. Gloria Anzaldua (2002) as I mentioned earlier suggests that minorities need to build bridges and work together for social justice because working in isolation does not give minority groups enough power to undo systems of injustice.

Native American scholars worry that their work is being appropriated unethically by whites. Devon Mihesuah (1998) disturbingly says that

> Many Indians would be satisfied if only Indians wrote about Indians. Some
> prefer not to read anything by white men and women, not understanding that
> having a command of the canon of the field is the only way to establish a
> point of departure. (p. 14)

I can understand the anger and frustration that indigenous peoples feel toward
whites. I can understand why they would not want to read work by whites and I can
understand why they do not want whites doing academic work about them.
American history is the history of genocide. This is a history that is not dealt with
enough or at all in American history classes at the secondary school level, or even
in college. We certainly need departments of Native Studies in American higher
education . However, I think that if white people are careful and honest and want to
give something back to the Native American community, then doing scholarship
on Native Americans is okay. I do not think that people own academic material.
But again, I understand the worries that Native Americans have about the unethical
appropriation of their materials.

One of the things that curriculum scholars worry about turns on issues of
representation. I have dealt with this in some detail in my book on the Holocaust
(2001) in relation to mis-representations of Jews in texts. These mis-represenations
are not in any way benign. Some argue that textual mis-representation led to the
annihilation of six million European Jews. There is a similar disturbing issue of
mis- representation of Native Americans. What images do mainstream Americans
have of Native Americans? John Wayne movies. Cowboys and Indians. Savages.
Popular culture is a text and these textual mis-representations have influenced
generations of Americans who grew up watching TV Westerns. But there is an
entire field that is dedicated to changing these stereotypes and it is called New
Western history. There are many in that field who are trying to undo negative
stereotypes about Native Americans. The New West studies, in many ways, is like
the work that is done in curriculum studies in that we look for who is left out of the
story. Race, class, gender and the history of differing oppressions are dealt with in
these New West studies. And in the New West studies the image of the cowboy is
debunked and his whiteness is challenged, so too are his oppressive ways. I think
there is a lot of promise in these new studies on the West. The idea of the West is
under the shadow of tremendous critique by scholars on the left, many of these
scholars are also ecologists, postcolonialists, critical race theorists, and the rest.
One of the problems with studies of the New West, is, as Devon Mihesuah (1998)
points out, that Indian "voices" get left out once again. We must work, then, to
include the voices of our Native American friends when we do try to understand
through academic work. If we do not include their voices, we only work to
colonize once again. Part of the problem, I think, is that most of us inside of the
United States academy are trained in European theoretical traditions. Much of my
work is steeped in the psychoanalytic tradition and this is clearly a European
tradition. So my theoretical framework might get in the way of understanding
Native Americans. Although I might use psychoanalysis to understand academic
questions, I also have studied the writings of Native Americans and have studied

some of the Native American mythologies, Native American fiction writers and scholars to better understand their struggles. In no way do I think that my work appropriates their material for academic gain. I am already a tenured professor with a career well in place. I have plenty of publications behind my name. My interest in Native American issues—especially the struggles that Native American scholars have—is one of social justice. As Paulo Freire has made clear, my work is work *"with"* other people, not *"for"* other people. That is, I would never say that I speak *"for"* my Native American friends, clearly that is a move of colonialism. I speak *"with"* them with great respect and empathy. Native American Sidner Larson (2000) talks to the issue of the difficulties that Native Americans have inside of the academy—and this is a difficulty that I can empathize with being on the margins myself as a queer Jewish intellectual in a very conservative rural area of the South. Larson talks about trying to change the conservative nature of the academy through trying to change curriculum. Larson states:

> Even in the most benign situations I have been unable to accomplish more than the most superficial changes in existing departmental infrastructures. Institutions with which I have interacted have consistently been interested in "opening up areas of study," but they have also been adamant in defining "opening up" as not including anything but the most facile criticism of mainstream styles and as hiring no more than the barest minimum number of ethnic faculty. (p. 14)

Institutions by their very nature are resistant to change. And if change does occur it takes a long time to implement. Programs that are in any way *"new"* or different have a harder time getting implemented because the nature of the university is to conserve tradition (Morris, 2006). The curriculum on university campuses reflect the larger cultural resistance to what is deemed different. Native American studies is a very important field that should be on every college campus and courses on Native Americans should be integrated into the curriculum. Native American students have to struggle with identity issues because they do not see themselves reflected in most university curricula. Vine Deloria and Daniel Wildcat (2001) call for "indigenizing education." Daniel Wildcat puts it this way:

> The problem with Indian education in America is really the problem of education in America, regardless of whether recipients of education are, figuratively speaking, red, yellow, black or white. Of course, the historically racist character of American education cannot and should not be minimized. (p. 8)

Curriculum scholars are particularly attuned to these problems and work to undo racist curricula. But again, institutions like universities and schools are difficult to change. And we curriculum scholars have little power to change public schooling in this country, so our work is done at the university level through our teaching and scholarship.

We are up against an extremely right wing fundamentalist culture that has a stranglehold especially on our public schools. The right wing fundamentalist stranglehold on American public schools is no secret. No wonder many Americans do not read, they are taught—through the degrading and hideous process of memorizing stupid 'facts' and spitting back 'facts' on high stakes tests. Maureen Corrigan (2005) tells us that

> Despite the proliferation of mega-bookstores and neighborhood reading groups, most Americans are indifferent to the lure of literature: in fact, according to a Wall Street Journal article a few years ago, some 59 percent of Americans don't own a single book. (xiv)

This is astonishing to me. My house is like the public library, books are overflowing everywhere. I cannot imagine a life without reading. But here is the problem. If Americans do not read, they do not have an understanding of what is wrong in America. In order to change things, we first need to know what the problems are and study them. If these same Americans who do not own a single book were victims of public schooling in this country and were undereducated or miseducated as most were and are, they know little about oppression and they probably know next to nothing about, for example, Native Americans or other minority groups. These 59 percent probably know next to nothing about the tyranny of whiteness or the insidious power of fundamentalism(s). What they know is what they see on TV and that amounts to basically nothing. Schooling in this country produces a nation of people who do not read and who do not want to read. It is no coincidence that 59 percent of Americans do not own books. Most Americans do not know their own history or the history of this country. And one of the extremely disturbing things about our history is the way in which public schooling has done violence especially to minorities. Here I am thinking of the Native Americans. As an example of this violence, I turn to Vine Deloria (1970) who reminds us of the complicity of public schooling with violence. In the case of Native Americans, he explains below:

> Indian children [during the latter part of the 1800s and on into the early 1900s] were kidnapped and taken thousands of miles away to boarding schools. Once there, they were whipped if they used their native languages or made any reference to their former mode of life. All religious ceremonies were banned on Indian reservations. Priceless objects of art were destroyed on the advice of missionaries and bureaucrats. . . . (p. 109)

If people do not read, they know little about this shameful history of America.

Destruction of cultures begin through schooling. Schooling continues to destroy cultures by the continuing absence of Native American representation in the curriculum. This continual erasure from history is another way to kill. Schools are still places where the underlying motive is assimilation into mainstream America. Is that not what standardization of knowledge is? Subjugated knowledges are hardly part of public schooling. Subjugated knowledges are hardly part of a college curriculum either. Courses in Western Civilization damage those who are not considered part of the West. Native Americans and other minorities are not represented in these kinds of courses and if they are they their representation is usually stereotyped or superficial. Subjugated peoples are not considered part of "civilization." Courses in World Religions damage those who are not thought to be part of the "great" religious traditions. Here again, we see the absence of the Native American traditions. And so we have generations of Americans who have had a particularly narrow education because what they know is white knowledge. White male knowledge that is. People who go to public school and then go to college and then become college professors turn around and repeat these patterns by teaching what they were taught, the great books tradition and the traditional canon. And when minorities are angry about the way they have been misrepresented or stereotyped, white people do not get it and accuse them of being "overly sensitive, without humor, taking things too seriously. . ." (Jackson & Jordon, 1999). Sandra Jackson and Jose Solis Jordan (1999) comment that professors of color walk on eggshells in the academy:

> Because of the barriers confronting scholars and professors of color in higher education we have learned how not to talk (about issues of race, sexuality and gender) because of the fiercely political, social and cultural environment of the academy. (p. 3)

Being a minority and being a professor is a very different kind of experience than being a white male in the academy. Not to say that white males do not have their share of problems in the academy, they do as I will touch on in a bit. But being a minority is especially difficult because of the ways racism, sexism and the rest gets played out behind the scenes and gets somehow mangled up in the tenure process. Now, there are some white male scholars who work very hard to think through their whiteness and fight for the rights of the subjugated. I am thinking here especially of Peter McLaren. I am thinking of Peter because of his far left position and his uncompromising Marxist revolutionary pedagogy. In a book called *Rage and Hope: Interviews with Peter McLaren on War, Imperialism and Critical Pedagogy* (2006) he talks to about the problems of white supremacy, racism, class, homophobia and sexism. He argues in this book that we must begin to see these things are real material lived experiences, not just as abstract concepts. He suggests that much of postcolonial theory misses the point because it obfuscates through abstractions. He is critical also of postmodern theories because they too miss the point about the material reality of subjugated peoples. It is one thing to talk about homophobia, but it is another thing to be a victim of it. McLaren even takes to task critical theory as it is done by most scholars of education. Here he suggests that "it nevertheless remains in danger of political domestication" (p. 22). McLaren argues— as does Vine Deloria—that when we talk about racism, sexism, homophobia, xenophobia we must understand it against a much broader cultural problem of imperialism, capitalism, globalization, economy, class and colonization. He says that it is not enough to "uncover" (p. 53) these oppressions but we must act in a "revolutionary" way to stop them. He models himself after Paulo Freire and Che Guevara who were both revolutionaries, albeit in very different ways. McLaren argues that it is not enough to teach against oppression, we must, he says, take to the streets and build coalitions of activists to fight against social wrongs. He calls his version of critical pedagogy, revolutionary. Now, McLaren is not calling for violence or for blowing up buildings. But he is calling for a revolutionary mind-set, which most professors do not have because they too have been domesticated—to use his word—by the academy. McLaren warns us that those of us on the left who argue in a Marxist fashion about the corrupt politics of our current disastrous government are in danger of having our work sabotaged or are in danger of losing our jobs. McLaren (2006) talks to the new McCarthyism as he states:

> I am worried about the newly established Office of Homeland Security and the possible consequences of new national security measures on civil liberties. I am referring here to wire taps, secret searches of citizens' residences, the imprisonment and deportation of immigrants without supporting evidence. . . . Non-citizens can be put under suspicion of terrorism, tried in secret by a military tribunal, and executed even if one third of the members of the tribunal disagree. . . . I am also worried about academic freedom, about the freedom of scholars to assess U.S. domestic and foreign policy without fear of retribution or censorship. (p. 90)

Since 9-11 the landscape of this country has changed and so too have the politics inside of the academy. Non-tenured faculty have to be very careful—especially if they are Marxist—not to be too vocal for fear of losing their jobs. The academy domesticates from day one. Young professors learn very early on that there is a politic to what can and cannot be said in the classroom and in the hallways. There is an air of paranoia too about scholarship and what they (the invisible power elite of the university) might or might not read and how that will affect a professor's career. So when we talk about the problems of racism and imperialism, globalization and the power of Marxist critique, McLaren warns professors that we could be under surveillance. I teach a course on power and schooling and in that course I devote much time to Che Guevara. One of my students remarked that her sister is in training to become a secret service agent and she worried that she would have to get rid of all her books on Che because they could jeopardize her sister's career. I was astonished at her worries. But she is not being ridiculously paranoid. McLaren points out that many people on the left are being monitored by the Bush Administration. It seems unbelievable and far fetched but it isn't.

At any rate, the academy is hardly a fair and equitable place. The academy is a mirror of the larger racist, sexist, anti-Semitic and homophobic society that is America.

Subjugated peoples, like the Native Americans, have an historically different kind of struggle within the university, than, say, someone like Wittgenstein, or William James or Ruth Benedict. The oppressions of subjugated groups differ and are probably much worse than the oppressions felt, by say, mainstream white European American men. A white woman, say, like Ruth Benedict, suffered from sexism at Columbia, but this kind of oppression is very different from the oppression that Native Americans suffer inside the academy. White men who are Marxist suffer from a very different kind of oppression than say African American professors. The academy mirrors the larger culture and it is a place that is far from utopian.

What kinds of knowledges count inside of the academy is an ongoing problem—especially for minority scholars. Native American scholar Duane Champagne (1998) claims that "[t]he efforts of American Indian Studies, however, are not valued within the academic arena". . . . (p. 188). And then there is the problem—as I mentioned earlier-- of white scholars appropriating Native American literatures for their own academic gain. Native American scholars, once again, feel as if white people are using them and stealing their (academic) property. Donald Fixico (2003) is very angry about this problem. He states:

American Indians have been exploited by non-Indians, who have established successful careers, won writing awards, have been called the nation's leading experts on Indians, and who have fed their families by writing "about" American Indians. (p. 126)

The question raised here concerns who has the right to write about whom. Many in the Native American scholarly community feel that white scholars have no business writing about Native American culture because they see it as yet another form of colonialism and abuse. Given the history of genocide of Native Americans in the United States I can appreciate and sympathize with their position on this issue. Curriculum scholar Nicholas Ng-A-Fook (2007) writes about the problems of the Houma Nation in Louisiana and states that these Native Americans were not even allowed to go to public school until the 1960s. In Ng-A-Fook's important ethnography he tells us of one Jason who expresses his grief over the many wrongs done to him and his people. Ng-A-Fook (2007) tells us that

Under the growing shadows of dusk, back on top of the levee, contrary to the tales found in Louisiana history textbooks, Joshua shares the tragic stories of his grandfather's stolen land, respective fishing and hunting rights taken away, the exploitation of human labor, the institutional implementation of racist identity policies, segregation inside and outside of public school walls, and the American government's continued denial of his indigenous identity. . . . (p. 10)

The legacies of colonialism, discrimination and genocide linger on in the Native American communities such as the Houma Indians. American public schooling has been complicit in this tragic history of colonialism. Native American scholars have much to be angry about. There is much prejudice inside of the academy and who decides what knowledge is most worth becomes a question of whether white knowledge has more weight than non-white knowledge when it comes to tenure decisions. Ng-A-Fook (2007) comments that this white knowledge is a "literature of dominance" (p. 26). Many white scholars take for granted their whiteness and do not even think about the ways in which the traditional canon of dead white men has anything to do with dominance and oppression. When we go to college and all we learn about is dead white men—as I did until my doctoral program—we tend to not even give it a second thought. It is as if that is the way the world is and that is that.

But for those of us who are minorities, this literature of dominance does strange things to our psyches. Where are we represented in that literature? Well, frankly we are not. And multicultural education is simply not enough. To reserve a course for minorities is as if the material were an aside. Integrating indigenous knowledges into the general curriculum is really what we should be doing, but rarely do I see any evidence of this especially when it comes to the literatures of the Native Americans. Now, who can write on Native Americans is the question that many of the Native American scholars raise as I've commented on earlier. Many are angry that white people would write on their struggles. I know that in the Jewish community, eyebrows are raised when non-Jewish scholars write about the Holocaust (Morris, 2001). Some Jewish scholars feel—as do the Native Americans about their culture—that non-Jewish scholars appropriate the Holocaust and use it to get academic recognition, they use it to make gains in their own careers, they make an industry out of the Holocaust. I must admit that when my students—who are Christian—want to write dissertations on the Holocaust, I wonder what stake they have in it, why would they want to write on a history that has nothing to do with them? But, then, again, my more rational side tells me that no one owns academic property and anyone can write on anything. But still there is a sensitivity there and I get a little bent out of shape when Christians begin displaying sentimental and patronizing philo-Judaism. This makes me very nervous and suspect of motives and intentions if Christians are writing on Jewish subjects. So I can empathize with the strong feelings that Native American scholars have about who can and cannot write about their history and culture. The scope of this book does not allow for me to go into much depth on the issue of Native American or Jewish scholarship (for more on this see Morris, 2006) but I bring these issues up to show that the academy is not a friendly place especially to minorities and that white scholars need to think about their privilege and whose knowledge is privileged inside the academy and why that might be so. How can we give a voice to those who do not have one? How can we make Native American Studies more visible and encourage our colleagues to take Native American scholarship seriously? There was a time in the history of the university both in Europe and in the United States when Jews were not welcomed in the academy. Women and African-Americans have had similar struggles. As I said earlier, Gloria Anzaldua (2002) suggests in her recent work that we need to build coalitions across cultures to try to undo the way in which the academy squashes minority voices. Anybody who is oppressed inside of the academy suffers psychically—and it is this psychic suffering that concerns me. We cannot afford to be isolationists in our sufferings anymore. The only way to get any sort of power is to band together as gays, lesbians bisexuals, straights, transgendered, whites, Native Americans, African Americans, Jews, Christians, Muslims and so forth to fight for an America that embraces social justice. No one group can do this work alone and I wholeheartedly agree with Anzaldua that we all need to work together on these issues.

ON HAVING TROUBLE WORKING: PSYCHIC SUFFERING AND INSTITUTIONS

Psychic suffering can cause one to not want to work, to not want to write, to not want to think. And the academy can squash us if we let it. If we feel that a psychic paralysis is coming on is there nothing to do to stop it or slow it or escape it? Or is it inevitable? Like Momady, Wittgenstein (1997)–in a letter to Bertrand Russell– complains of the inability to work. Wittgenstein (1997) says:

> Every day I was tormented by a frightful angst and by depression. . . . I was so exhausted that I wasn't able to think of doing a bit of work. It's terrifying beyond all description the kinds of mental torment that there can be! (p. 69)

Ray Monk (1990) suggests that Wittgenstein's troubles were twofold. He suffered from periods of not working, of psychic paralysis. He also suffered from being affiliated with an academic discipline that he loathed. Monk (1990) explains:

> What links this apocalyptic anxiety with his hostility to academic philosophy is his detestation of the power of science, which on the one hand encouraged the philosopher's craving for generality and on the other produced the atomic bomb. (pp. 484–485)

Wittgenstein felt that, among other things, students were not taught to do philosophy at Cambridge, but only to mimic and memorize. No real thought was going in philosophy classrooms at Cambridge. No doubt the institution disturbed him, but he was already psychically fragile. He complains throughout his letters of periods of psychic stasis when he was unable to work. In a letter to Keynes, Wittgenstein (1997) says:

> You ask in your letter whether you could do anything to make it possible for me to return to scientific work. The answer is no: there's nothing that can be done in that way, because I myself no longer have any strong inner drive. . . . (p. 207)

Having no inner drive is like sleep walking. What is it like to never have an inner drive?

Perhaps here is the beginning of Wittgenstein's turning. Turnings happen during crisis points in a life. He gives up on logic as science and starts to look at logic as mysticism. The language of logic—late Wittgenstein argued–was more like the language of the mystic. Perhaps his profound psychic paralyses allowed him to make that change from logician to mystical aesthete. Bertrand Russell (2002b) says in a letter to Ottoline Morrell that Wittgenstein

> has penetrated deep into mystical ways of thought and feeling, but I think (though he wouldn't agree) that what he likes best in mysticism is the power to make him stop thinking. (p. 199)

When thoughts become suffocating and overwhelming, depression looms because psyche overloads. This is what troubled Wittgenstein. As Russell points out, it was the mystical that made the obsessive thoughts stop. Stopping obsessive thought can relieve depression. Obsessive thoughts spiral out of control. Obsessive thoughts have their own thoughts and then those thoughts have their own thoughts and on and on. It is strange to think that someone as profound and as prolific as Wittgenstein had such trouble with thoughts. A philosopher tormented by thoughts. A curious thought. Wittgenstein managed to overcome his "crippling anxiety" (Monk, 1990, p. 89) to go on to produce some of the most important philosophical work of the twentieth century. Perhaps what saved him was quitting Cambridge. John Ryle (qtd. in Monk, 1990) says of Wittgenstein that

> he is so overcome by the deadness of the place [Cambridge]. He said to me, 'I feel I will die slowly if I stay there. I would rather take a chance of dying quickly.' And so he wants to work at some humble manual job in a hospital [During WWII]. (p. 432)

The deadness of the academy is not new by any means. Scholars have felt this for decades! Wittgenstein had such distain for the deadness of the academy that according to Allan Janik and Stephen Toulmin (1996), he told his students not to become academic philosophers. William Johnston (1972) reports that "[a]verse to professional philosophers, he [Wittgenstein] preferred to read cowboy stories and to quote remarks by his chambermaid" (p. 212). His hatred of academic philosophy combined with his already vulnerable psychic state resulted in periods of mental paralysis where he could do no work at all. Here I am reminded of Sack's (1999) descriptions of his patients who suffered from sleeping sickness. Immobility, trance, frozen, psychically dead. While reading Wittgenstein's letters to my doctoral students I raised the question about the possibility that he might have suffered bipolar disease. It crossed my mind that his patterns of work were either manic or nil. It was all or nothing for Wittgenstein. Bertrand Russell (qtd. in Monk, 1990) says of Wittgenstein:

> he has the artist's feeling that he will produce the perfect thing or nothing–I explained how he wouldn't get a degree or be able to teach unless he learnt to write imperfect things. (p. 57)

This all or nothing mentality is akin to the behavior of someone who suffers from bipolar disease. States of mania are followed by states of utter paralysis. And then the cycle continues. It sounds to me like Wittgenstein had a bit of this in him. What also strikes me in the above cited passage is Russell's comparison of the artist and scholar. He suggests that the logician is like the artist who wants only perfection in his work. Does the artist strive for the perfection? I would say that music conservatories demand perfection from their students. And that is partly what is wrong with conservatories. The pressure put on students is unthinkable. And then there are poets who want to craft the perfect poem. Here I am thinking of Anne Sexton. Sexton would revise some of her poems at least twenty times (Kumin, 1981). But when perfection does not come, and the obsessive thoughts get in the way of the perfect creation, one stops working, has a breakdown or gets medicated. Sexton got medicated. Then she committed suicide. Maxine Kumin (1981) says of Anne Sexton that

On thorazine, she gained weight, became intensively sun-sensitive, and complained that she was so overwhelmed with lassitude that she could not write. Without medication the voices returned [Sexton suffered from some psychotic breaks] As she grew increasingly more dependent on alcohol, sedatives, and sleeping pills, her depressive bouts grew more frequent. (xxxiii)

For Sexton, medicated or not, she had trouble writing because of her ongoing battles with depression and suicidal ideation. For a more in depth study of Anne Sexton, Paula Salvio (2007) has done an excellent job of unpacking the teacherly life of Sexton and her ongoing psychological problems.

The philosopher who comes closest to Sexton's struggles is William James. He too struggled with raging depressions and in fact had a nervous breakdown. He suffered from periods of not working, of not being able to write.

Alice James (cited in Strouse, 1980) comments of William that "[h]e spent long years unable to work" (xiii). Years! I am immediately reminded again of Sacks' patients who had sleeping sickness and sat frozen for years. Of course, James was not suffering from the sleeping sickness, but he did suffer mental paralysis of great magnitude, great enough to land him in breakdown. Like Sexton, James too struggled with suicidal ideation. Alice James (cited in Strouse, 1980) explains:

William too had been suffering mentally and physically all winter. . . . he wrote to a friend Tom Ward that he had been that year 'on a continual verge of suicide.' He was attending classes at medical school, arguing philosophy late into the night with the young Wendell Holmes, having trouble with insomnia, his back, his digestion, and his eyes. . . . (p. 110)

How can you work in the academy and be "on a continual verge of suicide"? What must that be like? What does it take to push someone who suffers suicidal ideation over the edge? The university is not exactly a friendly place for people who suffer mental illness. Some scholars do suffer from mental illness. This is a taboo subject that almost no one in the academy addresses.

It seems that James had a hard time making up his mind. Was his continual indecision part of his mental illness? Psychologist or philosopher? Medical degree or degree in philosophy? Indecision is enough to drive anyone mad. What is remarkable about James–like Sexton and Wittgenstein–is that he produced some of the most important intellectual work of the twentieth century despite his psychic and somatic difficulties. Like Wittgenstein, he also had the compounded problem of working inside of a killing machine, namely Harvard. In many of James' letters he complains about Harvard. He seemed only to have contempt for the place. He complained–like Wittgenstein–that what went on in the philosophy classes at Harvard was not philosophy at all but rubbish. Recall, Wittgenstein made a similar complaint about philosophy classes at Cambridge. In a letter to Charles Renouvier, James (1920) expressed his disappointment in academic philosophy. He states:

The philosophical teaching, as a rule. . . is in the hands of the president. . . that 'safeness' becomes the main characteristic of his tuition; that his classes are edified rather than awakened. . . lifeless discussions. . . and flabby formulas they [the students] have had to commit to memory. . . . (pp. 189–190)

Doing philosophy does not mean committing things to memory. Doing philosophy is not about learning formulas and memorizing the history of philosophy. Philosophy is the art of thought and that art—according to both James and Wittgenstein-- had to be done elsewhere, had to be done outside of the academy. The killing grounds of the academy do not welcome thought. A most curious thought. William James—an unusual philosopher for his time– wrote more like a novelist (like his brother Henry James) than a philosopher and for this he was ostracized from the academic philosophical community. At any rate, his writing was being continually interrupted. William complains to his brother Henry that his academic "*duties*" were getting in the way of doing philosophical work, of writing (1920). In more detail, James (1920) remarks to Renouvier that:

Our university moreover inflicts a monstrous amount of routine business on one, faculty meetings and committees of every sort, so that during the term one can do no continuous reading at all–reading of books, I mean. (1920, p. 45)

It is remarkable that Harvard–at least during the turn of last century–was no different from many universities today. Scholars have little time to do the real work of scholarship because of the "monstrous" amount of service work required for tenure and promotion—especially at regional or non-research institutions. And it is this ridiculous call to meaningless service that in the end harms the scholar. The damage done is psychological. When there is little time to do the work the scholar was called to do, anxiety and depression set in. This problem—for James— compounded with his already vulnerable psychic health nearly killed him. I believe that it is the compounding of these forces that make for certain disaster. James was not alone in his disdain for Harvard. Georg Santayana (2002) had similar problems. In a letter to George Herbert Palmer, Santayana says, "the routine of lectures and the general tone of the place were wearing me out and getting on my nerves more and more" (p. 2:94). In fact, he disdained Harvard so, that Santayana retired at forty eight (Holzberger, 2002b). He must have had money to retire that young!! Now, that's privilege. Like James and Santayana, recall that Emerson (2003) too was highly critical of Harvard. Again, he remarks in his famous speech "*The American Scholar*" that the academy is too conservative in that it is mostly concerned with tradition but not with the new, with experimental or forward looking thought. So people like Wittgenstein, James and Santayana had particular difficulties because they were all forward thinkers. Recall also that A.N. Whitehead (1929/1967)– also very critical of the academy–thought it " easy to produce a faculty entirely unfit" (p. 99). An unfit faculty is one that is not forward thinking. Margaret Mead, the world renowned anthropologist was also critical of Harvard but for a very different reason: its treatment of women. Mary Catherine Bateson (1984), Mead's daughter, remarks that

Harvard University was one of the few institutions She [Mead] had a continuing grudge against for discounting and exploitation of women. . . . . (p. 141)

Harvard wasn't the only Ivy League unfriendly to women, mostly all of them were. Ruth Benedict—Mead's lover of over twenty years—was treated badly at Columbia University and as Lois Banner (2003) points out:

Even when she [Benedict] served as de facto chair of the [anthropology] department for Franz Boas in the 1930s, she couldn't enter the Male faculty dining room, from which women were barred. . . . (p. 378)

I cannot even imagine this!! But then again, I can. I know how deeply entrenched sexism is not only in the academy but in the country at large. Columbia certainly did not make her life easier. Benedict struggled with two things, her own history of depression stemming from her father's death, and the problems she encountered at Columbia University associated with sexism. Hilary Lapsley (1999) tells us that for a while Benedict was a school teacher but found the job dreadful. Benedict suffered from depression most of her life and this teaching job did not help any. At one point in her life, Lapsley (1999) reveals a disturbing fact about Benedict:

Pushing back the feelings that threatened to overwhelm her, Ruth fantasized about "planning actual suicides. . . in very considerable detail". . . . (p. 50)

In the 1930s, women scholars like Benedict found little solace working inside of the university. Even though Benedict encouraged women students to come into the field of anthropology there was little hope of them actually landing positions in universities in those days. Hillary Lapsley (1999) points out that even Benedict's mentor, Franz Boas—who by the way was a champion of social justice and fought against racism and anti-Semitism— had little interest in undoing the ongoing sexism in the academy and in fact he was part of the problem. Lapsley states that:

However much Boas encouraged his women students, he was a man of his time in his attitude toward their work. He favored men when making recommendations for jobs and relied on women's willingness to work for little or no remuneration. (p. 60.)

It shocks that a man who fought for social justice for minorities was sexist. It is surprising to me that Boas treated women in this fashion knowing that both Benedict and Mead did groundbreaking work in anthropology and were highly respected by the scientific community. Lois Banner (2003) points out a curious fact about Benedict's well known book *Patterns of Culture* which was written in 1934. Banner is struck by the number of male scholarly references Benedict draws on in her work. It is as if she had to cite the works of men to be considered a legitimate scholar. This should come as no surprise because in the 1930s the academy had little regard for women scholars, even if they taught at places like Columbia. Banner (2003) tells us that

> In her [Benedict's] writing she cited male philosophers like Nietzsche and Santayana while overlooking feminist authors like Charlotte Perkins Gilman and Ellen Key. . . . She may have wanted to establish a male genealogy to ensure her acceptance as a theorist in a male intellectual world. . . . (p. 290)

For women scholars, even today, I do not think that things are much different as far as the question of whose knowledge is of most worth in the academy. Women are expected to quote male intellectuals and in fact much of university education—at least when I was a student—consisted of reading dead white men and quoting dead white men. When I was a student at Tulane University, we never read any books by women in my philosophy classes. In my masters program at Loyola University we rarely read women theologians. Again, it was expected that we quote men and read mostly men. I think that in most disciplines these trends are the rule and not the exception. It wasn't until I got into my doctoral program at Louisiana State University that I learned that women could be scholars, that gender mattered and that women's work should be studied and cited. It was in my curriculum studies program that I learned that gender mattered and that I began to think about my reading habits and how ingrained those sexist reading patterns were instilled in me because of the way I think I was (mis) educated. So I don't think that Benedict's situation was that different from the situation that many young women find themselves in today in the academy.

In the classical music world, as I mentioned earlier in this book, women have a hard time still. European orchestras are very reluctant to hire female musicians. It wasn't until the 1970s that it was thought to be okay for a woman to play the cello. Women conductors are rare as are women composers. I have talked with classical pianists who have told me that competitions are also sexist and more often than not male musicians win. When we think of famous women musicians, who comes to mind? Jacqueline du Pres, Martha Argerich, Ruth Laredo, Jesse Norman, Nadia Boulanger. The point here is that I cannot think of too many famous classical women musicians. The list of men, on the contrary, I can rattle off easily for pages and pages. The classical music world is hostile to women still. Nadia Boulanger is an interesting case here because she broke much ground for women in the classical music world in the early part of the 20th century and yet during her lifetime she was not respected by many male musicians as she should have been. Boulanger was one of the first women to conduct a symphony orchestra and she was a composer and pianist and organist. Many male musicians did not like being conducted by a woman. Leonie Rosenstiel (1998) tells us that when she conducted the New York Philharmonic Orchestra. . . "the instrumentalists not only ignored Nadia, they insulted her" (pp. 318–319). Boulanger is known mostly as a teacher, not as a performer or composer in her own right—which she was. She is remembered known primarily as a teacher. I find that it is interesting that one of the most talented women in music in the 20th century was not known as a conductor, composer or performer but teacher. Rosenstiel (1998) tells us that male composers like Saint-Saens were openly "hostile" to Boulanger. I want to cite the following passage in full below to expose the disturbingly sexist comments Saint-Saens made about women composers. It is remarkable to me that someone would openly make such repulsive statements about women. Rosenstiel (1998) explains:

> There was an additional chill from another quarter: Saint-Saens was hostile to her [Boulanger]. He was an influential member of the Prix de Rome Jury, and his distaste for women composers was well known. He had already been heard to remark that a woman composer was like a dog walking on his hind legs, a freak of nature, unnatural. . . . (p. 65)

In the 1920s it was unheard of to do what Nadia Boulanger did: she conducted and she composed. People were stunned by her boldness. When I was in the music conservatory, however, Nadia Boulanger's name came up all the time, but in a loving way. Everybody who knew everybody in the 20s' and 30s' studied with Nadia Boulanger.

At any rate, when I read about the struggles Boulanger had with her male colleagues in the classical music world, I was—to say the least—taken aback. Frankly, I was stunned. I had always heard her name mentioned with great reverence when I was in music school. It was just assumed that Boulanger was a superstar and did not have any struggles. The disturbing thing about Boulanger is that although she was clearly a feminist and fought for the rights of women to be conductors and composers, she was anti-Semitic—according to Rosenstiel (1998). This was not uncommon for the French especially with what we know about the Dreyfus Affair (Morris, 2001) and Vichy and the French complicity in the Holocaust. This is not to say that all French people were anti-Semitic, but there has been a long history in France of anti-Semitism (Morris, 2001). So here you have someone who fought for social justice for women, but not for Jews. I am reminded of Franz Boas who was Jewish but had little interest in fighting for rights for women.

I am curious as to why when many think of well known women scholars, we have trouble listing names. Off the top of my head, I think mostly of anthropologists like Mead and Benedict. I also think of other women who did their work as scholars who studied animal behavior like Jane Goodall and Dian Fossey. Of these women, Benedict probably spent the most time at the University while these other women spent most of their time out in the field. Is it an accident that the most well known women intellectuals spent most of their time away from the university? Is it that they could only have fame if they kept a distance between them and their jealous male colleagues? I wonder how far we have come since, say, the days of Nadia Boulanger and Ruth Benedict? Ruth Benedict suffered depression and struggled with suicidal ideation as I said earlier. Despite that, she went on to publish one of the most important books in the history of anthropology *Patterns of Culture* (1934).

The scholars who I've discussed in this chapter struggled to do their work—some suffered nervous breakdowns, depressions, and fought against working in oppressive environments—but somehow they did their work. William Pinar (1994) said in his early essay about the academy, that scholars must find a way out. The way out is the way back to work. On not being able to work is about finding ways to find a way back to the work.

AFTER THOUGHTS

I have been giving much (after) thought to the problems of not being able to do what you want to do. Part of the problem, I think, is that Americans are so monolingual. By this, I mean we are supposed to do one thing , not many. Mary Catherine Bateson (1989) comments on this and she tells us that many people who have their heart set on one career end up crashing and burning because that career did not work out. She suggests that we think more broadly about our lives. This is a hard prospect for Americans who live in one nation under one monotheistic god. While attending the Spoleto festival in Charleston, I had the opportunity to see Laurie Anderson perform. Now, I have been listening to her work for some twenty years and this was the first time I had ever seen her perform live. It was truly an amazing experience. What I learned from this was that she is NOT monolingual in any sense. She is a performance artist and does a variety of things. As I see it she is a poet, a storyteller, a musician, a visual artist, a cultural critic, a cultural studies scholar in fact. She sings, plays the electric violin, plays keyboards, does multimedia visuals, tells stories and comments on politics. She combines aesthetics and politics, music and theatre, talking and singing. I learned from watching her and listening to her that people are a lot more multi-lingual than we think. In the music world—the classical music world—you only play one instrument and you spend all of your time and energy mastering that instrument. It is almost anathema to try to play two. Well, some singers might play piano but they tend not to play well because they focus so much time and effort on their voice. But what if we were to play more than one instrument? What if we had more than one academic interest? A research agenda suggests that you have basically one interest and stick to that throughout your career. But what if we had many interests? Laurie Anderson breaks the rules, she has many interests and is good at doing many different things. What would it be like to be an academic who is a poet, a musician, a multimedia artist, a musician, a cultural critic? If you cannot think because you are psychically blocked you might think about playing; if you cannot play because you are injured you might think about writing. If your prose is stuck, you might turn to poetry. If you cannot write poetry, maybe you can sing. If you cannot sing, maybe you can paint. If you cannot paint maybe you can write cultural commentary. It is not so easy, however, to say to a musician who is injured, oh, just do something else!! If you have been trained since the age of 5 to be a classical musician and spend your entire life studying music, it is extremely difficult to turn around and do something else. This book has been highly autobiographical in that that is exactly what happened to me. It took me some ten years to get back on my feet after I hurt my arm and had to quit my music career. And then it was still another ten years before I found another career, or it found me!! I had many difficult years and I could have ended up in a gutter in New Orleans. But I didn't. It was because of the generosity and kindness of other people that I found my home in academe. In many ways, I owe my good fortune to the very special people I met in New Orleans who helped me get myself back on track. This book is dedicated to three of those people. I name them here: Mary Aswell Doll, William F. Pinar and Mary B. Virre.

REFERENCES

Abbey, E. (1971). *Desert solitaire: A season in the wilderness*. New York: Ballantine Books.

Abraham, N., & Torok, M. (1994). *The shell and the kernel* (Vol. 1, N. T. Rand, Ed. & Trans.). Chicago: University of Chicago Press.

Abram, D. (1997). *The spell of the sensuous*. New York: Vintage Press.

Abram, J. (2000). Editor's foreward. A kind of French Winnicott. In J. Abram (Ed.), *Andre Green at the squiggle foundation* (pp. xi–xviii). London: Karnac Books.

Adorno, T. (2004). *Philosophy of modern music* (A. G. Mitchell & W. V. Blomster, Trans.). New York: Continuum.

Alfred, T. (2004). Warrior scholarship: Seeing the University as a ground of contention. In D. A. Mihesuah & A. C. Wilson (Eds.), *Indigenizing the academe: Transforming scholarship and empowering communities* (pp. 88–99). Lincoln, NE: University of Nebraska Press.

Amos, T., & Powers, A. (2005). *Tori Amos: Piece by piece*. New York: Broadway Books.

Anderson, L. (1999). Laurie Anderson. In W. Duckworth (Ed.), *Talking music: Conversations with John Cage, Philip Glass, Laurie Anderson, and five generations of American experimental composers* (pp. 268–385). New York: Da Capo Press.

Andreas-Salome, L. (2003). *You alone are real to me: Remembering Rainer Maria Rilke* (A. von der Lippe, Trans.). Rochester, NY: BOA Editions, Ltd.

Anzaldua, G., & Keating, A. L. (Eds.). (2002). *This bridge we call home: Radical visions for transformation*. New York: Routldge.

Aoki, T. (2005). *Curriculum in a new key: The collected works of Ted Aoki* (W. F. Pinar & R. L. Irwin, Eds.). Mahwah, NJ: Lawrence Erlbaum and Associates Publishers.

Appelbaum, P. (2008). *Children's books for grown-up teachers: Reading and writing curriculum theory*. New York: Routledge.

Arendt, H. (1976). *The origins of totalitarianism*. Harcourt Brace & Company.

Arrau, C. (1991). Claudio Arrau. In E. Mach (Ed.), *Great contemporary pianists speak for themselves* (pp. 1–11). New York: Dover.

Arrau, C. (1992). *Conversations with Arrau*. Interviews conducted with and written by Joseph Horowitz (pp. 11–194). New York: Dover.

Atkins, C. (1992). Chet Atkins by Don Menn, October 1979. In D. Menn (Ed.), *Secrets from the masters: Conversations with forty great guitar players* (pp. 7–18). San Francisco: Backbeat Books.

Azerrad, M. (2001). *Our band could be you life: Scenes from the American Indie underground 1981–1991*. New York: Little, Brown and Company.

Bachelard, G. (1988a). *The flame of a candle* (J. Caldwell, Trans.). Dallas, TX: The Dallas Institute.

Bachelard, G. (1988b). *The right to dream* (J. A. Underwood, Trans.). Dallas, TX: The Dallas Institute.

Bachleard, G. (1990). *Fragments on a poetics of fire* (K. Haltman, Trans.). Dallas, TX: The Dallas Institute.

Bachelard, G. (1994). *The poetics of space: The classic look at how we experience intimate places* (M. Jolas, Trans.). Boston: Beacon Press.

Bachelard, G. (1999). *Water and dreams: An essay on the imagination of matter* (E. R. Farrell, Trans.). Dallas, TX: The Dallas Institute.

Bachelard, G. (2000). *The dialectic of duration* (M. M. Jones, Trans.). Manchester, England: Clinamen Press.

Bachelard, G. (2002a). *Air and dreams: An essay on the imagination of matter* (E. R. Farrell & C. Frederick Farrell, Trans.). Dallas, TX: The Dallas Institute Publications.

Bachelard, G. (2002b). *Earth and reveries of will: An essay on the imagination of matter* (K. Haltmann, Trans.). Dallas, TX: The Dallas Institute Publications.

Baker, K. (1988). *Minimalism: Art of circumstance*. New York: Abbeville Press.

REFERENCES

Balint, E. (1993). *Before I was I: Psychoanalysis and the imagination* (J. Mitchell & M. Parsons, Eds.). London: Free Association Books.

Balint, M. (1992). *The basic fault: Therapeutic aspects of regression*. Evanston, IL: Northwestern University Press.

Balint, M. (2000). *The doctor, his patient and the illness*. New York: Churchill, Livingstone.

Banner, L. W. (2003). *Intertwined lives: Margaret Mead, Ruth Benedict, and their circle*. New York: Vintage.

Barzun, J. (2002). *The house of intellect*. New York: Perennial Classics.

Batchelor, D. (1996). *Minimalism*. New York: Cambridge University Press.

Bateson, M. C. (1984). *With a daughter's eye: A memoir of Margaret Mead and Gregory Bateson*. New York: Perennial.

Bateson, M. C. (1989). *Composing a life*. New York: Grove Press.

Bauman, B. (2002). Preserving the Chicago public school murals. In H. Becker (Ed.), *Art for the people: The rediscovery and preservation of progressive and WPA-era murals in the Chicago public schools 1904–1943* (pp. 6–40). San Francisco: Chronicle Books.

Bazzana, K. (2007). *Lost genius: The curious and tragic story of an extraordinary musical prodigy*. New York: Carroll & Graf Publishers.

Beck, J. (1992). Jeff Beck by Jas Obrecht October 1980 & November 1958. In D. Menn (Ed.), *Secrets from the masters: Conversations with forty great guitar players* (pp. 19–27). San Francisco: Backbeat Books.

Becker, H. (Ed.). (2002). *Art for the people: The rediscovery and preservation of progressive and WPA-era murals in the Chicago public schools, 1904–1943*. San Francisco: Chronicle Books.

Beckett, S. (1958). *Waiting for Godot*. New York: Grove.

Beethoven, L. V. (1972). *Beethoven's letters* (A. Eaglefield-Hull, Ed., J. S. Shedlock, Trans.). New York: Dover.

Benedict, R. (1943/2005). *Patterns of culture*. New York: Houghton Mifflin Company.

Bennett, A. (2001). *Cultures of popular music*. UK: Open University Press.

Bergmann, M. S. (2001). The dynamics of the history of psychoanalysis: Anna Freud, Leo Rangell and Andre Green. In G. Kohon (Ed.), *The dead mother: The work of Andre Green* (pp. 193–204). New York: Brunner-Routledge.

Bernstein, L. (1976). *The unanswered question: Six talks at Harvard*. Cambridge, MA: Harvard University Press.

Berry, W. (1981). *Recollected essays 1965–1980: The selected essays of Wendell Berry*. San Francisco: North Point Press.

Bion, W. (1990). *Brazilian lectures*. London: Karnac.

Bion, W. (1991). *Learning from experience*. London: Karnac.

Bion, W. (1993). *Second thoughts*. London: Karnac.

Bion, W. (1994). *Cogitations*. London: Karnac.

Bion, W. (2000). *Clinical seminars and other works*. London: Karnac.

Bleandonu, G. (2000). *Wilfred Bion: His life and works 1897–1979* (C. Pajaczkowska, Trans.). New York: Other Press.

Bleuler, E. (1950). *Dementia praecox or the group of schizophrenias* (J. Zinkin, Trans.). New York: International Universities Press.

Block, A. (1997). *I'm only bleeding: Education as the practice of violence against children*. New York: Peter Lang.

Bollas, C. (1987). *The shadow of the object: Psychoanalysis of the unthought known*. New York: Columbia University Press.

Bollas, C. (1989). *Forces of destiny: Psychoanalysis and human idiom*. London: Free Association Books.

Bollas, C. (1996). *Cracking up: The work of unconscious experience*. New York: Hill And Wang.

Bollas, C. (1997). Christopher Bollas. In A. Molino (Ed.), *Elaborate selves: Reflections and reveries of Christopher Bollas, Michael Eigen, Polly Young-Eisendrath, Samuel & Evelyn Laeuchi and Marie Coleman Nelson* (pp. 1–60). New York: The Hawthorn Press.

Bollas, C. (1999). Dead mother, dead child. In G. Kohon (Ed.), *The dead mother: The work of Andre Green* (pp. 87–108). London: Routledge.

Bollas, C. (2000). *The mystery of things*. New York: Routledge.

Bowles, P. (1977). *The sheltering sky*. New York: The Ecco Press.

Brackett, D. (2000). *Interpreting popular music*. Berkeley, CA: University of California Press.

Brenner, W. H. (1999). *Wittgenstein's philosophical investigations*. Albany, NY: State University of New York Press.

Brinkely, D. (2000). Introduction. In *Edward Abbey's The monkey wrench gang* (pp. xv–xxiv). New York: Harper Perennial.

Broyard, A. (1992). *Intoxicated by my illness and other writings on life and death* (Compiled and edited by Alexandra Broyard). New York: Fawcett Columbine.

Buber, M. (2002/1947). *Between man and man*. New York: Routledge.

Camus, A. (1956). *The rebel*. New York: Vintage.

Camus, A. (1989). *The stranger*. New York: Vintage.

Camus, A. (1995). *A happy death*. New York: Vintage.

Carr, I. (1992). *Keith Jarrett: The man and his music*. New York: Da Capo.

Carr, V. S. (2004). *Paul Bowles: A life*. New York: Scribner.

Carretto, C. (2002). *Letters from the desert*. Maryknoll, NY: Orbis Books.

Casals, P. (1959). *The memoirs of Pablo Casals as told to Thomas Dozier*. New York: Time Inc.

Cavanagh, J. (2003). *33 1/3: The piper at the gates of dawn*. New York: Continuum.

Chabon, M. (2000). *The amazing adventures of Kavalier & Clay*. New York: Picador.

Champagne, D. (1998). American Indian studies is for everyone. In D. A. Mihesuah (Ed.), *Natives and academics: Researching and writing about American Indians* (pp. 181–189). Lincoln, NE: University of Nebraska Press.

Chomsky, N. (2000). *Noam Chomsky: The architecture of language* (N. Mukherji, B. N. Patnaik, & R. K. Agihotri, Eds.). New York: Oxford University Press.

Collingwood, R. G. (1958). *The principles of art*. New York: Oxford University Press.

Coltart, N. (2000). *Slouching towards Bethlehem*. New York: Other Press.

Cooke, D. (2001). *The language of music*. New York: Oxford University Press.

Cooke, J. F. (1999). *Great pianists on piano playing: Godowsky, Hofmann, Lhevinne ,Paderewski and 24 other legendary performers*. Mineola, NY: Dover Publications.

Coppela, F. F. (1983). *Koyaanisqatsi: Life out of balance*. Produced and directed by Godfrey Reggio. Music by Philip Glass. MGM Entertainment. #1003766.

Corredor, J. M. (1956). *Conversations with Casals* (A. Mangeot, Trans.). New York: E.P. Dutton.

Corrigan, M. (2005). *Leave me alone, I'm reading: Finding and losing myself in books*. New York: Vintage.

Cross, A. (1981). *Death in a tenured position*. New York: Ballantine.

Davis, B. (1996). *Teaching mathematics: Toward a sound alternative*. New York: Garland Publishing.

Deleuze, G., & Guattari, F. (2000). *Anti-Oedipus: Capitalism and schizophrenia* (R. Hurley, M. Seem, & H. R. Lane, Trans.). Minneapolis, MN: University of Minnesota Press.

Deloria, V. (1970). *We talk, you listen: New tribes, new turf*. Lincoln, NE: University of Nebraska Press.

Deloria, V., & Wildcat, D. (2001). *Power and place: Indian education in America*. Golden, CO: American Indian Graduate Center and Fulcrum Resources.

Derrida, J. (1976). *Of grammatology* (G. C. Spivak, Trans.). Baltimore: The Johns Hopkins Press.

Derrida, J. (1988). *The ear of the other: Otobiography, transference, translation* (C. McDonald, Ed., P. Kamuf, Trans.). Lincoln, NE: University of Nebraska Press.

Derrida, J. (1991). From Plato's pharmacy. In P. Kamuf (Ed.), *A Derrida reader: Between the blinds* (pp. 112–139). New York: Columbia University Press.

Derrida, J. (1992a). *The gift of death* (D. Wills, Trans.). Chicago: University of Chicago Press.

Derrida, J. (1992b). *The other heading: Reflections on today's Europe* (P.-A. Brault & M. B. Nass, Trans.). Bloomington, IN: Indiana University Press.

REFERENCES

Derrida, J. (1994). *Specters of Marx: The state of the debt, the work of mourning, and the new international* (P. Kamuf, Trans.). New York: Routledge.
Derrida, J. (1995). *Points: Interviews 1974–1994* (E. Weber, Ed., P. Kamuf and others, Trans.). Stanford, CA: Stanford University Press.
Derrida, J. (2000a). *Limited inc.* Evanston, IL: Northwestern University Press.
Derrida, J. (2000b). *Of hospitality* (R. Bowlby, Trans.). Stanford, CA: Stanford University Press.
Derrida, J. (2002). Derrida. Zeitgeist Video. Jane Doe Films. A Film by Kirby Dick and Amy Ziering Kofman. #9597510473.
Dewey, J. (1991). *How we think.* Buffalo, NY: Prometheus Books.
Dichter, M. (1991). Misha Dichter. In E. Mach (Ed.), *Great contemporary pianists speak for themselves* (pp. 63–73). New York: Dover.
Dickens, C. (2005). *Bleak house.* New York: Barnes and Noble.
Dillard, A. (1998). *Pilgrim at tinker creek.* New York: Harper Perennial.
Dimitriadis, G., & McCarthy, C. (2001). *Reading and teaching the postcolonial: From Baldwin to Basquiat and beyond.* New York: Teachers College Press.
Dimitriadis, G. (2005). *Performing identity/performing culture: Hip hop as text, pedagogy and lived practice.* New York: Peter Lang.
Dimmitt, M. A. (2000). Biomes & communities of the Sonoran desert region. In S. J. Phillips & P. Wentworth Comus (Eds.), *A natural history of the Sonoran desert* (pp. 3–18). Berkeley, CA: University of California Press.
Dixson, A. (2006). The fire this time: Jazz, research and critical race theory. In A. Dixson & C. Rousseau (Eds.), *Critical race theory in education: All god's children got a song* (pp. 213–230). New York: Routledge. Taylor and Francis Group.
Doll, M. A. (1995). *To the lighthouse and back: Writings on teaching and living.* New York: Peter Lang.
Doll, M. A. (2000). *Like letters in running water: A mythopoetics of curriculum.* Mahwah, NJ: Lawrence Erlbaum and Associates Publishers.
Doody, F. (2002). New class curriculum. In H. Becker (Ed.), *Art for the people: The rediscovery and preservation of progressive and WPA-era murals in the Chicago public schools, 1904–1943* (pp. 21–22). San Francisco: Chronicle Books.
Dreiser, T. (1914/1965). *The titan.* New York: A Signet Classic.
Easton, C. (1989). *Jacqueline du Pre: A biography.* New York: Da Capo Press.
Eco, U. (2004a). *On literature.* New York: A Harvest Book. Harcourt, Inc.
Eco, U. (2004b). *The mysterious flame of queen Loana.* New York: Harcourt.
Edelson, M. (1975). *Language and interpretation in psychoanalysis.* Chicago: The University of Chicago Press.
Eigen, M. (1993). *The electrified tightrope.* Northvale, NJ: Jason Aronson Inc.
Eigen, M. (1996). *Psychic deadness.* Northvale, NJ: Jason Aronson Inc.
Eigen, M. (2001a). *Damaged bonds.* New York: Karnac.
Eigen, M. (2001b). *Toxic nourishment.* New York: Karnac.
Eigen, M. (2004). *The sensitive self.* Middletown, CT. Wesleyan University Press.
Eigen, M. (2005). *Emotional storm.* Middletown, CT. Wesleyan University Press.
Einstein, A. (1976). *Out of my later years.* New York: Citadel Books.
Eisler, B. (2003). *Chopin's funeral.* New York: Knopf.
Emerson, R. W. (2003). *Selected writings of Ralph Waldo Emerson* (W. H. Gilman, Ed.). New York: A Signet Classic.
Epstein, M. (1996). *Thoughts without a thinker: Psychotherapy from a Buddhist perspective.* New York: Basic Books.
Epstein, M. (1999). *Going to pieces without falling apart: A Buddhist perspective on wholeness.* New York: Broadway Books.
Fadiman, A. (1998). *Ex libris: Confessions of a common reader.* New York: Farrar, Straus & Giroux.
Fanon, F. (1963). *The wretched of the earth* (C. Farrington, Trans.). New York: Grove Press.

Feliciano, H. (2004). Jose Feliciano: My deliverance. In J. A. Schroeter (Ed.), *Between the strings: The secret lives of guitarists* (pp. 207–209). Colorado Springs, CO: John August Music.

Fink, R. (2005). *Repeating ourselves: American minimal music as cultural practice.* Berkeley, CA: University of California Press.

Fisk, E. (2004). Eliot Fisk: Guitar divine. In J. A. Schroeter (Ed.), *Between the strings: The secret lives of guitarists* (pp. 218–224). Colorado Springs, CO: John August Music.

Fitzgerald, F. S. (1993). *The crack up* (E. Wilson, Ed.). New York: A New Directions Books.

Fixico, D. (2003). *The American Indian mind in a linear world: American Indian studies and traditional knowledges.* New York: Routledge.

Fleisher, L. (2008). Maestro Leon Fleisher uses "Two Hands" to Thank NIH. In *National institute of neurological disorders and stroke* (pp. 1–2). Retrieved from www.ninds.nih.gov/news_an_events/news_articles

Flemming, R. (1997). Preface. In R. Kostelanetz (Ed.), *Writings on glass: Essays, interviews, criticism* (pp. vii–x). Berkeley, CA: University of California Press.

Forte, D. (1992). Michael Hedges by Dan Forte February 1985. In D. Menn (Ed.), *Secrets from the masters: Conversations with forty great guitar players* (pp. 109–111). San Francisco: Backbeat Books.

Fox, M. (2006). *The a.w.e. project: Reinventing education.* Copperhouse.

Freud, S. (1900/1960). *The interpretation of dreams.* London: Standard Edition.

Freud, S. (1959). *Inhibitions, symptoms and anxiety.* London: Standard Edition.

Freud, S. (1960). *Jokes and their relation to the unconscious.* London: Standard Edition.

Fricke, D. (1997). Pink Floyd—the inside story. In B. MacDonald (Ed.), *Pink Floyd through the eyes of the band, its fans, friends and foes* (pp. 3–18). New York: Da Capo Press.

Frith, S. (1996). *Performing rites: On the value of popular music.* Cambridge, MA: Harvard University Press.

Furth, H. G. (1966). *Thinking without language: Psychological implications of deafness.* New York: The Free Press.

Ginsberg, A. (2000). *Deliberate prose: Selected essays 1952–1995, Allen Ginsberg.* New York: Perennial.

Giroux, H. (2004). *The abandoned generation: Democracy beyond the culture of fear.* New York: Palgrave Macmillan.

Glass, P. (1987). *Music by Philip Glass* (R. T. Jones, Ed.). New York: Harper and Row.

Glass, P. (2004). *Philip Glass: Looking glass.* A Film directed by Eric Darmon. Written by Eric Darmon & Franck Mallet. Arte France. #9913200010.

Gliserman, M. (1996). *Psychoanalysis, language and the body of the text.* Jacksonville, FL: University Press of Florida.

Good, M. J., Brodwin, P. E., Good, B. J., & Kleinman, A. (Eds.). (1994). *Pain as human experience: An anthropological perspective.* Berkeley, CA: University of California Press.

Gould, G. (1991). Glenn Gould. In E. Mach (Ed.), *Great contemporary pianists speak for themselves* (pp. 89–113). New York: Dover.

Gramsci, A. (1919/2000). *The Antonio Gramsci reader* (D. Forgacs, Ed.). New York: New York University Press.

Gramsci, A. (2005). *Selections from the prison notebooks* (Q. Hoare & G. Nowell Smith, Eds.). New York: International Publishers.

Green, A. (1993). *On private madness.* Madison, CT: International Universities Press.

Green, A. (1999a). The greening of psychoanalysis: Andre Green in dialogues with Gregorio Kohon. In G. Kohon (Ed.), *The dead mother: The work of Andre Green* (pp. 10–58). London: Routledge.

Green, A. (1999b). *The work of the negative.* New York: Free Association Books.

Green, B. (2003). *The elegant universe: Superstrings, hidden dimensions, and the quest for the ultimate theory.* DVD # 8342136779. Boston: WGBH.

Greene, M. (1995). *Releasing the imagination: Essays on education, the arts, and social change.* San Francisco: Jossey-Bass.

REFERENCES

Groddeck, G. (1977). *The meaning of illness: Selected psychoanalytic writings*. New York: International Universities Press.

Hagberg, G. L. (1995). *Art as language: Wittgenstein, meaning, and aesthetic theory*. Ithaca, NY: Cornell University Press.

Halliwell, M. (1999). *Romantic science and the experience of the self: Transatlantic crosscurrents from William James to Oliver Sacks*. Sydney: Ashgate.

Hargrove, J. (1991). *Pablo Casals: Cellist of conscience*. Chicago: Childrens Press.

Harris, J. (2005). *The dark side of the moon: The making of the Pink Floyd masterpiece*. New York: Da Capo.

Hawkins, A. H. (1993). *Reconstructing illness: Studies in pathography*. West Lafayette, IN: Indiana University Press.

Head, H. (1963). *Aphasia and kindred disorders of speech*. New York: Harpers Publishing Company.

Hedges, M. (1992). Michael Hedges by Dan Forte February 1985. In D. Menn (Ed.), *Secrets from the masters: Conversations with forty great guitar players* (pp. 109–111). San Francisco: Backbeat Books.

Hedges, M. (2005). Michael Hedges. In *The guitarist book of acoustic* (p. 70). Bath, UK: Future Publishing Limited.

Heidegger, M. (1971). *Poetry, language, thought* (A. Hofstadter, Trans.). New York: Harper & Row.

Heidegger, M. (2004). *What is called thinking?* (J. Glenn Gray, Trans.). New York: Perennial.

Heine, H. (1995). Heinrich Heine: Letters on the French Stage, 1837. In J. Amis & M. Rose (Eds.), *Words about music: A treasury of writings* (p. 2). New York: Marlowe & Company.

Hesmondhalgh, D., & Negus, K. (Eds.). (2002). *Popular music studies*. New York: Oxford University Press.

Hibbert, T. (1997). Who the hell does Roger Waters think he is? In B. MacDonald (Ed.), *Pink Floyd through the eyes of . . . the band, its fans and foes* (pp. 144–151). New York: Da Capo Press.

Hillier, P. (2002). Introduction. In *Steve Reich's Writings on music 1965–2000* (pp. 1–10). New York: Oxford University Press.

Hillman, J. (1975). *Re-visioning psychology*. New York: Harper & Row.

Hillman, J. (1997). *Suicide and the soul*. Putnam, CT: Spring Publications, Inc.

Hillman, J. (2004). *Healing fiction*. Putnam, CT: Spring Publications, Inc.

Hoare, Q., & Smith, G. W. (2005). General introduction. In Q. Hoare & G. Nowell Smith (Eds.), *Selections from the prison notebooks of Antonio Gramsci* (pp. xvii–xcvi). New York: International Publishers.

Hobson, J. A. (1999). *Dreaming as delirium: How the brain goes out of its mind*. Cambridge, MA: The MIT Press.

Holzberger, W. (Ed.). (2002). Introduction. In *The letters of George Santayana, Book Two 1910–1920* (pp. xxxvi–lxii). Cambridge, MA: The MIT Press.

Holzberger, W. (Ed.). (2002). Preface. In *The letters of George Santayana, Book Two 1910–1920* (pp. xi–xvi). Cambridge, MA: The MIT Press.

Hopkins, L. (2006). *False self: The life of Masud Khan*. New York: Other Press.

Horowitz, J. (1999). *Arrau on music and performance*. Mineola, NY: Dover.

Huebner, D. E (1999). *The lure of the transcendent: Collected essays by Dwayne E. Huebner* (V. Hillis, Ed., Collected by W. F. Pinar). Mahwah, NJ: Lawrence Erlbaum and Associates Publishers.

Huxley, A. (2004). *The doors of perception: Heaven and hell*. New York: Harper Perennial.

Isaacson, W. (2007). *Einstein: His life and universe*. New York: Simon & Schuster.

Jackson, S., & Jordan, J. S. (1999). Being in higher education: Negotiating identity and place. In S. Jackson & J. S. Jordan (Eds.), *I've got a story to tell: Identity and place in the academy* (pp. 1–7). New York: Peter Lang.

Jacoby, R. (2000). *The last intellectuals: American culture in the age of academe*. New York: Basic Books.

James, W. (1890/1950). *The principles of psychology* (Vol. 1). New York: Dover Publications.

James, W. (1920). *The letters of William James* (Henry James, Ed.). Boston: The Atlantic Monthly Press.

James, W. (1998). *Pragmatism and the meaning of truth*. Cambridge, MA: Harvard University Press.

Janik, A., & Toulmin, S. (1996). *Wittgenstein's Vienna*. Chicago: Ivan R. Dee, Publisher.

Jankelevilch, V. (2003). *Music and the ineffable* (C. Abbate, Trans.). Princeton, NJ: Princeton University Press.

Jardine, D. (2000). *Under the tough old stars: Ecopedagogical essays*. Brandon, VT: A Solomon Press Books.

Jagodzinksi, J. (2005). *Music in youth culture: A Lacanian approach*. New York: Palgrave Macmillan.

Jensen, D. (2006). *Endgame volume 11: Resistance*. : Seven Stories Press.

Johnston, W. M. (1972). *The Austrian mind: An intellectual and social history, 1848–1938*. Berkeley, CA: University of California Press.

Jourdain, R. (1998). *Music, the brain and ecstasy: How music captures our imagination*. New York: Harper Collins.

Jung, C. (1963). *Memories, dreams and reflections*. Recorded and edited by Aniela Jaffe. (Richard & Clara Winston, Trans.). New York: Pantheon Books.

Jung, C. (1976). *The symbolic life: Miscellaneous writings* (R. F. C. Hull, Trans.). Princeton, NJ: Princeton University Press.

Jung, C. (1977). *The archetypes and the collective unconscious* (R. F. C. Hull, Trans.). Princeton, NJ: Princeton University Press.

Jung, C. (1983). *The essential Jung: Selected writings* (A. Storr, Ed.). Princeton, NJ: Princeton University Press.

Khan, M. M. R. (1989). *The long wait and other psychoanalytic narratives*. New York: Summit Books.

Kirsch, A. (2005). *The wounded surgeon: Confession and transformation in six American poets*. New York: W.W. Norton.

Klosterman, C. (2005). *Killing yourself to live: 85% of a true story*. New York: Scribner.

Kogan, J. (1989). *Nothing but the best: The struggle for perfection at the Juilliard school*. New York: Limelight Editions.

Kohon, G. (1999). Introduction. In G. Kohon (Ed.), *The dead mother: The work of Andre Green* (pp. 1–9). London: Routledge.

Kostelanetz, R. (1999). Philip Glass (1979). In R. Kostelanetz & R. Flemming (Eds.), *Writings on Glass: Essays, interviews, criticism* (pp. 109–112). Berkeley, CA: University of California Press.

Krall, F. R. (1994). *Ecotone: Wayfaring on the margins*. Albany, NY: State University of New York Press.

Kristeva, J. (1984). *Revolution in poetic language* (M. Waller, Trans.). New York: Columbia University Press.

Kristeva, J. (1989). *Black sun: Depression and melancholia* (L. S. Roudiez, Trans.). New York: Columbia.

Kumin, M. (1981). How it was: Maxine Kumin on Anne Sexton. In *Anne Sexton: The complete poems* (pp. xix–xxxiv). Boston: Houghton Mifflin.

Lange, A. (1999). Chronicle, 1977–1980. In R. Kostelanetz & R. Flemming (Eds.), *Writings on Glass: Essays, interviews, criticism* (pp. 87–93). Berkeley, CA: University of California Press.

Lapsley, H. (1999). *Margaret Mead and Ruth Benedict: The kinship of women.*

Larrocha, A. D. (1991). Alicia de Larrocha. In E. Mach (Ed.), *Great contemporary pianists speak for themselves* (pp. 53–61). New York: Dover.

Larson, S. (2000). *Captured in the middle: Tradition and experience in the contemporary Native American writing*. Seattle, WA: University of Washington Press.

Lasch, C. (1991). *The culture of narcissism: American life in an age of diminishing expectations*. New York: W. W. Norton.

Latta, M. M. (2001). *The possibilities of play in the classroom: On the power of aesthetic experience in teaching, learning, and researching*. New York: Peter Lang.

REFERENCES

Leclaire, S. (1998). *A child is being killed: On primary narcissism* (M.-C. Hays, Trans.). Stanford, CA: Stanford University Press.

Le Rider, J. (1993). *Modernity and crises of identity: Culture and society in Fin-de-Siecle Vienna* (R. Morris, Trans.). New York: Continuum.

Lewis, S. (2005a). *Babbitt*. New York: Barnes and Noble.

Lewis, S. (2005b). *It can't happen here*. New York: Signet Classics.

Luria, A. R. (2002). *The man with a shattered world* (L. Solotaroff, Trans.). Cambridge, MA: Harvard University Press.

Lussia, A. (2001). The dead mother: Variations on a theme. In G. Kohon (Ed.), *The dead mother: The work of Andre Green* (pp. 14–162). New York: Brunner-Routledge.

Lynch, D. (2005). *Eraserhead 2000*. Film Absurda. Subversive Cinema Inc. #5833400103.

Lyotard, J.-F. (1991). *The inhuman: Reflections on time* (G. Bennington & R. Bowlby, Trans.). Stanford, CA: Stanford University Press.

Mabey, R. (2005). *Nature cure: A story of depression and healing*. Charlottesville, VA: University of Virginia Press.

Macdonald, J. (1996). *Theory as a prayerful act: The collected essays of James B. Macdonald* (B. J. MacDonald, Ed.). New York: Peter Lang.

Malcolm, J. (2007). *Two lives: Gertrude and Alice*. New Haven, CT: Yale University Press.

Malott, C., & Pena, M. (2004). *Punk rockers' revolution: A pedagogy of race, class, and gender*. New York: Peter Lang.

Mann, K. (1995). *Mephisto*. New York: Penguin.

Mann, T. (1999). *Doctor Faustus: The life of the German composer Adrian Leverkuhn as told by a friend*. New York: Vintage.

Marcuse, H. (1991). *One-dimensional man*. Boston: Beacon Pres.

Mason, N. (2004). *Inside out: A personal history of Pink Floyd* (Philip Dodd, Ed.). San Francisco: Chronicle Books.

Mattiessen, P. (1987). *The snow leopard*. New York: Penguin.

Maycock, R. (2002). *Glass: A portrait*. Surrey, UK: Sanctuary Press.

McCarthy, C., Hudak, G., Miklaucic, S., & Saukko, P. (Eds.). (1999). *Sound identities: Popular music and the cultural politics of education*. New York: Peter Lang.

McDonald, M. (1990). Transitional tunes and musical development. In S. Feder, R. L. Karmel, & G. H. Pollock (Eds.), *Psychoanalytic explorations of music* (pp. 79–95). Madison, CT: International Universities Press.

McLaren, P. (2006). *Rage and hope: Interviews with Peter McLaren on war, imperialism and critical pedagogy* (P. McLaren, Ed.). New York: Peter Lang.

McLaughlin, J. (1992). John McLaughlin by Don Menn, Chip Stern August 1978 and by Jim Ferguson September 1985. In D. Menn (Ed.), *Secrets from the masters: Conversations with forty great guitar players* (pp. 140–151). San Francisco: Backbeat Books.

Merleau-Ponty, M. (1968). *The visible and the invisible* (C. Lefort, Ed., A. Lingis, Trans.). Evanston, IL: Northwestern University Press.

Methany, P. (1992). Pat Methany by Dan Forte December 1981. In D. Menn (Ed.), *Secrets from the masters: Conversations with forty great guitar players* (pp. 152–157). San Francisco: Backbeat Books.

Meyer, J. (Ed.). (2000). *Minimalism*. New York: Phaidon.

Middleton, R. (2002). *Studying popular music*. Philadelphia: Open University Press.

Middleton, R. (2003). *Reading pop: Approaches to textual analysis in popular music*. New York: Oxford University Press.

Mihesuah, D. (1998). Introduction. In D. Mihesuah (Ed.), *Natives and academics: Researching and writing about American Indians* (pp. 1–54). Lincoln, NE: University of Nebraska Press.

Miller, A. (1990). *For your own good: Hidden cruelty in child-rearing and the roots of violence*. New York: Farrar, Straus & Giroux.

Miller, A. (1991). *The untouched key: Tracing childhood trauma in creativity and destructiveness.* New York: Anchor Books.

Miller, A. (1997). *The drama of the gifted child: The search for the true self.* New York: Perennial.

Miller, A. (2001). *The truth will set you free: Overcoming emotional blindness and finding your true self* (A. Jenkins, Trans.). New York: Basic Books.

Miller, A. (2005). *The body never lies: The lingering effects of cruel parenting.* New York: W.W. Norton.

Miller, D. (2005). Dominic Miller. In *The guitarist book of acoustic magazine* (pp. 92–95). UK: Future Publishing Limited.

Mills, C. W. (2000). *The power elite.* New York: Oxford University Press.

Milner, M. (1957). *On not being able to paint* (also under the name Joanna Field). Boston: Houghton Mifflin Company.

Milner, M. (1987). *The suppressed madness of sane men: Forty-four years of exploring psychoanalysis.* New York: Routledge.

Mitchell, S. A. (1993). *Hope and dread in psychoanalysis.* New York: Basic Books.

Mitchell, S. A. (1999). Preface. In S. A. Mitchell & L. Aron (Eds.), *Relational psychoanalysis: The emergence of a tradition* (pp. ix–xx). Hillsdale, NJ: The Analytic Press.

Modell, A. H. (1999). The dead mother syndrome and the reconstruction of trauma. In G. Kohon (Ed.), *The dead mother: The work of Andre Green* (pp. 76–86). London: Routledge.

Mogenson, G. (1992). *Creating the angels: An imaginal view of the mourning process.* Amityville, NY: Baywood Publishing Company.

Momady, N. S. (1990). *The ancient child.* New York: Harper.

Monk, R. (1991). *Ludwig Wittgenstein: The duty of genius.* New York: Penguin.

Moore, T. (2004). *Dark nights of the soul. A guide to finding your way through life's ordeals.* New York: Gotham Books.

Morris, D. B.(1993). *The culture of pain.* Berkeley, CA: University of California Press.

Morris, M., Doll, M. A., & Pinar, W. F. (Eds.). (1999). *How we work.* New York: Peter Lang.

Morris, M. (2001). *Curriculum and the Holocaust: Competing cites of memory and representation.* Mahwah, NJ: Lawrence Erlbaum and Associates Publishers.

Morris, M. (2006). *Jewish intellectuals and the university.* New York: Palgrave.

Mowat, F. (2006). *No man's river.* New York: Carroll& Graff Publishers.

Mulligan, B. (1997). Waters' view—just too black to be credible. In B. Macdonald (Ed.), *Pink Floyd through the eyes of . . . the band, its fans, friends and foes* (pp. 177–178). New York: Da Capo Press.

Nabhan, G. P. (2000). Welcome to the Sonoran desert. In S. J. Phillip & P. Wentworth Comus (Eds.), *A natural history of the Sonoran desert* (pp. 1–2). Berkeley, CA: University of California Press.

Nasio, D. J. (2004). *The book of love and pain: Thinking the limit with Freud and Lacan.* Albany, NY: State University of New York Press.

Nass, M. (1990a). On hearing and inspiration in the composition of music. In S. Feder, R. L. Karmel, & G. H. Pollock (Eds.), *Psychoanalytic explorations in music* (pp. 179–193). Madison, CT: International Universities Press, Inc.

Nass, M. (1990b). Some considerations of a psychoanalytic interpretation of music. In S. Feder, R. L. Karmel, & G. H. Pollock (Eds.), *Psychoanalytic explorations in music* (pp. 39–59). Madison, CT: International Universities Press, Inc.

Negus, K. (1996). *Popular music in theory: An introduction.* Middletown, CT: Wesleyan University Press.

Ng-A-Fook, N. (2007). *An indigenous curriculum of place: The United Houma Nation's contentious relationship with Louisiana's educational institutions.* New York: Peter Lang.

Noy, P. (1990). The development of musical ability. In S. Feder, R. L. Karmel, & G. H. Pollock (Eds.), *Psychoanalytic explorations in music* (pp. 63–77). Madison, CT: International Universities Press.

Page, T. (1997). Philip Glass (1989). In R. Kostelanetz & R. Flemming (Eds.), *Writings on Glass: Essays, interviews, criticism* (pp. 3–11). Berkeley, CA: University of California Press.

REFERENCES

Parsons, M. (1999). Psychic reality, negation, and the analytic setting. In G. Kohon (Ed.), *The dead mother: The work of Andre Green* (pp. 59–75). London: Routledge.

Parsons, M. (2000). *The dove that returns, the dove that vanishes: Paradox and creativity in psychoanalysis*. London : Routledge.

Patel, A. D. (2008). *Music, language, and the brain*. New York: Oxford University Press.

Perna, A. D. (2002). Mysterious ways. In J. Kitts & B. Tolinski (Eds.), *Guitar world presents Pink Floyd* (pp. 1–47). New York: Hal Leonard Corporation.

Peterson, D. (2005). *On the wild edge: In search of natural life*. New York: Henry Holt & Company.

Phillips, A. (1995). *Going sane: Maps of happiness*. New York: Fourth Estate, an imprint of Harper Collins.

Phillips, A. (1996). *On flirtation*. Cambridge, MA: Harvard University Press.

Phillips, A. (1997a). *On kissing, tickling and being bored.: Psychoanalytic essays on the unexamined life*. Cambridge, MA: Harvard University Press.

Phillips, A. (1997b). *Terrors and experts*. Cambridge, MA: Harvard University Press.

Phillips, A. (2000). *Darwin's worms: On life stores and death stories*. New York: Basic Books.

Phillips, A. (2001). *Promises, promises: Essays on psychoanalysis and literature*. New York: Basic Books.

Phillips, A. (2002). *Equals*. New York: Basic Books.

Piaget, J. (2007). *The language and thought of the child* (Marjorie & Ruth Gabin, Trans.). New York: Routledge.

Pinar, W. F. (1994). *Autobiography, politics and sexuality: Essays in curriculum theory 1972–1992*. New York: Peter Lang. "Death in a Tenured Position" in this volume dated 1984.

Pinar, W. F., Reynolds, W. M., Slattery, P., & Taubman, P. M. (1995). *Understanding curriculum: An introduction to the study of historical and contemporary discourses*. New York: Peter Lang.

Pink Floyd. (2004). *Inside Pink Floyd: A critical review, 1967–1996*. A Film. Ragnarock Films made in the Czech Republic. # 2388005004.

Poe, E. A. (1976). *The science fiction of Edgar Allan Poe*. New York: Penguin.

Poe, E. A. (2006). *The fall of the house of Usher and other tales*. New York: Signet Classics.

Potter, K. (2000). *Four musical minimalists: La Monte Young, Terry Riley, Steve Reich, Philip Glass* (pp. 1–20). New York: Cambridge University Press.

Powers, A. (2001). *Weird like us: My bohemian America*. New York: Da Capo Press.

Proust, M. (2003). *In search of lost time volume 1: Swann's way*. New York: The Modern Library.

Ramachandran, V. S., & Blakeslee, S. (1998). *Phantoms in the brain: Probing the mysteries of the human mind*. New York: Quill.

Rank, O. (1993). *The trauma of birth*. New York: Dover.

Reed, J. (1919/1977). *Ten days that shook the world*. New York: Penguin.

Reich, S. (2002). *Writings on music, 1965–2000. Steve Reich* (P. Hilier, Ed.). New York: Oxford University Press.

Rey, R. (1995). *The history of pain* (L. E. Wallace, J. A. Cadden, & S. W. Cadden, Trans.). Cambridge, MA: Harvard University Press.

Rich, A. (2001). *Arts of the possible: Essays and conversations*. New York: W.W. Norton.

Richardson, J. (1999). *Singing archaeology: Philip Glass's Akhnaten*. Hanover: Wesleyan University Press.

Riesenberg-Malcolm, R. (2000). *On bearing unbearable states of mind* (P. Roth, Ed.). New York: Routeldge.

Rilke, R. M. (1985). *The notebooks of Malte Laurids Brigge* (S. Mitchell, Trans.). New York: Vintage International.

Rilke, R. M. (1987). *Rilke and Benvenuta: An intimate correspondence* (Magda von Hattingberg, Ed. under the same name as Benvenuta, J. Agee, Trans.). New York: Fromm International Publishing Corporation.

Rilke, R. M. (2004). *Auguste Rodin* (D. Slager, Trans.). New York: Archipelago Books.

Rilke, R. M. (2005). *The poets guide to life: The wisdom of Rilke* (U. Baer, Ed. & Trans.). New York: The Modern Library.

Romano, R. (2002). *A pedagogy that presupposes passion.* In E. Mirochnik & D. Sherman (Eds.), *Passion and pedagogy: Relation, creation, and transformation in teaching* (pp. 365–377). New York: Peter Lang Publishers.

Rorem, N. (2000). *The later diaries of Ned Rorem: 1961–1972.* New York: Da Capo Press.

Rose, B. (2001). Barbara Rose. In *Lea Vergine's art on the cutting edge: A guide to contemporary movements* (p. 132). New York: Abbeville Publishing.

Rose, G. J. (2004). *Between couch and piano: Psychoanalysis, music, art and neuroscience.* New York: Brunner-Routledge.

Rosenstiel, L. (1998). *Nadia Boulanger: A life in music.* New York: W.W. Norton.

Rothko, C. (2004). Introduction. In *Mark Rothko's The artist's philosophies of art* (pp. xi–xxxi). New Haven, CT: Yale University Press.

Royce, J. (1988). *Josiah Royce: Selected writings* (J. E. Smith & W. Kluback, Eds.). New York: Paulist Press.

Russell, B. (2002a). *The selected letters of Bertrand Russell: The private years, 1884–1914* (N. Griffin, Ed.). New York: Routledge.

Russell, B. (2002b). *The selected letters of Bertrand Russell: The public years, 1914–1970* (N. Griffin, Ed.). New York: Routledge.

Russell, B. (2002c). *Unpopular essays.* New York: Routledge.

Sacks, K. S. (2003). *Understanding Emerson: "The American scholar" and his struggle for self-reliance.* Princeton, NJ: Princeton University Press.

Sacks, O. (1995). *An anthropologist on mars: Seven paradoxical tales.* New York: Vintage.

Sacks, O. (1998). *The man who mistook his wife for a hat and other clinical tales.* New York: Touchstone Books.

Sacks, O. (1999). *Awakenings.* New York: Vintage.

Sacks, O. (2000). *Seeing voices.* New York: Vintage.

Sacks, O. (2007). *Musicophilia: Tales of music and the brain.* New York: Alfred A. Knopf.

Saint-Exupery, A. D. (1986). *Wartime writings 1939–1944.*

Saint-Exupery, A. D. (1992). *Wind, sand and stars.* New York: Harcourt.

Salvio, P. (2007). *Anne Sexton: Teacher of weird abundance.* Albany, NY: State University of New York Press.

Santayana, G. (2002). *The letters of George Sanatayana, Book Two, 1910–1920* (W. G. Holzbeberger, Ed.). Cambridge, MA: The MIT Press.

Sartre, J. P. (1964). *Nausea.* New York: New Directions.

Scarry, E. (1985). *The body in pain: The making and unmaking of the world.* New York: Oxford University Press.

Schaffner, N. (1991). *Saucerful of secrets: The Pink Floyd odyssey.* New York: Delta.

Scharfstein, B. A. (1993). *Ineffability: The failure of words in philosophy and religion.* Albany, NY: State University of New York Press.

Schreber, D. P. (2000). *Memoirs of my nervous illness.* New York: NYRB Classics.

Schreiner, S. (1995). *Henry Clay Frick: The gospel of greed.* New York: St. Martin's Press.

Sedgwick, E. (1999). *A dialogue on love.* Boston: Beacon Press.

Segal, H. A. (2000). *Dream, phantasy and art.* New York: Routledge.

Segal, J. (1995). *Phantasy in everyday life: A psychoanalytic approach to understanding ourselves.* Northvale, NJ: Jason Aronson Inc.

Sekoff, J. (1999). The undead: Necromancy and the inner world. In G. Kohon (Ed.), *The dead mother: The work of Andre Green* (pp. 109–127). London: Routledge.

Selzer, R. (1996). *Mortal lessons: Notes on the art of surgery.* New York: A Harvest Book.

Sharpe, E. F. (1968). *Collected papers on psycho-analysis.* London: Hogarth Press.

Shostakovich, D. (2000). *Testimony: The memoirs of Dmitri Shostakovich as related to and edited by Solomon Volkov* (A. W. Bouis, Trans.). New York: Limelight Editions.

REFERENCES

Shuker, R. (2003). *Understanding popular music*. New York: Routledge.

Sinclaire, U. (1906/2006). *The jungle*. New York: Penguin.

Sinclaire, U. (1922). *The goose step: A study of American education*. New York: Kessinger Publishing.

Smith, M., Veth, P., Hiscock, P., & Wallis, L. A. (2005). Global deserts in perspective. In P. Veth, M. Smith, & P. Hiscock (Eds.), *Desert peoples: Archaeological perspectives* (pp. 1–13). Malden, MA: Blackwell.

Solms, K. K., & Solms, M. (2002). *Clinical studies in neuro-psychoanalysis: Introduction to a depth neuropsychology*. New York: Karnac.

Sowell, J. (2001). *Desert ecology: An introduction to life in the arid Southwest*. Salt Lake City, UT: The University of Utah Press.

Standiford, L. (2006). *Meet you in hell: Andrew Carnegie, Henry Clay Frick and the bitter partnership that changed America*. Pittsburgh: Three Rivers Press.

Stanton, M. (1997). *Out of order: Clinical work and unconscious process*. London: Rebus Press.

Stern, D. B. (1997). *Unformulated experience: From dissociation to imagination*. Hillsdale, NJ: The Analytic Press.

Sternberg, H. (2002). One of the most vital cultural movements in America, the WPA/FAP. In H. Becker (Ed.), *Art for the people: The rediscovery and preservation of progressive and WPA-era murals in the Chicago public schools, 1904–1943* (pp. 80–81). San Francisco: Chronicle Books.

Stolorow, R. D. (2007). *Trauma and human existence: Autobiographical, psychoanalytic, and philosophical reflections*. New York: The Analytic Press. Taylor & Francis Group.

Storr, A. (1992). *Music and the mind*. New York: Ballantine Books.

Stravinksy, I., & Craft, R. (2002). *Memories and commentaries: Igor Stravinsky and Robert Craft*. New York: Faber and Faber.

Strickland, E. (2000). *Minimalism: Origins*. Bloomington, IN: Indiana University Press.

Strouse, J. (1999). *Alice James: A biography*. Cambridge, MA: Harvard University Press.

Sumara, D. (1996). *Private readings in public: Schooling and the literary imagination*. New York: Peter Lang.

Sumara, D. (1999). Inventing subjectivity in post-Holocaust times: A narrative of catastrophe and slow accumulation. In M. Morris & J. Weaver (Eds.), *Difficult memories: Talk in a (post) Holocaust era* (pp. 141–155). New York: Peter Lang.

Symington, J. (2000). *Imprisoned pain and its transformation*. London: Karnac.

Thomas, G. (1946/2006). *The dark philosophers*. Trinity College, Carmarthen: The Library of Wales.

Thoreau, H. D. (2000). *Walden and civil disobedience*. New York: Houghton Mifflin Company.

Tolstoy, L. (1995). *What is art?* New York: Penguin.

Tyler, R. (1959). *Basic principles of curriculum and instruction*. Chicago: The University of Chicago Press.

Umwerth, M. V. (2005). *Freud's requiem: Mourning, memory and the invisible history of a summer walk*. New York: Riverhead Books.

Van Dusen, W. (1999). Wu-wei, no-mind and the fertile void in psychotherapy. In A. Molino (Ed.), *The couch and the tree: Dialogues in psychoanalysis and Buddhism* (pp. 52–57). San Francisco: North Point Press.

Vygotsyk, L. S. (1981). *Thought and language* (E. Hanfmann & G. Vakar, Trans.). Cambridge, MA: The MIT Press.

Wall, P. (2000). *Pain: The science of suffering*. New York: Columbia University Press.

Waller, D. (2002). *Art therapies and progressive illness: Nameless dread*. New York: Brunner-Routledge.

Waters, R. (1999). *Pink Floyd: The Wall*. A Film. Produced by Alan Marshall. Screenplay by Roger Waters. Directed by Alan Parker. Film music produced by Roger Waters, David Gilmour and James Guthrie. Sony BMG Music Entertainment. #58163.

Watkinson, M., & Anderson, P. (2001). *Crazy diamond: Syd Barrett and the dawn of Pink Floyd*. New York: Omnibus Press.

Watts, A. (1991). Andre Watts. In E. Mach (Ed.), *Great contemporary pianists speak for themselves* (pp. 179–189).

Webber, J. A. (2003). *Failure to hold: The politics of school violence.* New York: Rowman & Littlefield Publishers.

Weschler, L. (2006). *Everything that rises: A book of convergences.* San Francisco: McSweeny's.

Whitehead, A. N. (1929/1967). *The aims of education and other essays.* New York: The Free Press.

Willis, T. (2002). *Madcap: The half-life of Syd Barrett, Pink Floyd's lost genius.* Surrey, London: Short Books.

Wilson, A. C. (2004). Decolonizing and the recovery of indigenous knowledge. In D. A. Mihesuah & A. C. Wilson (Eds.), *Indigenizing the academy: Transforming scholarship and empowering communities* (pp. 67–87). Lincoln, NE: The University of Nebraska Press.

Wilson, E. (1998). *Jacqueline du Pre: Her life, her music, her legend.* New York: Arcade Publishing.

Winnicott, D. W. (1990). *Home is where we start from: Essays by a psychoanalyst.* New York: W.W. Norton.

Winnicott, D. W. (1992). *Psychoanalytic explorations: D.W. Winnicott* (C. Winnicott, R. Shepherd, & M. Davis, Eds.). Cambridge, MA: Harvard University Press.

Winnicott, D. W. (2005). *Playing and reality.* New York: Routledge.

Wittgenstein, L. (1958). *Philosophical investigations* (G. E. M. Anscombe, Trans.). Upper Saddle River, NJ: Prentice Hall.

Wittgenstein, L. (1965). *The blue and brown books.* New York: Harper Torchbooks.

Wittgenstein, L. (1980). *Culture and value* (P. Winch, Trans., G. H. Von Wright, Eds., in collaboration with Heikki Nyman). Chicago: The University of Chicago Press.

Wittgenstein, L. (1997). *Ludwig Wittgenstein: Cambridge letters.* Correspondence with Russell, Keynes, Moore, Ramsey and Sraffa (B. McGuinness & G. Henrik von Wright, Eds.). Malden, MA: Blackwell Publishers.

Wolff, K. (1972). *Schnabel's interpretation of piano music.* New York: W.W. Norton.

Woolf, V. (1993). *Mrs. Dalloway.* New York: Alfred A. Knopf.

Woolf, V. (2004). *The voyage out.* New York: Barnes and Noble.

4008 030

Printed in the United States
140577LV00002B/33/P

9 789087 907754